P9-CSH-375

THE ATLANTIC CIVILIZATION

EIGHTEENTH-CENTURY ORIGINS

THE

Atlantic Civilization

EIGHTEENTH-CENTURY ORIGINS

Michael Kraus

Cornell Paperbacks

Cornell University Press

ITHACA, NEW YORK

CORNELL UNIVERSITY PRESS

First published for the American Historical Association, 1949
First printing, Cornell Paperbacks, 1966

PRINTED IN THE UNITED STATES OF AMERICA
BY VALLEY OFFSET, INC.
BOUND BY VAIL-BALLOU PRESS, INC.

FOR VERA

Preface

THE concept of the Atlantic community is much in evidence in our present-day consciousness. Journalists and historians have been giving it increasing attention, sometimes treating it as a startling discovery. But there have been students writing on various phases of this theme for many years, enriching our understanding of Europe's contribution to America and, more rarely, America's contribution to Europe.

It has been my consistent aim to point up the impact of the New World upon the Old, because I believe that historians have too often neglected this phase of American-European history. The moral force that America exerted upon Europe in the eighteenth century bore little relation to the economic strength of the colonies. Europeans, who were well aware of the assault of American ideas upon old traditions, were mindful as well of the potentially vast economic power arising overseas.

This study reveals that the American colonies contributed their goodly share to that synthesis called "the Atlantic civilization," which, though fundamentally European, was undergoing transformations resulting from New World influences. These economic, social, scientific, and psychological changes were in the direction of a more democratic society, and to this end North America lent its vigorous weight. American creativeness in generating new attitudes in social relationships, particularly, had a contagious vitality. This youthful energy communicated its strength to Europe where it stimulated further thought and action. The conventional interpretation which pictures America as the terminal in the transit of European civilization needs to be broadened to include the idea of a return trip. America did much to give greater substance to such concepts as political and religious freedom, economic opportunity, and humanitarian ideals; and she hurried the Western World to the realization of them. But it is hoped that this narrative does not exaggerate the contributions of the New World. Building the Atlantic civilization has been, and will continue to be, a joint enterprise. It is one of the most remarkable developments in world history.

The research for this book has been spread over many years. Portions of the work have appeared in the *Mississippi Valley Historical Review* (March, 1936), *Pennsylvania Magazine of History and Biography* (January, July, 1936), *Bulletin of the History of Medicine* (May, 1940), *Scientific Monthly* (September, 1942), and *William and Mary Quarterly* (July, 1944). I wish to thank the editors of these publications, who have kindly given permission to use the materials already published. I should add, however, that these materials have undergone many changes before inclusion in the present text. My thanks go also to the Massachusetts Historical Society for permission to quote from the published Copley-Pelham letters (*Collections,* LXXI) and to the *New England Quarterly* for permitting quotation from its issue of January, 1930.

Several of my colleagues at City College, New York, have read portions of this manuscript to its advantage—Professors Nelson P. Mead, J. Salwyn Schapiro, Richard B. Morris, Joseph E. Wisan, and Louis L. Snyder. Professor Bailey W. Diffie was a patient reader of an earlier draft of the entire text and was generous in his encouragement. The library staff at City College eased my task considerably. Professor Herbert W. Schneider and Dean Harry J. Carman of Columbia read the manuscript and made helpful suggestions. To all I wish to express my gratitude. I also wish to thank the Social Science Research Council and the American Philosophical Society for grants to pursue this study. I like to remember at this time the stimulation of my former teachers, Professors William R. Shepherd and Evarts B. Greene of Columbia.

The Carnegie Revolving Fund Committee of the American Historical Association (Professor Ray A. Billington of Northwestern University, chairman) has given me the benefit of incisive criticism, which is much appreciated.

I feel certain that the coming years will see this rewarding sub-ect studied with ever greater intensiveness. My own purpose has been to draw attention to the wide ramifications of this theme as one worthy of further investigation.

With a deep sense of what this book owes to the good-humored patience and intelligence of my wife, Vera Edelstadt, I have dedicated it to her.

MICHAEL KRAUS

Stony Point, New York
August, 1949

Contents

THE ATLANTIC CIVILIZATION

EIGHTEENTH-CENTURY ORIGINS

CHAPTER I

The Beginnings of an Atlantic Civilization

THE Atlantic civilization resulting from the interrelationship of the Old World and the New belongs in the sequence of civilizations which originated in the region of the Mediterranean and which go back to Sumer and the valley of the Nile. To the Mediterranean heritage was added a rich inheritance that drew from all the lands and peoples bordering the Atlantic. Experience with the ocean itself and the impressive rivers and seas that emptied into it evoked awesome wonderment and powerful poetic response. The whole stage for business enterprise was vastly enlarged in the fifteenth and sixteenth centuries, and the relations between states were profoundly altered. The areas which had been peripheral to the Mediterranean center turned the political and economic world inside out and became themselves a new and greater center of trade and politics. Adam Smith thought that the discovery of America and the opening of a route to the East Indies by way of the Cape of Good Hope were the "two greatest and most important events recorded in the history of mankind." [1] The great expansion of trade that followed was a chief cause of the accelerated growth of economic individualism in western Europe. In a comparatively short time the everyday life of people was deeply affected by the streams of precious metals which spread from Spain to the rest of Europe, inflating prices and accelerating the rate of change in a slow-moving economy. The financial structure, which had stood for several centuries with a fairly stable bimetallic ratio, was completely overturned.

American treasure surely expanded the dreams of Hapsburg im-

[1] H. M. Robertson, *Aspects of the Rise of Economic Individualism* (Cambridge, Eng., 1935), chap. vii, "The Influence of the Discoveries."

perialists, and it strengthened Spanish militancy against Protestants and Mohammedans. Gold and silver made it glitteringly easy to equip armies and shed Spanish blood on remote European battlefields. It appears an inescapable conclusion that the wealth from the West Indies ultimately had evil effects upon the old homeland. This treasure from overseas helped create at home an illusion of prosperity which encouraged extravagance. Successful Spaniards, returned from the New World, endowed themselves with titles of nobility, to the shocked surprise of familiar neighbors. Wage earners suffered deeply during the price revolution, although Spanish workers were not affected as much as those elsewhere in Europe. Urban workers in Spain were one-fourth less well off in the last years of the sixteenth century than in the first years. Their position was, however, improved in the early part of the seventeenth century. Prices for merchandise at home, said one contemporary, reached fantastic figures, because of the heavy exports to the Indies.[2]

Class relationships in western Europe were altered, and established social institutions faced a challenge which grew sharper as men's knowledge grew wider and deeper. That knowledge was gained from contact with a new world of nature and new societies foreign to European experience. It shook minds out of their doubtlessly comfortable ruts and forced them on to strange and often fearsome pathways. A highly prized medieval inheritance was not discarded, of course, but its dominance was lessened in an increasingly secular world. The rediscovery of the Greek heritage and the discovery of a new world were together a powerful lever lifting the medieval mind to new planes of achievement. The embryonic Atlantic civilization looked also toward the older civilizations in the Orient and drew from them artistic inspiration and philosophic insights as well as material wealth.

In the long run it was, however, the impact from the new lands in the Atlantic littoral that shook more profoundly the structure of European society. Apart from Oriental material products, much that came from the East remained exotics, or at best adornments of a speculative, aristocratic society with only transient significance for the generality. The mass of Europeans were not much affected by

[2] E. J. Hamilton, *American Treasure and the Price Revolution in Spain, 1501–1650* (Cambridge, Mass., 1934), 44–45, 70, 279, 281, 290.

ıpper-class devotion to Chinese gardens, furniture, or philosophy. Vhat came from the New World, especially that which was distilled rom the experiences of fellow countrymen transplanted, was em-edded more certainly in the pattern of European life. The revolu-ions of the sixteenth and seventeenth centuries—political, scien-ific, religious, and commercial—made for a remarkable fertility of peculation and social reorientation. While the eighteenth century lid not add much depth to this speculation it did broaden its area, nd it definitely altered the outlook of societal institutions. The era of democratization was thus well begun, and this, truly, was in large measure the creation of the Atlantic civilization.

The story begins with the transplanting of peoples and their institutions to the Western Hemisphere—to North and South America and the islands between. Spain, Portugal, France, and the Netherlands established colonies on which the impress of the characteristics then dominant in the homeland was easily discerned. These colonies, like those of the English, were primarily for exploitation. To this immediate end, however, there was added another in the English and Spanish settlements—a permanent habitation for those leaving the homeland, willingly and unwillingly. Emigrants from the Continent in this early period were not numerous, and the impact on European homelands was less on the minds and spirit of the people than it was on their economy. But in the British Isles (which had sent a large number of emigrants overseas, in proportion to their population) the reaction created by these newer regions was deeper, more lasting, and more generally pervasive. There, while the effect of overseas settlement was equally great upon material well-being, the life of the imagination responded more quickly, more sympathetically to the fresh winds that blew from the West. More directly than other European peoples, the British, because of their large contingent abroad, absorbed into their own consciousness the hopes and frustrations of transatlantic settlers.

The interrelationship between the peoples of the Western World and their Old-World homelands, gradually, almost imperceptibly, produced a new civilization. As an eighteenth-century publication expressed it, the discovery and exploitation of these vast western regions extended geographical knowledge, "perfected navigation opened new sources of commerce, and gave a new face even to the affairs of Europe." [3] A new moral order had evolved, begun with the discovery of America, and the seal of its establishment was the American Revolution.

The discovery of America was a powerful stimulus to the imagination. The imaginative realm ruled over by the magisterial mind of Francis Bacon was greatly enlarged by the new phenomena of men and nature brought within his ken. "Nor must it go for nothing," he wrote in the *Novum Organum,* "that by the distant voyages and travels which have become frequent in our times, many things in nature have been laid open and discovered which may let in new light upon philosophy. And surely it would be disgraceful if, while the regions of the material globe; that is, of the earth, of the sea and of the stars—have been in our times laid widely open and revealed, the intellectual globe should remain shut up within the narrow limits of old discoveries." The Italian historian, Francesco Guicciardini, writing of the discoveries, expressed the common reaction when he said, "It is manifest that the Antients were mistaken in many Things relating to the knowledge of the Earth"; for example, the torrid zone *was* habitable.[4]

Many questions were asked. Did American Indians live longer because they painted their skin? And did the sun's heat blacken the African Negro? If so, why then did not the same happen to the glass blowers working under intense heat? The unusual phenomena of American nature, strange to European senses, "display a fertile field for a creative, fanciful genius to explore," said one traveler,

---

[3] D. Fenning and J. Collyer, *A New System of Geography . . .* (London, 1766), II, 625; *Le Triomphe du Nouveau Monde: Résponses Académiques formant un nouveau système de Confédération fondé sur les besoins actuels des Nations Chrétiennes . . .* (Paris, 1785), II, 295–297; see also E. A. Baker, *The History of the English Novel* (London, 1924–1939), II, chap. iv, "Utopian fiction."

Pedro Henriquez-Ureña, *Literary Currents in Hispanic America* (Cambridge, Mass., 1945), chap. i, "The Discovery of the New World in the Imagination of Europe," says, "On the whole the Americas occupy much less space in Spanish (and Portuguese) literature than might have been expected."

[4] *Works of Francis Bacon* (Spedding ed., Boston, 1860–1864), VIII, 117; F. Guicciardini, *The History of Italy* (London, 1753), III, bk. VI, 311.

"and may give rise to the most novel, elegant and beautiful flights of imagination, and the brightest, most ingenious and splendid embellishments of fiction." [5] Few countries, thought another writer, afforded more striking inspiration for the poet than North America. New ideas of grandeur and beauty were evoked by this exotic world.

The reaction to the discovery of America was immediate in the field of historiography. Accounts of overseas voyages and discoveries appeared in rapid succession. In belles-lettres America was an important part of that new and stimulating atmosphere which the voyages to remote and mysterious lands brought to the work of dramatists and poets. There have been many springtimes of the imagination, but few have surpassed in splendor and luxuriance of growth the Elizabethan age. Historians of literature, said Professor Walter Raleigh, "have been wont to treat the imaginative growth of the Elizabethan age as if it were a problem of skilful gardening, an instance of high success in the mysteries of transplanting, grafting, forcing, and the like. But what nourished the pale slips brought from abroad? They struck their roots deep in a soil rich with the matter of life, and breathed a genial and stimulating air. The dramatists and poets were the children and inheritors of the Voyagers." [6] For the voyagers themselves wrote in a language, naïve and racy, of a new and scarcely credible world.

In the years that intervened until Coleridge's work appeared, the lands overseas and the waters between furnished materials to literary craftsmen. The sea freshened Elizabethan literature, but it was not until the second quarter of the eighteenth century, when the novel became a recognized literary form and mariners became novelists themselves, that the sea found fuller expression in literature. On one occasion when Wordsworth was busy on a major work, he asked a friend to collect for him books of travels, "as without much of such reading," he wrote, "my present labours cannot be

---

[5] J. F. D. Smyth, *A Tour in the United States of America* (London, 1784), I, 165–166; see also J. Belknap, "Has the discovery of America been useful or hurtful to mankind?" *Boston Magazine*, I (1784), 281; J. E. Gillespie, *The Influence of Oversea Expansion on England to 1700* (New York, 1920), 208–209.

[6] Walter Raleigh, *The English Voyages of the Sixteenth Century* (Glasgow, 1910), 151–152; R. R. Cawley, *Unpathed Waters: Studies in the influence of the Voyagers on Elizabethan Literature* (Princeton, 1940), 117–170.

brought to any conclusion." [7] Coleridge's *The Rime of the Ancient Mariner* is the finest achievement of that eighteenth-century spirit which was nurtured by tales of adventure. And when the slow flame of inspiration had done its work, the product bore the marks of its origins, for running through the *Ancient Mariner* are the words of the voyagers themselves.[8]

Richard Hakluyt had gathered the voyagers' tales for the English, and others followed him in making similar collections. It was not long before such literature passed from the workshop of the litterateur and from exclusive libraries to a wider reading public. Every type of writer—scientist, social scientist, rationalist—made use of travel literature, with the result that literary expression itself was changed. The Royal Society, sponsor of so much of the intellectual activity of the period, disapproved of "a glorious Pomp of Words," indicating a strong preference for a "close, naked, natural way of Speaking," the language of "Artizans, Countrymen, and Merchants" rather than of "Wits, or Scholars." [9] In the middle of the seventeenth century the French were reading *The Jesuit Relations,* which came from the press at the rate of a volume almost every year. A contemporary observed the change in tastes of French readers, who were showing greater interest in voyages.[10] Swift was a close reader of such material and modeled certain characters after the monstrosities occasionally depicted by voyagers. In John Locke's opinion it was very important for gentlemen to read history, geography, and travels better to fit them to be the ruling class. These subjects, it may be noted too, furnished much of the recreation of American readers.

It was a reading of travelers' descriptions that prompted Sir William Temple to speak of "the fundamental moral beliefs which

---

[7] Lane Cooper in *Mod. Lang. Notes,* XXII (1907), 110, March 6, 1798.

[8] J. L. Lowes, *The Road to Xanadu* (Boston, 1927), 323; see also Sister Eugenia, "Coleridge's Scheme of Pantisocracy and American Travel Accounts," *PMLA,* XLV (1930), 1069–1084.

[9] R. W. Frantz, *The English traveller and the movement of ideas, 1660–1732* ("Univ. of Nebraska, Univ. Studies," XXXII–XXXIII, 1934), 59; F. Christensen, "John Wilkins and the Royal Society Reform of Prose Style," *Mod. Lang. Quart.,* VII (1946), 179–189, 279–291.

[10] G. Atkinson, *The Extraordinary Voyage in French Literature before 1700* (New York, 1920), 7 note 10, 11.

are shared by all men" despite their differences in government and social custom. Perfection was a fleeting thing "approached now in this part of the world, now in that, only to depart again." It was his study of Inca civilization, along with that of other peoples, that led him to support a cyclical theory of history. Montaigne, in his essay *On Carriages,* had preceded Temple in an appreciation of the superior achievements of early American civilizations, and he, too, was led to speculate on their cyclical nature. Travel books promoted the growth of humanitarianism, toleration, and cosmopolitanism, but it should be noted there was a body of opinion that condemned them for their aid to skepticism.[11]

Fictitious narratives of travels to little-known lands, whose happy inhabitants were contrasted with Europeans, added to the great mass of this literature; over two hundred such voyages have been listed by a recent student.[12] England read large quantities of imaginary as well as genuine accounts, and to supply this market enterprising publishers paid large sums to the authors who garnered travelers' reports. These appealed to children as well as to adults. W. H. Dilworth, whose school books were used extensively, brought this literature to the attention of British boys and girls, with publications on the buccaneers of America and the conquerors Pizzaro and De Soto. A German writer of children's books, which were translated into other languages, described the world that Columbus found, the New World from which came strange products unknown to Europe.[13]

Thus those who stayed at home escaped provincialism by vicarious voyages to distant places. Among those places was America, whose distance from Europe was lessened when emigrants began sending letters home. New expressions enriched the vocabulary of later voyagers, who were keener observers than their predecessors and gifted with more facile pens.[14] They fed the public taste for

---

[11] Clara Marburg, *Sir William Temple* (New Haven, 1932), 36, 61–63, 71.

[12] P. B. Gove, *The Imaginary Voyage in Prose Fiction* (New York, 1941).

[13] J. H. Campe, *The Discovery of America, for the Use of Children and Young Persons* (London, 1759).

[14] G. Chinard, *L'Amérique et le Rève Exotique dans la Littérature Française au XVIIe et au XVIIIe Siècle* (Paris, 1934), 28; Mary Serjeantson, *A History of Foreign Words in English* (London, 1935), 195–197, and *passim.*

romance with stories of explorers and filibusterers. This literature was more than a *divertissement,* for it made a deep impression on the consciousness of Europe and was an influential factor in the development of romanticism and philosophical radicalism. It was inevitable that the differences met with in foreign civilizations should have made Europeans more conscious of their own deficiencies—failings which were accented by contrast with the imputed superiority of exotic peoples.

The "noble savage" was constantly held up as an inspiration. During the three centuries that preceded the French Revolution, one can trace a continuous development of this literary convention. Columbus, in his earliest narratives, illustrates a step in the growth of the "noble savage" idea with its accompanying stress on sensibility. The natives and their king "shed tears in abundance," wrote the discoverer. "They are a very loving race, and without covetousness," they lived nakedly and innocently, but there was not "a better people in the world than these." In France, J. B. Du Tertre in his *Histoire Générale des Isles . . . dans l'Amérique,* probably did more than anyone else to fix the traits of the "noble savage"; and in the second half of the seventeenth century this idealization of the primitive, with other literary exports, was sent across the channel to England.[15] The great Spanish poem *Araucana* (now the epic of Chile) by Alonso de Ercilla, which celebrated the defense of their homeland by native chieftains, added lustre to the legend of the "noble savage."

The drama, too, reflected American exoticism. The life of frontier Virginia was portrayed on the London stage in 1613, six years after the Jamestown settlement. More than half a century earlier, Brazilian aborigines had participated in a noted fête in Rouen, France. A professor at William and Mary College sent an example of Indian eloquence to England where it was hailed as a masterpiece: "It is the eloquence of *sentiment,* and penetrates through the soul. . . ." [16] Treaties between Indians and whites in North Amer-

[15] *Journal of First Voyage to America by Christopher Columbus,* with introduction by Van Wyck Brooks (New York, 1924), 145; Chinard, 39; H. N. Fairchild, *The Noble Savage* (New York, 1928), 34, 362.

[16] Quoted in *Mass. Hist. Soc., Proc.,* ser. 1, XV (1876–1877), 230 ff. On the

ca were a highly expressive form of drama, costumed and ritualized y Indian custom.

Rationalistic satirists, like Swift and Voltaire, merely used the avage as a weapon of attack upon the foibles of humanity, but the omanticists saw in him "an embodiment of a creed." The early eriod was distinguished for its suspicion of the ideals of rationalsm and for its criticism of urban civilization. Although Rousseau vas not so enthusiastic about primitives as is commonly believed, is contemporaries seized upon this aspect of his thought, which nade the "noble savage" a warning symbol to the later half of the entury. The Lake Poets invoked the support of the "noble savage" or their nature philosophy, but by the early nineteenth century his literary convention had exhausted its appeal, for science was psetting the pictures painted by the romanticists.[17]

At the height of its influence, however, the romantic attractiveess of the Indian was well-nigh irresistible. The tale of a white nan's love for a savage woman in "Inkle and Yarico" (containing lso a criticism of urban life) was remarkably popular; indeed many riginal works based on this theme appeared in eighteenth-century urope. One reviewer remarked that "no story has ever taken so irm a hold on the public attention as this." [18] In Germany, the rench Chateaubriand's *Atala* led readers to much Indian literature, lthough earlier works had already prepared the way for its recepion. Kotzebue's dramas used the theme of the "noble savage," and ranslations of American and English books had acquainted Gernan readers with the Indians.[19] Some American writers likewise ell under this spell. Philip Freneau, in *Tomo Cheeki, the Creek ndian in Philadelphia,* was another critic of the white man's civiliation, speaking through the red man. The Indian stimulated

rama of Indian treaties, see Constance Rourke, *The Roots of American Culure* (New York, 1942), 61–69.

[17] Fairchild, 41, 45, 48, 52, 60–62, 124–139, 362–363.

[18] B. Bissell, *The American Indian in English Literature of the Eighteenth Century* (New Haven, 1925), chap. vi; L. M. Price, *Inkle and Yarico Album* Berkeley, 1937), 138. German interest exceeded that of other peoples (*Eur. Mag. and London Rev.*, XXXV [1800], 256).

[19] P. A. Barba, *The American Indian in German Fiction* ("German-Amerian Annals," n.s., XI, 1913).

thought and furnished entertainment to readers of magazines an newspapers; he remained first-page copy throughout the eighteent century.[20]

The Indian enriched the languages of Europeans as well as thei spirits. All the European nations, engaged in overseas expansion an settlement, experienced linguistic changes. Even those countri not so directly involved were affected; Germany, for example, too over Spanish, Portuguese, and other foreign words derived fro native American Indian expressions. The Dutch who lived i northern New York sometimes spoke and wrote "Mohawk Dutch, a combination of their original tongue and the Indian languag Names all over the land of the Western World are a living India inheritance.[21] The English too, took over many words from th Spaniards and Portuguese, who had first ingested them in the Ne World. New products, new animals, new people, characterized i aboriginal language, were found sometimes disguised in newe dress, in the tongues of Europe. Not the least of the riches brough back by explorers, adventurers, and traders were the words t weave their experiences into the pattern of European imagination

America as a geographical and ethnographical novelty was por trayed in numerous European publications. Pictures accompanie the text and reinforced the impression America made on Europ One of the earliest works, a poem on the discovery of the Ne World, included an illustration which seemed to set a model fo those that followed, a kind of Eden populated with many Eves. Col lections of voyages, such as Giambattista Ramusio's, and Sebastia Munster's *Cosmography* contained illustrations of the new lands t the west. It was not until near the end of the sixteenth century tha the engraver's art was applied on a lavish scale to illustrate Amer ican subjects. The finest work in this period was the product of th family headed by Théodore de Bry. His edition of Hariot's *Vir ginia,* with engravings made from John White's water colors o

[20] Some interesting details will be found in C. T. Foreman, *Indians Abroa 1493–1938* (Norman, Okla., 1943).

[21] W. Kurrelmeyer, "American and other loan words in German," *Jou Eng. and Germ. Philology,* XLIII (1944), 286–301; *Amer. Hist. Assn., Ann Report,* I (1931), 363.

merican Indians (1585), had wide circulation. Niagara Falls ap-
eared for the first time in Louis Hennepin's *Carte de la nouvelle*
rance. . . . Enterprising publishers in the Netherlands brought
ut half of the illustrated books on America issued in the seventy-
ve years after 1550. For a century thereafter the Dutch continued
) produce the major portion of illustrated Americana, most of
hich was devoted to the West Indies, reflecting Dutch interests
iere.

Slowly the English press began to contribute an increasing share
f titles in this field. Narratives of travels remained the most pop-
lar (and exotic views made the literary far fields appear even
reener). But the publication of specialized scientific works grad-
ally increased, notably, beautifully illustrated volumes on botany.
Iark Catesby's work *The Natural History of Carolina, Florida and*
he Bahama Islands (London, 1731–1743), with two hundred col-
red plates, is but one of a number of exceptional publications. The
cenagrafia (London, 1768) was composed almost exclusively of en-
ravings with numerous views of Canada and other British colonies.
t least one London tradesman used a cut of an Indian chieftain
obed in royal raiment to advertise his dry goods at "Ye Indian
ing" in Holborn.[22]

There were not many paintings of Indians, but some were to be
ound in private collections. Jacques Le Moyne, who came with
René G. de Laudonnière's French expedition to Florida in 1564,
ainted pictures of the Indians, which were engraved by Bry. A
icture of a West Indian scene by F. Post, which this writer saw in a
Iunich museum, was an early, unreal representation of American
ndians.[23] Shortly after Post, an important Dutch artist, Albert
ckhout, who had gone to Brazil with Count Maurice, painted
outh American aborigines and transplanted African Negroes. His
nany pictures, some of which still hang in European museums, in-
luded representations of the fruits and plants of the New World.

---

[22] J. F. Hunnewell, "Illustrated Americana," *Amer. Antiq. Soc., Proc.*, VI
1889–1890), 72–77, 283–294; Ambrose Heal, *London Tradesmen's Cards of*
he XVIII Century (London, 1925), plate LXIII; Stefan Lorant, *The New*
World: The First Pictures of America (New York, 1946).

[23] See also *Catalogue of Exhibition of Dutch Art* (1450–1900), Royal Academy
of Arts, Burlington House, London, 1929, painting by Jan Mostaert.

Another companion of Maurice was Frans Post, who painted lan
scapes and Brazilian natives. Paintings by these and other artis
made more vivid to European eyes the lushness of tropical scener
and the exoticism of strange people.[24] Over sixty landscapes b
Post have survived, some painted while he was in Brazil, others aft
he had returned to Europe. A modern critic speaks of several c
these landscapes as having "a quality completely alien to the spir
of early seventeenth century painting in Europe, a strange qualit
which relates them curiously to modern painting." Post's decor
tions in the Dutch castle of Ryksdorp (Wassenaar) synthesize th
prosperous civilization of the Dutch-Portuguese colony, "set in
grand framework of indigenous birds, insects and flowers." Mauric
said of this work by Post, that if a man should see it, "he would no
have to cross the seas to behold the fair land of Brazil," which, hi
soaring rhetoric claimed, had "no equal beneath the heavens."

Rubens made a copy of Titian's painting of Adam and Eve i
the Garden of Eden, and he added something to the original—
flaming red parrot, a macaw, among the trees. Titian's painting an
the copy by Rubens, it has been suggested, reveal how the art of th
Renaissance passed over into the baroque; "very appropriately, th
symbol of that momentous change in the history of art is a bir
from the fantastic forests of tropical America." [25]

Many years later Indians were painted by C. W. Peale in Phila
delphia and by Benjamin West in London, who included the Amer
ican primitive in his noted historical picture, "The Death of Gen
eral Wolfe." Romney painted Joseph Brant (Thayandenagaea), th
famous Mohawk who had been brought to London; and the por
trait was a complete visual image of the "noble savage." Reynold
and other contemporary artists also painted primitives.[26]

Scientists, as well as dramatists, poets, historians, and artists wer
drawn to this new area of investigation. From the lips of Dutc

---

[24] Thomas Thomsen, *Albert Eckhout, ein Niederländischer Maler . . . ei Kulturbild aus dem 17 Jahrhundert* (Kopenhagen, 1938); R. C. Smith, "Fran Post," *The Art Quarterly*, I (1938), 247–259.

[25] Henriquez-Ureña, 29.

[26] H. C. Hunter, "The American Indian in Painting," *Art and Archaeolog* VIII (1919), 81; C. B. Tinker, *Painter and Poet: Studies in the Literary Rela tions of English Painting* (Cambridge, Mass., 1938), 56–58.

merchants returned from Brazil to their native Amsterdam, a young German student, George Marcgrave, heard stories that aroused his curiosity so that he asked for a place in Count Maurice's expedition to South America in 1638. Here he stayed for several years making observations of all kinds and gathering large collections of the fauna and flora of Brazil. Although he died before he could put his material in shape for publication, others took up the task. Johannes De Laet of the West India Company edited some of Marcgrave's work which appeared in Leyden under the title, *A Natural History of Brazil.* In this book were more than six hundred and fifty forms, nearly all new to science; some four hundred of them were figured from the drawings left by Marcgrave. When Count Maurice, leader of the expedition, returned to Holland, he brought back a collection so rich in specimens that he had enough for his own museum and those of other private individuals, besides supplying two universities. By common consent of leading authorities, Marcgrave is accorded a high place for his contributions to ichthyology. Four charts of Brazil done by Marcgrave were etched on copper by the order of Count Maurice, and copies of these were to be seen on the walls of aristocratic Dutch homes.[27]

Almost a century before Marcgrave left for Brazil, André Thevet had gone there with a French group to build a settlement, and his observations were included in works published on his return to France. He wrote one of the earliest notices of the toucan and the three-toed sloth, and his description of tobacco was the first in French.[28]

In the large commercial warehouses of seaport towns were gathered goods from the ends of the earth, and here and there among the products of trade could be found curiosities—fossils, sea shells and what not—all calculated to provoke the imagination. Merchants stole time from more prosaic pursuits to write letters which transported them to distant realms. Peter Collinson, the London merchant and naturalist, writing to John Bartram, the Pennsylvania botanist, apologized for the repetition in some of his letters; "a multitude of affairs divert my memory, and my letters are not

27 E. W. Gudger in *Popular Science Monthly,* LXXXI (1912), 250.

28 Manoel da Silveira Cardozo, "Some Remarks concerning André Thevet," *The Americas,* I (1944), 35.

worth copying—being mostly writ behind the counter." There were many of the type of Collinson who were included in the membership of the scientific societies then rapidly spreading over Europe. From the start these organizations had revealed a cosmopolitan outlook. One of the earliest, established at Rome in 1600, had a plan to locate groups everywhere in the world for scientific co-operation. Among its publications was a *Thesaurus Mexicanus,* a description of plants and animals in Mexico.[29] Other societies were founded on Italian models and followed their lead.

The most famous of these organizations was the Royal Society in England. Its influence was world-wide, and its publication, the *Philosophical Transactions,* was the most distinguished forum available to scientific opinion. The Society sought information on the natural history and physical condition of foreign lands, and to that end a correspondence with other societies was early established. This correspondence was read at the meetings, and it made the Society more of an international than a local English group; "every important experiment, every important article, was communicated to it almost as soon as it was published." [30] French, German, and Russian societies were likewise established before the first quarter of the eighteenth century was over. Not until the second half of the century were similar organizations formed in English America, although many years earlier Increase Mather had gathered together a small group fairly regularly to discuss philosophical problems and to add "to the Stores of Natural History." [31]

Although organized efforts in behalf of science came comparatively late in the English colonies, individual initiative, in co-operation with European societies, made up for this lack. Secretary Henry Oldenburg in 1667 wrote to John Winthrop, the earliest American member of the Royal Society, asking for communications: "You will please to remember that we have taken to taske the whole Universe, and that we were obliged to doe so by the nature of our Des-

---

[29] William Darlington, *Memorials of John Bartram and Humphry Marshall* (Philadelphia, 1849), 134, Sept. 2, 1739; M. Ornstein, *Scientific Societies in the 17th Century* (New York, 1913), 74–76.

[30] Ornstein, 124, 127; *Philosophical Transactions, passim* (hereafter *Phil. Trans.*).

[31] K. B. Murdock, *Increase Mather* (Cambridge, 1925), 147–148.

ein. It will therefore be requisite that we purchase and entertain a ommerce in all parts of the world with the most philosophicall and urious persons to be found everywhere." Four years earlier, Olden-urg had confidently written Winthrop that the Society expected rom him a better description of "the remarkables (of New England) han is any yet extant, concerning the mappe of the country, the his-ory of all its productions, and particularly of the subterraneous ones . . likewise a relation of the Tides upon your coast, together with he course of your rivers, but especially and above all, a full account f your success in your new way of salt-making, whereof we could ot compasse the experement here, as was much desired." Olden-urg joined with Winthrop in ridiculing "the notional and dis-utaceous school philosophy" and urged him to foster "this reall xperimental way of acquiring knowledge, by conversing with, and earching into the works of God themselves"; the youth of New ngland should be "seasoned and possessed with the same." [32] Ol-enburg urged that a natural history of New England be written. ears later the grandson of Winthrop was honored by the dedica-ion to him of a volume of the *Philosophical Transactions* for his umerous contributions to mineralogy.[33]

One of the chief intellectual results of the discovery of the New World was the blow it dealt the patristic tradition in matters of cience. The first polygenist doctrines of modern times now ap-eared, and Paracelsus seems to have been the earliest to assert the lurality of the races of mankind.

In the middle of the seventeenth century, Isaac Peyrere published *rae-Adamitae,* attempting to prove that Adam and Eve were not he first human beings on earth. Men were here long before Adam, e argued, and as for the New World inhabitants they were pre-damite in origin. This pre-Adamitic heresy, as it was called, ngendered much controversy. Incidentally, it was at this time that he word "anthropology" was incorporated into the English lan-uage, and it was defined as a "history of human nature." A few

[32] *Mass. Hist. Soc., Proc.,* ser. 1, XVI (1877–1878), 211, Oct. 13, 1667, Aug. 5, 663, Mar. 26, 1670.

[33] Vol. XL; see long dedicatory notice to John Winthrop, F.R.S., Aug. 15, 741.

years later, in 1677, Sir Matthew Hale published *The primitive origination of mankind considered and examined according to the light of nature,* which states that the discovery of America had induced many to doubt the descent of all men from one pair, and in the course of his discussion he raised the question of the peopling of the New World. Long before Hale wrote, it had been argued tha America had very likely been peopled from eastern Asia. The famed Hugo Grotius traced a Nordic ancestry for people north of Panama whereas the Peruvians, he said, were kin to the Chinese.[34] Attempt were now made by scientists to catalogue types of men, and one manner of classification was a division into groups marked by differing hirsute characteristics.

The New World, said one writer, abounded with such variety of inhabitants and new animals unknown to Asia, Africa, or Europe that their origin was very unclear and certainly challenged the theory that all the earth was planted from one little spot: "The grea zeal to maintain a Jewish [i.e., biblical] tradition, put many learned Christians upon the rack to make it out." Noah is irreverently treated in these speculations which lead close to the borders of irreligion.[35]

The influence of anthropology was strong in the development of political theory. Long before Rousseau it was clear that the discoveries of new societies were being carefully applied in the construction of philosophical systems. Hobbes and Locke, especially show a familiarity with the social structure of American Indians which they used to good purpose. Each of the English political scientists wrote in a period of crisis, and in the search for a more valid ordering of society the American Indian was believed to have found many of the answers. The writing of P. J.-F. Lafitau on the American Indians, it has been stated by an eminent modern anthropol

[34] Edw. Brerewood, *Enquiries touching the diversity of languages, and Religions throughout the chief parts of the World* (London, 1614), 96; Grotius *De Origine Gentium Americanorum,* 1642 (E. Goldsmid, Eng. trans., Edinburgh, 1884).

[35] T. Bendyshe, "The History of Anthropology," *Memoirs of the Anthropological Society of London,* I (1863–1864), 352–365; see also José de Acosta *The Natural & Moral History of the Indies* (C. R. Markham, ed., London 1880), I, 45.

gist, was significant for a "synthetic ethnology." His influence on nglish writers and Montesquieu was recognizable, for his work romoted a comparative point of view.[36] Cadwallader Colden, a ersatile personality in colonial New York and historian of the oquois, believed that the society of Indians in their native state ould tell us more of the original political and social structure of all eoples than is to be found "in the most curious speculations of the earned . . . ; the Patriarchal and other Schemes in Politicks are o better than Hypotheses in Philosophy, and as prejudicial to real nowledge." [37]

The impact of the New World, subtle and devious as it somemes was on the *imagination* of Europe, was obvious and drastic on er *economy*. Imports of tobacco, coffee, sugar, furs, various woods, nd vast quantities of silver radically affected the peoples of Europe. verseas commodities became available to greater numbers of eople in the eighteenth century. Items like tea and sugar, once ixuries, became familiar to all. Cotton, first from the East and then om America, was a major factor, because of its cheapness, in ringing about the gradual disappearance of class distinction in ress.

Maize, which was the most widely cultivated New World plant, as introduced to Europe almost immediately after the discovery nd, along with tobacco and the sweet potato, quickly spread over ie earth; the Irish potato, as it was later known, was adopted much iore slowly. By the seventeenth century maize had become firmly stablished as the staple of the diet among the lower classes in southastern Europe. From Spain, which by the 1570's was serving the otato in large quantities in its public institutions, the rest of Europe gradually acquired its use. It was not, however, until the eightenth century that the potato was widely accepted; from then on, mong the poor, it became the first, and too often the last, line of efense against hunger. It was the potato which made life secure

---

[36] J. L. Myres, *The Influence of Anthropology on the Course of Political cience* ("Univ. of Calif., Publ. in Hist.," IV, no. 1, 1916).

[37] C. Colden, *The History of the Five Indian Nations* (New York, 1727), vii.

enough to support the vast increase in population of the eighteen and nineteenth centuries. Ireland and the German states in parti ular made it the main support of the poor.[38]

Great quantities of salt were transported from Venezuela in hu dreds of Dutch ships early in the seventeenth century. Dutch shi ping, in fact, was heavily engaged in New World trade at this tim some fifteen ships were built annually for the Brazil trade alon The sugar that came to Holland in this trade kept twenty-nine sug refineries busy.[39]

Naturally it was Spain, first in possession of western lands, whi was the earliest to experience the reaction to overseas influence- notably in her price revolution—a revolution which was to sprea with comparative rapidity to other countries in Europe in the si teenth century. The measure of the importance of this Indies trea ure in the lives of the Spanish people may be seen by a reference the rate paid for labor. The average annual receipts of America gold and silver (1591–1595, for example) were equivalent to abo twenty-one days' work of all the salaried employees and wage earne in the country. Largely as a result of the imports of precious metal the level that prices reached at this time in Spain and througho Europe was approximately the same that was maintained throug most of the eighteenth and nineteenth centuries. The mint ratio gold to silver was raised from about 10.00 to 1 to about 15.50 to the center, roughly, for the oscillations in the next two centuries. I Spain during the first quarter of the seventeenth century pric were almost three and one-fifth times as high as a century earlie In France prices had almost doubled. England's prices had mo than doubled by the end of the sixteenth century, and during th first part of the Puritan Revolution prices were close to three tim

[38] D. D. Brand, "The Origin and Early Distribution of New World Cu tivated Plants," *Agricultural History*, XIII (1939), 109–117; H. E. Jacob, *S Thousand Years of Bread* (New York, 1944), 205, 213. A Hessian officer duri the American Revolution spoke of potatoes as a blessing to Germany an added, "Columbus brought in exchange for this very useful food venere diseases, a deplorable bargain for the Americans!" (*The Siege of Charlesto . . . Diaries and Letters of Hessian Officers* [B. A. Uhlendorf, ed., Ann Arbo 1938], 340).

[39] E. Sluiter, "Dutch Maritime Power and the Colonial Status Quo, 158 1641," *Pacific Historical Review*, XI (1942), 32, 35.

what they were in 1500.[40] The startling character of these price rises is made manifest by a comparison with United States figures for 1820–1920, which include the peak prices of World War I, and which show a price rise of less than half what Spain experienced in the sixteenth century. Slowly wage rates were adjusted to commodity price increases.

Europe's foreign trade grew steadily in the seventeenth century and then with great rapidity in the eighteenth. The mines of Spanish America in the second half of the eighteenth century produced more than half the world's output of precious metals, and the bullion was coined mainly in Spanish mints on both sides of the Atlantic. Spain's national money, because of its volume and relative stability, had a pre-eminent position in world commerce. It is not surprising that the diplomacy of Europe should often have been concerned with the ways and means of separating Spain from her American treasure.[41] England and France, the dominant western powers, grew fat on this world trade, which far outstripped the growth of internal commerce. Not all of this trade was with America, but a very large fraction of it was, especially with the West Indies and the southern American colonies.

The English and French watched each other hawklike, and proposals for one to outdo the other in overseas trade came from the press like a rain of paper. One of the many English pamphlets said that to beat France, labor must be secured cheaply in the colonies, and manufacturers in England and planters in America must be eased of burdensome taxes and unnecessary restrictions on trade so that goods might be sold more cheaply at home and abroad. The expansion of trade would promote employment in England, cut down poverty and highway robbery, and lift relief burdens from the parishes.[42] Always the internal situation was coupled in the minds of economists with transatlantic realities. Some years earlier, toward the end of the seventeenth century, Sir Josiah Child esti-

---

[40] Hamilton, *American Treasure and the Price Revolution,* 34–35, 72, 207, 208, 210. England's prices 1593–1602 were 2.14 times those of 1501–1510.

[41] E. J. Hamilton, "Monetary Problems in Spain and Spanish America," *Journal of Economic History,* IV (1944), 21–22.

[42] *The Present State of the British and French Trade to Africa and America Consider'd and Compar'd . . .* (London, 1745), 3, 4, 9.

mated that the plantation colonies, mainly the West Indies, wer already giving employment to 200,000 persons in England.

England's exports doubled in the forty years after 1720, and i the period 1762–1792 they doubled again from £14,000,000 t £31,000,000. Imports in the same period increased from almo £10,000,000 to over £37,000,000. The shipping required to tran port this greatly increased trade kept pace with its changing dime sions. More than one and one-quarter million tons of ships cleare from British ports in 1800 as against fewer than half a million i 1760. The proportion that went to ports outside of Europe ros from less than one-quarter in 1700 to one-half during the course c the eighteenth century; total British shipping in foreign trade quac rupled in the eighteenth century. Just before the American Rev lution great quantities of tobacco and rice were sent from the co onies to England and Scotland: 100,000,000 pounds of tobacco i one year, and most of it, like the rice, was re-exported, thus addin large profits to British commerce. English exports to the continent colonies were also steadily rising, and in the period 1761–1765 the almost doubled the imports of over £5,400,000 from the same are

France's overseas economic relations were similar to Great Bri ain's. Both their fortunes in this period were heavily involved in th West Indian trade. The French trade with the Antilles in suga coffee, cocoa, indigo, spices, drugs, and cottonwood was about on fourth of her whole volume of foreign commerce just before he Revolution. In the half-century before the Seven Years' Wa France's foreign trade had tripled, reaching a figure of 600,000,00 francs. Her merchant marine and trade underwent great destru tion in that struggle, but in less than twenty-five years it was mor than restored.[43]

The French and British were acutely conscious of the role c overseas trade in their economy. From it there arose large cities or or close to, the Atlantic Ocean. Improvements in harbor faciliti were made with an eye to increased ocean-going trade. Merchant shippers, bankers made great fortunes out of this trade, a centr feature of which was the traffic in Negro slaves. Africa, too, is a essential ingredient in the creation of the Atlantic civilization. E

[43] L. Gershoy, *From Despotism to Revolution* (New York, 1944), 298, 30 308.

pe's population in the sixteenth and seventeenth centuries could
ɔt readily supply the large mass of labor required for the staple
ops of sugar, tobacco, and cotton.

Postlethwayt estimated the annual gain to England by Negro
bor in her colonies at £3,000,000. Even if it were possible for
hites to work in place of Negroes, he thought it unwise from the
ercantilist view, for it would drain off farmers, laborers, and ar-
sans. This loss of labor would in time interfere with home manu-
ctures, which would be reason enough to dread the prosperity of
ritish colonies. But, Postlethwayt concluded happily, "While we
n be well supplied with Negroes, we can be under no such Appre-
ensions; their Labour will confine the Plantations to *Planting*
nly; which will render our Colonies more beneficial to these King-
oms than the *Mines* of *Peru* and *Mexico* are to the Spaniards." [44]

When Postlethwayt was writing, nearly five hundred slave traders
ere listed in Bristol, London, and Liverpool, half of them in the
st named. In 1771, 190 ships sailed from British ports for Africa
ith a capacity of 47,000 slaves. It has been estimated that in the
ntury before the founding of the federal government over two
illion slaves had been imported into all the British colonies in
merica.[45] British slave traders supplied French and Spanish sugar
anters with half a million Negroes in the eighteenth century. By
e end of that period Liverpool, which earlier had outstripped her
vals, controlled more than half of the British slave trade and a
ttle less than half of the whole European trade in slaves. Despite
casional losses of ships the trade was immensely profitable, bring-
g into Liverpool alone a net annual profit of £300,000 in the
780's. At the close of the century Pitt believed that the annual
come from West Indian plantations was £4,000,000, and it was
is accumulation of capital that helped finance the Industrial Revo-
ution. One estimate has it that the supply of capital in Great
ritain, apart from land, multiplied five times in the sixty years
ter 1740. There was no doubt of the contribution to that supply
ade by overseas trade.[46]

---

[44] M. Postlethwayt, *The African Trade, the great Pillar and Support of the
ritish Plantation Trade in America* . . . (London, 1745), 14, 15.

[45] C. M. MacInness, *England and Slavery* (Bristol, 1934), 89–90.

[46] E. J. Hamilton, "Profit Inflation and the Industrial Revolution, 1751–

West Indian nabobs flaunted their wealth in England, and thei
entrance into politics raised the price of seats in Parliament. Fo
years the very powerful West India interest fought abolition of th
slave trade and any curbs on their monopoly in the home marke
but the American Revolution gave their position a severe blow
The French sugar islands, notably Santo Domingo, now far su
passed their British competitors in profitableness and productivit
French colonial exports and imports at this time needed 164,00
tons of shipping with 33,000 sailors. France took the sugar marke
away from Britain, and this colonial product enabled her to balanc
her world trade favorably. British commercial interest began t
turn more to the independent United States and to India. When th
sugar trade declined cotton more than made up for it; in a trul
impressive manner the Old World economy was bolstered onc
again by the New.[47]

The psychology of class relationships was changed by trade, whic
made society more fluid. It gave "a new face to the whole nation,
said Henry Fielding, "and hath almost totally changed the manner
customs, and habits of the people, more especially of the lower sort"
their humility was changed into pride, "and their subjection int
equality." [48] But it was in lands across the sea that a greater libera
tion of man's spirit was achieved. The westward tide of European
into the regions which produced so much of the new wealth of th
world, and which offered new homes for religious and political dis
senters, grew to respectable size in the seventeenth century, and i
the following years the emigrant ships arrived in steadily increasin
numbers.

1800," *Quarterly Journal of Economics,* LVI (1942), 263. The profits of trad
with India, in Asia, were also of fundamental importance in financing th
Industrial Revolution.

[47] Eric Williams, *Capitalism and Slavery* (Chapel Hill, 1944), 32, 34, 36–37
52, 53, 58, 96, 124, 145.

[48] Quoted in J. B. Botsford, *English Society in the Eighteenth Century as in
fluenced from Oversea* (New York, 1924), 146.

CHAPTER II

Communications and Social Relations

HE terrors of uncertainty in an unknown world were offset by fa-
iiliarity with the certain risks at home. In words that spoke the
iinds of succeeding generations of adventurers, William Bradford
eported the conclusion reached by his fellow Pilgrims; "It was an-
wered, that all great & honourable actions are accompanied with
reat difficulties, and must be both enterprised and overcome with
nswerable courages. It was granted the dangers were great, but not
esperate; the difficulties were many, but not invincible." [1]

Private and governmental enterprise joined hands for diverse
easons in hurrying, sometimes harrying, the people out of Europe,
hough in later years obstacles were placed in the path of skilled
abor proposing to emigrate. After emigrants reached the promised
and, for some the promise was a betrayal. But for many, and their
oices were louder and more numerous, *New England's First
ruits,*[2] as well as those of a later vintage, were indeed sweet.

The literature, often highly colored, reciting the advantages of
merica appeared in many places. Dissenting opinions were few
nd unheeded. Among the publications that moved the world in the
arly years of the eighteenth century was Daniel Falckner's *Unusual
News from Pennsylvania;* this was a collection of answers to ques-
ions propounded by August Hermann Francke, the noted German
eligious leader.[3] In 1704 the three works of most importance in
timulating German emigration appeared together in a single vol-

[1] William Bradford, *History of Plymouth Plantation* (Boston, 1899), 34.

[2] *New England's First Fruits* (London, 1643), 20, 25.

[3] On Falckner, see the translation and introduction by J. F. Sachse in *Penn. Germ. Soc., Proc.,* XIV (1905).

ume; with Falckner's were bound the *Detailed Geographical A* *count* of Francis D. Pastorius and a translation of the *Account* Gabriel Thomas. Some time earlier the writings of William Pe had been translated for German and Dutch readers, who receiv them from his agents scattered throughout the Continent. A go part of the early German literature on America was in fact, devot to the specific object of encouraging emigration, particularly Pennsylvania.

This comparative trickle of publications, partisan or disinterest in intent, was succeeded by a flood of words in the eighteenth ce tury. More newspapers and magazines, more frequent travel ar better postal facilities made America a topic of everyday convers tion. In the *Edinburgh Magazine and Review,* edited by Dav Hume, Adam Smith, and others, a writer stated in 1774: "T knowledge of distant countries is now become general. Those wh in the last wars had occasion to see the continent of America, a other parts, have diffused this knowledge among their countryme . . . Ships of merchandise frequently pass and repass by the weste parts of Scotland and frequent commerce with these inspires th inhabitants with a romantic turn for voyages." And with the cyn cism sometimes born of extended travel, he concluded, "The le they generally see of the world, the greater share of curiosity the have." [4]

There were in the Anglo-American colonies some two hundre thousand people at the end of the seventeenth century, and the numbers were to be rapidly augmented in the following decades. region like New England, which had had few additions from abroa since the first great wave of immigration in the 1630's, began to a sorb different strains—from Ireland and elsewhere—into its bod politic.

The tempo of European transplantation in the eighteenth ce tury appears incredibly slow to a modern mind conditioned by th speed of radio communication and fast airplanes. Because of th very slowness we tend to exaggerate the isolation of each part of th older world from the other, and we assume that their contacts wer

[4] "An Essay on Emigration," in the *Edinburgh Magazine and Review,* (1774), 564.

ecessarily few and infrequent. But if we remember that people ıen did not count on the frequency of communications which we .ke for granted, and that they adjusted their thought and behavior :cordingly, it is fair to say that populations living on the rim of the .tlantic world were in constant touch with each other and were ›nscious of residing in a common community. The Reverend Arch- ›ald Laidlie, accepting a call to a church in New York, reassured is brother in Scotland before he left: "As to the Distance from ·reat Britain, that is not so great as to prevent our frequently hear- ıg from one another as there is a Packet Boat once a month to and 'om New York." [5]

It is natural in looking back to emphasize what is exceptional in ıe past—to single out, for example, those circumstances which ›mpare unfavorably with modern travel developments. Thus many 'riters note the dangers of ocean, as well as land travel, in the ighteenth century. Surely it was, and is, no pleasure trip to cross the .tlantic in a boat of two hundred tons or less, and there were many ıtalities. But modern historians have tended to magnify the dan- ers and the deaths, many of which were due to epidemics which ıight have taken their toll just as well on land. The historian has too ften taken the unusual for the normal, and this is true also in xaggerating the length of the ocean voyage.

The ordinary individual who made an ocean trip generally did ıot care to repeat the experience, but William Bryant, a distin- uished navigator who on occasion acted as postman for Lewis 1orris, made fifty-five voyages between New York and London.[6] In he middle of the eighteenth century Bristol was the port whence nost of the merchandise for America was shipped, and this voyage vas considered sufficiently safe to warrant an insurance rate of but per cent.[7] Trips of four weeks or less were not uncommon, al- hough for poor, unfortunate immigrants the voyages were often nuch longer. Jefferson once made a remarkably fast trip from Bos-

[5] Archibald Laidlie papers, N.Y. Hist. Soc., Dec. 1, 1763.

[6] "Papers of Lewis Morris," *N.J. Hist. Soc. Colls.,* IV (1852), 46 note.

[7] *Scots Magazine,* XVII (1755), 428. Insurers, no doubt, were thinking of rivateers as well as disasters from natural causes. See also Virginia Harrington, *The New York Merchant on the Eve of the Revolution* (New York, 1935), 55–156.

ton to Portsmouth in nineteen days, which included three day spent in fishing on the Newfoundland banks while becalmed. Th prevailing winds generally made the westward voyage the longe one. Franklin said that Nantucket captains, who knew well the Gul Stream, averaged twenty to thirty days across, whether going east o west.

Communications, as might be expected, were more frequent be tween the colonies and England than they were between the col onies and any other part of Europe. For many years letters to an from England were carried by the captains of private vessels. A ba was hung up in a well-frequented coffeehouse to receive letter which the ship's master would transfer across the ocean for a penny or twopence if it were a double letter or parcel. By the end of th seventeenth century provision was made for a general letter office i New York at which all incoming letters were to be deposited an from which outgoing letters were to be sent. The English practic of using postmarks soon spread to the colonies. In the early years o the eighteenth century a proposal was made for a monthly packe service from England to New York, leaving from Bristol, but noth ing was done about it at this time.[8]

Dissatisfaction with existing arrangements led to a reorganizatio in 1711 when the entire postal system was placed under the Londo postmaster. The chief letter offices were in Edinburgh, Dublin, Ne York, and the West Indies under deputy postmasters-general. Rate for a single letter (one sheet of paper) were fixed at one shilling be tween New York and London; New York to Boston, Newport Portsmouth, or Charleston likewise cost a shilling. Ship captains paid one penny for each letter carried, were expected to delive them to the postmasters at port towns and get a receipt for them There was, however, no regularity in postal arrangements. Prob ably the nearest thing to a packet service in the earlier period wa the regular sailing of the fleet from Maine with masts for the Nav and of the tobacco fleet from Virginia.[9] The fairly regular sailin

[8] *Mss. Treasury Letter Books,* IV, 137–138, G.P.O., London.

[9] W. E. Rich, *The History of the United States Post Office to the Year 182* ("Harvard Econ. Studies," XXVII, 1924), 24–26.

of the tobacco fleet helps to account for the comparatively large number of Virginians who made the trip to England.

During the time Franklin was in the postal service a packet line, direct from Falmouth to New York, was established in 1755. Increased trade and pressing need for more frequent contact with provincial governors dictated this improvement. Four vessels, at first small, then later of some two hundred tons, each manned with a crew of thirty, were in the packet service. Soon a line was added to run between Falmouth and Charleston, but this was withdrawn in 1782. A regular service also went to the West Indies. The time allotted for the round trip between Falmouth and New York was four months, but the packets were slower than merchantmen, and their captains disregarded Franklin's instructions on navigation which would have speeded their voyage. The deputy postmaster in New York, Alexander Colden, advertised in the local papers that mails for England would be made up regularly on the second Saturday of every month.[10] After some years had passed the ship captains may have improved their navigation, for the "Speedy Packet" brought the mail to Falmouth from New York in twenty-seven days.[11]

The Anglo-American postal service, though costly, continued to expand. Like so many postal systems, this too operated at a deficit. In the seven years after 1755, the cost of the service between New York and Falmouth was over £62,000, while the revenue was under £13,000. But the service was popular, the increase in American wealth, trade, and population demanded it, the revenue had begun to increase, and a successful effort was made to reduce the cost. Most letters were undoubtedly single-sheet; at 2*d* a letter, £13,000 means at a maximum 1,560,000 letters, which would include intercolonial as well as transatlantic mail. Add to these letters the large number handled privately by ship captains and passengers from ports other than New York, and we see that England and the colonies were not so far apart in space and time as we generally imagine. Demand for the New York to Falmouth service was sufficiently great by 1770 to require that a fifth boat be added to the packets. A monthly service was now in effect, and it was proposed to institute the same arrange-

10 *Holt's N.Y. Gazette,* May 12, 1763.

11 *Public Advertiser,* May 5, 1787.

ment for the southern colonies and the West Indies.[12] The post master-general, Anthony Todd, asked his deputy in New York to send by each packet the very latest American newspapers.[13] Improved facilities also increased the correspondence between the Pennsylvania Dutch and their coreligionists in Europe, although the exchange of letters never reached large proportions.[14]

Franklin had urged that charges for letters be reduced from two pence to a penny to build up volume, and soon thereafter Parliament did reduce the rates, although not to the extent requested.[15] A few years after the Revolution when a discussion arose over the function of a postal system, that constant friend of America, Thomas B. Hollis, wrote to President Willard of Harvard: "I hope the Americans will never raise taxes from the post office, no more than is necessary to defray the expense of carriage of letters, which will be but trifling. Every other charge will operate as a licence upon the press increase the expence of printing and prevent the communication of sentiments which is the life and soul of a republick. Look around you and observe how the press is burdened watched and cramped in the European states." [16]

Postal service between the colonies and the European continent was not very regular (letters generally going via England), although a French packet ran for a time between L'Orient and New York. After the Revolution, in a correspondence between British Postmaster-General Todd and Franklin, it was remarked that the French were about to establish a monthly packet service between L'Orient and New York. Franklin wanted to know England's intentions, and he was informed she would maintain the same service, a vessel leaving from New York the first Wednesday in every month. The French planned to sail every third Wednesday in the month.[17]

---

[12] *Treasury Letter Books,* VIII, 260–263, 264, 301–302; *Treasury Letter Book,* June, 1760–March, 1771, 259–264, 301–302.

[13] *American Letter Book, 1773–1783,* 43, July 6, 1774, Oct. 5, 1774, G.P.O., London.

[14] H. W. Kriebel, "The Schwenkfelders in Penn.," *Penn. Germ. Soc., Proc.,* XIII (1904), 183–185.

[15] *Treasury Letter Book,* June, 1760–March, 1771, 65–66; Wm. Smith, *History of the Post Office in British North America* (Cambridge, Eng., 1920), 35.

[16] "Willard Letters," *Mass. Hist. Soc., Proc.,* XLIII (1909–1910), 622.

[17] *American Letter Book, 1773–1783,* 301–302, 318–320.

Franklin had pointed out that this arrangement would make it possible for Europeans and Americans to write to each other every fortnight. His agile mind frequently sought improvements in navigation: one of his suggestions was for the use of bulkheads in ships to make them less liable to sinking. He sent to a French correspondent a chart of the Gulf Stream for the benefit of navigators.[18]

New Yorkers complained in the 1790's that the service was not nearly so speedy and dependable since the packets began to touch at Halifax, and their request that the direct route be re-established was endorsed by British officials.[19] A proposal was made in the 1790's to open direct communication with the interior of Europe through Hamburg, but nothing was then done about it.[20]

Even in the early years of the eighteenth century North America's ties with Europe were a matter of deep concern to both areas. A crop failure in Europe would draw off so much wheat that embargoes were necessary to prevent hardship in the colonies. American wheat arriving in European ports in quantity forced a lowering of its price. Richard Champion, a Bristol merchant trading to America in the Revolutionary era, emphasized the value of American grain to England. Just prior to the beginning of hostilities he spoke of the shortage in England which had been partly relieved by American shipments: "Had it not been for these supplies," he wrote, "we should have been in great distress." [21] The refusal of the colonies to provide food for the empire in the winter of 1774–1775 would result, said Lord North, in higher prices and a precarious situation in military and civilian supplies. To make up this deficit in overseas shipments an embargo was therefore suggested on Irish exports to the rest of the world in order to save them for the exclusive use of the British

---

[18] Franklin to M. G. Jean de Crèvecoeur, 1783, in A. H. Smyth, *The Writings of Benjamin Franklin* (New York, 1905–1907), IX, 148; hereafter Smyth, *Franklin, Writings.*

[19] New York mechants to British Minister Hammond, Jan. 27, 1792, Pub. Rec. Off., Foreign Office Rec., *Amer. Corr.*, 14.

[20] Rich, 60, 103.

[21] C. K. Shipton, "The Shaping of Revolutionary New England 1690–1740," *Pol. Sci. Quart.*, L (1935), 584–597; G. H. Guttridge, ed., *The American Correspondence of . . . Richard Champion* ("Univ. of Calif., Publ. in Hist.," XXII, no. 1, 1934), 24, 26, 41–42.

Empire. American flour meant much to the Irish, for it had kept down the price of provisions in their country.[22]

Colonial ships ranged far afield, and just before the Revolution it was estimated that of the vessels under British registry, about one-third had been built in the colonies. Transatlantic shipping between Great Britain and the thirteen colonies totaled almost 200,000 tons, about one-sixth of the whole merchant marine possessed by the mother country. The transport of tobacco and rice alone required 80,000 tons of shipping. English shipowners handled 80 per cent of Anglo-American commerce, and the restraints placed upon colonials in this trade were very heavy.[23] British merchants were so intimately tied to American economy that many of them were bankrupted because of the Revolution.

Ships of varying sizes were the links that joined together the Atlantic ports. In the 1760's some two hundred of them a year sailed from London alone for the thirteen colonies.[24] Most of the vessels were between two and three hundred tons; when transporting people, a rough computation assumed loading capacity of one person per ton, although many ships packing them in even more tightly had a heavier passenger list. Large numbers of emigrants left in the 1760's and 1770's; from Irish ports in the five years prior to 1774, 152 ships sailed with nearly 44,000 people, most of whom were in their twenties.[25] Earlier in the century the German Palatine migration moved regularly from Rotterdam to Philadelphia, with the same ships appearing so often that it was in the nature of a ferrying job. In the quarter-century following 1702 nearly fifty thousand Germans left for America. Ninety-five shiploads arrived at Philadelphia between 1727 and 1742. Most of the Germans paid for their passage by selling themselves as indentured servants.[26]

---

[22] M. Kraus, "America and the Irish Revolutionary Movement in the Eighteenth Century," in *The Era of the American Revolution: Studies inscribed to Evarts B. Greene* (New York, 1939), 342; *Hibernian Magazine,* V (Oct., 1775), 610.

[23] L. A. Harper, "Mercantilism and the American Revolution," *Canadian Hist. Rev.,* XXIII (1942), 4 and note 4; Harper, "The Effect of the Navigation Acts in the Thirteen Colonies," in *The Era of the American Revolution.*

[24] Brit. Mus., Add. Mss., 38341 (f. 125).

[25] *Gentleman's Magazine,* XLIV (1774).

[26] H. E. Jacobs, "The German Emigration to America 1709–1740," *Penn.*

Before this, large numbers of Scotch-Irish had begun to arrive at Atlantic ports, and within a comparatively few years fifty-four ships came to New England from Ireland. Even larger numbers went to ports in the middle colonies and South Carolina. Over half of the European emigrants went to the colonies as bound labor; many of them from Britain were convicts. The large Irish immigration to New England overwhelmed Puritan society, and along with new manners, trades, and interests, it introduced a hatred of England which was not present in the older stock.[27]

The price of passage varied. We read that one shipload of Huguenot refugees bound for Virginia at the beginning of the century paid five pounds sterling for adults and fifty shillings for children under twelve.[28] When William Penn was seeking settlers for his colony his prospectus provided for passage of adults at five pounds a head, children under ten, fifty shillings, and babies nothing. Forty shillings per ton was charged for their freight, but one chest free was allowed to every passenger. At the end of the eighteenth century superior accommodations for cabin passengers cost twenty-five guineas or more, for which sum they were supplied with everything except bedding and linen; steerage was eight to ten pounds but sometimes much less, children at half-price. The Reverend Henry Toulmin was at great pains to arrange details for a more agreeable trip; a stock of raisins, prunes, lemons, oranges, and apples, he found, added much to its pleasure. The traffic lanes were busy at this time, for more than 1,800 ocean-going vessels arrived at New York and Philadelphia in 1788.[29]

Germ. Soc. Proc., VIII (1898), 144; C. Bridenbaugh, *Cities in the Wilderness 1625–1742* (New York, 1938), 409; see A. E. Smith, *Colonists in Bondage* (Chapel Hill, 1947); R. B. Morris, *Government and Labor in Early America* (New York, 1946), 319, 392.

[27] C. Wittke, *We Who built America* (New York, 1939), 49; C. K. Shipton, "Immigration to New England 1680–1740," *Jour. Pol. Eco.*, XLIV (1936), 234, 239; Morris, 315, 316 note 3.

[28] *Virginia Hist. Soc., Colls.*, n.s., V (1886), 16.

[29] J. L. Mesick, *The English Traveler in America 1785–1835* (New York, 1921), 18; *Rev. Henry Toulmin's Journal 1793–1794*, II, Huntington Library Mss.; F. B. Dexter, ed., *The Literary Diary of Ezra Stiles* (New York, 1901), III, 341, Feb. 20, 1789 (hereafter Stiles, *Diary*).

Although many Englishmen had left their homeland with few regrets it is clear that their thoughts often turned to the mother country. Their conversation and their letters reveal this nostalgia. For some Americans engaged in business, study, or promoting closer religious association between the ocean-separated sects, there were opportunities to travel and savor the life of London and other capital cities. Colonials regretted, especially in earlier years, a certain sparseness in their cultural milieu; "unfurnisht America," with its unpolished airs, said one, denied the posterity of Englishmen an opportunity to acquire praiseworthy accomplishments.[30]

Many colonials took advantage of their stay in England to engage in genealogical research and were delighted when they discovered near or even distant relatives. One Winthrop had complained to another early in the eighteenth century that Americans were very careless of genealogies, which, he prophesied, would be highly esteemed in another generation.[31] Franklin looked up the family tree, and so did less famous Americans. The former found the ancestral home and carefully deciphered the family names and dates on the worn, moss-covered gravestones. He told his sister, Jane Mecom, that very few Franklin kin were left in England, and he drew a genealogical chart of the family for her. In passing, he referred to Cotton Mather's *Magnalia* as a valuable aid in genealogical researches.[32] The Tilghman families in England and America exchanged gifts and genealogical information, and members of the colonial branch who traveled abroad were made welcome in the old home. An English Tilghman thought heavy taxes in the mother country might drive people to America. Writing in 1743, he believed it probable that the colonies within ten years would be "Eligible for freedom and opulence & become more populous than the old Island." [33]

When visitors to the colonies arrived from England they too sought out relatives with whom they joined in pleasant family re-

[30] J. W. to Gov. Fitz-John Winthrop, no date, early eighteenth century, Winthrop papers, IX, 7, Mass. Hist. Soc.

[31] Feb. 2, 1709/10, Winthrop papers, IX, 16.

[32] George Boyd to John Wendell, London, Aug. 26, 1774, *Mass. Hist. Soc., Proc.*, XLVIII (1914–1915); Carl Van Doren, *Benjamin Franklin* (New York, 1938), 280; Jane Mecom Mss., Amer. Phil. Soc., Nov. 11, 1758, July 17, 1771.

[33] H. Tilghman, ed., "Letters between the English and American Branches of the Tilghman Family 1697–1764," *Maryland Hist. Mag.*, XXXIII (1938), 148, 163–164.

unions. On his grueling journey through America in 1755, Samuel Fothergill found rest and a warm welcome in the homes of cousins in Newport. He wrote to his wife that he was sending home dried apples and peaches, "and perhaps some fruit trees and should be glad they might be planted in the Garden untill my return." [34] The Scots were told of an American recipe which enabled housewives to provide light cakes for their visitors and friends in a few minutes. Peter Collinson urged John Custis in Virginia to raise fox grapes for wine. He wrote also that tomatoes, "apples of love," were much used in Europe; Italians, who called them "tamiatas," put them into broths and soups to give them "a pretty Tart Taste." Collinson himself planned to try the experiment. The interrelationship between England and foreign lands was reflected even in playing cards which taught Britons the geography of the Americas; the queen was Elizabeth and the knave was a cannibal representing the Caribbean Islands.[35]

Gifts were frequently sent to friends overseas. John Fothergill sent candlesticks to William and James Logan: "They save the eyes very much," he wrote, "and make either reading or writing by candle-light much more easy." [36] A less useful gift, two turtles, was sent by the Boston Sons of Liberty to their London idol, John Wilkes.[37] Apples as gifts from America are often mentioned in correspondence, melons were requested (although it was pointed out they would not keep beyond ten days), and Indian bows and arrows, buckskin, etc., were prized souvenirs. Michael Collinson said that great quantities of American apples had been imported, they were better than Europe's finest but were too expensive for common eating.[38] Business and friendship often blended. Thomas Longman, the London publisher, received from Henry Knox, the Boston

[34] Crosfield Mss. (43), June 27, Sept. 30, 1755; also Port. 22 (50), June 5, 1755, Friends House, London.

[35] *Scots Magazine,* LXI (1799), 827–828; Curwin papers, II, Amer. Antiq. Soc., Jan. 25, 1738/39, Feb. 6, 1742/43; W. H. Willshire, *A Descriptive Catalogue of Playing and other Cards in the British Museum* (London, 1876), 236, also p. 28 of supplement.

[36] Port. 38 (82), Fothergill to W. Logan, Friends House, London.

[37] Wilkes corr., July 26, 1769, Brit. Mus., Add. Mss., 30870 (f. 171).

[38] *Correspondence between William Penn and James Logan* ("Hist. Soc. Penn., Memoirs," IX, 1876), 231, 3d 2d mo. 1703, Penn to Logan; Logan to Penn, Sept. 2, 1703; Darlington, 454, Feb. 25, 1773.

bookseller, a gift of "three pair of Ducks"; in response he sent a watch.[39] People from all walks of life, acquaintances and unknowns, were forever sending things to Franklin in his European homes. Some sought his favor to advance business interests, others were "headhunters," most people simply adored him.

Americans in London could keep in touch with their home communities in the several coffeehouses named after their provinces, where fellow colonials regularly met. Peter Manigault of South Carolina, then studying law in London, wrote he had met a friend at the Carolina Coffee House. Apparently not much impressed by England, he told his family he saw nothing there that would make him quit his native country. Those having contacts with Pennsylvania found it convenient to meet in the Pennsylvania Coffee House in Birchin Lane, London; it was here that Franklin usually received his mail. Almost a century before, on a trip to London, Increase Mather found congenial companions from Massachusetts at the New England Coffee House and gossiped about home with old Harvard men living in England.[40] The noted scientist, Sir Hans Sloane, smoothed the way for two generations of one American family. Zabdiel Boylston, the elder, who fought for the new method of attacking smallpox by inoculation, remembered Sloane's kindness and commended his son to him. The younger man was going to London to study medicine, and the father spoke of him proudly as "the first fruits of Inoculation in the American World." [41]

Homes of distinguished Americans abroad, Franklin's and later John Adams', and the residences of close friends of Americans, such as Dr. John Fothergill's, were meeting places for travelers, students and just homesick colonials. A lady from the Old Dominion, married to a London merchant, made a practice of filling her house every Christmas with Virginia dinner guests. Edward Dilly, the noted bookseller, entertained Americans whom he introduced to England's celebrities. The friendship between Edward and Charles

---

[39] H. Cox and J. E. Chandler, *The House of Longman, 1724–1794* (London, 1925), 12.

[40] *So. Carolina Hist. and Geneal. Mag.*, XV–XVI (1914–1915), 114–115, June 26, 1750.

[41] Murdock, 263; Sloane Mss., Brit. Mus. 4055 (f. 238), Dec. 14, 1726; (f. 248), Dec. 19, 1737.

)illy and Benjamin Rush, the noted doctor from Philadelphia, ex-
ended over a period of more than thirty years.[42] Abigail Adams in
London saw plenty of her own countrymen; "I hardly know how
o think myself out of my own country," she said, "I see so many
Americans about me." The journal of Adams' daughter, under date
of November 1, 1787, mentioned that representatives of seven states
at down together to dinner, and some of them topped off the re-
union with a theater party.[43] On another occasion Miss Adams was
n a gathering in Paris and to her dismay (for she wanted to learn
about Europeans) found they were mostly Americans. The wealthy
William Bingham and his wife were the center of an American
group in Paris. Englishmen traveling in America were less likely to
run across familiar faces. One Englishman, John Bernard, an actor
at the end of the century, did have the thrill of meeting London acquaintances in a Boston theater.[44]

Londoners were asked to act as guides to Americans anxious to
see the sights. Dr. Alexander Garden, of Charleston, wrote to the
noted naturalist John Ellis, asking him to shepherd some friends
who wished to see the British Museum.[45] The must list of sights
for the modern tourist was already part of the schedule of the
eighteenth-century visitor. When John Adams' daughter was leaving for England, he told her to see Westminster Abbey, St. Paul's,
the British Museum, Josiah Wedgwood's earthenware factory, and
the famous actress, Mrs. Siddons. Of the latter Miss Adams wrote,
"I could see her forever, and still behold her with new delight and
satisfaction." Mrs. John Adams spoke of visiting the church at Leyden "in which our forefathers worshipped when they fled from
hierarchical tyranny and persecution. I felt a respect and venera-
tion upon entering the doors," she said, "like what the ancients paid

---

[42] H. R. Marraro, trans., *Memoirs of the Life and Peregrinations of the Florentine Philip Mazzei 1730–1816* (New York, 1942), 165–166; Dilly to Rush, April 26, 1770, Feb. 13, 1771; Jan. 6, 1795, Rush corr., Ridgway Library.

[43] Quoted in E. B. Greene, *The Revolutionary Generation* (New York, 1943), 419; K. M. Roof, *Col. William Smith and Lady* (New York, 1929), 67, 187.

[44] Mesick, 8.

[45] J. E. Smith, *A Selection of the Correspondence of Linnaeus and other Naturalists . . .* (London, 1821), I, 583, Garden to Ellis, Jan. 26, 1771 (hereafter, Smith, *Corr. of Linnaeus*).

to their druids." [46] Drawing up a list of "objects of Attention for an American," Jefferson urged his compatriots traveling in Europe to concentrate on the useful arts, industrial and agricultural. Painting and statuary were worth seeing, he added, but not worth studying because America, he thought, was as yet too poor to support artists.[47]

Friendships begun in America or England were kept alive by transatlantic correspondence. Quaker homes like that of the bookseller James Phillips were familiar stops for Americans. The home of Adey Bellamy in England was a gathering place for American Friends, and when they returned to their own land they prized the memory of its associations. "Your house I remember with pleasure," wrote Samuel Emlen, "the kindness Ye shewed me will I hope be a means of exciting my Care to be useful & a means of Encouragement to Strangers when they fall in my Way in this Land." [48] The Fothergill home was a mecca for Americans, who remembered warmly its kindness.[49] A visitor, returned to Philadelphia, tells Ann Fothergill that he is writing "at the convenient Desk" furnished him by her generosity. More than thirty years after attendance together at the University in Edinburgh, Benjamin Rush and Joshua Dixon were exchanging writings and recalling student days.[50]

Englishmen were urged to travel in America, as well as in Europe, for pleasure and instruction. It was pointed out that hunting in America was excellent, with plenty of deer, bear, buffalo, wolves, and foxes. Wild turkeys were numerous and wild pigeons "in prodigious great flocks." And the Izaak Waltons were lured with tales of the quantity and variety of fish to be had. Governor Gooch of Virginia thought English doctors would benefit by traveling through the colonies, learning about native plants and their medical uses.[51]

---

[46] Roof, 54, 152; Edward Dumbauld, *Thomas Jefferson, American Tourist,* (Norman, 1946), 116.

[47] G. Chinard, *Thomas Jefferson* (Boston, 1929), 165; but Jefferson himself was an art enthusiast.

[48] Gibson Mss., I, 107, Philadelphia, May 5, 1773, Friends House, London.

[49] Port. 22 (147), R. Jones to Ann Fothergill, Dec. 4, 1788, Friends House, London.

[50] T. J. Pettigrew, *Memoirs of John Coakley Lettsom* (London, 1817), III, 385, 387, Aug. 22, 1800.

[51] John Clayton to S. Durrent, Mar. 21, 1739, *Va. Mag. Hist. and Biog.*, VII

One of London's greatest doctors, John Fothergill, never got to America, but he had many friends there whose communications were a substitute for travel. Of a recent trip he had taken to the Continent he wrote to Israel Pemberton, in Philadelphia, that it enabled him "to judge of other nations without prejudice" and to study the history of man with more exactness.[52] Crèvecoeur criticized European travelers interested in the dead civilizations of an older Italy, urging that they spend their money and time more profitably in America. Only there, he said, might the traveler "contemplate the very beginnings and outlines of human society." [53]

Apparently not very many cared to make the ocean trip as tourists, but some who did published their impressions and thus gave us a varied picture of eighteenth-century America. Over eight hundred travelers in North America, from 1700 to the Revolution, left accounts which mixed the veracious with the fallacious in proportions familiar to travelers since Herodotus. Travel reports by Englishmen, Germans, and others were supplemented by over one hundred accounts written by Frenchmen after their American journey.[54]

Those Europeans who did visit America found enough of a cosmopolitan society in the coastal towns to make them feel at ease. There were intelligent conversation, an appreciation of the latest literature, and sufficient sophistication to make the time pass quickly for the traveler. The speed with which the latest fashions were imported from the mother country was a matter for astonished comment; "I am almost inclined to believe," wrote William Eddis from Maryland, "that a new fashion is adopted earlier by the polished and affluent Americans, than by many opulent persons in the great metropolis [London]. . . ." He was delighted and surprised to find good theatrical performances in the colonies, consid-

(1899), 172–174; Gov. Wm. Gooch to Bishop of London, June 29, 1729, *ibid.*, XXXII (1924), 229.

52 Port. 38 (81), Jan. 28, 1741, Friends House, London.

53 J. H. St. John Crèvecoeur, *Letters from an American Farmer* (New York, 1925), introductory letter.

54 J. R. Masterson, "Records of Travel in North America 1700–1776," *Harvard Univ., Summaries of Theses, 1936* (Cambridge, 1938), 339; F. Monaghan, *French Travellers in the United States 1765–1932* (New York, 1933).

ering them equal at least to those in English provincial theaters.[55]

Even the physical surroundings, especially in Philadelphia, Ne
York, Boston, and Charleston (the South Carolina town, said La
fayette, was "one of the most beautiful cities he had ever seen"), im
pressed visitors as eminently suitable for pleasurable living. Phila
delphia, wrote one observer in the middle of the century, neede
only the streets to be paved "to make it appear to advantage, fo
there is few towns if any in England that are better Illumin'd wit
Lamps, & those of the best Sort, nor their watch better regulated."
New York's houses were said to compare favorably with those of th
empire's capital, and her streets were believed to be better pave
than London's.[56] The popular *Gentleman's Magazine* told its read
ers that only London's structures exceeded the size and quality o
Boston's.[57] Jefferson, an excellent observer, thought Philadelphi
handsomer than Paris or London. The architecture of these Euro
pean capitals was in the "most wretched style" he had ever seen, "no
meaning to except America, where it is bad." [58] Benjamin Silliman
the Yale professor traveling in England at the turn of the centur
believed Liverpool's residences to be inferior to those of New York
Philadelphia and Boston, but he did think her public building
"elegant." Like other Americans, he too felt more at ease with Eng
lishmen in country districts and in the smaller towns. Bristol wa
especially favored by New Englanders who found in the seaport'
customs and manners a strong similarity to their own.

An English botanist wrote to a correspondent in Charleston ad
vocating the creation of public gardens, parks, and the like to beau
tify American communities. The always benevolent Peter Collin
son wrote to John Custis in Virginia that rows of horse-chestnu
trees planted in the streets of Williamsburg "would have a fine Ef

---

[55] Wm. Eddis, *Letters from America . . . 1769 to 1777 . . .* (London, 1792) 93, 112.

[56] *Some Cursory Remarks made by James Birket in his Voyage to North America 1750–1751* (New Haven, 1916), 67; *Scots Magazine,* XVII (1755), 75–76; L. Gottschalk, *Lafayette joins the American Army* (Chicago, 1937), 7.

[57] *Gentleman's Magazine,* XXV (1755), 15–18.

[58] A. A. Lipscomb, ed., *The Writings of Thomas Jefferson* (Monticello ed., Washington, D.C., 1904), V, 304–305, to John Page, May 4, 1786; Benjamin Silliman, *Journal of Travels in England, Holland, Scotland . . . 1805 and 1806* (New York, 1810), I, 49; II, 50.

ect"; they are, he added "very good natured Trees grow in any Soil nd in any Place." Collinson also recommended the early-flowering nagnolia to Custis.[59]

There are no statistics on travel in this period, though there are ndications that it increased considerably toward the end of the entury. Early in the nineteenth century William Tudor boasted of Boston's many travelers. Certainly among its wealthier citizens, he aid, it would be difficult to find a group of half a dozen in which ome, if not most of the party, had not visited Europe. Business, leasure, and study drew them, particularly to England; women also raveled. "You might find a large circle of both sexes," he said, "who ave not only seen London and Paris, but Rome and Naples." [60]

The Earl of Buchan thought nothing was more valuable for Brit-in's peace, industry, and happiness "than an interchange of citi-ens with congenial America, and whoever discourages that inter-hange must be considered as no friend to the happiness of either ide of the Atlantic or the interests of humanity at large." [61] The amous philologist, Sir William Jones, told Arthur Lee that if young Englishmen had "any English spirit, they would finish their educa-ion by visiting the United States, instead of fluttering about Italy; and strive to learn rather political wisdom from republicans, than to pick up a few superficial notions of the fine arts, from the poor hralls of bigotry and superstition." [62]

An interchange of ideas and products aided in the beautification of many homes, rural as well as urban. William Hamilton, from Pennsylvania, was so impressed by the "natural style of landscape-gardening" he saw on a visit to England after the Revolution that on his return he remodeled his own place so that it was said to be the best example of landscape gardening in America. Far-sailing ship captains and correspondents in all parts of the world sent him speci-mens for his gardens. Hamilton took note in England of the pleasing

---

59 Smith, *Corr. of Linnaeus,* I, 459, Ellis to Garden, Aug. 25, 1759; Curwin papers, II, Oct. 20, 1734, April 2, 1744.

60 Wm. Tudor, *Letters on the Eastern States* (New York, 1820), 317.

61 *Gentleman's Magazine,* LXIV (1794), 587, letter to editor, July 12, 1794; also *The Bee* (Edinburgh), XVII (Jan. 1, 1794), 323.

62 A. B. Shepperson, *John Paradise and Lucy Ludwell of London and Williamsburg* (Richmond, 1942), 177.

effect of ivy climbing over buildings and arches, and he ordere
some for a new bridge on his estate.[63]

Homes in America and Europe were made safer through the us
of Franklin's lightning rod and were made more comfortable b
his stove. Both improvements were adopted by Englishmen, and i
time they found their way to other parts of Europe. A notice of a
English adaptation of the stove, which changed the design a lit
tle, emphasized that it was based on Franklin's, which was adver
tised as the "most effectual and elegant mode of warming a larg
Room." [64] Letters from Lord Kames, Turgot, Gronovius, the Dutc
botanist, and many others all attest to a wide European interest i
the new stoves. A request came from Florence for them, and unde
Franklin's direction a craftsman began their manufacture. A Mil
anese periodical carried a long description of the stove; in a shor
time, said a contemporary, they were being sold in Italy and ex
ported to other countries.[65]

A gift of a silk-grass hammock was sent to an English botanis
from Carolina; "It will be at least a curiosity," wrote Alexande
Garden good-naturedly, "and a proof to your infidels what Americ
can produce." Franklin was proud to send his friend Peter Collinso
some candles which he thought gave a flame nearer to natural ligh
than any he had ever seen. He included also a few cakes of America
soap "made of Myrtle Wax, said to be the best Soap in the Worl
for Shaving or Washing fine Linnens, etc." Hand soap from Vir
ginia sent to Bristol was judged equal to the best Castile.[66] It is cer
tainly odd to read now of Jefferson's dilemma in Paris; because h
couldn't get "good & genuine Madeira wine" there, he was import
ing it from New York, "where it is generally to be had good." [67]

Women of fashion in England were said to have borrowed fo

---

[63] *Penn. Mag. of Hist. and Biog.*, XXIX (1905), 70.

[64] A. Walker, *A Philosophical Estimate of the Causes, Effects, and Cure o Unwholesome Air in Large Cities* . . . (London, 1777), 15.

[65] Marraro, 165; *Scelta di opuscoli interessante tradotti da varie lingue* (Milan), I, 15–83.

[66] Smith, *Corr. of Linnaeus*, I, 513, Garden to Ellis, Feb. 26, 1762; Smyth, *Franklin, Writings*, III, 262, June 26, 1755; *Scots Magazine*, XXVIII (1766), 271.

[67] Jefferson to F. Lewis, Feb. 9, 1786; Lewis sent it, May 9, 1786, Jefferson papers, Mass. Hist. Soc.

headdress during the Revolutionary era the Indian mode of wearing feathers for decoration. American beaver hats and some especially fine examples of cotton manufacture were admired in London. But English productions in turn captured American fancy. They were of all sorts which went to enrich the material culture of people overseas—clothing, furnishings, etc.; and a new type of lamp that Jefferson had seen in London was speedily dispatched to his friends in America.[68]

The colonies were more appreciated for their production of wealth for England than for their physical charms. According to one statement America had become the "fountain" of her riches; "for with America," it said, "our greatest trade is carried on. . . ." The *London Magazine* acknowledged that a very considerable part of England's wealth and much of her employment were supported by the American colonies, especially the West Indies, "yet there is a set of people over here who grudge every expence we are put to for [their] support. . . ." Another British periodical said that the English colonies "were always of great Consequence but they are now [1756] of the *utmost* Consequence to the Nation; for at least one Half of our Commerce depends upon them." [69] English exports to the colonies in general greatly exceeded imports, except for Virginia and Maryland, which shipped large quantities of tobacco, but even these, after the Revolution, took far more from England than they sent to her.[70] Adam Smith was of the opinion that trade with America was more valuable to Europe than that with the East Indies.

In his defense of the rights of the colonists, James Otis reminded the Old World that from the New "as from an endless source, wealth and plenty, the means of power, grandeur and glory in a degree unknown to the hungry chiefs of former ages, have been pouring into

[68] *Scots Magazine,* XXVI (1764), 454; Jefferson, *Writings,* V, 294, April 22, 1786.

[69] *Scots Magazine,* XVII (1755), 77–78; *London Magazine,* XXV (July, 1756), 328–331; *Monthly Review,* XIV (1756), 29–37.

[70] See tables in Charles Whitworth, *State of the Trade of Great Britain . . . from the year 1697* (London, 1776), with pencil notations of trade figures to 1801, in Public Record Office copy; Prof. L. A. Harper of Berkeley, California, kindly showed me his notes on this.

Europe for three hundred years past." [71] This reminder by Ot. seemed hardly needed, for British periodicals in these years gav greatly increased space to news of American manufactures, popul: tion, politics, and the like, which made the colonies themselve conscious of their growing importance.

After the Seven Years' War, it was argued in Britain that trad with America should be an alternative for England's commerc with the Continent, "where we have Competitors to encounter." One writer proposed that Anglo-American political-economic rel: tionships be so intertwined as to make for a sounder imperial struc ture. England's surplus capital, he believed, should be invested i American lands; "If every *man of property* in *England,"* he said "was under some *political necessity* of having an *estate in America* we could have no dispute about rights of legislation or taxation because we should then truly be but one people, in interest as wel as in blood." American demand for English manufactures (if mor money had been invested in the colonies) would have increased s fast that "we should long since have wanted no other market.' Rather than have speculation in government funds, which raisec the price of labor and necessaries, the writer suggested that in th future no one who did not own sufficient arable land in Americ: should be elevated to the peerage, or hold any important appointiv office, or be permitted to sit in the House of Commons. Restriction were to be placed on further purchases in England by any individ ual until he had acquired lands in America and Ireland. Thus, con cluded the argument, no restraints would need to be placed or colonial trade, "the gains of America would be understood . . . tc be the gains of Great Britain; For it would be no longer the interes of the man who had an estate in Middlesex to prevent the product o his other estate in Virginia from coming directly to the best marke and at the least charge." [73]

---

[71] M. C. Tyler, *Literary History of the American Revolution* (New York 1897), I, 49.

[72] Thomas Whately, *Considerations on the Trade and Finances of thi Kingdom* . . . (3rd ed., London, 1769), 20.

[73] *Political Speculations, or an Attempt to discover the Causes of the Dear ness of Provisions, and High Price of Labour, in England; with some Hint for remedying those Evils* (Part the Second, London, 1767), 52–62.

Another writer, evidently representing a different level of British society, contrasted the virtues of small holdings in New England with the iniquities of large landholdings at home. This, he maintained, was the basis for the greater liberty enjoyed by the New Englanders. He believed that the grant of small allotments was the right way to settle Canada.[74]

It was widely recognized that the increase of American population would be a great addition to English power and wealth. It is, said a contemporary, "the only equivalent . . . for that great superiority in numbers, which our enemies have over us in Europe." America would thus in truth enable England to maintain the traditional balance of power.[75] In an argument favoring a conciliatory policy toward America at a time when tempers were rising, Caleb Evans quoted Lord Chatham to the effect that the profit to Great Britain from her trade with the colonies was £2,000,000 annually; "THIS," said Chatham, "is the fund that carried you triumphantly through the last war." [76]

The uneasy in mind feared America as an economic competitor whose full strength was soon to be revealed. The farther-seeing ones in America and in England, with a vision of Anglo-American destiny, had almost grasped the true nature of an Atlantic commonwealth on the eve of the Revolution. Many publications during the era of the American Revolution indicate the fertility of political thought in the Anglo-American world, with their plans for autonomous dominions and international co-operation, but more than half a century passed before these theories found some fulfillment in the famed Durham Report.[77]

---

[74] *Memoirs of Thomas Hollis* (London, 1780), 661, appendix, paper signed Marcus Aurelius, Jan. 23, 1767. He also criticized large holdings in New York and the South.

[75] John Mitchell, *The Present State of Great Britain and North America with regard to Agriculture, Population, Trade, and Manufactures* . . . (London, 1767), viii–lx.

[76] C. Evans, *A Letter to the Rev. Mr. John Wesley* . . . (London, 1775), 20.

[77] *The American War of Independence, its History, Origin and Progress as revealed by Contemporary Books, Pamphlets, Manuscripts, Maps and Plans* (London, 1931), introduction by R. G. Adams; J. P. Boyd, *Anglo-American Union: Joseph Galloway's Plans to preserve the British Empire 1774–1788* (Philadelphia, 1941), 7, and *passim;* C. F. Mullett, "English Imperial Thinking," *Pol. Sci. Quart.*, XLV (1930), 548–579.

CHAPTER III

Religious Relations

THE lines of communication and business enterprise that joined the widely dispersed areas of the Atlantic community were reinforced by a whole cultural complex which picked a lonely scientist, artist, or religious leader out of his colonial isolation and made him part of a larger fraternity of like-minded people. Colonials in pre-Revolutionary years, measuring themselves against the great of Europe, sometimes exaggerated their own limitations, almost as if to say: "We are pretty good, don't you think, considering our handicaps?" This sense of inferiority was deepened when, by a laudable ambition, colonials compared their communities to the capitals of Europe, rather than to provincial towns alongside of which they would have shown to much better advantage.

It is a mistake to picture the colonists as merely awaiting the continued flow of civilization from abroad. They were, as we have already indicated in their economic and social affairs, active contributors to its further creation; but as befitted their secondary position in this early period they were rarely the prime movers. In general the cultural activities of the colonies reflected the strength or weakness of similar patterns in the homelands. In the power of their religious ideas, however, and in the novelty of their practical application of such beliefs as separation of church and state, the American colonists were conscious of being in the vanguard of eighteenth-century progress.

The cross-fertilization of religious thought and the mutual support each region accorded the other in effecting changes in religious life are striking features of European-American cultural relations in the eighteenth century. Local forces generating a renewal of spiritual life in both Europe and America were strengthened by migrant beliefs and believers moving overseas in both eastward and westward directions. The complacency and placidity of old-established churches were shaken by the bubbling enthusiasm that welled up from the lower depths. National boundaries, as well as class divisions, were ignored in the creation of the city of God that transcended geography. Rationalists and like bold spirits, who were aliens in the new city of God, also sought communion with their fellows in near and distant lands.

In emphasizing that the eighteenth century was an age of reason, and at times antireligious, we forget too often the powerful ties which were then binding the religious life of two continents. These ties were made of many strands. The Anglican Church had in A. W. Boehme a very close link with German Protestantism. He was pastor of the Court Chapel, a pupil of the great A. H. Francke, and brought to the attention of English and German churches authoritative works which promoted friendlier relations between them. Boehme was indeed an important factor in fostering union between the Church of England and German Protestantism. He also promoted German migration. With great regularity ships went back and forth transporting Palatines to the New World. The earliest records of their churches, and indeed of all other churches in the colonies, show how dependent, financially, such institutions were upon the Old World for building construction, books, and guidance.

Heinrich M. Mühlenberg, leader of the American Lutherans, who was trained at Halle and Göttingen, retained his close ties with Halle, whose institutions exerted a profound influence in the colonies. It is worth noting that all three of his sons were also trained at Halle. The Lutherans in New York maintained fraternal relations continuously with ecclesiastical bodies in Europe, but they emphasized religious autonomy as against the direction exercised by the consistory at Amsterdam.[1] The Reformed Church in Pennsylvania was always in close touch with the classis in Holland. Ministers coming and going through the colonies kept the scattered

[1] A. J. Van Laer, trans., "The Lutheran Church in New York 1649–1772. Records in the Lutheran Church Archives at Amsterdam, Holland," *N.Y. Pub. Library, Bull.*, XLVIII (1944), 31–60, 409–418, 471–484, 761–776, 907–929.

flocks in America in touch with one another but also preserved the ties with the mother church in Europe.

The threads that linked believers in this Atlantic world ran through luxurious churches and humble chapels on the Continent in Britain, and in her imperial possessions. A list of English ministers (including schoolmasters) receiving the King's bounty of £20 for passage to the continental and West Indian colonies showed more than twelve hundred emigrants in the eighteenth century. Many of those on the list were born in the colonies and had gone to England for holy orders.[2] In the previous century twenty-seven Harvard-trained ministers went to England before 1660, and Cotton Mather asserted that from the founding of Harvard "Old England had more ministers from New than our New-England had since *then* from Old." A recent student asserts that some sixty New Englanders went to England in the seventeenth century to serve in the ministry. Some played important parts on the Puritan side during the period of the Commonwealth.[3] The treasured *Bay Psalm Book* of Massachusetts ran through eighteen editions in England (the last in 1754) and twenty-two in Scotland by 1759. Richard Baxter, the greatest of English Puritans, evidently admired Increase Mather, to whom he dedicated his *The Glorious Kingdom of Christ . . .* (1691). Mather's own writings had a small but appreciative audience in London, and editions of his *De Successo Evangelii* (1688) were published for German, French, and Dutch readers.[4]

It was the nonconforming sects, generally, which supplied the motive power for religious change and adjustment. The Dissenters were far and away the most politically minded people of their day. The challenge that was flung at authoritarianism in politics and economics was thrown also at the established churches. At first the challenge was rather timidly offered, but soon after the middle of the century the revolutionary ferment at work in politics and economics gave strength as well to religious dissent. Apparently it

---

[2] G. Fothergill, *A List of Emigrant Ministers to America 1690–1811* (London, 1904).

[3] T. G. Wright, *Literary Culture in Early New England 1620–1730* (New Haven, 1920), 22, 62, 92; W. L. Sachse, "The Migration of New Englanders to England 1640–1660," *Amer. Hist. Rev.*, LIII (1948), 251–279.

[4] Murdock, 266, 271.

was the Dissenters, particularly in New England, who inoculated George Whitefield with "strong prejudices" against the Established Church.[5]

Quaker influence also weakened Establishments. The vigorous English Quaker, Thomas Story, holding a meeting in Stamford, Connecticut, at the end of the seventeenth century, read the local officials a lesson in religious freedom. In answer to the warrant estopping his Quaker services, he "stood up," his journal reads, and "acquainted the People with the Law of Toleration in England . . . and that they of Connecticut ought not (by their Charter) to have any Law there to the contrary." But the independent colonial officials said they "did not depend upon the Laws of England, but stood upon their own Foundation; and they had a Law, that no Quakers should have any Meeting . . . and none there should be." Despite the sharp exchange of words, however, the meeting was held and thus, in this group, made up of diverse believers, the leavening influence of toleration was allowed to work its beneficent way.[6]

A New England Congregational publication by Samuel Mather, dedicated to Samuel Holden, a director of the Bank of England, noted the libertarian sentiments on both sides of the ocean and emphasized that the liberties of the colonial churches "must be deem'd to be as sacred things as the Ecclesiastical Liberties of the National Churches of England and Scotland." [7] John Erskine, of Scotland, warned Mather against the interference of the Anglican Church. The latter, said Erskine, apparently believed it was rendering a greater service to God by converting "Presbyterians and Congregationalists to Episcopacy . . . than Heathens to Christianity." [8]

It was not, obviously, the exclusive prerogative of the colonies to set an example of toleration. The more liberal attitude of the English government, inspired in part, no doubt, by mercantilist considerations, led to a warning by the Board of Trade against Vir-

---

[5] Luke Tyerman, *The Life of the Rev. George Whitefield* (London, 1876–1877), I, 334 and note.

[6] *A Journal of the Life of Thomas Story* . . . with original Ms. letters interleaved (New Castle upon Tyne, 1747), 178–179.

[7] Samuel Mather, *An Apology for the Liberties of the Churches in New England* (Boston, 1738), dedication.

[8] Erskine to Mather, March 16, 1764, Curwin papers, II, 128.

ginia's harsh treatment of Dissenters. Religious liberty, said the Board, was "essential to the enriching and improving of a trading nation." English sympathizers won a measure of relief for New England religious minorities, notably Episcopalians, and the Privy Council intervened to release Dissenters who had been imprisoned for opposing assessment of church taxes.[9]

Lest we think it an age of continuous controversy, it should be pointed out that denominations occasionally did have friendly intercourse one with another. Sometimes a visitor, freed from the blighting effects of ingrown antipathy, braved the briery road to church reconciliation. Increase Mather, who on a trip to England once sought to bridge over the differences between the Presbyterians and the Congregationalists, thought he would have been successful had it not been for the opposing views of church organization.[10] Mather's son, Cotton, numbered among his many projects one for a union of American and European Christians.[11]

The Anglo-American world of which we speak was Protestant, for the Jews were few, and Roman Catholics were likewise comparatively small in number, although increasing toward the end of the eighteenth century. Episcopalianism had a preferred position in many of the colonies, and even in New England by the early years of the eighteenth century much of the militant hostility to Anglicanism had softened. Indeed, as the career of Samuel Johnson of Connecticut reveals, the transition to Anglicanism was already being made. In the eighteenth century, of some eighty Episcopal missionaries in New England on the list of the Society for the Propagation of the Gospel, more than one-fourth had been brought up as Dissenters. Puritan New Englanders, grown wealthy, were ready to forget the radical Levellers of the seventeenth century, and their antipathy to English religious traditions wore thin when Whig bishops filled the sees of the homeland.[12]

---

[9] E. B. Greene, *Religion and the State: The Making and Testing of an American Tradition* (New York, 1941), 68–69.

[10] Murdock, 281.

[11] H. C. Rice, "Cotton Mather speaks to France," *New Eng. Quarterly*, XV (1943), 198–233.

[12] C. F. Pascoe, *Two Hundred Years of the Society for the Propagation of the Gospel in Foreign Parts* . . . (London, 1901), 44; Shipton, "The Shaping of Revolutionary New England 1680–1740," *loc. cit.*

The sun of the Establishment shone brightly over most of the home fields, and it cast its warm rays on distant adherents. Wealth was hers, and large sums were sent from Britain to strengthen the established organization and revitalize the fading faith of back-sliders. That well-known institution, the Society for the Propagation of the Gospel in Foreign Parts, performed such a splendid task as a missionary enterprise that its achievement as an educative force should not be overlooked. Dr. Bray's activities were as much educational as they were religious, and they brought the lamp of learning to dark and obscure places. Hundreds of inexpensive books were sent over to the colonies yearly, and some itinerant missionaries were provided with copies of the *Husbandman's Manual* and Tillotson's *Works* (in twelve volumes). In a rural society the *Husbandman's Manual* quite aptly used agricultural terms to cultivate the religious spirit. Mastery of the materials sent over by the S. P. G. library would have made for a clergy well versed in theology and ecclesiastical history, but there is little evidence that many were masters.[13]

Colonial Anglicans were shepherded in England by Dr. Zachary Grey, who acted as a rallying point for Anglo-American orthodoxy. "It is astonishing," wrote one Massachusetts divine to him, "to reflect on the impudent affronts Christianity has received in a Christian country. I have read Woolston [*Six Discourses on the Miracles of Christ*] with horror and think the Devil has left him a great deal of his wickedness, but none of his wit. . . . Tindal . . . seems to me a more formidable Atheist by his first book; I wish his powers may be weakened in his second." At a little later date Timothy Cutler was again bewailing the importation of books of infidelity which spread their "poison among us." The evangelist preachers George Whitefield and Gilbert Tennent were described in hostile language. And Daniel Neal, too, the historian of New England, came under Cutler's ban. Neal is very popular with dissenters, Cutler told Dr. Grey, "the more venomous a book is, the more sweetly do Dissenters suck at it." [14] Although Cutler was fearful about the

---

[13] *Grants of books 1739–1790*, Mss. in S.P.G. library, London.

[14] John Nichols, *Illustrations of the literary history of the eighteenth century* (London, 1817–1858), IV, 290, April 20, 1731; also 268, 271, 283, 295, 298, 299, 304.

decay of religion in New England, he thought it not likely "to ru into such refined Atheism and Deism" as existed among the Eng lish; "our poor starved Colleges will not afford us anything eithe for or against Religion." The S. P. G. sent books to Cutler in Bosto to counteract the influence of Whitefield who was undermining th bulwarks of orthodoxy.[15]

Anglicanism had made its uneasy peace with dissent during th Restoration, but in the eighteenth century the surface smoothnes of decorous observance was shattered by the crudities of Wesleyan ism. Even before Wesley, the German-born Dr. Andrew Horneck along with English preachers, had been exhorting young men t meet in religious societies for self-improvement.[16] Wesleyanism wa imbued with the need to make religion intimate, yes, even "enthu siastic." Wesley himself experienced a genuine spiritual rebirth o his voyage to Georgia in 1735, for on shipboard he met the Mora vians, and in the colony he faced new situations which shaped th character of the church he made thereafter. To converse with th Moravians, Wesley learned German, and they in turn studied Eng lish. He was deeply moved by the simplicity of their church organ ization. It almost made him forget, said Wesley, "the seventeen hun dred years between, and imagine myself in one of those assemblie where form and state were not, but Paul the tent-maker or Peter th fisherman presided. . . ."[17]

Wesley shortly turned to a study of German psalmody, realizing its great emotional value, and his translations were so good that one student says they have never been surpassed. These translations, revealing Wesley to be a poet of strong imagination, were used not only in Methodist services but among Episcopalians, Baptists, and the Dutch Reformed as well.[18] Psychologists pay high tribute to Wesley's keen understanding of the value of congregational sing-

[15] John Nichols, *Literary Anecdotes of the Eighteenth Century* (London, 1812), I, 481–482; II, 545 note; Percival Merritt, *The Parochial Library of the eighteenth century in Christ Church* (Boston, 1917), 14–15.

[16] J. S. Simon, *The Revival of Religion in England in the Eighteenth Century* (London, 1911), 125.

[17] N. Curnock, ed., *The Journal of John Wesley* (London, 1938), I, 170, Feb. 28, 1736.

[18] J. T. Hatfield, "John Wesley's Translations of German Hymns," *PMLA*, XI (1896), 171–180.

ing.[19] The crowning achievement of his experience in Georgia "was the slow molding of the Methodist system. The circuit, the society, the itinerant ministry, the class-meeting, the band-meeting, the love feast; leaders and lay assistants; extempore preaching and prayer, and even the building of a meeting-house—all this, and much else in the form and spirit of early Methodism, came to John Wesley in Georgia, and transplanted by him to English and Irish cities and villages." [20]

Back in London after difficult personal trials in Georgia, Wesley met Peter Böhler, who was an important influence in the formation of the "Fetter Lane Society" in the spring of 1738. And when Böhler left for Carolina Wesley was greatly moved. "Oh what a work hath God begun, since his coming into England! Such an one as shall never come to an end till heaven and earth pass away." [21] But conversations in Georgia and London with religious leaders were not enough for Wesley. He felt the need to seek the truth in Holland and Germany, for there he believed welled up the clearest waters of evangelicalism. In Rotterdam, Dr. John de Koker and Wesley exchanged thoughts, and in time Koker translated the latter's writings, which familiarized the Dutch with the Evangelical Revival in England. A visit to Zinzendorf and lodgment with the Moravians confirmed Wesley in his belief in the power of faith. The Halle Orphan House left him ecstatic: "Surely, such a thing neither we nor our fathers have known as this great thing which God has done here." [22] The orphan houses later established by Wesley and George Whitefield had their origin at Halle, whose influence on religious charity was profound in Britain and America.

Cotton Mather, like Wesley, sought inspiration from Halle. In his formidable style, he said he was in correspondence "with the Most Illustrious Frederician University in the Lower Saxony where the most glorious design that ever was managed in the World, is now under a notable prosecution"; and this literary exchange, he stated, had been of great advantage to him. In addition to A. H. Francke,

[19] S. G. Dimond, *The Psychology of the Methodist Revival* (London, 1926), chap. v.

[20] Curnock's estimate in *Wesley's Journal,* I, 426.

[21] *Ibid.,* 458.

[22] *Ibid.,* II, 3 note 1, 4, 8, 13, 17 note 1.

Mather corresponded with Anthony W. Boehme and others, and their German pietism strengthened an influence already at work in the colonies. Writings were exchanged between Boehme and Mather, and through the latter Americans sent contributions to Halle.[23] The prophecy of Cotton Mather was now being fulfilled He had written enthusiastically on one occasion of Francke's schoo at Halle and added: "The World begins to feel a Warmth from the *Fire of God,* which thus flames in the Heart of *Germany,* beginnin to extend into many Regions; the whole World will e're long b sensible of it." [24]

It was from this and similar sources that Wesley drew strength and he was not long back in England when he wrote to Herrnhu about his "Fetter Lane Society," formed with the advice of Böhle and functioning much like the Moravian groups. "We are endeav ouring," he wrote, "to be followers of you, as ye are of Christ." [2 But Wesley's inspiration came not from the European continen alone. Griffith Jones stirred many hearers in Wales, thousands o whom learned to read the Bible in Welsh after he established "ci culating schools" there.

America too was a source of religious reinvigoration. Reviva there, begun by the preaching of Gilbert Tennent and Jonatha Edwards, preceded those in England.[26] In a sincere tribute to Te nent's "little Logg House," a companion of Whitefield with who he visited the school said it had produced more "Godly Ministers in the previous ten years than both Oxford and Cambridge.[27] A na rative of the Edwards' revival in Northampton had been publishe in London with a strong endorsement by Dr. Isaac Watts and D John Guyse. The English writers hoped that this example of peop

---

[23] Mather to Ashurst, March 5, 1715/16, Huntington Lib.; Boehm-Math Corr., Curwin papers, IV, 49, 51, 52, Amer. Antiq. Soc.

[24] C. Mather, *Nuncia Bona E Terra Longinqua* (Boston, 1715), 9; K. Franc "Cotton Mather and A. H. Francke," *Amer. Germanica,* I (1897), 58; a *Harvard Studies and Notes in Philology and Literature,* V (1896), 57–67.

[25] Curnock, II, 91 note 2, 121 note 2.

[26] Simon, 135.

[27] William Seward, *Journal of a Voyage from Savannah to Philadelphia, a from Philadelphia to England* (London, 1740), 12.

turning "from a formal, cold and careless Profession of Christianity" would be an inspiration for the mother country.[28]

In these days Wesley was reading the narrative of the conversions then taking place during the revival in Northampton, New England. "Surely," he wrote in his diary, "this is the Lord's doing, and it is marvellous in our eyes." Within a few years another American, David Brainerd, was to act as a living force on the mind of Wesley.[29] The latter had now come to realize the gulf that separated him from he Established Church. In the late summer of 1739 he was describng to his hearers, "in very plain terms," as he notes in his diary, 'the real difference between what is generally called Christianity, and the true old Christianity which, under the new name of Methodism, is now also everywhere spoken against." Although almost rresistibly drawn to the Moravians, Wesley ultimately retained an ndependent religious position. But through his own movement and he shining Christianity of Moravianism arid sections of English reigious life were brought to flower once again with the fertilizing deal of the brotherhood of man.[30]

Although the Moravians stirred the souls of many Englishmen, n some instances only the ire of legislators was aroused. James Hutton, who championed the cause of the Moravians, wrote to Zinzendorf in strong opposition to New York's discrimination against this roup. Hutton hoped that New York would be restrained by the nore tolerant spirit prevailing in England. On another occasion ressure exerted from Pennsylvania assisted in liberalizing the position of Moravians in England. Zinzendorf was anxious to procure egal standing and protection for his congregations throughout the British Empire, and, in support, the act of 1743 in Pennsylvania was uoted. "Foreign Protestants, who, like the Quakers," it ran, "reused to take an oath [i.e., had religious scruples against oaths] hould be permitted like them to be naturalized in the North Amer-

---

[28] *A faithful Narrative of the Conversion of many hundred souls in Northnpton* . . . (London, 1737).

[29] Luke Tyerman, *The Life and Times of the Rev. John Wesley A.M.* (2nd l., London, 1871), II, 606; III, 535.

[30] Curnock, II, 278, Sept. 16, 1739; 441, April 6, 1741; 500 note 1; and Simon, ap. ix.

ican colonies, on certain conditions." Although assured that this included his denomination, Zinzendorf and his supporters pushed fo
a specific reference to Moravians. Finally by 1747, after constan
pressure by James Oglethorpe and others, the precedent of th
Pennsylvania act of 1743 was successfully invoked to exempt Moravians from taking an oath.[31]

The Moravians were good organizers in most respects. The grou
in Pennsylvania had several vessels built to carry their coreligionists from Europe; one of the ships, the "Irene," a fast boat, crosse
the Atlantic twenty-four times and made other trips as well. Th
Moravians took such good care of the passengers (and luck no doub
was with them that scarcely any fatalities occurred during the man
ocean voyages, a fact of which they were justly proud.[32]

The religious revival that swept over Europe and America linke
them both in anxious concern, and George Whitefield, a powerfu
preacher, stirred the Anglo-American world in a common emotion
Whitefield had been invited to Boston by Dr. Benjamin Colman
who had been corresponding with Britishers on the progress of th
Great Awakening.[33] The excitement of the revival in the Britis
Isles and America gave birth to the first Scottish religious periodicals.[34] Contemporaries were aware of the interrelationship of th
movement in Germany, Britain, and America, and each reprinte
the stories from distant lands that joined them all in a contagiou
enthusiasm. In all this literature the reader is especially consciou
of the central place occupied by the American colonies.[35] Althoug
Whitefield's Calvinism came to sudden birth in England in 1739
it was, his biographer asserts, "cradled and greatly strengthened i
America." [36] The preaching of Gilbert Tennent in New Yor

---

[31] Daniel Benham, *Memoirs of James Hutton* (London, 1856), 171, 206–20

[32] J. W. Jordan, "Moravian Immigration to Penn., 1734–1765," *Penn. Ma of Hist. and Biog.*, XXXIII (1909), 230–248.

[33] "The Glasgow Weekly History, 1743," *Mass. Hist. Soc., Proc.*, LIII (1919 1920), 192.

[34] W. J. Couper, *The Glasgow Periodical Press in the Eighteenth Centu* (Glasgow, 1929); Couper, *The Edinburgh Periodical Press* (Sterling, 1908), I 86–89.

[35] *E.g.*, Rev. John Gillies, *Historical Collections relating to Remarkable Per ods of the Success of the Gospel* . . . (Glasgow, 1754; appendix, 1761).

[36] Tyerman, *Whitefield*, I, 274.

pened new vistas of religious experience to him. Never before had e heard "such a searching sermon." Tennent convinced him that we can preach the Gospel of Christ no further than we have expeenced the power of it in our own hearts." [37]

Whitefield felt America to be a spacious land for his energetic acvity, and many plans were projected for religious asylums and :hools in the colonies. "Fear not to speak the truth," he wrote to a reacher in Yorkshire, "if driven out of England, here is a noble inge for you in America." In this communion of religious fellowaip the Reverend Ralph Erskine and his friends in Scotland were piritual kin to Wesley and Whitefield. The latter on his return om America in 1741 wrote to Erskine, "Your 'Sonnets and Serions' have been blessed to me and many. The former are reprinted 1 America." [38]

Whitefield's return to England did not cut him off from the wakening in America. He corresponded with Tennent, Thomas rince, and others scattered over the colonies.[39] During a trip that Vhitefield made to Scotland several pamphlets were issued telling f his work in New England, but evidently this served mainly to rouse the antagonism of Presbyterians against him.[40]

Publications came in profusion from presses on both sides of the tlantic—in German too—telling of the religious revival. Wesley imself republished in London an abridgment of Jonathan Edards' *Thoughts concerning the Present Revival of Religion in Iew England* (1745).[41] Isaac Watts had asked that news be sent over London where publications dealing with the revival would, he elieved, be very popular.[42] A London reprint of a Boston narrative as highly recommended by Dr. Isaac Watts, who told of receiving iany communications, published and in manuscript, from New ngland, "most of which agree in attesting to the great Work of

---

[37] *Ibid.*, 328.

[38] *Ibid.*, 355, 377–378, 419; letter to Erskine, Feb. 16, 1741, 461.

[39] *Ibid.*, 476, 509, 539.

[40] *Ibid.*, II, 13, 14.

[41] See too, *Glaubwürdige Nachricht un dem herrlichen werck Gottes* (Magebburg, 1738).

[42] "Letters of I. Watts and Elisha Williams," *Mass. Hist. Soc., Proc.*, ser. 2, X (1894–1895), 335.

God in the conversion of Souls throughout that Country from meer formal Profession to real inward Religion and Godline . . . 'Tis much the same Doctrine which prevails in Scotland."

Watts's testimonial to a Boston publication was an appropria exchange for the enthusiastic endorsement Massachusetts gave his writings: "I can assure you (without a compliment)," wro Jonathan Belcher, "all Dr. Watts' works are had in great esteem ar honour amongst us." [44] His *Hymns* had once been recommended an antidote to the "foolish Songs and Ballads" which were bei peddled around the countryside and allegedly corrupting t people. His writings were said to command in America three tim their London selling price.[45]

Watts followed the New England revival closely and stimulat Americans to literary composition; his sermons, said the Rector Yale, had done "great service" to Connecticut youth. After inclu ing news of the local religious awakening, Elisha Williams soug comfort from Watts because word had just been received that Pa liament had rejected the application of Dissenters to have the Co poration and Test Acts repealed. "I had hoped by this time," wro Dr. Williams, "that the just notions of liberty had so far prevailed the nation, as to have delivered as good subjects as any the King h from a part at least of that persecution they had long felt. Are t adversaries of truth and liberty still so strong as to discourage ar further attempt?" [46] The reverence for the memory of Watts w deep enough for Americans of later years to visit his home in pio pilgrimage.

Orthodox believers, opponents of religious "enthusiasm," tri to maintain their structure unimpaired by disparaging the evang lists or even by interfering with their meetings. Clergymen in En land and Scotland, anxious for the orthodoxy of their own congr

---

[43] *The Testimony and Advice of an Assembly of Pastors of Churches in Ne England . . . July 7, 1743 . . . With a Recommendation . . .* by the Rev Dr. Watts (London, 1744).

[44] T. Milner, *The Life, Times and Correspondence of the Rev. Dr. Isa Watts, D.D.* (London, 1834), 459, 469, 498.

[45] C. H. Firth, *An American Garland; being a collection of Ballads relati to America 1563–1759* (Oxford, 1915), xlii–xliii; *Gentleman's Magazine,* LX (1796), 916.

[46] Milner, 530, 543, May 24, 1736.

tions, were obviously pleased to have counterblasts to claims of e Whitefield supporters sent from America. A Boston correspond- t wrote that, far from benefiting religion, the revival had stimu- ted superstition and disorders and certainly did not generate "a ore Christian Love" among neighbors; "instead of being more nd and gentle, more full of Mercy and good Fruits, they are more tter, fierce and implacable." The conservative writer indicated at his basic fear was that these developments would lead to "Quak- ism and Infidelity." [47] Another writer was hostile to Whitefield, arging him with inspiring Negroes with hatred against whites.[48] he widely read *Gentleman's Magazine* reprinted a letter from a oston newspaper describing unsympathetically the physical excita- on attending revivals.[49]

Whitefield had spread with eloquent zeal the evangelical message, d from America he reported his successes to Wesley. But the reli- ous spirit ebbed and flowed unevenly in the colonies. Tennent rote despondently from Philadelphia in 1750, "Religion at pres- t is very low in general in this country." [50] Some years later, after reading of Thomas Prince's *Christian History,* telling of the reli- ous awakening in New England, Wesley was moved to soliloquize:

hat an amazing difference is there in the manner wherein God has rried on His work in England and America! There, above a hundred the established clergy, men of age and experience and of the greatest te for sense and learning . . . are zealously engaged in the work. ere, almost the whole body of the aged, experienced, learned clergy, e zealously engaged against it; and few, but a handful of raw young en, engaged in it, without name, learning, or eminent sense. And yet, that large number of honourable men, the work seldom flourished ove six months at a time, and followed a lamentable and general cay, before the next revival of it; whereas that which God had rought, by these despised instruments has continually increased for teen years together.[51]

[47] *A Letter from a Gentleman in Boston, to Mr. George Wishart . . . of dinburgh, concerning the State of Religion in New England* (Edinburgh, 42). A similar publication appeared the same time in Glasgow.

[48] *Scots Magazine,* III (1741), 367.

[49] *Gentleman's Magazine,* XI (1741), 651.

[50] Tyerman, *Whitefield,* II, 267, Dec. 15, 1750.

[51] Tyerman, *Wesley,* I, 506; II, 162–163.

Despite the contempt in which Wesley's movement was held b
the Establishment, grudging tribute was sometimes paid it by th
scoffers, and more rarely even sincere recognition of the value of hi
work might be the testimonial. An Anglican clergyman, the Reve
end John Newton, paid the Methodists a warm tribute in a letter t
the Earl of Dartmouth: "Surely had not the Lord seasonably inte
posed by raising up what is called Methodism, the knowledge of th
true Gospel had been by this time well nigh lost out of our land.
Samuel Davies, a Presbyterian, collecting funds for Princeton, me
Charles and John Wesley in England. With all their weaknesses th
"despised Methodists," said Davies, seemed "to have more of th
Spirit of Religion than any Set of People in this Island." [52]

Quakers too were swept along in this religious revival. The note
London doctor, John Fothergill, wrote to Israel Pemberton i
Philadelphia of the flurry of interest in the religious news from Ge
many. He was himself prejudiced in favor of German religious en
thusiasts and, as he expressed it, "far from being uneasy that
people not bearing our name should have made such eminent ad
vances in piety and virtue as the reports gave room to hope for." D
Fothergill had gone to the continent, where he had an opportu
nity to learn at first hand about the sources of German spiritua
strength.[53] English Friends spoke with one another of the close af
finity between Moravians and Methodists, and in sympathetic lan
guage described their temper. The Moravians were held up a
examples to themselves; "May they be a means to provoke us t
greater diligence," wrote one Friend, "I am sure the Day calls fo
it." [54] The noted Thomas Story reported to James Logan in Penn
sylvania that the stirrings in the religious world had affected th
young people: "It looks like a fresh Spring a coming on by thos
budds, Sprouts & Blossoms in so many places & forms." [55]

No religious group had closer transatlantic ties than did th
Quakers. The numbers who went back and forth across the ocea

---

[52] Davies, *Diary, 1753–1755,* II, 85, Princeton Library; *Hist. Mss. Commis sion,* Earl of Dartmouth, Mss., III, 199, Nov. 11, 1772.

[53] Mss. Port., 38 (81), London, Jan. 28, 1741, Friends House, London.

[54] Gibson Mss. I, 243, Josiah Martin, London, Sept. 18, 1739, Friends House London.

[55] *Journal of Thomas Story,* appendix, Nov. 2, 1739.

seem astonishingly large in a sailing-ship era, and when personal visits were lacking written communications kept up the intimate association. Over one hundred and fifty ministering Friends (one-third of them women) left Europe to visit America. Some of them made two or more trips.[56] American Friends had a regular correspondence with booksellers in England who were coreligionists and received from them the latest religious as well as secular books. From their earliest days in America Quakers in their voluminous records tell a story of continuous intercourse with the homeland. The spread of missionary activities to the mainland of continental Europe broadened considerably the area of Quaker enterprise.

A large number of influential ministers were produced in the colonies at a time when Quakerism was passing through lean years in England. "As to the state of our Society, as a religious people, it is but low at present everywhere. The life of the word of God is too little known, and less obeyed amongst us" came the news from England.[57] As a result of the initiative of American Friends, women in England won the same right to greater participation in Quaker activities that their American sisters already enjoyed.[58]

Samuel Fothergill did as much as anyone to revitalize the religion of his fellow Quakers. He traveled through the whole length of the colonies and in warm letters to his family in England wrote modestly of his work. Preachers in America journeyed prodigious distances by horseback; 2,500 miles or more was not unusual.[59] Fothergill told of traversing some six thousand miles of American roads and trails in twelve months. He spoke gratefully too of one favorite horse who carried him more than a third of the way and with whom he often shared his scanty rations. In Boston's Town Hall on three hours' notice the Quaker held a meeting attended by two thousand people.[60] He wrote to his brother, Dr. John Fothergill, that discipline had been much neglected among New England Friends, and

[56] See list in *Journal of the Friends Historical Society*, X, no. 3 (1913), 117–133. The period covered 1656–1793.

[57] W. Armistead, *Memoirs of James Logan* (London, 1851), 115–117, 1735.

[58] R. M. Jones, *The Later Periods of Quakerism* (London, 1921), I, 105, 113–115, 117 note 2.

[59] Gibson Mss., II (37), John Oxley to John Gurney, May 1, 1771.

[60] Crosfield Mss. (33–48), letters from America, Oct. 3, 1754, to Oct. 3, 1755, Friends House, London.

that "the Revival thereof is no small part of my concern & Labour." [61] Samuel Fothergill's personality left its impress upon Americans long after he returned home.[62] While English Friends revived waning spirits in the colonies, Americans were performing a like service in England.

As did other sects, Friends on both sides of the ocean observed closely the progress of religious freedom. "Be assured," came the word from London, "that we shall watch with Great Attention & do everything that lies in our power to secure your civil and religious Liberties on their ancient Foundation." [63] Fearing that their religious privileges might be affected, a standing committee of correspondence was appointed to deal with such subjects in Pennsylvania.[64] Frequent correspondence revealed the sense of injustice expressed by Quakers who felt aggrieved at supporting the Establishment in Virginia and paying taxes in lieu of serving in the military.[65] A more cheerful report came from Rhode Island where as the expression ran: "Friends [were] generally free from suffering on account of Priest Rates," and payments in place of military service were slight. Indulgent officials, notably in Virginia, were lenient in enforcing the military service act upon Quakers. Similarly from North Carolina came the grateful words: "The Hearts of those in Authority seem soft towards us, insomuch that they are gentle and kind." [66] In fact the substance of most statements on the subject sent from the colonies reveals that provincial officials were lax in their demands of military service upon the Friends.

Wise James Logan, although confident of the ultimate progress of "true Religion," wrote, rather pessimistically, to Thomas Story that it could occur only as the aftermath of a revolution against the forces of reaction, which were thoroughly entrenched in church and state.[67] Word came to a New York correspondent from London that

---

[61] Port. 22 (30), June 13, 1755, from Newport, R.I.; Port. 22 (157), Susanna Fothergill to Samuel Fothergill, Jan. 10, 1756, Friends House, London.

[62] Gibson Mss., IV (59), Nov. 9, 1756; Mary Pemberton to John Fothergill, June 13, 1756, in Dreer Coll., Hist. Soc. Penn.

[63] *Letters to and from Phila.*, Mss., I, Feb. 15, 1765, Friends House, London.

[64] Mss. Port. 21 (81), Phila., May 21, 1756, Friends House, London.

[65] *Ibid.*, 27 (55), July 21, 1740; (56), July 19, 1742; (57), July 20, 1741.

[66] *Ibid.*, 27 (65), April 15, 1741; (110), Aug. 2, 1743.

[67] After appendix in *Journal of Thomas Story*, May 12, 1736.

ı accordance with an old law, Quakers in the American province ɔuld serve on juries without swearing an oath.[68] Quakers on both des of the ocean continued to be concerned with each other's atus, and for long years thereafter they maintained a lively corre- ɔondence on questions of religious freedom.[69]

Friends sent over to Pennsylvania large quantities of religious terature to be used in proselytizing non-English-speaking peoples. tandard Quaker writings like Barclay's *Apology* were requested in ;erman, Spanish, and French. Dissatisfied with the German transla- ion, London sought with apparent success for a better one from ennsylvania. After long delays Philadelphia sent over two hundred opies of its new translation to the British capital.[70] London kept 'hiladelphia informed about the progress of proselyting among the 'rench, to whom many books in their own language were being ent.[71]

Attendance at each other's meetings deepened their significance ɔr local residents, who were thus made to feel they belonged to a roader fellowship. Quaker schools in England used Woolman's *ournal* and Lindley Murray's books, and occasionally American hildren were enrolled in the overseas classes. More than any other ect the Friends maintained a continuity of close transatlantic asso- iation, which the American Revolution itself did little to impair.

Other groups besides the Anglicans, Methodists, Congregational- sts, and Quakers were closely knit. Baptists and Presbyterians tried o hold together their widely dispersed flocks, some of whom it was eared were being shepherded into the fold of Methodism. Early in he eighteenth century Pennsylvania Baptists opened a correspond- ence with London ministers. One correspondent assured his English eaders that the American ministers were "all sound in the faith" nd practiced "most things like the British churches." Books which vere requested were sent, and in response word came from Phila- lelphia that a little library would be formed so that the public

[68] *Letters to and from Phila.*, I, Dec. 7, 1764.

[69] *Ibid.*, March 17, 1797.

[70] *Ibid.*, April 7, 1759, Oct. 14, 1768, July 29, 1769, Oct. 2, 1772, Nov. 30, 775, Nov. 21, 1776, Dec. 5, 1783.

[71] *Ibid.*, London to Phila., July 29, 1791.

might use the volumes.[72] Thomas Hollis, who scattered books a
Andrew Carnegie scattered libraries, sent many works to Abel Mo
gan in Pennsylvania.[73] The Hollis family came to the rescue of Bos
ton Baptists at the same time, sending funds to enlarge and repai
their meeting house. Thomas Hollis replied to a complaint abou
taxes with the reminder that they were not to be thought of as
burden. "It is giving tribute or tithes to whom tribute is due, unles
the taxes do oppress you unequally, because you are Baptists an
Separatists; if so, then let me know," wrote Hollis, "and I will en
deavor to have a word spoken for you to the Governor, that you ma
be eased." [74]

Much of the energy of Presbyterians and Baptists was directe
toward liberalizing relations between the dissenting sects and th
state. Two representatives went over to London from Connecticu
to protest against taxation of Baptists for the benefit of the estab
lished colonial church, saying it was a violation of the provincia
charter. A central committee for Dissenters in London wrote to th
Connecticut government against oppressions. Under the auspices o
the Warren Association, Baptists in many of the colonies joined i
an appeal to the King in Council for relief from taxation for th
established churches.[75]

The American and Scottish Presbyterians were in particularl
close association. The events of the Great Awakening illustrate it
as does the powerful transatlantic influence exerted on one anothe
by prominent preachers and writers during the whole of Scottish
American religious history. Probably no name is more significan
in this story than that of Jonathan Edwards. The impact of hi
thought on Scotland is well known to historians of religion.

A biography of Edwards, published in London in 1785, spoke o
his transatlantic reputation and referred to him as "one of th
greatest . . . and most useful of men, that have lived in this age."
The Dutch as well as the Scots, were deeply appreciative of him, and

---

[72] Joseph Ivimey, *A History of the English Baptists* (London, 1823), III, 126-129.

[73] *Memoirs of Thomas Hollis,* appendix, 596.

[74] Isaac Backus, *A History of New England . . . Baptists* (Newton, Mass. 1871), I, 485–490, 509–510.

[75] *Ibid.,* II, 101, 155–156.

› more than a few Scotsmen he was the "greatest divine this age ıad] produced." [76] Among a list of American authors recomıended for young Baptist ministers, the works of Edwards were ngled out with high praise.[77] The name of David Brainerd too 'as intimately familiar to those who cherished a saintly life. Among vangelists in all sects, especially those who labored in the missions › the Indians, his name was freshly remembered. Wesley tells of ıaking a collection for Indian schools in America, but he was oubtful of its value. "Will money convert heathens?" he asked. Find preachers of David Brainerd's spirit," was his answer, "and ıothing can stand before them; but without this, what will gold or ilver do? No more than lead or iron." [78] Years later, the noted Aethodist leader, Dr. Thomas Coke, aboard ship to America, testiıed again to the continuing inspiration of Brainerd's life: "His ıumility, his self-denial, his perseverance, and his flaming zeal, vere exemplary indeed." [79] Jonathan Edwards wrote a biography f Brainerd which was published in Edinburgh, and Wesley used it or his own narrative of the American missionary. His religion, Vesley instructed his readers, "did not consist only in *experience,* feeling] without practice [application]." [80]

While records of contacts between distinguished individuals are airly familiar, the incidents revealing the friendly relationship beween large groups and the sympathetic response of each to the ther's problems are less well known. An instance of this association s revealed in the news item telling of a collection taken up in Scotish churches (May, 1760) for the relief of Presbyterian ministers ınd their widows and orphans in Pennsylvania and Delaware. This ıction was taken at the suggestion of a corporation founded in the :olonies and based upon the prior example of the Church of Scotand.[81]

---

[76] *The Life and Character of . . . Jonathan Edwards . . .* (London, 1785), ›reface, 104.

[77] John Rippon, *The Baptist Annual Register* (London, 1790–1793), I, 255.

[78] Tyerman, *Wesley,* II, 606, quoting *Wesley's Journal,* Aug. 8, 1767.

[79] *Extracts of the Journals of the Rev. Dr. Coke's Five Visits to America* (Lonlon, 1793), 9; date was 1784.

[80] Edwards' biography appeared 1765; Wesley's in 1771.

[81] *Scots Magazine,* XXII (1760), 265–268.

It was in the Revolutionary era that the interrelationships of th Anglo-American religious groups found broader expression in join campaigns for religious, humanitarian, and political ends, and it a striking testimony to her creative vitality that so much of the in tiative emanated from America.

CHAPTER IV

On Books and Learning

THE religious life of America was always closely interwoven with
hat of Europe and while there was frequent dependence on Old
World traditions in New World settlements, the latter did seek out
novel and untried highways. The pattern is repeated in education,
a field in which Americans adapted an old inheritance to changing
situations and at the same time revealed their willingness to experiment with new ideas. On the lower levels of education they opened
wider the doors of their schools. They also definitely broadened the
curriculum of the colleges, although practice fell short of progressive theory. British financial support fostered higher education
overseas, and education in all branches in the colonies benefited
rom transatlantic associations.

A considerable number of the teachers in colonial schools and
homes were recently arrived immigrants from Scotland or Ireland,
ome of them indentured servants poorly prepared for teaching.
Anthony Benezet of Philadelphia wrote his friend, Samuel Fothergill, that in the colonies any person of "tolerable morals, who can
read & write" was thought sufficiently equipped to teach, "when
ndeed the best and wisest Men are but sufficient for so weighty a
charge." If governments were influenced by true wisdom, he went
on to say, "they would have made the proper education of the Youth
heir first & special care." And Benezet concluded with his usual
sincere plea, "I earnestly desire our Friends both here [in America]
and amongst you, would consider of it." He counted on Fothergill,
ecently returned to England from America, to help supply teachers
for Pennsylvania.[1] Materials for young scholars, such as ink powder,

[1] Crosfield Mss., Nov. 27, 1758; I. Pemberton to I. Wilson, July 1, 1755, Gibson Mss., II, 17.

paper for copybooks and the like were ordered from London. It was not unusual for southern plantation owners to send to Scotland for tutors, but when American youngsters began to acquire the "burr" of the Scots their popularity waned. Eventually, colonial colleges helped to supply tutors for Southerners.[2]

Benezet was an educational reformer with an excellent understanding of the need for pedagogical changes. Always the indefatigable propagandist, he urged his European correspondents to seek higher standards in pedagogy. Teaching, he said, was constantly to be directed toward humane ends, with a special emphasis on the horrors of war.[3] A transplanted German Mennonite schoolmaster, Christopher Dock, noted that because of the broader humanitarian sentiments in America, schoolmasters could not be as strict with children as they were in the Old World. Hugh Jones said that Virginia children found "*Grammar* Learning taught after the common round about Way . . . not much beneficial nor delightful." They believed that the arts and sciences could all be studied in English rather than in Latin or Greek. The classical tongues, it may be noted, were under frequent attack in America in the eighteenth century. It is clear that a number of colonials had departed from conventional pedagogy.[4]

American children read books published in London along with their own widely used *New England Primer*. In both Europe and America the hornbook was the favorite instrument for initiating children to formal education. When the Pilgrims were in Holland hornbooks were in wide use for Dutch youngsters, and these seem to have been the source for many of the early hornbooks used in England. In later years hornbooks were frequently advertised for sale in many colonial newspapers, and although some were made locally most of them were imported from Europe.[5]

---

[2] T. J. Wertenbaker, *The Old South: The Founding of American Civilization* (New York, 1942), 31.

[3] Benezet to Barclay, 1782, in R. Vaux, *Memoirs of Anthony Benezet* (Philadelphia, 1817), 19, 24; see also G. S. Brookes, *Friend Anthony Benezet* (Philadelphia, 1937), 29–60.

[4] M. Curti, *The Growth of American Thought* (New York, 1943), 62; H. M. Jones, *Ideas in America* (Cambridge, Mass., 1944), 270.

[5] G. A. Plimpton, "The Hornbook and its use in America," *Amer. Antiq. Soc., Proc.,* XXVI (1916), 268.

Mother Goose, brought to England from France, was made famous by the noted publisher of children's books, John Newbery. His volumes, which gave children works of greater permanence than the popular chapbooks of the day, were familiar to Americans. A Boston publication, *The Famous Tommy Thumb's Little Story-Book . . .*, was a reprint of the English original by Newbery. James Rivington, the New York printer, republished many books for children and sent one, *Robinson Crusoe,* to Henry Knox in Boston; Rivington said his price was lower than that of books imported from London.[6] The energetic Isaiah Thomas, after the Revolution, reprinted children's books from Newbery's list, including a number of editions of Mother Goose *Melodies.*

Englishmen, not always accurately informed, spoke of the devotion of the colonies to the education of children, particularly in New England where free schools were established by law. Schools here were said to be superior to those anywhere in Europe, and educational standards in some of the colonial schools were judged to be higher than in similar institutions in England. At the end of the century, in his very widely used compilation of history and geography the British author William Guthrie told his readers that in New England, learning was "more generally diffused among all ranks of the people, than in any other part of the globe." A mature person who was illiterate was a rarity, said Guthrie. Thirty thousand copies of newspapers were printed weekly in New England.[7] This was enough for one-fourth of the families, but it should be remembered that a single paper circulated beyond the subscriber's immediate family. The *Encyclopedia Britannica,* in words that were repeated for more than a century, said that "notwithstanding their peculiar addiction to those occupations of which lucre is the sole object, Americans were duly attentive to cultivate the field of learning, and they have ever since their first foundation been particu-

---

[6] W. H. Whitmore, *The Original Mother Goose's Melody* (Boston, 1892); see also Charles Welsh, *A Bookseller of the Last Century . . . John Newbery,* (London, 1885), 91; "Henry Knox and the London Bookstore in Boston 1771–1774," *Mass. Hist. Soc., Proc.,* LXI (1927–1928), 225 ff., March 1, 1774.

[7] W. Guthrie, *Geographical, Historical and Commercial Grammar* (17th ed., London, 1798), 867. He copied this from Jedidiah Morse, *American Geography* (London, 1792), 145–146.

larly careful to provide for the education of the rising progeny." [8]

Several American authors were known to British students. Samuel Johnson's *Elements of Philosophy,* with its advanced pedagogical views, was presented in a London edition (1754). After the Revolution more Americans were introduced to young English readers, and one, Lindley Murray, became a best selling author. Another American, Robert Davidson, wrote *The Elements of Geography* (1787), an excellent volume presenting its lessons in rhymed verse, which was introduced to English readers with the hope that they would have "Humility and good Sense enough to learn from an American." "True genius," the introduction continued, "knows no Party in Politics, it scorns all the Quarrels of Kingdoms and States, as utterly unworthy of a Moment's Regard." It required a broad outlook to reprint this volume for use in English schools at this time, for many lines in it are a glowing eulogy of America. Benezet's *The Pennsylvania Spelling Book or Youth's Friendly Instructor,* published in Philadelphia, appeared in a Dublin edition, 1800. In some remarks on the education of youth included in this volume, Benezet joined other contemporaries in expressing skepticism about the value of including Latin in a general curriculum.

English texts for children drew on Franklin's life for inspiration. To promote "vigilant observation" Franklin's experiments on the effect of pouring oil on water were quoted. Dr. Thomas Percival, author of one of these books and friend of Franklin, wrote in one passage, "I cannot conclude, without noticing the illiberal censures we are apt to pass on those pursuits of knowledge which do not seem immediately subservient to the benefit of mankind." Franklin's work in electricity was thereupon referred to as an excellent instance of the union between the theoretical and practical.[9]

Lindley Murray is in a class by himself. He had grown up as a Quaker in America (Long Island, New York), and according to one contemporary, had gone to England soon after the Revolution for reasons of health. His books, written in England, were widely used

---

[8] Third ed., 1797, 574. The *Encyclopedia,* like Guthrie, took its material from Morse.

[9] T. Percival, *A Father's Instructions; Consisting of Moral Tales* . . . (London, 1789; earlier ed., 1775), 66–67, 152.

there as well as in Ireland and America. The *Grammar,* one of his most famous books, said by Scotsmen to be the best ever written, learned on earlier models, especially John Burn's *A Practical Grammar of the English Language* (Glasgow, 1766). It was said that the profits of Murray's work were devoted to charitable purposes, including aid to the education of poor children. His background in America helps explain the many references to American scenes and themes to be found in his books. Idealization of the Indian, "the noble savage," appeared in the *Introduction to the English Reader* (York, 1801). A naturalistic explanation is given of the differences between Negroes and whites, and a strong antislavery sentiment is implanted. A very friendly tone toward America pervades Murray's writings, and this, it will be recalled, during a period of painful Anglo-American readjustment. Murray maintained a correspondence with Americans who used their influence to promote his publications in his native land. Quite naturally, he told Jedidiah Morse that the extensive circulation of his books in America gave him great satisfaction. He aimed always, he said, to stress virtue and religion along with his literary instruction.[10]

Sunday schools, first established in the 1780's by Robert Raikes in Britain, were quickly copied in America. A writer who asked that they be instituted in Boston, spoke of their recent adoption in England and Ireland, saying they were "highly worthy of imitation here." In England it was thought that they performed a useful function in social indoctrination, for students would learn to have an "obedient carriage to those above them." [11] Booksellers looked with unrestrained delight on the growth of Sunday schools, for it was believed that they would diffuse knowledge and promote the sale of books—which prompted the publisher, James Lackington, to invite all booksellers "to unite in a hearty amen." [12]

In a retrospective view covering a score of years, the resourceful Lackington, writing toward the close of the eighteenth century, believed that the sale of books had grown enormously in England; in

[10] Mss. Port. 17 (93), Friends House, London; Lindley Murray to Morse, Dec. 26, 1806, Morse papers, Yale Library; Silliman, *Journal of Travels,* II, 294.

[11] A. Mathews, "Early Sunday Schools in Boston," *Col. Soc. Mass., Trans.,* XXI (1919), 283; W. Jesse, *Importance of Education* (Kidderminster, 1785), 29.

[12] *Memoirs of James Lackington* (London, 1794), 243–244.

fact he estimated a fourfold increase. He himself was selling over a hundred thousand volumes annually. A much wider reading audience now existed there: "The poorer sort of farmers, and even the poor country people in general" who formerly "spent their winter evenings in relating stories of witches, ghosts, hobgoblins, etc., now shorten the nights by having their sons and daughters read romances, etc., and on entering their houses you may see Tom Jones, Roderick Random, and other entertaining books, stuck up on their bacon-racks, etc." The young people on their visits to town were reminded to bring home the best novels. "In short," wrote Lackington, "all ranks and degrees now read." [13] In similar vein the popular William Guthrie said, with exaggeration, that learning in England was no longer restricted to the few: "It is become as universal as it is useful." [14] Books were now written to the popular taste, and reduced in price. "It is to books of this kind," he said, "more than to the works of our Bacons, our Lockes, and our Newtons, that the generality of our countrymen owe that superior improvement which distinguishes them from the lower ranks of men in all other countries."

On the higher levels of education the ties between America and Europe have always been fairly close. Schools in Maryland and Virginia staffed by Anglican ministers were modeled after the famous English public schools. Some Southerners went to Cambridge or Oxford, as well as to Edinburgh, Aberdeen, and the Inns of Court in London. The numbers were not large—fewer than three dozen from Virginia matriculated at Oxford or Cambridge before the Revolution—but they included her leading families. The founding of all the colleges in the colonial period was made easier by British support, and in their early years these colleges received funds and books and scientific equipment from friends in the homeland. The fact that so large a proportion of New England's first settlers were college-bred undoubtedly explains the early establishment of Harvard. At least one hundred and thirty alumni of Oxford and Cambridge came to New England before 1646—a very high proportion of university-trained men for the population of those times. Many of these university men had studied at Emmanuel College, Cam-

---

[13] Quoted in Cox and Chandler, 14–15.

[14] W. Guthrie, *A New Geographical, Historical and Commercial Grammar*, (4th ed., London, 1774), iii–iv.

bridge, which had in their day been rededicated to the intellectual life in the spirit of Plato. Along with other tendencies moving in the same direction, Cambridge Platonism exerted a powerful force on eighteenth-century rationalism, deism, and tolerance. It was due to Locke's spreading influence that the Cambridge seed "grew at length into a great tree." [15]

Harvard graduates living in England saw to it that her requirements were kept before the most prominent Dissenters in the mother country. The legendary pride of Harvard's sons was a distinct characteristic even in her very early years. Cotton Mather felt that Harvard was superior in scientific teaching to English universities, and Benjamin Colman was of the same mind. In a letter to Bishop White Kennet, Colman said, "When I visited yr famous Universities & private Academies . . . I was proud of my own humble Education here in our Cambridge because of the Catholic Air I had there breathed in." But in the 1720's the serenity of academic life was shattered, said Colman, "by a parcel of High-Flyers" who had "poison'd & stagnated it, by leading us into a course of angry controversy wch has alarm'd & sorrowed us." [16]

Throughout the colonial period well-educated men coming from Europe made their mark in American education and politics. A considerable number of them came over in the quarter-century before the Revolution, and four of them became college presidents —William Smith, of the College of Philadelphia (later the University of Pennsylvania), Witherspoon, of Princeton, Myles Cooper of King's College (later Columbia), and John Horrocks, of William and Mary. The possibility of adding Joseph Priestley to an American faculty came under discussion. In response to a query from Franklin, John Winthrop, Harvard's distinguished professor, said that Priestley would be a valuable addition to any American college, but that probably none would accept him because of his unorthodox religious views.[17] The growth of skepticism at William

---

[15] S. E. Morison, *Puritan Pronaos* (New York, 1936), 16; F. J. Powicke, *The Cambridge Platonists* (London, 1926), 3, 198, 210, 212.

[16] S. E. Morison, *Harvard College in the Seventeenth Century* (Cambridge, Mass., 1936), II, 390; Colman to Kennett, Dec. 17, 1725, Mass. Hist. Soc., Mss.

[17] J. Sparks, ed., *Benjamin Franklin, Works* . . . (Boston, 1836–1840), VI, 375, March 4, 1773.

and Mary before the Revolution frightened many of the parents with sons at the school.

Continental scholars looked to green pastures in America. A number of German literati planned to establish a nonsectarian college overseas but, as they wrote to Franklin, they contemplated that at first they would teach only Germans until they had mastered the English language. Johann Christoph Kunze, late from Halle, established a "Seminarium" in Philadelphia in 1773, whose curriculum, conducted in German, was based entirely on that of the school in Germany. English was soon added because of the strong Anglicizing forces operative among the Germans in America.[18] Included in the lengthy correspondence between Ezra Stiles and Christophe D. Ebeling, the German historian of America, were the details of the course of study at Yale and the numbers graduated from the college during the century. Up to 1793, said Stiles, some twenty-three hundred had been educated and graduated.[19] Frenchmen, too, were making plans for the education of Americans, and one European schoolman proposed taking the Genevan academy in its entirety to America.[20]

The records of the colleges in the colonies reveal the close dependence on the homeland for support. The donations to Yale and Harvard are fairly familiar, but not so well known are the gifts granted to representatives of other American colleges soliciting aid in European countries. King's College and the College of Philadelphia sent a group to England; and others, too, had their agents abroad asking for funds. The colleges in New York and Philadelphia, under strong Anglican influence, felt they could make an appeal to England on religious grounds. A brief in their support mentioned the need to combat the emissaries of Catholicism, and it also pointed out that diverse peoples had settled in the colonies to whom the true faith must be brought. The next spring (1762) James

[18] I. M. Hays, ed., *Calendar of Franklin Papers* (Philadelphia, 1908), I, 481, J. D. Simon to Franklin, Aug. 22, 1778; C. F. Hausman, "Kunze's Seminarium . . . ," *Amer. Germanica,* XXVII (1917), 16–37.

[19] Stiles to Ebeling, Feb. 20, 1795, Yale Library.

[20] *Calendar of Franklin Papers,* II, 158, Jules, Comte de Montfort, Oct. 19, 1779; Jefferson, *Writings,* IX, 291, Nov. 22, 1794.

Jay and others were designated to collect funds for King's College; the Royal Society was asked to contribute. Lord Bute and his fellows among England's ruling group made donations.[21] The Archbishop of Canterbury took a deep interest in the American colleges and authorized a house-to-house canvass for funds.[22] The New York and Philadelphia colleges fared handsomely in England, sharing over fourteen thousand pounds between them; the collections in Oxford and Cambridge were £350.[23]

A Yorkshire vicar, Daniel Watson, preached a sermon in support of the two American colleges. The latter were a means of instructing the Indians, Watson believed, and he took care to state that in the schools Protestants of all denominations were welcome. "This circumstance," he observed, "will open a free communication of sentiments, and tend to wear off that sourness of party which has been the disgrace of the *Reformation*." And Watson concluded with the same sentiments, almost with the same words, as those of Bishop Berkeley, "not only true religion, but all arts and sciences had their dawning in the East, have hitherto travelled Westwards, and seem to be still in the same direction." [24]

George Whitefield sought aid for Princeton in Scotland and urged that an appeal be made in person by an American spellbinder. A delegation did arrive in Scotland in 1754, made up of Gilbert Tennent and Samuel Davies. They solicited funds in London, too, where some eighty contributors gave nearly five hundred pounds for the New Jersey college. Davies, who kept a diary of the trip, was delighted with the generosity of the much-maligned Scots. The collections were sufficient to pay for the erection of the earliest college buildings. Whitefield also interceded with noted Englishmen on behalf of other American schools, the College of Philadelphia,

---

[21] *Church Brief*, B, II, 9, Aug. 19, 1761, Brit. Mus. Mss.; Letters and Papers, decade IV, 148, May 14, 1762, Royal Soc. Library; *N.J. Hist. Soc., Colls.*, II (1847), 64 and note, letter to Bute, May 24, 1762.

[22] American Colonies Mss., III, 257, 270, Lambeth Palace Library.

[23] A. F. Gegenheimer, *William Smith, Educator and Churchman* (Philadelphia, 1943), 72–73; *Collections in England for the Colleges of Philadelphia and New York, 1763*, Am 325, Hist. Soc. Penn., Mss.

[24] D. Watson, *A Sermon Preached on Occasion of the Brief for the American Colleges* (London, 1763), 31, 34.

Harvard, and Eleazar Wheelock's Indian School (Dartmouth).[2
Harvard students on one occasion graciously presented a poetica
offering to the King but at the same time could not resist speakin
of the progress their college had achieved without much aid fron
the mother country.[26]

After the Revolution the American colleges, in straitened cir
cumstances, again made appeals to Europeans. They even believed
with excessive optimism, that England too would aid them, but the
were reminded that she was burdened with war debts and heav
taxes. Franklin was one intermediary who, it was hoped, woul
prove the open sesame to educational philanthropy; but he depre
cated, as injurious to American prestige, wholesale academic beg
ging in Europe. John Wheelock, collecting for Dartmouth, reporte
that the Prince and Princess of Orange approved of his work, bu
while Haarlem responded well, Amsterdam gave him no encour
agement. John Wheelock (successor to his father Eleazar at Dart
mouth) was given a note of introduction from John Adams to th
distinguished Dutch patriot, F. A. Van der Kemp.[27] Brown Univer
sity sought the patronage of Louis XVI to establish a chair in th
French language and history. The King replaced the house of th
president of William and Mary, burned down while French troop
were billeted there. Princeton commissioned Witherspoon (agains
his better judgment) and General Joseph Reed to secure benefac
tions in France and England. The latter country, Witherspoon be
lieved, offered no prospects. Newer colleges, Bowdoin in Maine an
Dickinson in Pennsylvania, sought support from old friends o
America in London.

More frequent than solicitations for funds were the requests fo
books, and they rarely went unanswered. It must be remembered

[25] Tyerman, *Whitefield,* II, 227, 251; Davies, *Diary, 1753–1755;* also Davie
and Tennent, *A General Account of the . . . College . . . in New Jerse*
(London, 1754), 8 postscript. Both items are in the Princeton Library.

[26] *The Monthly Review,* XXIX (1763), 22–26, quoting preface of *Pietas e*
Gratulatio Collegii Cantabrigensis, apud Novanglos, Bostoni Massachusetten
sium.

[27] *Calendar of Franklin Papers,* III, 73, June 12, 1783; Adams to Van de
Kemp, Feb. 18, 1783, Hist. Soc. Penn.; for Franklin's criticism, see J. P. Boyd
Report to the Thomas Jefferson Bicentennial Commission (1943), note 3 o
insertion following p. 19.

hat expensive books and those with a limited audience were not as et generally published in America. Until the early years of the ineteenth century most books used in American colleges were mported. Granville Sharp sent over two cases of books for Dickinon, picking them out himself, and, as he told Benjamin Rush, at a ow price, "for otherwise (to tell you the truth) I could not have fforded to send you so many." [28] In 1785, Thomas Brand Hollis, he last of this noted family of philanthropists, sent over a box of ooks to be divided between Harvard and the American Academy f Arts and Sciences. Dr. John C. Lettsom could always be counted pon for aid to American learning, and he responded freely to these equests from the young colleges.

Long before the newer colleges were founded, Yale and Harvard ad counted on many benefactors to enrich their libraries. Harvard ent to England one hundred copies of its library catalogue (1723), vhich unquestionably stimulated interest and brought additions to t from overseas. Yale's library, in 1742, owed much to gifts that had een sent from England from its founding. Jeremiah Dummer's ift of eight hundred volumes—literature, science, and theology— lonated by himself and others, was a princely offering in 1714. Jonahan Edwards, Yale 1720, spoke of reading Locke's *Human Understanding* in the Dummer collection and said he had "more satisfacion and pleasure in studying it, than the most greedy miser in athering up handfuls of silver and gold from some new discovered reasure." Samuel Johnson, in after years president of King's College, also testified to the invigorating quality of Dummer's books. The best writers of England were now available to him, said Johnson; "all this was like a flood of day to his low state of mind." It is a moving experience for present-day booklovers to see many of these original volumes of the reconstructed library of 1742, tucked away in a tiny corner of the large, modern Yale structure.[29]

The Reverend Benjamin Colman, sending books to Elisha Williams, Rector of Yale, said they had come from Samuel Holden, Governor of the Bank of England, and he urged that they be so inscribed. With a sentimental note, Colman spoke of Holden as the

---

[28] Sharp to Rush, Sept. 29, 1783, Mss. 28–92, Ridgway Library.

[29] Articles on the Dummer library in *Papers in Honor of Andrew Keogh* . . . (New Haven, 1938).

son of the landlady at whose house he had lived when in London; she "was a mother to me," he told Williams. The practical Colman suggested that Williams maintain a correspondence with various well-wishers in London; "Who knows of what Benefit it might be to you?" [30] The widow of Samuel Holden sent funds to Harvard for a beautiful chapel which was put up in 1744. Not long before this a London paper reported the gift of "a box of very choice Books" sent to Colman by Hollis, intended ultimately for Harvard.[31] Bishop Berkeley sent a valuable collection of Greek and Latin classics to Harvard (1773), and to Yale he donated some thousand volumes as well as a deed to his estate. Berkeley's gift to Yale was believed to be the finest collection of books that had yet been brought to America.[32] Yale also received books from the Reverend John Erskine of Edinburgh, who was always friendly to America. In fact, he was said to have distributed more books there than any other European. He maintained a large correspondence with Americans, writing to more than twenty of them.[33]

Probably no name is more important in this story of bibliophilanthropy than that of Hollis. It appears again and again in gifts to educational and religious organizations. Thomas Hollis (1659–1731) was the oldest of a family to whom Harvard owed a great debt of gratitude. He was a London merchant and a Baptist, who believed that a liberalized Harvard was worthy of his benevolence. He gave hundreds of pounds for scholarships and endowed the professorship of divinity which was graced with his name. Hollis definitely broadened the outlook of Harvard Congregationalism and aided in the process of bursting the narrow bounds of provincial thought. He founded a professorship of mathematics and natural philosophy (1727) with an endowment of £1,200 and apparatus to go with it, truly a "landmark in the history of the teaching of science in America." The first holder of the chair, the erratic Isaac Greenwood, who had had experience with English methods of teaching science by

---

[30] Colman to Williams, Nov. 30, 1732, Sprague Mss., Congregational Library, London.

[31] *The Weekly Journal; or the British Gazetteer*, Jan. 11, 1729.

[32] Andrew Keogh, *Bishop Berkeley's Gift of Books to Yale in 1733* (Oslo, 1933).

[33] Samuel Miller, *Memoir of Rev. Charles Nisbet* (New York, 1840), 194.

observation and experiment, was a vigorous stimulus to scientific study in the colonies.[34]

Greenwood's letter to Colman recommending himself for the post was a gem of academic correspondence. "I need not observe," he goes on to observe,

> that the greatest impediment to the increase of good literature in all nurseries of learning has been that those who taught have not had encouragement enough to determine on their studies for life, but only so long as that they might be able to provide for themselves better, & consequently have been for the most part, only carefull to instruct themselves in so far as to discharge their Duty without disgrace; whereas such as have engaged in the profession for all their Days, are naturally ambitious to excell & render themselves an ornament to it. . . .

In other words, Harvard needed a scholar as well as a teacher, and Greenwood was the man.[35]

The compiler of the memoirs of a younger Thomas Hollis says that he sent to the colonies those books which were most useful to the community (and not necessarily most acceptable to particular persons). Always a vein of high regard for public liberty motivated his gifts. He was drawn to Jonathan Mayhew because of the latter's position against political authoritarianism and maintained a lifelong correspondence with him. Hollis saw to it that American colleges got his new edition of Locke's *Two Treatises on Civil Government,* and he also sent to America literature on Milton, whom he looked upon as the fount of English and American liberty. In a copy of Milton's prose presented to Harvard, Hollis had written, "Reader, observe, reverence this the genuine full character, of the matchless John Milton." [36]

Hollis was in effect the London agent for the Harvard library,

---

[34] S. E. Morison, *Three Centuries of Harvard 1636–1936* (Cambridge, Mass., 1936), 58, 66–69, 79; "Charles Morton's Compendium Physicae," *Col. Soc. Mass., Trans.,* XXXIII (1940), xxxi; T. Hornberger, *Scientific Thought in The American Colleges 1638–1800* (Austin, 1945), 44–45. The whole of chap. v in Hornberger's book is very important.

[35] Greenwood to Colman, London, Dec. 20, 1725, Colman Mss., I, 1697–1734, Mass. Hist. Soc.

[36] *Memoirs of Thomas Hollis,* vi–vii, 92–93, 239; R. D. Havens, *The Influence of Milton on English Poetry* (Cambridge, 1922), 42 note 4.

and with some pride he wrote Mayhew that the books he had sent to the college were collected and even packed by him. In the period of rising tension with the homeland, in the 1760's, Hollis wrote Mayhew that more books, especially on government, were on the way: "Should those go safe, it is hoped that no principal books on that First subject will be wanting in Harvard College, from the Days of Moses to these times. Men of New England, Brethren, use them for yourselves, and for others; and God bless you!" After Mayhew's death, Dr. Andrew Elliot continued the correspondence with Hollis. The latter, when sending additional books for Harvard, wrote to Elliot that these, like earlier volumes, related mainly to civil and religious liberty. "We are entering, I doubt, to live in bad times, and I have been willing to contribute my mite . . . toward your getting stocked with books on these two most precious subjects." [37]

After the disastrous fire at Harvard in 1764, Hollis subscribed £200 for new apparatus and stirred friends to make contributions. When Franklin was in England he supervised the purchase of scientific instruments for Harvard. Hollis' will set aside £500 for the Harvard library, and his philanthropy also embraced Rhode Island College (Brown) and Wheelock's school. Before the Revolution William and Mary had made arrangements to import the best current books, particularly the publications of European philosophical societies. William and Mary's purchases of scientific apparatus abroad gave her equipment equal to that of Harvard. The war interrupted the program, but it was to be resumed as soon as practicable.[38] Louis XVI sent over five hundred volumes for the college library.

Americans gave as well as received, although when they sent books to Europe it was generally to individuals. Universities in Germany were anxious to add the new American books and magazines to their libraries and were ready to subscribe for them. Christophe D. Ebeling was the channel through which the American Philosophical Society's *Transactions* were distributed to various

---

[37] *Memoirs of Thomas Hollis,* 335, 319, 396.

[38] Stiles, *Diary,* II, 445, July 11, 1780.

German societies.[39] While the preponderant influences in education were from Europe to America, it has been suggested that Jefferson's ideas in his *Notes on Virginia* may have had weight with the French when they adopted their system of free elementary schools, their lycées, competitive scholarships, and fellowships. Joel Barlow described to France, reconstructing her society during the Revolution, the educational system of Connecticut where, he said, nearly everyone could read and write and "cast accounts." [40]

Libraries, and literary and scientific societies which were instruments of adult education (and sometimes the only substitutes for schools), were modeled on European precedents. As the Reverend John Lathrop, of Boston, wrote to Dr. John Lettsom after the Revolution, "To you more particularly we look for examples; from you we are constantly receiving aids; and from those aids, which can only be derived from older countries, and from societies matured with age, if we are not wanting to ourselves, our progress will be vastly more rapid than it could be were we left wholly to ourselves." Like other critical Americans he acknowledged his country's lag in intellectual achievement, but he added, "The disposition which prevails in all parts of America, to follow the example of Europe, in forming Societies, will greatly facilitate improvement," so that "in a few years we shall begin to make a figure." [41]

Libraries and learned societies were relatively more important in the education of adults in the eighteenth century than they are in the twentieth. Sometimes these societies were substitutes for advanced education, and they also furnished a kind of post-graduate study for people already college-trained. The early story of American libraries is filled with names of English benefactors. One historian of libraries says "it is preeminently a record of reciprocal good offices between some of the best men of both countries." [42]

---

[39] E. L. Bradsher, *Mathew Carey* (New York, 1912), 53, Ebeling to Carey, March 20, 1794; Amer. Phil. Soc., Mss., April 18, 1803.

[40] Chinard, *Thomas Jefferson,* 98; Barlow, *Advice to the Privileged Orders,* (London, 1792), pt. I, chap. iv.

[41] Pettigrew, II, 443, 445, Nov. 9, 1790, Nov. 16, 1791.

[42] E. Edwards, *Memoirs of Libraries,* quoted in B. C. Steiner, "Rev. Thomas Bray and his American Libraries," *Amer. Hist. Rev.,* II (1896–1897), 61.

Probably no one did more to stimulate the growth of libraries than the Reverend Thomas Bray. As a leader in the Anglican Church he was, of course, thinking mainly in terms of parochial libraries, but his vision was not bounded by religious considerations alone. In his *Essay towards promoting all Necessary and Useful Knowledge* . . . (1697), he advocated for Britain and the colonies the establishment of free circulating libraries, to be used by the gentry as well as by ministers. Maryland, to which Bray was assigned for clerical duty, proposed to set apart public funds for the support of a free public library. Bray himself said that in four years £2,400 worth of books had been shipped to the colonies, thus furnishing assistance for thirty libraries, and foundations for seventy more. In 1723 he named several men to aid him in carrying out his work; they were later called "Dr. Bray's Associates for founding clerical libraries and supporting negro schools." His energy in behalf of libraries bore rich fruit in both England and Wales, where some eighty of them were established before his death in 1730. Within another seven years an additional twenty-three were founded.

Isaac Watts, having learned of a proposal to establish a library in Connecticut, sent to Benjamin Colman the rules of a circulating library set up by Samuel Fancourt, a dissenting minister. The library, said Watts, was of great use to country ministers and gentlemen in the community. He sent books as well as rules and, because of a mix-up in the ownership of the volumes, which were claimed by another library, in Lyme, Watts had to send additional books to satisfy both communities. Postage and other expenses were a burden to Watts, and his New England correspondents were sensitive about the costs to him—"but you gladly spend," said Colman, "and are spent, for the many at home and abroad." [43] Within a short period, by the middle of the century, seventeen subscription libraries had been founded in various American towns and villages, possibly surpassing in number those in England.[44]

---

[43] *Mass. Hist. Soc., Proc.*, ser. 2, IX (1894–1895), 368–369, Oct. 12, 1739; A. S. Pratt, *Isaac Watts and his Gift of Books to Yale College* (New Haven, 1938), 3, 56.

[44] J. T. Adams, *Provincial Society* (New York, 1928), 305. E. Edwards, *Memoirs of Libraries* (London, 1859), II, 183, says no town in England had a

The Library Company of Philadelphia, one of America's earliest and best libraries, was indebted to Peter Collinson, in London, for intelligent choice of its books; he was its agent for thirty years. Its annual purchases overseas in the early years averaged twenty pounds, said Franklin.[45] In a tribute to Collinson, Franklin said that Philadelphia's success, which owed much to him, encouraged the opening of other libraries, so that at the time of writing (1769) there were over thirty of the type scattered through the colonies.[46] A noted colonial institution was the Redwood Library in Newport, to which Catharine Macaulay sent her works. The Charleston Library Society, a main center of the intellectual life of the community, had a large collection, for its day, of over six thousand volumes, many of which came from foreign sources. After the Revolution a newly established Massachusetts town named for Franklin received, through the efforts of the good doctor and of Richard Price of England, a selection of books "most proper to inculcate Principles of sound Religion and just government." It was this library which helped furnish the early education of Horace Mann.[47]

Libraries grew comparatively slowly until the time of the Revolution, but then they picked up momentum so that by 1800 there were more than a hundred circulating libraries in Connecticut alone, and they continued to grow at a fast rate into the nineteenth century. The usual cost for shares in a library, from one to five pounds, began to decline very rapidly.[48]

The great majority of books offered for sale in early America were imported from the mother country, which sent all kinds of literature to enrich libraries of schools, communities, and private homes. Recent studies show that a considerable proportion of New Eng-

---

subscription library at the time when the Library Company of Philadelphia was formed, 1731.

45 Smyth, *Franklin, Writings,* Franklin to Strahan, II, 296, Dec. 11, 1745.

46 Wertenbaker, *The Old South,* 46; Smyth, *Franklin, Writings,* to Michael Collinson, V, 185; F. P. Bowes, *The Culture of Early Charleston* (Chapel Hill, 1942), 61.

47 Quoted in Greene, *The Revolutionary Generation,* 391; E. I. F. Williams, *Horace Mann, Educational Statesman* (New York, 1937), 6–7.

48 "The 'Trumbull Manuscript Collections' and early Connecticut libraries" in *Papers in Honor of Andrew Keogh.*

landers of all classes owned books. Henry Knox, a large importer of English books, sold them on long credit to country booksellers, hawkers, and other buyers. The coastal communities in the South were continuously supplied—so well, in fact, that one modern student believes "literary London was far nearer Williamsburg than Boston." Americans who wished to secure books from abroad got them through personal correspondents or through publishers with whom they had opened an account. Thomas Evans, in Paternoster Row, was the agent for Isaiah Thomas in the 1780's. Thomas in turn recommended new outlets for British books in American towns.[49] The London agents for the Philadelphia Library Company in later years were Joseph Woods and William Dillwyn. Southern planters regularly received from their factors in England standard works as well as new publications. A detailed examination of book ownership in colonial Maryland shows a much wider distribution than has generally been believed.

John Clark was the London agent for Lewis Morris, whose orders included the works of Milton, and some history and law books which Americans read in great quantities. Edward and Charles Dilly kept Benjamin Rush abreast of the latest publications, particularly in medicine. In return, Rush was asked to send one hundred copies of the forthcoming *Transactions* of the American Philosophical Society for sale in England.[50] John Stockdale was entrusted with the task of keeping Thomas Jefferson supplied with books, old and new. Renewed English interest in Shakespeare was similarly reflected in colonial reading. Some Americans were interested, too, in beautiful imprints, and Baskerville's *Milton*, for example, was an acquisition highly prized. Franklin lent encouragement to Baskerville by sending his products to American printers. James Phillips was the London agent for a number of Americans, particularly fellow Quakers, whom he sometimes entertained on their visits to London. His overseas correspondents placed much reliance on his judgment in choosing books for them.

---

[49] Isaiah Thomas papers, e.g., Feb. 2, 1785, Amer. Antiq. Soc. More complete documentation for this section will be found in M. Kraus, "Literary Relations between Europe and America in the Eighteenth Century," *William and Mary Quart.*, ser. 3, I (1944), 227–231, from which most of this is taken.

[50] Rush corr., Ridgway Library.

Periodicals have always been read in large quantities by Americans, and such was their significance that a close student of early New England believes that they were "the most important missionary of European culture." Over two hundred copies of various magazines were listed in one invoice sent by Thomas Longman for Henry Knox's "London Book Store" in Boston.[51] The *Monthly Review* was one of the periodicals imported, and, though not as widely read as its competitors, appealed to Americans because of its disapproval of the government's handling of the colonies. Samuel Miller, a judicious historian of eighteenth-century civilization, said in writing of his own time, that it should be called "the age of periodical publications." Though he granted that periodicals were of tremendous influence in the democratization of culture, he believed they were unfavorable to "real scholarship." They discouraged, said Miller, habits of "connected reading and of patient *systematic* thinking."

Enterprising American printers were kept posted on the latest publications by their London contemporaries. William Strahan was one of the London printers most active in his associations with Americans. Franklin wrote to him, in 1744, that he had long wanted a dependable friend in London to send him "from time to time such new pamphlets as are worth reading on any subject (religious controversy excepted) for there is no depending on titles and advertisements." For many years he supplied Franklin and David Hall with English newspapers, magazines, and books. To set up a nephew in business in New Haven, Franklin asked Strahan to send over "a complete good new press," ink, one thousand pounds of type, and other materials. Strahan arranged to have English provincial papers sent to Hall and also full materials on the Parliamentary sessions which he frequently attended. In response to an apparent scolding from "Davie" Hall, Strahan promised to send all new books and to forward more promptly the latest magazines and pamphlets. The Library Company of Philadelphia as well as prominent individuals like Joseph Galloway utilized the services of Strahan.

American printers were still importing their presses in the second half of the eighteenth century, although by 1769 the first press and

[51] "Henry Knox and the London Book-Store in Boston 1771–1774," *Mass. Hist. Soc., Proc.,* LXI (1927–1928), 253. This correspondence is one of the best sources on transatlantic bookselling.

the first type created by local craftsmen were in use. The output o
colonial presses was considerable, at least in quantity; Boston a
the beginning of the eighteenth century was the outstanding pub
lishing center, after London, in all the British Empire.

Franklin was the most important link between the presses of Eu
rope and America. All kinds of requests from European publisher
and authors came to him: for American news, for information abou
America as a market for European publications, and for permissio
to dedicate books to him. Writers who were planning histories o
America asked him for bibliographies; one wanted details for a wor
on the "Illustrious Men of America." Franklin, Jefferson, and other
gave advice to writers on the American Revolution. Jefferson con
gratulated one writer on his decision to go to America to gathe
materials, for, as he remarked, although much of the subject matte
could be found in England, "the greatest mass of important event
were transacted in America." There, he wisely added, "the ver
ground itself will give you new insight into some of the most inter
esting transactions." European printers planning to migrate t
America sought advice at home and abroad; to meet their need
Henry Lemoine, a noted English bookseller, contributed a length
letter to the *Gentleman's Magazine* on the state of printing an
bookselling in the United States.

The rapid growth of an English-speaking population overseas wa
looked upon as a boon to the booksellers of England, although pi
rated American editions moderated this prospect for authors an
publishers. Before the middle of the century Franklin had writte
to Strahan that English authors little appreciated the fame they ha
in America: "We are a kind of Posterity in respect to them," h
observed. Forty years later he wrote to the same friend that a vas
American audience was assembling for "English Authors, ancient
present, and future . . . and this will demand large and of cours
profitable impressions of your most valuable Books."

Observers on both sides of the Atlantic thought the time not fa
distant when English would displace French as the most popula
language for international usage. "Let the French . . . triumph i
the present diffusion of their tongue," wrote Hume to Gibbon i
1767, "our solid and increasing establishments in America . .
promise a superior stability and duration to the English lan-

guage." [52] An Edinburgh periodical proudly looked forward to the time when all over America, "in the days of our grandsons, the language and writings of Washington, Franklin, Dryden, and Shakespeare, will be studied and revered." To his diary Ezra Stiles confided his belief that English would probably "become the vernacular Tongue of more people than any one Tongue on Earth, except the Chinese." And when John Adams urged Congress to establish an institution similar to European academies to maintain standards for the national tongue, he also wrote that English would be in the future "more generally the language of the world" than were Latin or French in ages past. Quite probably it was dislike of the prospect of the rising tide of nationalism that prompted a Frenchman to send Franklin a plan for a universal language.[53]

In America the pressure of English upon other immigrant tongues was steady, and the latter struggled with varying success against submersion. German held out stubbornly in Pennsylvania, but elsewhere it gradually gave way. The needs of business enterprise often prompted the transition to English. Dutch lingered on in the villages of the Hudson Valley, but within a generation after the founding of the federal government English had largely triumphed over its rivals. In the intimacy of the home, Dutch, and even more tenaciously German, held out for decades thereafter.

The London booksellers were clearly alive to the possibilities of the American trade. According to Lord Sheffield this book trade was very large and would continue to favor England because of the higher American labor costs. In particular he thought schoolbooks could be sent more cheaply from England than they could be printed in America. Bibles had been sent in such "immense quantities" at twenty shillings a dozen that they "formed a great article of commerce" before the Revolution. The Longmans, Rivingtons, and the brothers Dilly were very active in this trade. Edward and Charles Dilly were more than publishers and booksellers; as part of the circle of Price, Rush, Franklin, *et al.*, they acted as the electric wire transmitting the current of European and American thought. Stockdale, Debrett, and Phillips did most of the London reprints of

---

[52] H. Roumigière, *Le Français dans les Relations Diplomatiques* ("Univ. of Calif., Publ. in Mod. Philology," XII, 1926), chap. v and 315.

[53] See *Amer. Phil. Soc., Trans.*, IV (1799), 162.

American editions. A flattering English survey of the American literary scene near the end of the century stated that the largest booksellers in the coastal cities were stocked with nearly all publications available in Europe, except the more expensive ones: "Their sales are very great, for it is scarce possible to conceive the number of readers with which even every little town abounds."

An American newspaper in 1810 pointed out that for ten years after the Revolution books were imported and sold more cheaply than they could be printed in the United States, and not until the outbreak of war in Europe (coupled with an added duty on paper) could American booksellers compete with English. After the turn of the century the Americans, among whom Mathew Carey was a leading spirit, sought to advance their interests by organizing book fairs modeled after more famous predecessors at Leipzig and Frankfort.

Many of the books published in Europe and sent to America were histories, travel reports, etc., of the New World. So numerous had they become, even at an early date, that bibliographies were needed to guide readers to these materials. White Kennett assembled one of the earliest American bibliographies which he hoped the Society for the Propagation of the Gospel would adopt for the creation of a "perfect American library." He believed that it would be of great service to missionaries, mariners, and merchants. Historians, heralds, and statesmen could also make use of this library of Americana, which Kennett urged might become "the common Fund and treasury of all the Remains of that Country, and of all the following Discoveries and Remarks that shall be hereafter made upon it." He hoped that his catalogue, which contained about fifty tracts relating to Virginia and one hundred to New England, would stimulate some publisher to make a collection of American travels.[54] In the

[54] W. Kennett, *Bibliothecae Americanae Primordia* . . . (London, 1713) Almost a century before, works on America had been included in the bibliography by Antonio R. de León Pinelo, *Epítome de la Bibliotheca Oriental y Occidental*. . . . (Madrid, 1629; reprinted Buenos Aires, 1919). Fuller documentation on this section will be found in Kraus, "Literary Relations between Europe and America in the eighteenth Century," *loc. cit.*, 219–227. *The Bibliotheca Americana*, 1789, generally attributed to A. Homer, was compiled by L. T. Rede; see S. C. Sherman, "Leman Thomas Rede's Bibliotheca Americana," *William and Mary Quart.*, ser. 3, IV (1947), 332.

latter part of the eighteenth century a *Bibliotheca Americana* appeared in London. It justified itself on the ground that "America was a very considerable portion of the known world, and a most important field for historical investigation." It listed hundreds of publications and manuscripts available to English scholars, and its introduction was a friendly estimate of American culture.

The literature on America, mainly by Europeans, had thus grown extensive enough to require guides, and at the same time the products of American writers themselves were given more space, as well as critical attention, in the periodicals of Europe. This attention was not always flattering. In January, 1810, the *Edinburgh Review* said: "America has done nothing, either to extend, diversify or embellish the sphere of human knowledge. Though all she has written were obliterated from the records of learning there would, (if we except the works of Franklin) be no positive diminution either of the useful or agreeable." Other observers were more favorably impressed. A German dictionary of English, Irish, and American writers listed over three hundred American authors whose work had appeared in their own country or in Europe, and sometimes in both, between 1790 and 1803. Most of these Americans, like the English named, were writers of articles contributed to periodicals. This is significant, for it reveals the emphasis placed on periodical literature in the eighteenth century, especially by scientists. It indicates too that we need to readjust our perspective of America in the eighteenth century. Historians of culture, when treating of literature, usually place so much stress on belles-lettres that the comparative absence of the latter has put early America on a relatively low plane. The important fact to note, however, is that her contemporaries were interested in all kinds of literature—political and scientific as well as belletristic. The generation after the Revolution is often depreciated because of the absence of important names in belles-lettres, but in reality this was a seedtime for the future. The main contribution of these years was the democratization of culture.

Americans in the era of the Revolution were pleasantly conscious of the heightened literary reputation they enjoyed in Europe after their political writings were published abroad. A recent student of Anglo-American literary relations expressed the belief that the literature of the American Revolution was "the most magnificent irruption of the American genius into print." America, he said, has never since equaled that tremendous display of power. The American mind marshaled all its force to one end; "the protection of national rights, and the expression of an ideal." The American state papers, he reminds us, "have been justly described as the first authoritative presentation to the Old World of the intellectual and political condition of the New." [55]

Even a prejudiced critic like the writer in the *Edinburgh Review* who belittled American authors was obliged to make an exception in favor of Franklin. If a complete bibliography of Franklin were ever compiled, it would include, besides collections of his works, the hundreds of articles, anecdotes, and poems by him, about him, and ascribed to him that appeared in the newspapers and magazines all over Europe. A London magazine said he was better known abroad than in his native country; this publication alone had over twenty-five items on Franklin in its volumes. "With what avidity," one of its writers stated, "must the public expect the memoirs of this very extraordinary man." The editors revealed their own impatience at the delay of an English edition by printing extracts from Franklin's autobiography which had already appeared in French; these were promptly copied by the *Scots Magazine*. Readers of modern best sellers wait no more anxiously for the latest works of their favorite authors than did their ancestors for Franklin's autobiography. "We have in no small degree shared the impatience with which the public has for some time been expecting a full and authentic narrative of his life," confessed one reviewer. Critical comment was heavily in his favor in Germany too, where Herder strongly praised the *Autobiography*: "I scarcely know a more modern book for the young," he wrote, "which could give them such complete instruction in industry, wisdom and morality as this one."

It was counted as an important scoop to print any of Franklin's writings not included in his collected works. His humor was highly appreciated, and a reviewer of one of his publications wrote of his "garrulity which, in an old man, and such an old man, is not only excused, but approved." On the alert for a fresh manuscript, Charles Dilly asked Rush if Franklin had "any literary work that he had

[55] G. S. Gordon, *Anglo-American Literary Relations* (London, 1942), 27–28; this short book is a quick survey of a large subject.

houghts of giving to the world before he makes his exit?" [56] The German magazines lost little time in publishing Franklin's writings, which they usually reprinted from English publications. A Franklin mprint from France appeared in a London edition with the explanation that "the most trifling miscellaneous productions of that distinguished author will be agreeable to the public." Franklin's eputation in Italy prompted an admirer to send him Comte de Carli Rubbi's *Lettere Americanae*. Word came to him of election to he Royal Academy of History in Madrid, and of the translation of his writings into Spanish. The *Sentimental and Humorous Essays, Conducive to Economy and Happiness* by Noah Webster were likewise assured a kindly reception, for their indebtedness to Franklin was acknowledged, although one reviewer did credit Webster with a fair share of originality. Their popularity in America was thought sufficient reason for introducing Webster to English readers.

Washington and Jefferson also received some attention in European publications, Washington not so much for his writings as for his character and influence in American life. An English life of Washington, which included anecdotes of other eminent Americans of the Revolutionary period, was frankly eulogistic. Jefferson's *Notes on Virginia* was given considerable notice, although English reviewers treated it rather caustically because of his pro-French bias. John Stockdale, who published it in London, was doubtful of its sale. He said it was well spoken of in England "except those points that relate to our country." [57]

Morse's *American Geography* was widely acclaimed, and the *Monthly Review* pointed out that for information on various phases of American life: "We must no longer consult British writers but have recourse . . . to the Americans themselves." When asking Richard Price to arrange for English publication of the geography, Morse had revealed his anxiety lest his language describing the "late war" offend British readers; he left it to Price to erase offensive words or to substitute "softer language." [58] Shortly before this, Ramsay's history of the Revolution in South Carolina had been

[56] Dilly to Rush, May 5, 1786, Rush corr., Ridgway Library.

[57] Stockdale to Jefferson, Aug. 8, 1786, July 10, 1787, Jefferson papers, Mass. Hist. Soc.

[58] Jan. 30, 1789, Morse Mss., Yale Library.

turned down by Dilly as too personal for the English public; in fact he said it would be "dangerous to publish [it] in this Country." [59] A more favorable reaction was accorded Belknap's *History of New Hampshire* and Gilbert Imlay's *A Topographical Description of the Western Territory of North America.* The latter may well have influenced the dream of a utopian Pantisocracy nurtured by some of the Lake Poets.[60]

William Bartram's descriptions of his travels in the southern states were well known to European readers, who were attracted as much by his vivid romantic narrative as they were by his keen observation. Coleridge knew Bartram's *Travels* well, and a recent student of the poet thinks that of all the books he was reading "during the gestation of 'The Ancient Mariner' " none "left more lively images in his memory" than Bartram's. Wordsworth, a poet whose teachers were nature and solitude learned also from contemporary students similarly instructed, and it is therefore not surprising to find that he knew Bartram's work almost by heart. In some parts of "Ruth," the poet "follows Bartram word for word," says Lane Cooper, and in "The Prelude," the theme of the "noble savage" is supported by the adaptation of a scene from the American naturalist. As in Coleridge's experience, this reading lay dormant for years in the mind of Wordsworth. The work of Chateaubriand, particularly his *Atala,* the most important book in the literature of American exoticism, reveals his debt to Bartram and Imlay, who gave him the color to enrich his background and sometimes even the text to tell his story. The romantic appreciation of nature in England sometimes attributed to the influence of Wordsworth, certainly arose earlier and owes a good deal to America's startling scenery which evoked rhapsodical comments from travelers. As one tourist in the South phrased it, the scenery was "romantically pleasing" and rendered "the imagination sick with wonder."

Poetry written by Americans, sometimes reprinted in Europe, was not highly regarded abroad although, on occasion, it did receive compliments. Richard Lewis, a former Etonian, resident in Maryland, contributed to the *Gentleman's Magazine* a poem "Description of the Spring," which won some popularity in England. The

[59] July 5, 1786, Rush corr., Ridgway Library.

[60] O. F. Emerson, "Notes on Gilbert Imlay," *PMLA,* XXXIX (1924), 427.

poetry of youthful Thomas Godfrey, of Philadelphia, was appreciated in England more perhaps as the creation of supposed untutored genius than for its high literary merits. John Trumbull's *McFingal,* which had a London edition, was favorably reviewed. *A Poem, addressed to the Armies of the United States of America,* by David Humphries (reprinted in Paris and London) had many faults, wrote one reviewer, but it revealed "the true spirit of poetry." His *Poem on the Happiness of America* was less favorably received. Barlow was given more notice than the other American poets; it was frequently favorable, but criticism was sometimes leveled at his bombastic language. In the *Amerikanisches Magazin,* a long article, probably by Professor C. D. Ebeling, leniently appraised American poetry. It was heavily dependent on English models, he said, but it already had a distinctive character, and, although inferior to that of England in the power of its imagination, it excelled in genuine feeling. Barlow was the most original of the American poets, the writer thought, and America would in time learn from the poetry of other nations as well as from England, but would eventually go her own way.

But Europe's way, for the most part, was America's way in this early period. Addison and Steele, Pope and Milton, all had their echoes, faint though some of them were, in American newspapers and magazines. A student periodical, *Telltale,* modeled after Addison's *Spectator,* circulated in manuscript at Harvard in 1721. A reviewer of Franklin's collected works remarked that although "the Doctor's style [was] original, and unique," it also showed Addison's influence. A recent student of Franklin's earliest writing confirms in detail this eighteenth-century judgment. Colonial newspapers reprinted whole numbers of the *Spectator,* while Pope's *Essay on Man* and Butler's *Hudibras* were widely quoted. When Timothy Dwight in his *Conquest of Canaan* and Joel Barlow in his *Columbiad* modeled their poems on Milton, they were in the company of many Englishmen who acknowledged *Paradise Lost* as the greatest epic in a modern tongue. *L'Allegro* and *Il Penseroso* were imitated frequently in England and America, and in general it is fair to say that Milton was known equally well on both sides of the Atlantic.

Thomson too, had his admirers, and American Quakers were strongly appreciative of Cowper. A bond of sympathy existed between Americans and Thomson (who has been called the leader of the ethical movement in English poetry), for in his poems he encouraged the philanthropy of James Oglethorpe and his associates. In France, too, the followers of Thomson expressed strong humanitarian sentiments in their poetry. Franklin's letter to his London agent William Strahan is well known: "Whatever Thomson writes send me a dozen copies of. I had read no poetry for several years, and almost lost the Relish of, till I met with his Seasons." A Philadelphia Quaker wrote to Cowper that he had frequently read *The Task*: "There are in this city, and in the circle of my acquaintance, many . . . who love thee with true affection." Wordsworth, too, found his most enthusiastic American supporter in a Philadelphian, the distinguished editor Joseph Dennie.

American literature toward the close of the eighteenth century reflected the English vogue of sentiment and sensibility and the emphasis on narratives of seduction. In the novels of the period the influence of Richardson and Sterne was obvious. While American periodicals contained contributions of moral tales, which told of seductions and their aftermath of misery, there was vigorous censure of this reading matter by the keepers of the public morals.

The introduction of literature from Germany was facilitated by the large German population already established in America. Barlow wrote to Ezra Stiles from Hamburg in 1794, regretting that a language difference should raise a barrier between Americans and German literature. "We have been content to borrow from them their improvements in science," he added, "without being able to relish the beauties of their writers. These are more numerous, and perhaps more excellent, than those of any other modern nation." But Barlow himself underestimated American familiarity with German writings.

As far back as the seventeenth century many books by German authors were found in New England libraries. John Winthrop the younger was in close touch with the current of German thought through books and correspondence. During the eighteenth century this American contact with German intellectual life grew slowly, but in the Revolutionary era it was more frequent and sustained. German writers in larger number were introduced to America, where interest in this literature was largely a reflection of England's interest. The works of Solomon Gessner, Lessing, Schiller, and Goethe were known overseas in American reprints as well as by performances of their dramas.

Charles Brockden Brown, a keen observer of literary trends, was very much interested in German literature, to which his *Monthly Magazine* devoted some attention. Another American who was asked to give his reasons for studying German answered, for "intellectual pleasure and improvement." He himself wished to read "this Kotzbue they talk so much of; this Gessner; this Wieland, this Haller, this Schiller, and this Goethe." Years before George Ticknor "discovered" German culture, his predecessor, William Bentley, of Salem, together with Christophe D. Ebeling in Hamburg, had promoted a strong interest in American-German relations. New England's flowering owed much to these pioneers.

The knowledge of French among the educated classes in America, particularly in the later years of the eighteenth century, led to the importation of many works in history and travel, while the interest in the sentimental novel was stimulated by the arrival of increasing numbers of émigrés. French literature was imported in considerable quantity by New York and Philadelphia booksellers who hurried their orders as soon as the publications were available. In translations (mostly in extracts) or in originals, many of the works of Montesquieu, Burlamaqui, Voltaire, and others were known to Americans. Of Voltaire's writings his histories were the most popular in America. They were published before his philosophical writings, of which the favorite was the *Philosophical Dictionary*. A rapid growth of interest in Voltaire in the decade before the American Revolution may be traced in booksellers' lists, library catalogues, almanacs, and magazines. This interest showed no abatement in the postwar era, and in the period of the French Revolution it was very great, although then he was more frequently the object of vituperation than of admiration. The interest in French drama (mainly through English adaptations) was considerable in this period.[61]

Significant as was this appreciation of Continental literature, it

[61] L. P. Waldo, *The French Drama in America* (Baltimore, 1942), 212–213.

would be a distortion of emphasis to overlook the continuing powe
of the English tradition, which was the main stream in America
culture. Comparable groups on both sides of the Atlantic rea
similar titles with the same relish—or equal discomfort. There wa
indeed (apart from the drama in the seventeenth century) a clos
correlation between American and English reading tastes through
out the colonial and early national periods.

The colonial era was one of dependence upon the homeland fo
literary and educational stimulation. If the standards of Britis
schools were not high the American institutions could not hav
been expected to achieve distinction. But apparently the prep
aration that young men received in America was adequate fo
advanced studies—in law and medicine, for example. The accom
plishments of British and American students seem comparable, an
if the latter are to be believed they worked harder at their studies.

The pressure among Americans was always for broadening th
opportunities to reach a larger audience. This was a tendency com
mon to Britain as well, but the pressure there was not so strong. Th
Americans were proud of their democratization of educational in
stitutions—schools, libraries, and the like. Enlarging the area o
educational opportunity was already a fixed objective in the schem
of the Atlantic civilization.

CHAPTER V

Graphic Arts, Music, and Architecture

THE migrant European preserved much of his cultural heritage in his overseas home in spite of adverse circumstances. He himself, especially in a retrospective view, was hardly aware of how much he had brought with him and how much he had saved. His descendants of the nineteenth century, with different tastes, depreciated his artistic achievements, but in the twentieth these are so fully appreciated they almost run the risk of overpraise.

In recent years we have learned that appreciation of aesthetic values by Americans, even in their earlier colonial period, was much deeper and finer than is generally understood. Reputed Puritan hostility to "art" is another of the many historical judgments which requires serious modification. England itself was heavily in debt to the Continent for her painters, architects, and musicians. If England was comparatively infertile in the arts the colonies could hardly be expected to prove fertile. Thus it was not necessarily Puritan opposition to the fine arts which was the main deterrent but rather the lack of a strong support at home.[1] It is of course true that utilitarian standards always condition a society struggling to make its adjustment to new physical surroundings, but even under such circumstances there are individuals whose aesthetic sense is never so dulled as to be unappreciative of beauty in its diverse manifestations. "After the first Cares for the Necessaries of Life are over, we shall come to think of the Embellishments," wrote Franklin to Mary Stevenson. "Already some of our young Geniuses begin to lisp Attempts at Painting, Poetry and Musick." [2]

---

[1] See M. Rouquet, *L'Etat des Arts en Angleterre* (Paris, 1755).

[2] Smyth, *Franklin, Writings,* IV, 193, March 25, 1763.

Where English achievement in the arts and crafts was of a high order, such as in silversmithing and in the making of fine furniture colonial standards revealed the impress of the parent pattern. Where the native English tradition was spare and too exclusively aristocratic, as it was in painting, no strong development could be expected in early colonial society, undistinguished and unburdened by a hereditary aristocracy.

But even so the modern student finds much to admire in seventeenth-century American portrait painting. With the growth of wealth and the secularization of life that are apparent before the middle of the eighteenth century, many more (and better) portraits of colonial worthies were painted.[3] Provincial artists worked in a new medium as early as, if not earlier than, European contemporaries. Henrietta Johnston was making creditable pastels in South Carolina in 1710, preceding Rosalba Carriera, of Venice, who is often referred to as the inventor of pastels. Miss Johnston, probably English-trained, was the earliest of a line of artists who worked in pastels; Copley was the most distinguished among them in provincial America.[4]

Opportunities for artists, so limited in earlier decades, noticeably expanded by the middle of the eighteenth century. Painters, uncertain of a future in the homeland, visited the colonies as itinerants and sometimes remained as permanent residents. They taught as well as painted, and whatever instruction some of the native artists received came from these wanderers. John Wollaston, in New York from England in mid-century, was the community's first really fashionable portrait painter for whom the leading families sat. He went on to Philadelphia and then to South Carolina. During his seventeen years' stay in America he made several hundred portraits, some of them extant. His work, says a leading authority, left its mark on Benjamin West.[5]

Colonial artists, when corresponding with Europeans, were wont to say, a little defiantly, a little apologetically, that they were self-

---

[3] V. Barker, "Puritan Portraiture," *The American Magazine of Art,* XXVII (Oct., 1934), 507–514.

[4] M. Vaughan, "Pastels in Colonial America," *International Studio,* LXXXIX (March, 1928), 31–35.

[5] W. Sawitzky, "The American Work of Benjamin West," *Penn. Mag. of Hist. and Biog.,* LXII (1938), 440–443.

caught, forgetting an indebtedness, however slight, to their older contemporaries. It is worth remembering, for example, that Joseph Blackburn introduced a new note of grace into American portraiture which deeply impressed Copley. Robert Feke, acclaimed as America's finest portrait painter before Copley, and one of the real founders of the American tradition in art, also painted "subjects," i.e., scenes of work, etc., showing the influence of Flemish genre painting. Feke's more immediate indebtedness was to Smibert.[6]

John Smibert, who came to America with Bishop Berkeley, is one of the more famous of the transplanted group. Fairly well known in London, he was nevertheless conscious (according to gossip) of being a small frog in a big pond, and he believed removal to the colonies would make him the big frog. Berkeley, who did not remain long, tried hard to entice Smibert to return and settle in Ireland, where the Bishop was now located. Do "myrtles grow in or near Boston, without pots, stoves or greenhouses in the open air? I assure you they do in my garden. So much for the climate," said Berkeley. But though Smibert stayed on in Boston he kept in touch with English painters. He helped spread Hogarth's fame on this side of the Atlantic. In addition to filling commissions, he sold materials for painters, ordering large quantities of supplies from London. "Fann Paper" was called for in bulk. "There are many women that paints Fanns for the country use," said Smibert, "and as they buy the Colours of us the paper has of late come naturaly in to be an article in the Shop." He thanked his English dealer for sending "Landskips," saying they were the finest collection of such prints he had ever seen. The public was interested in them, they sold well; and Smibert's experience indicated that a considerable market for art products already existed in the colonies. Smibert, on one occasion, bewailing the lack of interest in art in England, wished that if the arts were about to leave Great Britain they might "take their flight into our new world that they may at least remain in some part of the British dominions." [7]

In a positive manner Smibert brought the British tradition to

---

[6] T. Bolton and H. L. Binsse, "Robert Feke, First Painter to Colonial Aristocracy," *The Antiquarian,* XV (Oct., 1930), 33; see J. T. Flexner, *American Painting: First Flowers of our Wilderness* (Boston, 1947), chap. vi.

[7] "Smibert-Moffatt Letters, 1735–1752," *Mass. Hist. Soc., Proc.,* XLIX (1915–1916), 23–42.

America. Soon after his arrival in Boston he held a showing of hi[s] originals and replicas, and it is believed that this was the first such exhibition in the colonies. In everything but in name, says a recent student, Smibert's house "was the first British academy in New England." [8] Smibert's own copies of old masters were Trumbull's teachers, and the line of continuity was maintained when Trumbull used his predecessor's studio.[9]

Where Smibert and others made the trip from east to west, Copley, Benjamin West, Mather Brown, and others made the voyage from west to east. Copley's talent was early revealed, and like so many other colonials he deplored the fate that had dumped him onto an aesthetic desert—but he looked forward to a greater fertility. In a letter to a well-known Swiss painter, J. E. Liotard, from whom he ordered art materials, Copley wrote defensively:

> You may be surprised that so remote a corner of the Globe as New England should have any d[e]mand for the necessary eutensils for practicing the fine Arts, but I assure You Sir however feeble our efforts may be, it is not for want of inclination that they are not better, but the want of oppertunity to improve ourselves. however America which has been the seat of war and desolation, I would fain hope will one Day become the School of fine Arts and monsieur Liotard'[s] Drawing with Justice be set as patterns for our ministration.[10]

On other occasions Copley was to admit that good taste (which he himself, did much to elevate) did exist in the colonies, and his many commissions indicated at least that his provincial contemporaries were interested in portraiture. "I have a large Room full of Pictures, unfinished," he wrote to a friend, "which would ingage me these twelve months, if I did not begin any others. . . ." He was conscious that he needed further study to improve his art, but he was not averse to making money at the same time. Painters, he said once, cannot live on art only, "tho I could hardly Live without it." [11]

---

[8] O. Hagen, *The Birth of the American Tradition in Art* (New York, 1940), 44–62.

[9] W. T. Whitley, *Artists and their friends in England 1700–1799* (London and Boston, 1928), I, 62–67.

[10] "Letters and Papers of John Singleton Copley and Henry Pelham 1739–1776," *Mass. Hist. Soc., Colls.*, LXXI (1914), 26, Sept. 30, 1762.

[11] *Ibid.*, 32–33, Copley to Thomas Ainslie, Feb. 25, 1765; 74.

It was the painting, "Boy with the Squirrel," which eventually gave a new direction to Copley's life. A ship captain with a discriminating eye saw to it that this appealing picture was exhibited in London in 1766. The praise heaped upon it was gratifying beyond measure. "It was universally allowed to be the best Picture of its kind that appeared on that occasion," wrote Captain R. G. Bruce. Joshua Reynolds said "that in any Collection of Painting" it would have passed for "an excellent Picture," but when he was informed of Copley's presumed disadvantages, he added that *"it was a very wonderfull Performance."* It was superior to any of West's portraits and, Reynolds went on, "he did not know one Painter at home, who had all the Advantages that Europe could give them, that could equal it." If such a work were the product of Copley's own untutored genius Reynolds said that with the advantages of European example and instruction the American could become "one of the first Painters in the World," provided he escaped early enough from the unpromising atmosphere of Boston. Reynolds was not all flattery. He found a little hardness in the drawing, coldness in the shading, and in general an overminuteness.[12]

Benjamin West, then in London, wrote in his ever generous way a detailed criticism of the picture, noting its virtues and defects. At first sight, he said, the picture struck the eye as too "liney," too much "neetness in the lines." In nature, said West, "every thing is Round, or at least Partakes the most of that forme which makes it imposeble that Nature, when seen in a light and shade can ever appear liney." West advised Copley what to paint for the following year's exhibit, and "be shure take your Subjects from Nature as you did in your last Piec, and dont trust any resemblanc of any thing to fancey" except the background. Copley was predisposed to this view, for he had given it as his firm belief that "all human productions fall infinitely short of the bea[u]tys of nature." And like Reynolds, West urged Copley to paint only in oil, as they both believed it superior to all other painting. West, too, added his voice to the others urging Copley to visit Europe for a few years to see the great masters.[13]

Copley, who was given the distinguished honor of election to the Society of Artists of Great Britain, at once felt he was moving in a

[12] *Ibid.*, 41–43, Aug. 4, 1766.

[13] *Ibid.*, 43–45, West to Copley, Aug. 4, 1766.

larger world. He agreed with West that in America, "there is
examples of Art, except what is to [be] met with in a few prints i
diferently executed, from which it is not possable to learn much
Copley clearly overlooked many examples of good painting
America, by Feke, Blackburn, and others, but quite possibly b
cause these were in private homes and never appeared in publ
exhibitions, his complaint may have had some justification. N
ture, he told West, "has hitherto been my only instructor." H
wanted to know what painters were doing in Italy and wheth
those living were as great as the masters of former years. Capta
Bruce assured Copley that English artists had already put him "on
footing with all the Portrait Painters except Mr. Reynolds." [14]

West gave Copley a correspondence course in painting. He r
minded him that Van Dyck, whom he called the Prince of Portra
Painters, managed by light and shadow and the color of draperies
make "the face and hands apear allmost a Disception. For in Po
trait Painting those are they Parts of most Consiquence and of cor
ought to be the most distinguished. There is in Historical Painting
West added, "this same attention to be Paid." Main characters mu
be singled out; otherwise all is confusion. Again Copley was urge
to travel abroad, letters to Italy were promised, and said West, "
you should Ever come to London my house is at Your Service." [15]

The pressure on Copley continued until his head swam. "I a
afraid," said Captain Bruce, "you will delay coming to Europe ti
the Force of your Genius is weakened, and it may be too late fo
much Improvement." London or Boston, which was it to be? I
America, Copley observed with some bitterness, people general
regarded painting as "no more than any other usefull trade, as the
sometimes term it, like that of a Carpenter tailor or shew maker, no
as one of the most noble Arts in the World." Artistic encourag
ment, he said inaccurately, came to him only from abroad. He di
admit that financially, America had been kind to him, for he wa
earning three hundred guineas a year. He had saved enough, h
said, to support him in London for some time, but he was fearfu
that he might not do as well in England. West did not relax the pre
sure, urging him to come to Europe at least for a year, with study i

[14] *Ibid.*, 50–51, Nov. 12, 1766; 55, June 11, 1767.

[15] *Ibid.*, 56–58, June 20, 1767.

aly too, adding lavishly, "tho perhaps amongs the liveing masters that Country you may not meet with a rival." [16]

But Copley stayed on, painting the leading citizens in the north-n towns and even executing commissions ordered from abroad. ohn Greenwood, a New England painter living in London as a ccessful art dealer, asked Copley to paint his mother and send the icture overseas. Copley also painted the portrait of a boy, Wilkes arber, and the picture was sent to London to John Wilkes, his amesake, who was then the stormy petrel of English politics and ero of New England radicals. It was left to West's judgment hether to exhibit it, but the cautious Copley desired to avoid any nputation of party spirit and wished it not to be shown if either de were offended. Political contests, he said, were "neigther pleas-g to an artist or advantageous to the Art itself." It was not shown.[17]

West recommended to a New England father that he send his son study with Copley; but he advised that the boy learn about colors rst and observe nature closely. West said his own experience had een valuable—"My having no other Assistance but what I drew om Nature"—gave him a good foundation, "while had I come to urope sooner in Life I should have known nothing but the Re-eipts of Masters." A relative, writing in approval of Copley's long-latured plan to study abroad made an observation that belongs in ie history of expatriation. He remarked that after contact with uropean society returned Americans do not find enough people at ome to satisfy their intellectual and artistic interests and therefore o overseas again, "so that our country is check'd in its improve-ient." "I hope," he told Copley, "better things of you, than a dis-osition which is rather selfish." [18]

As the time neared for Copley's departure (he finally decided to eave in 1773), West from his own experience sent him details on ow to study in Italy. West's first injunction was that Mrs. Copley e left at home, so that the artist husband could study without dis-raction! Ancient sculpture should be studied, Raphael, Michel-ngelo, "Corragio," Titian, "as the source from whance true tast in

[16] *Ibid.*, 59, June 25, 1767; 65, 72.

[17] *Ibid.*, 81–82, 95, 98, Nov. 24, 1770.

[18] *Ibid.*, 118–119, West to Shrimpton Hutchinson, June 18, 1771; 190–192, no. Clarke to Copley, Dec. 20, 1772.

the arts have flow'd." In good character sketches of their work, We
then explained why these artists were to be studied. Americans wh
had been to Italy and were familiar with art circles there we
pressed into service for letters of recommendation, which were du
forthcoming. There always seemed to be intermediaries who coul
be counted on to smooth the way. When Stuart was a young painte
struggling to establish himself in London, Benjamin Waterhou
asked Dr. John Fothergill to aid him. Dr. J. C. Lettsom assiste
him, too, by sitting for his portrait.[19] The English home of th
American wax portrait artist, Mrs. Patience Wright, was a cente
for artists of all nationalities, and she, too, helped ease the transitio
for transatlantic students into the sophisticated circles of Londo

Copley finally arrived in England in the summer of 1774, saw th
notables in the art world, and left shortly for Paris and Rome. Ra
phael was his delight, "the greatest of the Modern Painters"; but i
a more restrained mood he wrote to his half-brother, Henry Pelham
also a painter, that the works of the great masters were but picture
"and when a man can go but a very little beyond his cotemporar
he becomes a great Man." The difference between Raphael, Titia
Michelangelo, and the "common run of moderately good Artists,
said Copley, "is not so great as one would Imagin from the Prais
bestow'd on those Great Men. But they are the first Artists and the
merit the most elaborate Praises from the World." [20] Copley did no
fail to tell Pelham that Reynolds, West, and others had said h
would "be very rong" to alter his own style. But his style did chang
in the long years that remained to him in England, for he neve
returned to a Revolutionary America.

Copley had come to an England which was jealously familiar wit
the works of colonial artists. The principal attraction at the exhibi
of the Free Society in 1769 had been the portrait by Henry Ben
bridge of Paoli, the noted Corsican chieftain, symbol of liberal re
volt against tyranny. Bembridge, an American, had been commi
sioned by James Boswell to do the portrait, which was seen by a larg
number of people. A few years earlier, in 1764, West's picture c

---

[19] William Dunlap, *A History of the Rise and Progress of the Arts of Desig in the United States* (F. W. Bayley and C. E. Goodspeed, eds., Boston, 1918), 204.

[20] "Copley-Pelham letters," 330–343, July 2, 1775.

General Monckton, principal lieutenant to Wolfe at Quebec, created a sensation at the exhibit. West, who had come from Italy with the tag "the American Raphael" skyrocketed to fame in England. "The great crowd of the year is around Mr. West's pictures," said Joshua Reynolds in 1766. West had nine pictures in the 1771 exhibition and ten two years later. His genius was freely proclaimed, and it was prophesied that he would be "a much greater History Painter than England has ever yet bred." [21] Native artists resorted to the press to express their hurt:

> Every dauber from Rome is brought forward to view,
> But *an Englishman's* always kept down.

West became a popular idol, and his picture of the death of General Wolfe (1771) strengthened his position not only among the populace but with most of his fellow artists. It has often been spoken of as his best work. West capitalized on the general interest in Wolfe, for other artists had also been attracted to this popular theme.

A few years later Copley scored a tremendous success with "The Death of the Earl of Chatham" (1781). Some twenty thousand visitors paid to see it, and Copley was said to have cleared £5,000 by its exhibition.[22] People looked at it with great reverence in awesome remembrance of the chief architect of empire. In after years, even larger numbers of people went to see Copley's "The Defeat of the Floating Batteries at Gibraltar" and West's "Death of Nelson." Other Americans—Trumbull and the less famous Mather Brown—produced well-known historical paintings in their London studios, but West's pre-eminence in the art was everywhere recognized. He was one of the first, said a leading magazine, "who opened the eyes of the English to the merits of modern Historical Painting, and excited in them a desire of seeing it flourish in this happy Island." [23]

A present-day critic, however, argues that it was Copley, not West,

[21] C. I. Landis, "Benjamin West and the Royal Academy," *Penn. Mag. Hist. and Biog.* L (1926), 134–148, 241–253; *Reflections on the English Language* . . . (London, 1770), preface xxxiv–xxxv.

[22] Whitley, *Artists and their friends in England 1700–1799,* I, 187–197, 281, 357. For an appreciation of West's influence in historical painting, see C. Mitchell, "Benjamin West's 'Death of Wolfe' and the Popular History Piece," *Journal of the Warburg and Courtauld Institutes,* VII (1944), 20–34.

[23] *Eur. Mag. and Lond. Rev.,* XXVI (Sept., 1794), 163–166.

who brought about the revolution in historical painting. He it was, of all American artists, who made "the first great contribution . . . to the art of Europe," and it was Copley who became the true progenitor of European historical painters. From Philadelphia came a report from a Quaker correspondent that historical painting was popular there, "but we are too young and too poor, to shine in the fine arts," said the writer, "if we have plants of that genius amongst us they must be transplanted to a warmer and more luxuriant soil." [24]

It is worth noting that colonials, who apparently were more conscious of empire than resident Englishmen, did much to vitalize the imperial idea in their paintings. And it is ironic that this should have happened at the time the Empire was being reduced by the loss of the American colonies.

The emphasis in earlier decades of the eighteenth century was on portraiture; and, under fresh appraisal, American painting of this period has attained unwonted stature. The formality of English portraits deriving from a more aristocratically ordered society became, in the contemporary American paintings, simplified and more straightforward. English painting, thought of as being integrated with a paneled room, was decorative in effect. American portrait painters were seemingly more successful in revealing the inner nature of their sitters. This may have been due to the fact that in their travels through the colonies on commissions they probably lived for weeks in the homes of their patrons. In these years, says one critic America had in its portraits "an excellent and indigenous" style well represented by Robert Feke and the earlier work of Copley. It was to some extent distinguished from the British school and, generally speaking, "better the less closely" her art was imitated. English portraiture at this time, it is said, is "never so intimate a revelation, never so candid or unguarded in expression as the work of an American who is without English training." Gilbert Stuart, by bringing back to America the English mannered treatment, may be said to have marked a divergence from a simpler American tradi-

[24] Hagen, 133, and also 123, arguing that West's influence was fatal to the American tradition. Letter to Capel Lofft, May 8, 1788, in Young, *Annals of Agriculture,* XV (1791), 417.

›n. He persisted, "British fashion, in *making a picture.*" His set
eces and well-ordered arrangements are to be contrasted with the
›rks of such artists as Feke, Copley (in the American period), or
alph Earl, "who always seemed to surprise life itself without hav-
g first posed it." Copley, in his later English decadence, himself
lieved that his work done in America had been superior.[25]

Technically, Americans often gained a greater proficiency from
nglish academic training, but, as in the case of Trumbull, there
as a loss of warmth and inner glow. Trumbull's earlier work had
greater gift of communicating to the observer a sense of individ-
ality in the portraits. In his historical paintings, "Bunker Hill"
785) and the "Death of Montgomery in the attack upon Quebec"
786), he had already shown himself to be a better painter than his
entor, West. The latter with characteristic generosity told Benja-
in Silliman that Trumbull's paintings included some of the "great
ings of modern times." At that period, says a recent critic, Trum-
ull, modeling his style on Rubens, "was a man capable of forming
great idea, a master of the human figure and a colorist equal to the
st of his age. He, if anyone, might have created a monumental
storical art in the United States." But the attempt made by four
nerations of American artists ended at last in failure, and largely
cause architects did not create the monumental architectural set-
ng required for it.[26]

Trumbull himself, in after years, wrote discouragingly of histor-
al painting in America. Talent did abound, he wrote to Edward
verett, but without study and cultivation it availed as little in the
ts as in literature. "Portrait painters are many," he said, "but the
ifference between portrait and historical painting is almost the
me as that between a Cabinet maker and an Architect—a man may
roduce exquisite cabinet work who would be utterly incapable of
ombining the vast and varied magnificence of the Capitol." [27]

[25] This paragraph is much indebted to the text by Gordon Washburn in *The
atalogue of Old and New England—An Exhibition of American Painting of
olonial and early Republican Days together with English Paintings of the
me time . . .* in the Museum of Art of the Rhode Island School of Design
'rovidence, 1945).

[26] E. P. Richardson, *The Way of Western Art 1776–1914* (Cambridge, Mass.,
39), 39–42; Silliman, *Journal of Travels,* I, 215.

[27] Trumbull to Everett, Jan. 12, 1827, Trumbull Mss., Yale Library.

Ralph Earl, adjudged one of the best landscape painters in o history, refused to Anglicize himself during his years abroad. O enthusiastic American critic says that Earl "came closer to und standing the secret of being a good artist than the fastidious Re olds." He was the first American to break away from the conve tional contemporary landscape tradition, and he sought faithfu to portray the character of the landscape before him, "in the mo of a disciple rather than master of nature," writes a discrimin ing student. A number of English landscape painters were in t United States in the 1790's, and one of them, Francis Guy, has be highly praised for his freedom from scholastic traditions and achievement in actually painting nature as he saw it. Earl was, course, contemporary with the heralds of English and German manticism, and from his time a broadening stream of landsca and genre painting continued into the nineteenth century in Am ica.[28]

Some of American "folk art" in the eighteenth century is unli work found in contemporary Europe, and the portraits rank hi in the building of a native tradition. In general, however, folk cr tions, to judge from German peasant art in Pennsylvania, seem to have become cruder in a later generation, and the simpler d signs were not well executed.[29]

Charles W. Peale exhibited miniatures and oil portraits at Ro Academy shows in 1768 and 1769, but he did not enjoy his st abroad nor was its influence long felt. His work on his return see less suave than that of the portraits made in England. Gilbert Stu had marked success in Britain. He was called the Van Dyck of time, and for years the correct attribution of his and Raebur work was a problem even for experts. He was also influenced Gainsborough, but he said "I will follow no master; I wish to fi out what nature is for myself and see her with my own eyes." B

---

[28] Richardson, 95; J. H. Pleasants, "Four late Eighteenth Century Ang American Landscape Painters," *Amer. Antiq. Soc., Proc.*, LII (1942), 189–193.

[29] T. J. Wertenbaker, *The Founding of American Civilization: The Mid Colonies* (New York, 1938), 327. A higher opinion of folk art in Pennsylva is expressed in J. J. Stoudt, *Pennsylvania Folk-Art* (Allentown, 1948), wh stresses the factor of religious inspiration in the art of the Pennsylvania Dut

ıe pity is that English perspective apparently did distort his vi-
on.[30]

Benjamin West, who had gone abroad before Copley and who as the guardian angel to many Americans in London, never felt imself so deeply cut off from his native roots as Copley did. Perhaps /est's greater sympathy for democracy accounts for it. (It was partly :sponsible for his later loss of royal patronage.) New Englanders ansplanted to the homeland often find it harder to adjust them- :lves than do Americans from other regions. They seem to have ıore chips on their shoulders, they exaggerate the supposed sim- arities of New England to old England in life and custom, and are iscomfited to find on closer contact that there are many differences, hereas Americans from other regions apparently start with fewer resuppositions of similarities and therefore are less vulnerable to ıe shock of the unfamiliar.

West was, perhaps, in every respect the most successful of all .merican painters who have lived abroad, but his ties with his orig- ıal home were never broken. After the loss of royal favor, he ainted "Christ Healing the Sick" for the Pennsylvania Hospital in hiladelphia. This and his "Christ Rejected" were seen by multi- ıdes. The ardor and vigor of these pictures have won for them re- ewed appreciation. In the revaluation of earlier American civiliza- on, which is an important concern of the present-day mind, West ; accorded a more significant position than former critics have as- igned to him. His work, partly because of his subject matter, ap- ears less arid than the works of the French classicists with which it orresponds. In most of the historical painting of the day however, ıcluding West's, there was a fundamental weakness. English paint- ng, says Richardson, "was an art of sentiment, not of form, and entiment is not the foundation of monumentality." [31]

The brashness of some of these American invaders of the art vorld must have been disconcerting. Even Franklin, usually not hauvinistic, was carried away by excessive enthusiasm. "In England t present" (1783) he said, "the best History Painter, West; the best 'ortrait Painter, Copley; and the best Landscape Painter, Taylor,

[30] J. T. Flexner, *America's Old Masters, First Artists of the New World* (New 'ork, 1939), 187, 268.

[31] Flexner, 58, 84; Richardson, 30–31.

at Bath, are all Americans." [32] John Taylor, admired by Smolle
and Garrick, was known as the "gentleman artist of Bath." Math
Brown wrote home to Boston, "Nothing flourishes but Paintin
and he hoped "in the course of a few years to be [its] supreme di
tator." Brown was one of many Americans who studied with We
Portraits and historical paintings (he is best known for pictures co
nected with Lord Cornwallis' exploits in India) kept him very bus
and after a few years he seems to have dropped the chip from h
shoulder. It had once been a great weight: "I will let them see,
an obscure yankey Boy cannot Shine as great as any of them."
The astonishing fact is that a number of Yankee boys did shine i
surroundings already illuminated, and this, be it remembered, in
phase of culture supposedly deficient in America.

In other arts America's contribution to the common fund
eighteenth-century civilization was less that of creator than that
supplier of the raw materials for the artist as well as stimulus to th
artistic imagination. Blake's illustrations for his *America* represe
the newly risen, revitalized soul looking at heaven's bright daw
for there was indeed a new light in the world. In another field
creative achievement, ceramics, noted manufacturers in Englan
made porcelain and china ware of exceptional strength and beau
from Virginia materials.[34] British publications, always sensiti
to colonial rivalry, printed news of the manufacture of china i
Philadelphia, where it was claimed that the product was better tha
that of Bow or Stratford. Porcelain earth was sent from South Car
lina to Bristol, and there it may have induced Richard Champio
to manufacture china on a large scale. A local paper had noted th
arrival of porcelain ware from Georgia, and though the materia
were said to be good, the workmanship was judged less admirable.
Wedgwood had a keen understanding of America's role in th

---

[32] Smyth, *Franklin, Writings,* IX, 41, Franklin to Ingenhousz, May 16, 1783

[33] Mather Brown letters, copies of Mss., especially March 7, 1784, July 2
1784, Jan. 1, 1793, Mass. Hist. Soc. Brown painted the first portrait ever do
of Jefferson, getting £10 for it.

[34] Botsford, 103; *Scots Magazine,* XXIII (1771), 48.

[35] Hugh Owen, *Two Centuries of Ceramic Art in Bristol* . . . (Londo
1873), 7–9.

›rcelain trade. In the year of crisis, 1765, he was deeply worried ›out sales overseas. "Our home consumption," he wrote, "is very ifling in comparison to what is sent abroad." He feared the rising valry of colonial pottery manufactures, which he believed had 'ery resource readily available, "and as the cost of living increases :re [in England], many artists and manufacturers are leaving." [36]

The provocative course of America's development did much to .spirit European artists and craftsmen. Wedgwood ware and sim- ır products exploited popular interest in Anglo-American politics, ıd the motifs that were used to decorate the vast majority of the ıtput gave graphic support to liberal and radical views. It need ırdly be added that it was good business, for the English potters ıd a profitable trade with America. Wedgwood had catalogues rawn up for his agents in Europe and America, and the trade over- as was sufficiently large to require that specially designed crates ıd casks be made for it.[37] Franklin's portraits were everywhere, ıd even in England, during the war, his face was a familiar sight on laques, miniatures, etc. Washington, in later years, was well known › Englishmen; a Wedgwood portrait of him was owned by John laxman, the noted sculptor.[38] Pitt's support of the colonial cause ı the Stamp Act controversy led New York and South Carolina to rder statues of the famed leader, done by Joseph Wilton. A portrait f Lord Chatham, done by Peale in London, was sent to a group of dmirers in Virginia. "What do you think of sending Mr. Pitt upon rockery ware to America," Wedgwood asked his partner, Bentley. A quantity might certainly be sold there now & some Advantage ıade of the American prejudice in favour of that great man." [39]

Wedgwood's first portrait of Franklin was made from a wax ıodel by Patience Wright. A later one which achieved very wide opularity came from a model by Flaxman. A Washington portrait y Wedgwood was modeled from the dry-point etching by Joseph

[36] E. Meteyard, *The Life of Josiah Wedgwood* (London, 1865), I, 367.

[37] E. A. Jones, "Old Wedgwood Ware in America," *Art in America,* IX (1921), 46.

[38] *Catalogue of a Collection of old Wedgwood belonging to Arthur Sanderson* London, 1901), 39.

[39] C. H. Hart, in *Mass. Hist. Soc., Proc.,* XLVIII (1914–1915), 294–295; . T. H. Halsey, "Josiah Wedgwood, American Sympathizer and Portrait Maker," *Scribner's Magazine,* XLII (1907), 690; Meteyard, I, 468.

Wright, son of Patience. This period witnessed the highest achie ment in ceramic-medallion portraiture in northern Europe, a the popularity of American Revolutionary leaders was an importa element in the promotion of radical sentiment in England a France. Franklin wrote to his family that many medallions had be made of him, some to be put in lids of snuffboxes and some to be p in rings, and the numbers sold were incredible. "These, with t pictures, busts and prints (of which copies upon copies are spre everywhere) have made your father's face as well known as that the moon." But he added, with his usual good sense, "One is not expect being always in Fassion." [40]

The whole development of the art of caricature was greatly sti ulated by the intensity of British political life in the last third of t eighteenth century. Satirical artists had already won an appreciati audience, and their work in earlier years had begun to touch England's imperial struggles in America. In one print the Ang French rivalry in the Ohio Valley stirs an American response: "T Devil take 'em all for they have ruined our rich Country." As t editor remarks on this satire, the American colonists were the ul mate sufferers whether England or France was successful. The i creased activity of the political opposition in England, inspired events in America, tied in with demands for parliamentary a administrative reform and was reflected in numerous prints ar drawings. Artists were employed to advance the opinions of t opposition, and one print on the Stamp Act, "The Repeal," was popular and so widely circulated that hundreds of impressions a still in existence. Vast numbers of satirical prints, mostly politic appeared in these years, and to those separately issued must added the great many published in magazines and periodicals every variety. Publication of satirical prints was so lucrative as attract publishers for this field exclusively. The prints reveal a d cline in respect for royal dignity and power, and it is clear that t public mind was sympathetic to American discontent. In one etc ing, "Goody Bull," the "old woman" Britannia is said to have bee

[40] R. T. H. Halsey, "Ceramic Americana of the Eighteenth Century," *A in America,* IV (1916), 224–232; V (1916), 41–47; Franklin to Jane Meco Passy, Oct. 25, 1779, Amer. Phil. Soc., Mss.

ught wisdom because of the resistance of her buxom daughter. hatham, a hero in the Stamp Act episode, wears in one print an ıdian cap, alluding to his part in the repeal; he is named the \merican Colossus" in "Commonwealth." In another print Amer-a appears as an Indian warrior, who broke the yoke that bound .m and then trampled upon the Stamp Act.[41]

The series of crises connected with John Wilkes and his association ith American revolutionary thought are clearly revealed in the :ints. Villains are the same in England and America—Bute, North, ındwich, Germain. The strong feeling of antiepiscopacy (fear of ıe establishment of an Anglican bishopric in the colonies) had its ›unterpart in England. In fact, the no-popery agitation which led p to the Gordon riots was associated with the American Revolu-on. Hostility against Roman Catholicism was combined with al-gations of popery (religious authoritarianism) against the Church : England.

A representation of the Boston massacre was familiar in England, ıd in the following years there were many references to America ı published prints. As they were antiministerial, they were thus ro-American, reflecting what seems to have been a popular atti-ıde. In 1775 the impact of the Revolution was so great that nearly very political print related to America. In them the Western World ɔpears to be a combination of Amazon and noble savage, and on :casion an Indian wields a businesslike scalping knife. "Miss Amer-a" generally holds aloft the cap of Liberty. America "is the land f liberty and virtue, England that of corruption and slavery." A ımiliar theme of many of these prints is that of liberty taking flight › America.[42]

The late eighteenth century, England's great age of caricature, :presented pre-eminently by Gillray and Rowlandson, was often ›nservative in temper. Two of America's best friends, Richard

---

[41] F. G. Stephens, ed., *Catalogue of Prints & Drawings in the British Museum: ɔlitical and Personal Satires* (London, 1870–), III, pt. I (1734–1750), xx; III, t. II (1751–1760), 927, 928, no. 3280; IV (1761–1770), xxxvii, lxii, lxiii, cvi, cvii, 'iii, 368, no. 4140, 375, no. 4142; R. T. H. Halsey, *Impolitical Prints* (New ork, 1939).

[42] M. D. George, ed., *Catalogue of Political and Personal Satires . . . in the ritish Museum* (London, 1935), V (1771–1783), xiii–xxii and *passim*.

Price and Joseph Priestley, were the chief villains in a number satires directed against the Dissenters, who were compared with r publican sectaries of the Puritan Revolution. Paine was often sa irized during these years, but he did have his defenders. One of tl latter shows him asleep, wearing a cap inscribed "Libertas," an around his bed of straw is a flag on which is written "Vive l'Ame ica." Still revealing the Indian influence, America continued to b represented by a figure with a tuft of feathers on his head. A pri referring to Ireland's discontent told of her distressed manufactu ers adopting the American example of tarring and feathering tho who refused to join nonimportation and nonconsumption agre ments. A print of the early French Revolutionary period sho America represented by a woman in feathered headdress with bare breasts, a quiver attached to her shoulders, a portrayal similar to th Amazon of former years.[43] The prevailing Tory sentiment did n prevent the King from being portrayed as a figure of comedy, but is interesting to note that his popularity rose with the increase i hatred of Paine. Liberals feared the extension of liberalism to ra icalism, and in their recoil they thrust the political center of gravi to the right.

Thomas B. Hollis, in 1791, sent a number of prints to the Aca emy of Arts and Sciences in Boston to induce its members "to thin of the art of engraving." [44] Whether Hollis contributed anything t its development is not certain, but there was a spurt of America activity in engraving in the 1790's. Cornelius Tiebout, a native c New York, went to England for instruction in 1796 and is said t have been the first American engraver to do so. Alexander Ande son, who had studied the work of his older contemporary, Thom Bewick, England's most illustrious wood engraver, did much t raise the standards of the art in America. A young Englishma David Edwin, landed in Philadelphia in 1797, where a countryma in the publishing business immediately gave him some work. H achievements rank him, in the eyes of a historian of engraving, a "the first good engraver of portraits" to appear in America.[45] Ther

[43] *Ibid.* (1938), VI (1784–1792), xxii, xxv, and nos. 6397, 6650, 7694.

[44] "Willard Letters," June 18, 1791, *Mass. Hist. Soc., Proc.,* XLIII (1909 1910), 634.

[45] B. J. Lossing, *A Memorial of Alexander Anderson* (New York, 1872

was so much imitation of English pictures that a subscriber to a New York magazine (1794) asked for engravings from American materials. The publisher replied that if contributions came in he would be glad to use them; two then arrived with native designs. Twenty years before, in 1774, the publication of more than a score of copper plates in the *Royal American Magazine* is said to have "marked an epoch in magazine history in this country." [46]

Southern planters owned large numbers of engravings, and a local press notice (1784) spoke of the arrival of nearly five thousand prints.[47] When John Trumbull solicited subscriptions at three guineas each for prints of his paintings of Bunker Hill and Montgomery at Quebec, most of the well-known names in America responded. A few foreign subscribers in England and on the continent also listed their names.[48] Prints and engraved copper plates were in great demand in America, and the English export of large quantities after the Revolution was an important factor in transatlantic publishing.

Europeans brought their musical life to America, and in our own day the richness of this heritage in ballad and song is being rediscovered on stage and radio. This inheritance had been almost lost in an urbanized America, but again at long last it enriches her people. Herein lies another aspect of the general reinterpretation of Puritan civilization undertaken by many scholars in recent years. Historians of music have assumed that Puritans on both sides of the Atlantic disliked music and that therefore there was no musical history to record. These historians, too, were urban dwellers (or had urban attachments) and thus simply ignored folksong, folk dance, and the instrumental activity that once graced the lives of English villages. England flourished musically in the first half of the seventeenth century, and her music did not die in ships at sea.[49]

Iantle Fielding, "David Edwin, Engraver," *Penn. Mag. Hist. and Biog.*, XXIX .905), 80.

[46] F. L. Mott, *A History of American Magazines 1741–1850* (New York, 1930), 7–38, 86; *Gentleman's Magazine*, LXVI (1796), 916.

[47] Wertenbaker, *The Old South*, 56.

[48] John Trumbull (1790), HM 1781, Huntington Library.

[49] P. A. Scholes, *The Puritans and Music in England and New England* (London, 1934), 55–56, chap. vii *passim;* M. M. Knappen in *Tudor Puritanism*

Performers and teachers of secular music in colonial towns we generally French or Italian. Religious music was brought over fro Europe in the hearts and minds of all immigrant peoples. Just Falckner of Germantown wrote to a European Lutheran lead about religious conditions in Pennsylvania at the very beginni of the eighteenth century and suggested that music would contri ute greatly toward a good Christian service. "It would not only tract and civilize the wild Indian, but it would do much good spreading the gospel truths among the sects and others by attracti them." "Instrumental music," he said, "is especially serviceab here." He asked that an organ be sent over, and it was. A few yea later, Gustavus Hesselius, an organ builder who was also a paint came over from Sweden, and left a marked impress on colonial cu ture.[50] The music of the Ephrata Cloister under Conrad Johan Beissel won great renown. The Moravians at Bethlehem, Penns vania, in our times the seat of a Bach cult, added their distincti contribution to musical history in America. Tremendously stir ulating as this musical life was, it was unfortunately restricted to closely to the Pennsylvania Germans and thus was isolated from th main stream of American culture.[51]

Folk hymns were brought to the seaboard colonies by Engli Dissenters and spread slowly through the interior. In time, in reviv meetings, the songs became transformed into revival spirituals, an these, it is argued by one school of musicologists, are the true pare to religious folksongs of the Negro, with their call and respon patterns. Another school of music historians finds the roots of th Negro spirituals in the original African homeland, and the disti guished colored singer Roland Hayes prefers to call this mus "Aframerican religious folksongs." [52]

Orchestral performances and musical interludes were familiar audiences in colonial towns. Americans played the harpsichord an

(Chicago, 1939), page 431, reminds us that Puritans carefully distinguished b tween "music inside the church and music outside of it."

[50] *Penn. Mag. Hist. and Biog.*, XXI (1897), 221; XXIX (1905), 129.

[51] J. F. Sachse, "The Music of the Ephrata Cloister," *Penn. Germ. Soc., Pro* XII (1903).

[52] See G. P. Jackson, *White and Negro Spirituals* (New York, 1943); Rola Hayes, *My Songs: Aframerican Religious Folksongs* (Boston, 1948).

ute and occasionally composed music. Francis Hopkinson wrote to efferson that he had discovered a new way of quilling a harpsichord. Ie had sent to London for a new instrument—"a very excellent ouble Harpsichord made by Shudi and Broadwood and quilled in he new way." In a long letter (for which he apologized), Hopkinson ave a detailed description of the mechanics of the new type of arpsichord. His main delight was in his expectation of keeping it in asier repair. "To the Musical tribe," he said, the improvement vould appear significant. "Many Persons who play very well on the Iarp," he noted, "are not able to keep it in Order." Jefferson orered a pianoforte from abroad. It was to be a gift to a lady, he said, let the case be of fine mahogany, solid not veneered." [53] Franklin's nterest in Armonica glasses stirred up much activity in Europe. A nanufacturing establishment at St. Cloud making glasses for the Armonica wanted Franklin's advice in perfecting the process. A raftsman in Prague sent Franklin an account of his Armonica made rom the American's model. A Boston kinsman of Franklin, Josiah Williams, went to London to study music with John Stanley, the vell-known blind organist. Young Williams was a constant attendnt at musical events so that, as Franklin wrote to his father, "his hirst for music is in a way of being thoroughly satiated." [54]

William Bentley, correspondent of C. D. Ebeling, and likewise nterested in music, aided in introducing German music to New England.[55] Bentley and Samuel Holyoke, a native New Englander, organized an orchestra and choral group at Salem and gave concerts of German music long before the better-known Handel and Haydn ociety of Boston was created. A number of Europeans came to seaoard towns in the second half of the eighteenth century and deeloped a greater popular interest in music. They also imported good instruments, especially from Germany. William Tuckey, from England, was with Trinity Church in New York where, under his

[53] Hopkinson to Jefferson (really for Amer. Phil. Soc.), Nov. 1784, Mass. Hist. Soc., Jefferson papers; Jefferson to Thomas Adams, Feb. 20, June 1, 1771, Jefferson, *Writings,* IV, 229, 235.

[54] *Calendar of Franklin Papers,* III, 92, 188, Aug. 3, 1783, May 11, 1784; Smyth, *Franklin, Writings,* V, 310, Franklin to Jonathan Williams, March 5, 1771.

[55] H. S. Jantz, "German Thought and Literature in New England, 1620–1820," *Jour. Eng. and Germ. Philology,* XLI (1942), 41–42.

direction, Handel's "Messiah" was performed in 1770. Williar Selby was in Boston shortly thereafter, greatly enriching the musica life of the community. Alexander Reinagle, well known in Eurc pean musical circles, was in Philadelphia in the 1780's helping t set high the standard of local concert performances. Several men bers of the London Professional Concerts migrated in 1792, addin their stimulus to new-world music. Earlier in the century activ musical circles in Charleston and Williamsburg presented program which not long before had achieved sensational debuts in London.[5 Charleston's St. Cecilia Society has the honor of being the first mu sical organization in the colonies.

It is no accident that the native William Billings should have bee able to exert so much influence on American music in his own time In every phase of life this was an era of almost hurried maturation The Revolutionary period was itself a stimulus to the creation o numerous songs, some of which have lasted through the years Words for many new songs were written after 1760, sung generall to old English, Scottish, or Irish tunes.[57] European airs crossed th Atlantic as soon as they gained any popularity at home. Franci Hopkinson was familiar with the best that came from abroad, par ticularly from England. His famous "My Days Have Been So Won drous Free" had English antecedents, but Hopkinson's version ha more vigor and a more elastic line and is more in harmony with th meaning of the words. Hopkinson, too often singled out as almost a "sport" in colonial culture, may be only one of an obscure line o early American musicians.[58]

Franklin's daughter started to collect American music in ex change for a present of Scotch songs. "But Music," said Franklin meaning native compositions, "is a new Art with us." He and hi daughter played the Scotch tunes for their friends who though

---

[56] P. H. Lang, *Music in Western Civilization* (New York, 1941), 690–694 R. R. Drummond, "Alexander Reinagle and his connection with the musica life of Philadelphia," *Amer. Germanica,* n.s., V (1907); Drummond, *Earl German Music in Philadelphia* (New York, 1910), 43.

[57] Harry Dichter and Elliott Shapiro, *Early American Sheet Music, its lur and its lore 1768–1889* (New York, 1941).

[58] L. Keefer, "Hopkinson and the First American Art-Song," *Musical Amer ica,* LXII (Nov. 25, 1942).

.em "the finest in the World." Many years later Franklin was still .terested in American music. "As a small Curiosity," he sent to the bbé Morellet some American compositions, "the first Production : the kind that has appeared here." "I fancy," he said, "some of the Iusic may suit your taste, as it is simple and pathetic." [59]

The *Massachusetts Magazine* included original American music . its pages regularly. Most selections were sentimental songs, but .ere were also marches and anthems. Music publishing in the nited States begins in the 1780's, and, quite naturally, the pubshers, some of whom were transplanted Englishmen, copied Engsh models. Music for the dance was also part of the colonial eritage, and it comes with something of a shock to conventional nterpretations of our past to read that "dancing is the principal and .vourite amusement in New England." [60]

Long years were to elapse before music from America was to make .uch of an impression on Europe, but even in the eighteenth cenıry European music already revealed some awareness of the Amer:an scene. Dances and songs newly created in the colonies of Spain 'ere brought back to Europe where they had an enduring vogue. 'he "noble savage," celebrated in prose and poetry, was commemrated in song as well. "The Death-Song of the Cherokee Indians," :lling of the fearlessness of the warrior in the presence of his torırers, was brought to England in the Revolutionary era.[61] Ballads ɔld of the visit of Indian chieftains to England in 1710 and of the .nglo-French struggle for Canada. Just as American painting conributed to the imperial idea, ballads based on American themes lso inspired its growth. In the earliest years of colonial settlement, he satirical ballad "Summons to New England" was sung in Engish streets. "The Death of General Wolfe," more frequently called Bold General Wolfe," was one of a number of ballads relating to ncidents in America which were sung for years throughout Engand.[62]

---

[59] Smyth, *Franklin, Writings,* IV, 209, Dec. 11, 1763; IX, 690, Dec. 10, 1788.

[60] O. Strunk, "Early Music Publishing in the United States," *Papers of Bib- iog. Soc. of America,* XXXI (1937), 176–179; *Encyclopedia Britannica* (3rd ed., 797), 666.

[61] *The Bee,* II (March 23, 1791), 109.

[62] Firth, xlii.

Transplanted Europeans carried with them their architectur designs as well as other forms of art. Dutch influence in New Yo for example, was clearly marked, and the Huguenots left an ind ible French imprint on Charleston. By a strange growth of historic myth, it has long been assumed that log cabins were the earli homes of the colonists, but recent research has been upsetting th fable of colonial life as it has upset so many others. In general, col nists used the construction they used at home, which was not l cabin. Migrants, particularly in family groups, are usually conserv tive and cling very stubbornly to the familiar in an alien worl But the Swedes did have a tradition of log-cabin building, and a parently they, on the Delaware, were mainly responsible for intr ducing this form of architecture to the colonies in the seventeen century. It was found to be most adaptable to the frontier and, b the time of the American Revolution, it had become the typic dwelling of frontiersmen. White and Indian civilization occasio ally became so intermixed that the word "wigwam" was used inte changeably with "cabin." The term "log cabin," it seems, was n in use until about 1750.[63] Very slowly the architectural adjustme was also made in the South. Dr. Alexander Garden, writing fro Charleston to an English correspondent, wanted to know th proper ingredients which, added to lime made of oyster shells, wou make "a terrace-mortar, that will stand the sun and rain in Car lina, for flat roofs to houses. Flat roofs would be of the greatest ut ity to us in Carolina." Garden asked what material Mediterrane peoples terraced their roofs with—"and how make the floor to be that terrace?" [64]

Franklin discussed European housing with fellow American To a Philadelphia query he replied that the English sometim covered their roofs with copper, but evidently it was not a wid spread practice. To another American correspondent he praised th new method of English construction, substituting stuccoed walls fo wainscoting. It avoided fire peril, he said, and he was pleased whe he learned that Americans were following this procedure. An adve tisement in an English paper, selling cast-iron tiles for house

[63] H. R. Shurtleff, *The Log Cabin Myth* (ed. with introd. by S. E. Moriso Cambridge, Mass., 1939), 4, 24, 26, 55–56, 59, 123.

[64] Smith, *Corr. of Linnaeus* . . . I, 513, July 25, 1761.

aught Franklin's eye, and he proposed to introduce them to Phila-
elphia, that is, if they were cheap and efficient.[65] The cottage in
arly Virginia was English, but the differences in building materials
ocally available and the necessity of adapting houses to wide varia-
ions in temperature gave the structures an American individuality
which was distinctive. Artisans were often called over from England
o help build homes in Maryland and Virginia. Professor Werten-
aker believes that in Massachusetts a native style had evolved be-
ore the close of the seventeenth century. Modifications in the de-
igns of the Flemish cottage and medieval East Anglican two-story
ouse which the Puritans knew in England had gone far enough to
ive the new American structure a different appearance.[66]

Functional considerations and limited means dictated design in
arlier years, but in the colonies (as in England) the academic spirit
nd academic architectural forms gradually won the upper hand.
The emphasis was now transferred from considerations of function
o those of pure form, partly because of changing taste, partly be-
ause of a desire to display waste conspicuously. Royal governors
helped set the pace for the more elaborate structures, but possibly
he most important factor was the widespread use of handbooks, like
hat of James Gibbs. English and American houses though differing
n details quite naturally looked alike when they were built from
he same construction guides. "The ideal of the colonial style," says
Fiske Kimball, "remained always conformity to current English
usage."

Whatever America contributed to architectural style was a post-
Revolutionary development. In these years French influence began
o predominate, and the classic forms of antiquity, the temple and
he rotunda, took hold. The American search for architectural
beauty now was so vigorous that her adaptation of classical models
often preceded that of Europeans.[67] It is an interesting fact that
Hessian officers, after their return from service in the American

---

[65] Smyth, *Franklin, Writings,* V, 250, March 17, 1770; V, 265, June 26, 1770; V, 305, Feb. 10, 1771; IX, 277, Oct. 18, 1784.

[66] Wertenbaker, *The Old South,* 80; Wertenbaker, *The Puritan Oligarchy,* 123.

[67] Fiske Kimball, *Domestic Architecture of the American Colonies and of the Early Republic* (New York, 1933), 53, 55, 141, 145–146.

Revolution, built mansions and furnished them after the manner of fashionable colonial homes. Kassel, the capital of Hesse, contained many mementos of Hessian participation in the war overseas. The famous baroque masterpieces of South America, especially in Mexico, left their mark on the architecture of Spain itself, notably in the province of Andalusia.

Professional architects in larger number, first European, then native, practiced their art in America in this period. But for some time to come architectural handbooks continued to be widely used by home builders. British handbooks were used in America in both English and American editions. The first distinctly American work, by Asher Benjamin, appeared toward the very end of the eighteenth century.

The more elaborate homes on both sides of the Atlantic owed much of their charm to their fine woodwork. The American wood carvers were generally inspired by British models, which they followed closely. But there were some, and among them Samuel McIntire of Salem in particular, whose individuality could not be readily confined and who made distinctive contributions of their own.[68]

It was in the last resting places, the intimate graveyards, that the Puritan sculptors found most frequent outlet for their art; there are good portraits, flowers and fruits, ships, lettering, and even Adam and Eve in their garden undress. It is in the gravestone carvings, "often very beautiful, always thoughtful," writes an appreciative observer, that "we meet the most characteristic expression of the Puritan as artist." There was very little sculpture of the formal type produced in early America. Whatever appeared was generally of foreign creation and consisted of casts and copies of noted antique statues and busts, thus reflecting Europe's devotion to the classical tradition. But American taste had sufficient independence to urge that a projected statue of George Washington show him in modern rather than in classical garb.[69]

---

[68] A. J. Wall, "Books on Architecture printed in America 1775–1830," in *Bibliographical Essays: a Tribute to Wilberforce Eames,* 299–313; R. Caye "Decorative Wood-carving in Colonial and Post-Colonial America," *Arts and Decoration,* X–XI (Aug., 1919), 178.

[69] H. M. Forbes, *Gravestones of early New England and the men who made*

Franklin was asked if America could use the services of the distinguished Roman sculptor, Cerrachi, for the memorials she was expected to raise in honor of her great. Franklin's reply was discouraging for, he said, the best American artists go to Europe where people are rich enough to employ them.[70] Philip Mazzei was asked to supply sculptors from Europe to serve the newly established federal government in erecting public buildings in the capital and to work on the Capitol itself. Canova was to be asked to make a marble statue of liberty, in sitting position, seven feet high. Two Florentines, John Andrei and Joseph Franzoni, were induced by Mazzei to accept commissions for America.[71]

Mazzei's friend Thomas Jefferson was insistent that public buildings be a standing guide to architectural excellence. "How is a taste in this beautiful art to be formed in our countrymen," he asked, "unless we avail ourselves of every occasion when public buildings are to be erected, of presenting to them models for their study and imitation?" He was an enthusiast on the subject of the arts, he wrote to Madison, for his object was to improve the taste of his countrymen, "to increase their reputation, to reconcile to them the respect of the world, and procure them its praise." A few years later, the plan for the capital city drew commendation from the *Gentleman's Magazine,* which thought it resembled no other in the world.[72]

In a small circle American taste was of a standard comparable to the best European level. But the mass of Americans, like people elsewhere, had limited aesthetic experience, and even where a sense of beauty was well developed there were not always the means to indulge it. Although Americans were more appreciative of art than has generally been believed, it is true that even those with considerable education often betrayed a woeful misconception of the function of the creative imagination. Dr. Enoch Edwards, who visited

---

them 1653–1800 (Boston, 1927), 2; Dumbauld, *Thomas Jefferson, American Tourist,* 78–79.

[70] Ingenhousz to Franklin, April 29, 1783, *Calendar of Franklin Papers,* III, 57; Franklin to Ingenhousz, May 16, 1783, Smyth, *Franklin, Writings,* IX, 41.

[71] Marraro, *Memoirs of Mazzei,* 409, 413; see also F. Kimball, "The Beginnings of Sculpture in Colonial America," *Art and Archaeology,* VIII (1919), 185.

[72] Jefferson, *Writings,* V, 137, Sept. 20, 1785; *Gentleman's Magazine,* LXIII (1793), 434.

West's studio in England after he had called upon the painter's brother, a farmer in Pennsylvania, remarked, "I have seen very beautiful pictures yet I declare I never in my life, in any part of the world, saw a much more beautiful sight, than the bullocks—the flocks—the clover—the watered meadows—the orchards—and above all, the bower of Mr. West, in . . . Pennsylvania." [73] Slowly, an appreciation of art in all its varied forms spread among Americans, but for long years to come it too often waited upon European developments.

---

[73] Edwards to Sinclair, Sept. 14, 1796, *The Correspondence of Sir John Sinclair, Bart.* (London, 1831), II, 68–69.

CHAPTER VI

The Humanitarian Spirit

AN AWAKENED social conscience is one of the outstanding character-
tics of the eighteenth century. This is not to say that previous cen-
ıries made no provision for those members of society who had fal-
red and lagged behind in the pursuit of happiness. In medieval
hristendom the Church lent a helping hand to the disheartened,
nd when the unity of the religious world was shattered the state as
ell as the various churches ministered to the needy and discour-
ged. The second half of the seventeenth century saw the rise of
ertain organizations designed to prod a complacent society, but
heir effectiveness was strictly limited. Scattered individuals raised
heir small voices in a heedless world. But during the eighteenth
entury practical minds, skilled in the ways of propaganda, united
isparate voices into thunderous commands that shook indifferent
arliaments and peoples into humanitarian activity.

It is not easy to determine why the heart of man was so unusually
tirred during this century. English philanthropy was stimulated by
nore frequent intercourse with the continental countries, whose
nnovations offered encouraging precedents.[1] To the tolerance of
he Dutch was ascribed much of their commercial prosperity, and
he English were urged to take note. The *Pietas Hallensis* of A. H.
rancke in Germany, in the early days of the eighteenth century,
vas a powerful stimulant to humanitarianism, and the *Pietas Lon-
linensis,* published nearly one hundred years later, listed the large
umber of institutions established in the eighteenth century.[2] New

[1] B. Kirkman Gray, *A History of English Philanthropy* (London, 1905), 84–
5.

[2] Anthony Highmore, *Pietas Londinensis: History, Design and Present State
of the Various Public Charities in and near London* (2 vols., London, 1810).

religious forces wakened related impulses, and it is possible to sho
a close relationship between the growth of evangelicalism and th
deepening of the spirit of benevolence.[3]

The word "benevolence" itself was endowed with vigoro
vitality in the years after Shaftesbury in his *Characteristics* (171
had focused upon it the attention of the English literary worl
English literature, which during the Restoration had shown a
aristocratic indifference to the lower classes, now introduced altr
ism as a novel note. Charity, which in the hands of the Anglica
Church appeared to be a bargain with God, was now to issue from
genuine benevolence. James Thomson was among those who init
ated the ethical movement, and his poetry, which encouraged th
prison reforms of Oglethorpe and various other philanthropi
ventures, ranks him "the first humanitarian poet in English."

Hogarth's genius, along with that of Smollett, Fielding, and Gol
smith, promoted the general development of humanitarianis
Hogarth's painting of Thomas Coram, founder of the Foundlin
Hospital, is a fine expression of this spirit. Coram was a warn
hearted figure whose humanitarianism embraced both shores of th
Atlantic World. The broad area of his interests is revealed in H
garth's picture, which shows a globe turned to the Atlantic Ocea
and the continent of North America, for Coram had lived for te
years in New England; he had also been an active participant in th
founding of Georgia.[4]

The connection between the burst of humanitarian activity a
sociated with the names of Wilberforce, Howard, and others and th
constant poetizing of benevolence and charity is real. In fact it i
argued that the Romantic Revolt in English literature was itse
only one aspect of a more inclusive social movement, which ex
pressed itself politically in a reform of the suffrage franchise; re
ligiously, in the rise of evangelicalism and Methodism; ethically, i

[3] C. A. Moore, "Shaftesbury and the Ethical Poets in England 1700–1760,
PMLA, XXXI (1916), 281; V. W. Crane, "The Promotion Literature c
Georgia," in *Bibliographical Essays: A Tribute to Wilberforce Eames,* 281–29

[4] Tinker, *Painter and Poet; Studies in the Literary Relations of Englis
Painting,* 24, 40; V. W. Crane, "The Philanthropists and the Genesis c
Georgia," *Amer. Hist. Rev.,* XXVII (1921–1922), 68; Coram promoted shi
building in New England; see letter June 17, 1745, Ayer Coll. 188, Newberr
Library, Chicago.

ıe rise of humanitarianism; and aesthetically, in naturalism and ı romanticism of the remote.[5]

The prevailing temper espoused a kind of science or religion of umanity that sought to create a unity in a world of diversity. Per-aps it was a substitute for a vanished religious unity; perhaps it 'as the harbinger of a society that is yet to be. A German writer re-erred to Franklin as the "most humane and happiest of all who ave been chosen as contributors to the sublime work of inaugurat-ıg the Golden Age of Humanity." [6] The 1797 edition of the *En-yclopedia Britannica* stated that Philadelphia excelled all other ities in making "useful improvements . . . particularly in the cience of humanity." Herder played an important part in the for-ıation of a "Friday Society," which was influenced by Franklin's unto in Philadelphia. For the German group, which in Herder's yes was really a "Society of Humanity," the political philosopher rote the *Letters of Humanity,* largely inspired by the life of Frank-in. "Would to God we had in all Europe," he exclaimed, "a people who would read him, recognize his principles and act and live in ccordance therewith to their own best well-being; where would ve then be!" [7]

A Swiss writer believed there was a germ of perfection in man-ind that could be developed by cultivation. For such cultivation ıan must acquire knowledge which would contribute to the ad-ancement of society; America, he reasoned, could furnish valuable ata, and he therefore requested Franklin to name a correspondent who would forward helpful materials from time to time.[8] An Amer-can writer on government and education thought that history hould no longer be concerned with petty intrigues but rather with he "science of human nature." [9] In comparison with the eighteenth

---

[5] G. F. Richardson, "A Neglected Aspect of the English Romantic Revolt," *Jniv. of Calif., Pub. Modern Philology,* III (1915–1916).

[6] P. C. Weber, *America in Imaginative German Literature in the first half f the 19th Century* (New York, 1926), 18.

[7] M. D. Learned, *Herder and America* ("German-American Annals," n.s. I, no. 9, 1904), 554–559.

[8] *Calendar of Franklin Papers,* I, 466, Isaac Iselin, July 28, 1778.

[9] Nathan Chipman, *Principles of Government* (1793), quoted in A. O. Han-en, *Liberalism and American Education in the Eighteenth Century* (New ’ork, 1926), 99.

century and its cosmopolitanism, the twentieth century with it heritage of nationalism seems in some respects startlingly pro vincial.

The shifting economic bases of life in the eighteenth century like wise contributed to the growth of the philanthropic spirit; thi philanthropy was frequently the result of sheer necessity. Th changes in industry and agriculture dislocated many a routine lif that had hitherto been spent as a yeoman, or spinner, or weaver a home, and in the period of readjustment the body had to be fe and the spirit nurtured. Real wages in London showed a stead decline in the second half of the century, and public and privat charity often had to supplement the lower income.[10] Lifelines ha literally to be thrown to those who had been torn from their moor ings. And for those debtors who had been tripped by the law ther was a new sympathy because the principles of the law themselve were called into question. Rationalism, which was underminin traditional beliefs, knew no limits to its probing, and man's relation ship to man was subjected to sharper analysis.

With almost every phase of the philanthropic activity that w shall note in these years were associated one or more Quaker names These often led causes whose early hopelessness frightened th fainthearted, but whose gradual success attracted the waverer an then made of him a crusader. It is an instructive study—an examina tion of this comparatively small sectarian group, which seemed t be a conscience to the eighteenth century. Sometimes this con science was a guide, sometimes this conscience was deliberately un heeded, but its voice rarely failed to cry out against injustice.[11]

While the literature of the period inspired humanitarianism a well as reflected it, it was a group of spirited organizations whic sought more determinedly to ameliorate the sad lot of mankind One of these was the Society for the Propagation of the Gospel which helped educate the home front in England to call for a variet of reforms. In every parish people were more than passive partici

[10] Hamilton, "Profit Inflation and the Industrial Revolution," *Quarterl Journal of Economics,* LVI (1942), 260.

[11] Dietrich von Dobbeler, *Social-politik der Nachstenliebe dargestellt ar Beispiel der gesellschaft der freunde* (Goslar, 1912), an inadequate stud; A. Jorns, *The Quakers as Pioneers in Social Work* (New York, 1931), better.

ants in the humanitarian program. They not only read the mass of terature, tracts, sermons, and the widely circulated abstracts of roceedings, but they also contributed money and discussed new eps in advancing this movement.

Human life was more highly valued in the New World than in ie old. Pennsylvania had a criminal code in its earlier years which emanded the death penalty for but two offenses—murder and eason. The Quaker colony had perhaps the mildest code in the tlantic civilization in the seventeenth century. At an early period ie colonial code of Massachusetts reduced the number of offenses hat, in England, were punishable by death. These New England 'uritans were more humane, too, in drawing up laws protecting vomen, children, strangers, servants, and dumb animals. Almost lone among seventeenth-century legislative bodies, says Preserved mith, "the Massachusetts General Court forbade any man to exer- ise any tyranny or cruelty toward any brute creatures which are isually for man's use." [12]

Lahontan used the familiar device of a conversation with a "noble avage" to hold up to ridicule outmoded judicial and penal prac- ices. The American Indian pointed out the frequency of judicial rrors resulting in the death of innocent men and denounced the ise of torture in extracting confessions of imaginary crimes. He hought it absurd that in France two witnesses were sufficient to ondemn a man to death, and he had strong words for the exces- ive severity of punishments.[13] The popular *Gentleman's Magazine* poke of the presumed peacefulness of life among the Indians and y contrast said that in England "the great Inequality of Property was] the source of almost all Murders, Robberies, and other Vices mong ourselves." [14]

Fundamental changes in the character of the laws did not come

---

[12] P. Smith, *A History of Modern Culture* (New York, 1930), I, 497–498, quot- ng W. H. Whitmore, *The Colonial Laws of Massachusetts,* 43, 53; and F. J. Klingberg, "The Evolution of the Humanitarian Spirit in Eighteenth Century England," *Penn. Mag. of Hist. and Biog.,* LVI (1932), 266. In some nstances, however, English criminal law was less severe than that of Massa- chusetts; see R. B. Morris, "Massachusetts and the Common Law," *Amer. Hist. Rev.,* XXXI (1926), 449. H. W. Fitzroy, "The Punishment of Crime in Pro- vincial Pennsylvania," *Penn. Mag. of Hist. and Biog.,* LX (1936), 243.

[13] M. T. Maestro, *Voltaire and Beccaria* (New York, 1942), 22.

[14] *Gentleman's Magazine,* III (1733), 5.

until after the epoch-making works of Montesquieu and Beccari
Beccaria's essay with commentary by Voltaire was known to Ame
icans immediately after its appearance in France and in fact was th
first of Voltaire's works to be published in America.[15] From thes
sources a number of plans and discussions stemmed that calle
for a reconsideration of legal systems, particularly with reference t
crime and punishment. Jefferson made a careful study of Willia
Eden's *Principles of Penal Law* (London, 1772), and into his *Com
mon Place Book* the young Virginian copied long passages from *O
Crimes and Punishments* as well as extracts from Montesquieu. T
them he was indebted for his sentiment that "capital punishmen
should be avoided as much as possible, and punishments choser
which equally with death, restrain the delinquent from committin
the like crime a second time"; to Beccaria, also, Jefferson owe
much for his "Bill proportioning crimes and punishments." [16]

At a later date another Italian, Gaetano Filangieri, repaid th
compliment and in his examination of the systems of civil and crin
inal law turned often to Franklin for advice. He sent to the Ame
ican at Passy his *Scienza della Legislazione,* which brought the repl
that no laws needed reform so badly as the criminal laws. "They ar
everywhere in so great disorder, and so much injustice is com
mitted in the execution of them," wrote Franklin, "that I have bee
sometimes inclined to imagine less would exist in the world if ther
were no such laws, and the punishment of injuries were left to pri
vate resentment." [17] From the Economic Society of Berne came a
announcement of a contest for a prize essay on a scheme of legisla
tion for criminal affairs. Brissot de Warville and others scattere
over Europe sent to Franklin plans of works on penal laws an
prisons which they hoped might be adopted by the Ameri
cans.[18]

Sir Samuel Romilly, the noted law reformer, was another of th
many Europeans who fell under Franklin's spell. To an essay tha

[15] M. M. Harrison-Barr, *Voltaire in America* (Baltimore, 1941), 119.

[16] G. Chinard, ed., *The Common Place Book* (Baltimore, 1926), 38–39, 45–46, 102, 303–309.

[17] Smyth, *Franklin, Writings,* X, 361.

[18] *Calendar of Franklin Papers,* I, 298, Oct. 1, 1777; II, 39, 499, March 7, 177 Sept. 17, 1782; III, 5, 173, Jan. 13, 1783, March 3, 1784.

omilly had written on the need for penal and legal reform was ppended a letter on the same subject by Franklin to add strength the Englishman's position. Mirabeau translated the publication nto French.[19] Franklin exchanged tracts and sentiments on this ubject with a favorite English correspondent, Benjamin Vaughan, nd in one communication derided a pamphlet that urged hanging or all thieves. He favored (as did French reformers) proportioning unishments to offenses and wrote bitterly against capital punishnent for minor crimes.[20]

The seniors at Yale College debated whether the sentence of eath upon convicted criminals should be immediately executed or lelay granted. The college students approved the abolition of mprisonment for debt. On another occasion they questioned "Whether Criminal Law, or Punishment of Crimes be too severe & igorous in the United States for the present Stage of Society?" A Harvard thesis upheld the view of Henry Fielding that the effect of punishment depended on its certainty rather than on its severity. A raduating student at the Yale commencement debate opposed the egality of capital punishment, and his argument, which was taken argely from Beccaria, attracted some attention.[21] An evidence of he new American interest in penology is the space devoted by nagazines to descriptions of European penal conditions and argunents against public and capital punishments.[22]

With a wistful note an English penal reformer wrote to an Amercan, in whose country "old prejudices do not exist," telling him hat his task in introducing a system that would prevent crime vould be much easier of accomplishment than in Europe.[23] Some American states after the Revolution, because of hostility to British

---

[19] *Memoirs of the Life of Sir Samuel Romilly* (London, 1840), I, 69, 90; Romilly, *Observations d'un voyageur Anglais sur la Maison de Force appellée Bicêtre* . . . (Paris, 1788).

[20] Smyth, *Franklin, Writings,* IX, 292, March 14, 1785.

[21] Stiles, *Diary,* III, 118, April 20, 1784; III, 128, June 29, 1784; III, 209, Feb. 21, 1786; III, 328 note 2, Sept. 10, 1788; III, 346, March 9, 1789.

[22] *New York Magazine or Literary Repository,* V (1794), 425, Saxon state prison; *ibid.,* n.s., I (Jan.–July, 1796), 250, punishment of state criminals in Holland; Dr. Rush in *American Museum,* II (Aug., 1787), 142, IV (July, 1788), 78.

[23] S. L. Knapp, *The Life of Thomas Eddy* (New York, 1834), 187.

tradition, forbade counsel to cite decisions of the English court: The common law was criticized by Americans because of its sever punishments, its bias against debtors, and its doctrines of crin inal conspiracy and seditious libel.[24] On the other hand, in pre Revolutionary years the British Government exercised a modera ing influence on the colonies by instructing the royal governors t get laws passed to check brutality to indentured servants on sout ern plantations, where they were often badly treated.

On various occasions in the eighteenth century charitable im pulses prompted philanthropists to mitigate the harshness of prisoner's existence, particularly if he had been imprisoned fo debt.[25] When fortunes were made and lost, sometimes with grea rapidity, a debtor's plight might be anyone's, and sympathy for vi tims of misfortune was more easily aroused. In colonial societ where labor was scarce it was uneconomic to withdraw a workma from production. One British proposal that insolvent debtors b sent to populate America was a shrewd mixture of humanitarianis and mercantilism. Among its alleged advantages was mentioned th rapid rise in fortunes of the lowly.[26]

Penal reform in the last quarter of the eighteenth century di tated a shift from the emphasis on corporal punishment to impriso ment. The American Quakers made significant contributions t penology when they substituted imprisonment for corporal punis ment and combined the prison and the workhouse. It was a nove idea that punishment should consist of hard labor rather than th torture of enforced idleness.

It was the Englishman John Howard who most strikingly effecte a change in the systems of penology in Europe and America; in th young states overseas he gained perhaps his most enthusiastic dis ciples. The *Massachusetts Magazine* printed an article "Of th Cleanliness, order and Economy of Dutch Prisons (By the late cele

---

[24] J. A. Krout and D. R. Fox, *The Completion of Independence 1790–183* (New York, 1944), 288; Morris, *Government and Labor in Early America,* 206 207, 471.

[25] *New York Mercury,* Jan. 19, 1767, under Philadelphia news of Jan. 8.

[26] *A Letter to a Member of Parliament, relating to the Relief of Poor In solvent Prisoners for Debt . . .* (London. 1724). 6–7.

orated Mr. Howard)"; [27] his descriptions of the more modern prisons in Rome and Ghent were read in Philadelphia by Caleb Lownes and others, and the reforms undertaken in English prisons as a result of Continental influence became in turn the models for Americans. A Philadelphia pamphlet of 1790 which argued for prison reform included lengthy extracts from Howard's works.

Philadelphia, however, had an earlier tradition of penal reform that dated from the first days of the colony, although it should be mentioned that this progressive tradition had gone into eclipse for many years after 1718, only to emerge again during the Revolution. A local society to assist distressed prisoners had been formed in 1776 but was dissolved during the war that followed. Soon after the conclusion of the struggle, "The Philadelphia Society for alleviating the miseries of Public Prisons" was organized, and it was this group, a revival of the earlier organization, that followed Howard so eagerly.[28] They sent him their constitution and asked for communications. "With the friends of humanity in Europe," the Pennsylvanians acknowledged their obligations to him for drawing the attention of the public to prisoners and for attacking the problem of crime prevention. Dr. Rush sent Dr. Lettsom his own pamphlet on prisons and told him that the local institution was an outgrowth of Howard's "excellent history of Prisons." [29]

Dr. Lettsom kept the Philadelphia society informed of the activities of Howard, and the latter expressed his willingness to help support the Philadelphia society, whose work in changing prison administration was watched by other American states. William Bradford, the attorney-general, who was a leader in the movement for reform of prisons and the criminal code, wrote in 1793 that the religious principles of the Quakers had been opposed to a harsh code, "and as soon as the principles of Beccaria were disseminated, they found a soil that was prepared to receive them." [30] It is a fact of some

[27] II (1790), 685.

[28] Roberts Vaux, *Notices of the . . . Prison at Philadelphia . . . Criminal Code of Pennsylvania* (Philadelphia, 1826).

[29] Pettigrew, II, 429, May 18, 1787.

[30] H. E. Barnes, "The Historical Origin of the Prison System in America," *Journal of the American Institute of Criminal Law and Criminology,* XII (1921–1922), 36–51.

significance that at least three editions of Beccaria's treatise were issued in Philadelphia between 1778 and 1809; one other edition appeared as early as 1773 in New York.

Benjamin Rush, who participated in nearly all the reform movements of his day, was also active in presenting modern ideas on penology. A prison, he felt, must serve three purposes: reformation, the deterrence of others from crime, the protection of society from crime. His type of institution would provide for a classification of offenders and a rational system of convict labor, under which the prisoners were to grow their own food and to perform other tasks to pay for their upkeep. The idea of an indeterminate sentence (only recently put into practice) was another that was familiar to Rush.[31] He believed too that the use of convict labor in road building was bad for community morale because it rendered labor of every kind disreputable. He exchanged observations and publications with Englishmen, particularly Dr. Lettsom, on this and related subjects. Rush asked Lettsom to place in a London periodical his tract against capital punishment, and he sent to Dr. Price his pamphlet on the *Effects of Public Punishments upon Criminals and upon Society*.[32]

Granville Sharp, who also corresponded with Rush, disagreed with the argument that murder should not be punished with death. Rush stuck to his opinion, however, and sent a new edition of his essay against capital punishment to Lettsom. The American reported, optimistically, that his opinion, once unpopular, was gaining ground everywhere in the United States, and that Dr. Lettsom's fellow Quakers were openly advocating it. "I wish Christians of all denominations would unite in enforcing it," wrote Dr. Rush. "Death, for any crime, is certainly as contrary as war, to the spirit of the gospel." [33]

By common consent, Thomas Eddy, a New York Quaker, was called the "Howard of America." Eddy visited the Philadelphia

---

[31] O. F. Lewis, *The Development of American Prisons and Prison Customs, 1776–1845* (Albany, 1922), 19–22.

[32] "Price Letters," *Mass. Hist. Soc., Proc.*, ser. 2, XVII (1903), 366, April 6, 1787.

[33] Pettigrew, II, 235, Aug. 16, 1788; 435, Oct. 3, 1788; 438, June 8, 1789; 439, May 28, 1792; N. G. Goodman, *Benjamin Rush* (Philadelphia, 1934), 279–282.

prisons, received advice from Caleb Lownes, and corresponded with European philanthropists. In this way, writes a student of penology, he did much "to establish the cross-currents of penological influence between Europe and America that marked the first thirty years of the nineteenth century." Eddy came back from Philadelphia with a number of copies of the Pennsylvania criminal code which he distributed among the New York legislators. General Philip Schuyler, in the New York Senate, was interested in this problem, and with Eddy's assistance drew up a bill for establishing a penitentiary system based on that in Philadelphia. Eddy's plan for single cells was not adopted, but he sent it to his English correspondent, Patrick Colquhoun, a distinguished figure in penology, who was instrumental in having it introduced later by the London Society for Improving Prison Discipline. "Solitary Confinement, under certain regulations is excellent," wrote Colquhoun. From Paris, Jefferson sent plans to Virginia for the construction of a prison on the solitary-cell plan which a French architect had suggested.[34]

Eddy informed Colquhoun, who was in charge of the London police, of the many changes that were taking place in the American treatment of criminals, and Colquhoun answered with news of European accomplishments.[35] Europeans followed American experiments closely. The Philadelphia prison, wrote Colquhoun, "furnishes an irrefragable proof to all Europe, as well as America, that the great desideratum has been accomplished, of rendering the labour of criminals productive [self-supporting] . . . and what is more of importance, of restoring them again to society with amended morals . . . to become useful instead of noxious members of the community." Eddy's pamphlet on the New York prisons was read by the leading reformers in England, including Jeremy Bentham, who in exchange sent a packet of publications to the New Yorker.

Eddy's account of the New York prison included citations from and eulogies for Montesquieu, Beccaria, and Howard. But he reminded his readers that, while these names should be remembered, "the legislators and philanthropists of our own country deserve not

---

[34] Lewis, 43, 210; Misc. Papers, New York Public Library, C. Lownes to Eddy, April 19, 1796.

[35] Knapp, 41, 56–57, 76–77, 178 ff.

to be forgotten." In the judgment of Eddy, Beccaria's opinions had "the force of axioms in the Science of penal law," and he also praised very highly *A Treatise on the Police of the Metropolis* by his London correspondent, Colquhoun.[36] The latter returned in kind in a note to Lettsom wherein he referred to the valuable work that Eddy was doing in America.[37]

American disciples of Howard, though devoted to the master, were critical of some of his teachings. A visitor to the Philadelphia prison from South Carolina, R. J. Turnbull, who urged his state to follow the lead of Pennsylvania, quoted American experience to refute Howard's belief that some corporal punishment might be necessary. Howard was skeptical also about self-supporting prisons, but here too Pennsylvania experience had apparently proved them possible. The Frenchman Constantin F. de C. Volney, who was then in the South, wrote to a Charleston paper endorsing the sentiments of Turnbull.[38] A review of Turnbull's tract in the *Gentleman's Magazine,* noting that solitude was the main idea of the Philadelphia prison, observed that an important principle of Quakerism was the silence of solitude. "If this produces reformation," the reviewer continued, "it is an experiment worth trying. . . ." And with commendable reserve he added, "There is . . . a wide difference between speculative and practical reformation." [39] A review of Turnbull's publication in the *Monthly Review* led to self-criticism of English criminal jurisprudence, which the writer felt was barbarous in continuing to exact the capital penalty "for mere violations of property." [40]

It was another Frenchman who made the Walnut Street prison in Philadelphia better known to Europeans. The Duc de la Rochefoucauld-Liancourt published an account of the criminal jurisprudence of Pennsylvania and noted that the chief reformers were Quakers. The results that they achieved were compared with

---

[36] T. Eddy, *An Account of the State Prison . . . in New York* (New York, 1801), 64, 88.

[37] Pettigrew, II, 361, Jan. 19, 1803.

[38] R. J. Turnbull, *A Visit to the Philadelphia Prison* (Philadelphia, 1796); this appeared originally in the *Charleston Daily Gazette.*

[39] *Gentleman's Magazine,* LXIX (1799), 504.

[40] *Monthly Review,* XXIII (1797), 356.

those obtained in European systems, and in La Rochefoucauld's opinion Europe came off second best. The Americans had gone further than Howard who, it was noted, had a more inclusive list of crimes punishable by death. William Bradford had written a pamphlet opposed to capital punishment (except in case of premeditated murder), and the visiting nobleman believed that Bradford's ideas had gained wide circulation in America. To the New World he paid an eloquent tribute and called upon her to reverse the process of borrowing "illumination" from Europe and to "serve in her turn as a model to reform the criminal jurisprudence and establish a new system of imprisonment in the old world." He recalled that the ideas were originally European, but "the attempt at an almost entire abolition of the punishment of death, and the substitution of a system of reason and justice, to that of bonds, ill treatment and arbitrary punishment, was never made but in America." [41]

English interest in progressive penal legislation in America was in part satisfied by a notice in the *Gentleman's Magazine* of details in Pennsylvania's new code of 1794. It singled out especially the facts that only murder in the first degree was punishable by death and that "benefit of clergy was forever abolished." [42] English publications on America, especially the reports of travelers, often noted the superiority of American criminal codes. In *A Short View of the Administrations in the Government of America* George Henderson observed that some of the states, especially Pennsylvania, had codes "far less sanguinary than most known in other countries," and this had resulted in greater rather than less security for society. For particular commendation he singled out the laws for the relief of imprisoned debtors.[43] An authoritative descriptive geography said that in the South in the middle of the eighteenth century "few or no debtors [were] confined in prison above twenty-four hours." [44] The example of Massachusetts in making minor offenders engage in

---

[41] La Rochefoucauld-Liancourt, *On the Prisons of Philadelphia* (1796); B. Faÿ, *The Revolutionary Spirit in France and America at the End of the Eighteenth Century* (New York, 1927), 559 note 69.

[42] *Gentleman's Magazine,* LXIV (1794), 850.

[43] London, 1802, 35–36.

[44] Fenning and Collyer, II, 670.

profitable work while in prison was held up for emulation to European nations by another writer.[45]

John Walker, who was so bitterly critical of the Liverpool slave dealers, rejoiced with "the friends of humanity" that the American States were discarding the "barbarous and sanguinary code of laws which they derived from Europe." [46] The *Edinburgh Bee,* mindful of conditions at home, in 1791 was surprised to find that an American newspaper reported "not a single robbery or murder" for four months.[47] Young's *Annals of Agriculture* reprinted La Rochefoucauld's description of the prisons of Philadelphia.[48]

A London reprint of William Bradford's *An Enquiry how far the Punishment of Death is necessary in Pennsylvania* contained also an account of the Philadelphia prison by Caleb Lownes. The advertisement to this London edition indicated its value to an English audience, who were asked to "observe with pleasure the principles of philosophy and humanity practically combining their influence to enlighten the ignorant and to reform the vicious." Bradford's work caused the English to look critically at their own code, which demanded capital punishment in a great many instances. A notice in the *Monthly Review* of La Rochefoucauld's *Travels* mentioned "with peculiar approbation" the prisons in Philadelphia.[49]

A more tangible indication of American influence on English penal reform came as a result of the meeting of the two Quakers, William Savery of Philadelphia and Elizabeth Fry. It is the belief of Rufus M. Jones that it was most likely Savery who awakened Elizabeth Fry, later a most valuable servant in this work, to the condition of the degraded prisoner.[50] Other Americans supplied arguments for European reformers. A radical publication, *The Complaints of the Poor People of England,* which was critical of capital punishment, quoted in support Joel Barlow's remark in his *Advice to the Privileged Orders* that capital punishment was absent

---

[45] Samuel Stearns, *The American Oracle* (London, 1791), 258–259.

[46] J. Walker, *Elements of Geography and Natural and Civil History* (2nd ed., 1795), 567.

[47] V (1791), 239.

[48] XXVII (1796), 572–623.

[49] *Monthly Review,* enlarged ser., XXXV, 121.

[50] Jones, *Later Periods of Quakerism,* II, 356–357.

from Connecticut for 130 years after the founding of the settlement. The English writer credited such blessings, which included the absence of poverty, to the existence of representative government. "The American government," he continued, "has settled into a system of mercy." [51]

A French publication on English criminal law included a letter from Franklin which criticized the disproportion between the penalty and the crime, and in a footnote to the text the writer observed with favor the new name, more humane, given to Philadelphia prisons, now called "Bettering Houses" (*maisons d'amélioration*).[52] Franklin's support of the Masonic Lodge of the Nine Sisters in a campaign to moderate the French criminal law was very welcome.[53]

One British writer shortly before the Revolution thought banishment to a growing, prosperous America hardly a punishment, and he suggested therefore Hudson's Bay. In reply Lord Kames said that as civilization advances severity of punishment should be lightened. Transportation to America should, therefore, be continued for lesser crimes.[54] After the Revolution, the closing of America to British convicts made it imperative that new outlets be found, for the crowded conditions in English prisons were potentially dangerous to the community; therefore Sydney, Australia, was chosen as a new settlement.

A German periodical devoted to criminal law included articles on American penal legislation, frequently based on writings by American authors. One article, "Ueber die Amerikanische Criminalverfassung," pointed out that the states modeled a good deal of their legislation on that of England, but that many changes had been introduced. G. A. Kleinschrod, the writer, was certain that no American state had as good a system of criminal legislation as Pennsylvania. He noted how the total of criminals had fallen by comparing

---

[51] G. Dyer, *The Complaints of the Poor People of England* (2nd ed., London, 1793), 30–31.

[52] *Observations d'un Voyageur Anglais . . . sur la Législation Criminelle de la Grande-Bretagne*. Imité de l'Anglais. Par le Comte de Mirabeau. Avec une Lettre de . . . Franklin (1788), 21.

[53] Faÿ, 230.

[54] Lord Kames (Henry Home), *Sketches of the History of Man* (Edinburgh, 1774), I, 392 note.

the results of the last four years under the system in use in Pennsyl-vania before 1790 with the first four years of the new system.[55]

Slavery and antiquated penal legislation were objects of strong attack by social reformers whose critical pens were also directed against many other evils. Reformers were reminded by proslavery advocates of the "superior hardships of our own poor at home."[56] The title of one of Benezet's publications suggests the wide range of interests these humanitarians had: *An extract from a treatise on the Spirit of Prayer . . . with some Thoughts on war; Remarks on the Nature and bad effects of the use of Spirituous Liquors and Considerations on Slavery.*

Within the growing circle of influential humanitarians was Dr. Thomas Percival, of Manchester, whose *Moral and Literary Dissertations* treated many phases of reform, including the question of dueling. Franklin was one of his readers, and he agreed with Percival in condemning the "murderous Practice of Duelling."[57] Granville Sharp took time off from his antislavery crusade to tell Benezet that he had composed a tract strongly opposed to dueling; this was published with Beccaria's treatise in Philadelphia in 1778.[58] Sharp had earlier sent his pamphlet to Rush, with extra copies to be placed in the hands of persons *"who are liable to serve on Juries."*[59] Although dueling was illegal in England and America it was condoned by social convention. Throughout the eighteenth century many individuals, including Paine and Jefferson, voiced disapproval of the practice, but the social conscience in America was not profoundly stirred until after the tragedy of the Burr-Hamilton duel.[60]

The growing concern for human life was expressed in yet another manner, the organization of "humane societies," or lifeguards to

[55] E. F. Klein and G. A. Kleinschrod, *Archiv des Criminalrechts* (1799), bk. II, chap. i, 10–27; see also bk. I, chap. iv, 35.

[56] P. Hoare, *Memoirs of Granville Sharp* (London, 1820), II, 189, Sharp to Bishop of Salisbury, May 21, 1789.

[57] Smyth, *Franklin, Writings,* IX, 236, July 17, 1784.

[58] Hoare, I, 210, Jan. 7, 1774.

[59] Sharp to Rush, Jan. 10, 1774, Ridgway Library.

[60] E. B. Greene, "The Code of Honor in Colonial and Revolutionary Times," *Col. Soc. Mass., Trans.,* XXVI (1924–1926), 368.

esuscitate people apparently drowned. The British Royal Humane ociety was formed in 1774, seven years after its model in Amsteram. Americans were interested in this movement, for the *Royal merican Magazine* printed an account of "Dr. Tissot's Method of ecovering Drowned Persons," and one Bostonian was in correpondence with Dr. W. Hawes of the Royal Humane Society. Ten ears after the formation of the British Society, one of its active pirits, Dr. Henry Moyes, came to America to organize similar roups. In a short time he wrote to a London friend of his success n Boston; other cities along the Atlantic Coast likewise formed such ocieties.[61] Chastellux gave Benezet a box of apparatus and intructed him in French methods of resuscitation. A member of the Massachusetts society on a visit to London asked the Royal Humane ociety for assistance in setting up a lighthouse on Cape Cod; on nother occasion the English group sent a description of a new type f lifeboat, which was then copied by Americans.[62] In a comparaively short time many communities in Europe and America had rganizations to resuscitate the drowned.[63]

Americans who were interested in life insurance corresponded vith Dr. Richard Price, whose writings on the subject attracted vide attention. Price wrote to President Willard of Harvard College n the expectation of life among its graduates and gave advice to Massachusetts ministers who were planning to provide annuities or their widows.[64] Ezra Stiles told one correspondent that plans of his nature would require more complete records of births and leaths than New England had been accustomed to keep.[65] Franklin nad suggested that Price include in his volume on *Annuities* the xample of an arrangement in Holland, where a pension fund was ccumulated so that in old age people would be freed of poverty and

---

[61] *Gentleman's Magazine,* LVII (1787), 1154, Dr. Moyes to Dr. A. Johnson, Nov. 12, 1785.

[62] Vaux, *Memoirs of Anthony Benezet,* 104; M. A. DeWolfe Howe, *The Humane Society of . . . Massachusetts, 1785–1916* (Cambridge, 1918).

[63] R. P. Finch, D.D., *A Sermon . . . for the Benefit of the Humane Society,* London, 1788).

[64] "Price Letters," *Mass. Hist. Soc., Proc.,* ser. 2, XVII (1903), Wigglesworth o Price, 346, July 27, 1786; Willard to Price, 347, July 29, 1786.

[65] Emmet Collection, New York Public Library, 7914, Stiles to Rev. William Gordon.

have a place to live. From a village in Saxe-Weimar a plan for per
sioning widows and orphans was sent to Franklin. Plans to eliminat
poverty, for founding almshouses or state institutions for the in
digent and homeless, were also sent to him. Another philanthropi
gentleman acquainted Franklin with a plan to gather together al
the poor and transplant them to America.[66]

The orphan house that Whitefield had established in Georgi
before the middle of the century and that one visitor observed "ha
made such a noise in Europe" was based on the work of A. H
Francke in Germany. Over £5,000 was contributed by England an
Scotland, in addition to large sums by the colonies themselves, fo
Whitefield's orphan house.[67] The *Gentleman's Magazine* judge
highly of a Connecticut plan to prevent poverty, which it believed
however, to be unworkable in a large community. It seems that in
New London a strict watch was kept by the people over each other'
business affairs, and if any one neglected his business and becam
involved in "ruinous projects," he was judged unfit to manage hi
affairs any longer, and they were then taken over by the legally con
stituted authorities. A notice signed by three selectmen of the town
told of a sort of guardianship that had been placed over a local busi
nessman until his concern was once again put on its feet, thus pre
venting him and his family from becoming charges of the town.[6
When Philip Mazzei returned to Florence after a stay in America
he proposed to improve the handling of beggars by drawing on hi
experience as an administrator in Virginia.[69]

The question of poverty was attacked in a vigorous way by tha
versatile American expatriate, Count Rumford, who had entered
the service of the Elector of Bavaria. The city of Munich was di
vided into sixteen districts, every dwelling place was numbered, a
committee of charity was named for each district, and a doctor, a
citizen, a priest, a surgeon, and an apothecary were assigned to look

---

[66] Smyth, *Franklin, Writings,* V, 406, Franklin to Francis Maseres, June 17
1772; *Calendar of Franklin Papers,* II, 235, April 7, 1780; I, 395, April 14, 1778
I, 467, July 29, 1778; III, 152, A. F. Rühle von Lilienstern (circa 1783).

[67] *Georgia Hist. Soc., Colls.,* IV (1878), 16; E. M. North, *Early Methodis
Philanthropy* (New York, 1914), 89–98.

[68] *Gentleman's Magazine,* XXXV (1765), 123.

[69] Marraro, *Memoirs of Mazzei,* 258–259.

fter the poor without pay.[70] In a suburb of Munich he established beggars' home by refitting an old house, and certain economies he nstituted attracted unusual attention throughout Europe. He esablished school lunches in Munich to improve the diet of poorer hildren. Social improvements everywhere in Bavaria were stimuated by Count Rumford, and as a result of his experiments he wrote he *Fundamental Principles on which General Establishments for he Relief of the Poor may be formed in all Countries.* He realized hat his chances of success would be much greater if he could keep he costs down, so he turned his attention to studies of foods and heir nutritive values; he urged the use especially of the inexpensive merican Indian corn.

Rumford planned kitchens elsewhere in Europe, and in 1795 he vent to England to publish some of his writings, hoping thereby to lraw attention to his reforms already effected in Germany. In Engand and Ireland he supervised changes in many philanthropic intitutions. A Boston edition of his works appeared (1798–1799), but opies of the London edition had already found their way to Amerca. When he was leaving for the States in the early part of 1799 Rumford asked his English publishers to send him a dozen copies f his essay "bound in the best manner," to be used for gifts. It may e noted that the future American historian, George Bancroft, was ed in his youth according to the dietary innovations of Count Rumford.[71]

The *European Magazine* of London gave an enthusiastic recepion to Rumford's *Essays Experimental, Political, Economical and Philosophical.* The reviewer believed that property owners would e interested in Rumford's measures to benefit the poor and abolish eggary, especially since he had shown that no rise in taxation vould result. A later issue of the magazine contained an account of Rumford and suggested that many of his plans might be adopted in Great Britain "to the benefit of every class"; some of them, it said, ad already been cordially received.[72] One of Rumford's strongest

[70] G. E. Ellis, *A Memoir of Sir Benjamin Thompson, Count Rumford* (Boson, 1876), 178.

[71] Brit. Mus. Add. Ms., 34045; M. A. DeWolfe Howe, *The Life and Letters f George Bancroft* (New York, 1908), I, 16.

[72] *Eur. Mag. and Lond. Rev.*, XXIX (1797), 320–324; XXXI (1798), 83.

supporters was Thomas Bernard, son of the colonial governor o Massachusetts, Francis Bernard. Thomas Bernard became a frienc of Rumford, was a leader in English humanitarian movements, es pecially the Society for Bettering the Condition of the Poor, and, a a director of the Foundling Hospital, introduced Rumford's plan for diet and fuel.[73] This London Foundling Hospital was held up t Bostonians by the historian Jeremy Belknap, as worthy of imitation

The question of costs was always uppermost in the minds of re formers, which explains their preoccupation with inexpensive diets Henry Wansey, traveling in America at the end of the eighteentl century, had been much impressed by the use of parsnips in poor house meals. Apparently the vegetable was not well known in Eng land, and he gave directions for its planting. It kept a long time ir large stacks covered over, he said, and unlike other vegetables it wa immune to frost. "In these dear times," he wrote, "what a resourc would such a stock have been to our poor!"[74]

Another phase of human distress that interested philanthropist was the education of the deaf and dumb. Francis Green, an Amer ican, was inspired by the success of Scottish teachers in handling dea mutes and became the pioneer in establishing free schools for th afflicted in England and America.[75]

The problem of poverty was closely related to the question o temperance. In England the early decades of the eighteenth centur were particularly marked by excesses in drink, which exacted a vas toll in money and misery. Arguments for temperance were fairl common in the middle of the century, and they grew in volum toward its closing years. In this, as in other movements, the Amer ican Quakers led the way, for they were opposed to the increasin use of hard liquor, and after 1736 frequent warnings were issued tc Friends against excessive use of strong drinks. The Mathers in Nev England at an early day had favored temperance; the trustees of th Georgia settlement sent to the colony one hundred copies of an Eng lish pamphlet, Dr. Hale's *Friendly Admonition to the Drinkers o Brandy,* which urged the use of malt liquors. An attempt at prohi-

[73] James Baker, *Life of Sir Thomas Bernard* (London, 1819).

[74] Henry Wansey, *Thoughts on Poor-Houses . . .* (London, 1801), 28.

[75] A. G. Bell, "Francis Green, a Philanthropist of the last Century," *Amer Antiq. Soc., Proc.,* XIII–XIV (1900), 383–393.

bition, by law, of the sale or importation of ardent spirits in Georgia led to abuse and repeal of the act. Woolman advised Quakers against intemperate drinking, and Benezet, who was more vigorous in his attack, wrote a pamphlet against the habitual use of hard liquors. In the *Pennsylvania Spelling Book* Benezet included a list of questions which were in the nature of a catechism to promote the idea of temperance among children. He influenced the Quaker Yearly Meeting to resolve that members should not deal in spirituous liquors. The Methodists also took steps to discourage their members from participation in the hard-liquor business. In Connecticut a few influential men formed a group in 1789 that was the "first organized abstinence from ardent spirits." Although newspapers still advertised liquors, more and more they were printing items critical of their sale.[76]

English attention to American temperance statements indicated a concern over conditions at home. The *Scots Magazine* in 1795 printed an extract from Belknap's *History of New Hampshire* which attacked the very free drinking of hard liquor, and an earlier issue printed Dr. Rush's *Enquiry on the Effects of Spirituous Liquors upon the Human Body*. An extract from this essay was published again in a later issue of the *Scots Magazine* with much flattering comment.[77] Another periodical in Scotland, *The Bee,* gave a favorable review to Lettsom's *History of Some of the Effects of Hard Drinking*.[78] A London newspaper printed a letter from Boston telling of a tax to be laid on retailers of liquors to curb this evil.[79]

An American newspaper printed an extract from one of Lettsom's writings against spirituous liquors which won the commendation of Dr. Rush. Rush told Lettsom that a campaign in the newspapers against spirituous liquors, in 1788, had caused a drop of one-third in their use in Pennsylvania, but his co-workers in this campaign of education were less enthusiastic. Quakers, Methodists, and the local College of Physicians opposed their use, Rush wrote, and added that no object lay nearer his heart than the extirpation of spirituous liq-

---

[76] J. A. Krout, *The Origins of Prohibition* (New York, 1925), 51–83.

[77] *Scots Magazine,* LVII (1795), 82–85; XLVII (1785), 469–474; LVI (1794), 202–203.

[78] *The Bee,* X, 71–72, July 18, 1792.

[79] *The Morning Herald and Daily Advertiser,* Jan. 7, 1784.

uors.[80] The memorial of the Philadelphia College of Physicians t the legislature, largely inspired by Rush, urging the substitution c malt liquors for hard drinks, was reprinted in the *Scots Magazine*.[8 The temperance movement that was to gain increasing strength i the nineteenth century owed much of its original force to the vigo ous Dr. Rush.

Among the causes that appealed to a growing humanitarianisn was slavery. It was in North and South America that the most insis ent voices were raised in the slave's behalf. An Anglican divine Morgan Godwin, who was later to be quoted by Benezet, had show sympathy for the slave at the close of the seventeenth century. Chie Justice Sewall of Massachusetts wrote a significant tract which though it did not propose the abolition of slavery, criticized th traffic in slaves and the institution itself. Boston was already prepar ing to legislate against slavery when Sewall wrote his *Selling o Joseph.* American Quakers in 1729 agreed to oppose the further pu chase of slaves, and leaders with convictions as strong as those pos sessed by John Woolman and Anthony Benezet preached and wrot against slaveholding as unchristian. To the religious argument against slavery were added, during the Revolutionary period, thos derived from the doctrine of natural rights. A Harvard thesis denie that it was "lawful to subject Africans to perpetual bondage." Pro hibitive duties were placed on the importation of slaves into Penn sylvania, Rhode Island, and Connecticut, while Quakers in the Ne England and Middle Colonies began to disown their fellow sectar ians who persisted in holding slaves.[82]

In a correspondence covering many years, Quakers on both side of the Atlantic exhorted one another to hold fast to the determina tion to abolish the slave trade and slavery itself. Philadelphia Quak ers wrote in 1761 of a provincial tax on the importation of slaves and requested English support, lest an opposition group urge the repea

---

80 Pettigrew, II, 435, Aug. 16, 1788; Goodman, 274–278.

81 *Scots Magazine,* L (1788), 562.

82 A. Matthews, "Early Protests against Slavery," *Col. Soc. Mass., Trans* VIII (1902–1904), 288; *Mass. Hist. Soc., Proc.,* ser. 1, XVIII (1881), 139; M. S Locke, *Anti-Slavery in America, 1619–1808* ("Radcliffe Coll. monographs," no XI, 1901).

f the prohibitory duty. Members of other religious groups were lso converted to the Quaker position, wrote the Philadelphia riends.[83] From North Carolina and Virginia Quakers, too, came essages to London of opposition to the slave trade.[84] Further progess in the promotion of antislavery sentiment, especially among on-Quakers, was reported with satisfaction to London Friends up the outbreak of the War for Independence. Always there is reealed in the exchange of communications a belief in the need for o-operative action. Even during the war correspondence on the ubject was continued, and London Quakers acknowledged Amercan assistance in "discouraging the African Trade." [85]

Thus the movement gained impetus on this side of the Atlantic.)verseas in England and France opinion was formed more slowly, ut its shape was fashioned largely by America. An international ellowship of those who joined in the crusade against humanity's ls made one of its strongest fights against slavery. Anthony Benezet, he peace-loving Philadelphia schoolmaster, was one of the most ilitant crusaders. He appealed to the influential Franklin to do omething about this evil; to him and to important Londoners, Benzet sent his tracts on the slave trade, urging that the matter be rought up in Parliament. In support of reform he quoted liberal merican opinion, yet he realized the opposition that would be enountered from those "who sell their country and their God for old." In reply Franklin wrote to Benezet that he had made a short xtract of the reformer's writings and had published it in the *Lonon Chronicle*. Franklin mentioned that several selections against avery had been printed and assured Benezet that his "labours had lready been attended with great effects." Soon after, Franklin met ranville Sharp with whom he decided to co-operate in eradicating he slave trade.[86]

---

[83] *Letters to and from Philadelphia,* I, March 24, 1761, Friends House, Lonon.

[84] Port. 21 (31), Thomas Nicholson, Oct. 30, 1770, Friends House, London; 8 (19), Virginia, June 9, 1772; also S. B. Weeks, *Southern Quakers and Slavery* 'Johns Hopkins University Studies," extra vol. XV).

[85] *Letters to and from Philadelphia,* I, April 22, 1773; April 9, 1779.

[86] *Calendar of Franklin Papers,* I, 132, April 27, 1772; Smyth, *Franklin, Writgs,* V, 431, Aug. 22, 1772; VI, 9, Feb. 10, 1773.

Some letters indicating a strong hostility to slavery had alread appeared in several British publications. One contributor to a Edinburgh periodical in 1769 singled out American Negro slaver for particular condemnation.[87] A newspaper thirty years before ha printed as its leading article a long letter against slavery.[88] The sam year the *London Magazine* printed a strong attack on slavery whic rested its arguments on the natural right of an individual to free dom. Some time later another attack on slavery appeared in thi magazine; "Have Britons, who have so long tasted the sweets of lib erty forgot the relish of it?" The *Gentleman's Magazine* reprinte the resolution of the town assembly of Salem, Massachusetts, agains the importation of slaves as repugnant to the "natural rights c mankind." [89] Sharp reminded Philadelphia that many Negroes wer natives of the colonies "and consequently have *a natural right* to *free existence* therein, as well as the Landholders themselves." [90]

Thomas Day in answer to an American request for his opinion o slavery pointedly replied in 1776, "If there be an object truly ridic ulous in nature, it is an American patriot signing resolutions of in dependence with the one hand, and with the other brandishing whip over his affrighted slaves." Day's humanitarianism was greatl stimulated by association with Americans, especially John Lauren of South Carolina.[91] Sharp concurred with Day, saying that th "toleration of domestic slavery in the colonies greatly weakens th claim or *natural right* of our American brethren to Liberty." [92]

As early as 1727 London Quakers had distributed to other Englis Friends answers to queries of Philadelphia Friends about slave im portation, which was frowned upon as "not a commendable, nor al low'd practice." [93] In later years the *Scots Magazine* gave a very sym pathetic review to Benezet's *Historical Account of Guinea,* which i

[87] *The Weekly Magazine, or Edinburgh Amusement,* VI, Oct. 31, 1769.

[88] *The Old Whig; or, The Consistent Protestant,* March 16, 1737/1738.

[89] *London Magazine,* VII (March, 1738), 129–131; XXI (Oct. 1752), 47 *Gentleman's Magazine,* XLIII (1773), 358.

[90] *The Just Limitation of Slavery* (1776), appendix 6, July 18, 1775.

[91] T. Day, *Fragment of an original Letter on the Slavery of the Negroes wri ten in the year 1776* (London, 1794), 33.

[92] G. Sharp, *Declaration of the People's Natural Right to a share in the Le islature* (London, 1774), 28 note 25.

[93] Gibson Mss., III, 195, Friends House, London.

larkson's opinion did more than any other book to spread a knowl-
dge and hatred of the trade.[94] Benezet sent some copies of a treatise
n the slave trade to David Barclay to place in the hands of influen-
ial English citizens.[95]

The Philadelphia Yearly Meeting of Quakers sent to the London
early Meeting the tracts of Benezet which were to be reprinted
nd circulated, particularly among the students in English schools,
1 order, as Clarkson put it, "that the rising youth might acquire a
nowledge, and at the same time a detestation of this cruel traffic."
arliament members likewise received hundreds of copies. Rufus
I. Jones, perhaps the leading authority on the Quakers, believes
hat Benezet wielded greater influence through his personal correpondence. He selected prominent individuals or their friends,
ien like Robert Shackleton, who was close to Burke, as agents for
is propaganda. It was probably Benezet's work that aroused John
Vesley to strong comment against slavery. When the evangelist
rote a tract against the evil it was reprinted in Philadelphia by
enezet, with notes and additional material.[96] John Woolman,
hough he was with the English Friends but a very short time, left
iem with a renewed determination to fight against slavery.[97]

Samuel Johnson was one of a number strongly opposed to slavery,
ut the most effective champion in the earlier period was Granville
harp, who was a correspondent of Benezet. Sharp, in the Somerset
ase (which furnished the precedent for the Knight case in Scot-
ind), had helped outlaw slavery from the British Isles. An abridg-
ient by Benezet of Sharp's tract *On the Injustice of Slavery* was put
ito the hands of the judges and counsel who were concerned with
ie Somerset case. This case attracted the attention of American
uakers who then began a correspondence with Granville Sharp.
harp and John Wesley informed Benezet that they intended to

---

[94] *Scots Magazine,* XXXIV (1772), 486; Thomas Clarkson, *History of the
ise, Progress, and . . . Abolition of the African Slave Trade . . .* (London,
339), 118.

[95] Mss. Port. 38 (87), April 29, 1767, Friends House, London.

[96] Clarkson, 94; Jones, *Later Periods of Quakerism,* II, 318–321; Tyerman,
esley, III, 115, 183; see copy in New York Historical Society.

[97] Woolman Mss., Port., 6 (33), March 25, 1773; Yorkshire Quarterly Meeting,
riends House, London.

make weekly contributions to the newspapers on the slave trade to stir up public opinion.[98]

But trade in slaves was still carried on. As long as the trade wa supported "by authority on your side," wrote Philadelphia Friend to England, "Great Britain cannot be clear of a pollution," bu when word arrived of a petition to Parliament, the American Quak ers felt relieved. A report on the conditions of Negroes was drawn up in England and presented to each member of Parliament, and a copy was sent to America. Within a few months the Americans had reprinted five thousand copies of the report for general distribution throughout the States.[99]

The agitation against the slave trade, one half of which was car ried on in ships from Liverpool, was more impressive in the decade following 1783. *An Essay on the Treatment and Conversion of Afri can slaves in the British Sugar Colonies* by James Ramsay, whos firsthand experience enabled him to write with authority, presented most of the arguments used against slavery and slave trading there after. The *European Magazine* and the *Gentleman's Magazine* gav it favorable reviews.[100] Another writer, Anthony Stokes, in *A View of the Constitution of the British Colonies* . . . devoted a section to slavery, particularly in the West Indies. He claimed that white could work where Negroes worked, and he supported his statement with a reference to many poor whites in Carolina and Georgia who raised grain without slave assistance.[101]

The time seemed ripe in the 1780's for a popular attack, and so the Quakers determined on a campaign of public education in th spirit of modern propagandists. James Pemberton wrote to Phillips the bookseller, that the Pennsylvania Quakers had found it advan tageous to issue publications frequently on the slave question: "Th like means will I expect be useful in your kingdom." [102] Tracts and newspapers were pressed into service; a petition to Parliamen

[98] Hoare, I, 121–123, 143, 146, 149.

[99] *Letters to and from Philadelphia,* I, Aug. 15, 1782; July 17, 1783; Dec. 1783; Aug. 19, 1784.

[100] *Eur. Mag. and Lond. Rev.,* V (1784), 448; *Gentleman's Magazine,* LI (1784), 415.

[101] (London, 1783), 415.

[102] Ms. Port., 6 (152), July 22, 1783; Yorkshire Quarterly Meeting, Friend House, London.

:alled for the abolition of the trade. Twelve thousand copies were)rinted of *The Case of our Fellow-creatures, the oppressed Africans, espectfully recommended to the serious consideration of the Legisature of Great Britain, by the people called Quakers.* James Philips, who did most of the printing for the Quakers, listed seventeen itles of antislavery publications, "lately published" by him; M. Gurney, another Quaker bookseller, also published many of these racts.[103]

Benjamin Rush was pleased to learn that English Dissenters of all lenominations had joined with the Quakers in petitioning Parlianent to end the slave trade. "We perceive already the good effects of the abolition of negro slavery in Pennsylvania," he told Price. 'The slaves who have been emancipated among us, are in general nore industrious and orderly than the lowest class of white peo)le." [104] English Friends circulated the work of Benezet on the conlition of Negro slaves in the British colonies.[105] They reported to Philadelphia that various essays were appearing on the subject in England, and that increased public attention was focused on it, but orrowfully they added, "Deep rooted ideas of interest however misaken, still silence the call of humanity on many minds." [106]

In 1786, Clarkson, who was to gain great fame in this movement,)ublished *Is it lawful to make men slaves against their will?* The next year Wilberforce announced himself the champion of the :ause in Parliament, and the Negroes' case was further strengthened)y the formation of a Society for the Abolition of the Slave Trade, with Granville Sharp as president. Richard Price informed Frankin of the organization of the London Society whose papers he had earlier forwarded. At the same time he acknowledged his election o the Pennsylvania Abolition Society, of which Sharp was also a corresponding member.[107] Englishmen requested copies of the contitution of the Pennsylvania Society and called on their native land

---

[103] See list at end of James Ramsay, *Objections to the Abolition of the Slave Trade, with Answers* (2nd ed., London, 1788).

[104] *American Museum,* I (Oct. 15, 1785), 125–126.

[105] *Letters to and from Philadelphia,* I, Nov. 3, 1786.

[106] *Ibid.,* Dec. 2, 1785.

[107] *Calendar of Franklin Papers,* III, 364, Jan. 10, 1788; Sparks, *Franklin, Works,* X, 320, Price to Franklin, Sept. 26, 1787.

to imitate the North Americans, her late enemies, in the extirpation of slavery. Thomas Percival of Manchester wrote to his friend Franklin: "It will afford you much satisfaction that the people of Great Britain are now awakened by the example of America to a just sense of the iniquity and cruelty of the Slave Trade." He hoped that passage of the bill then before Parliament would hurry along abolition of the trade. Sharp was glad to hear that slavery had been abolished in the northern states and he counseled non-co-operation in returning fugitive slaves to the South.[108]

The Pennsylvania Abolition Society funneled information from Europe to other American communities which it fired with its own fervor. Dr. Lettsom, who was in frequent correspondence with Americans, was the center in his own country of many humanitarian movements, and writers in various parts of England informed him of the progress of antislavery activity.[109] It was suggested that committees of correspondence, patterned on those formed by the colonials in the American Revolution, be organized to bring pressure on Parliament by an aroused public opinion; all the abolitionist agencies were to be joined together in a vast network.

Granville Sharp was in correspondence with the New York Anti-Slavery Society, of which John Jay was president; the latter was informed that the English group had been in communication with French reformers. Sharp thought Jay could assist in extending the "sphere of action" to include France. At the same time he sent to New York the recent tracts against slavery and added that petitions from various towns and religious bodies had been sent to Parliament.[110]

It was believed that a universal abolition of the slave trade might be secured by treaty among interested powers, including France, for she, too, was the center of lively reform agitation. The American Quakers, in fact, gave renewed power to an antislavery sentiment that had been slowly gaining strength in France. Emancipation of slaves by Quakers in Pennsylvania stimulated the French to a dis-

---

[108] Percival to Franklin, June 25, 1788, Amer. Phil. Soc.; Sharp to Rush, Oct. 10, 1785, Ridgway Library.

[109] Pettigrew, II, 238, 320, 370, 432.

[110] H. P. Johnston, *John Jay, Correspondence and Public Papers* (New York, 1890–1893), III, 329, May 1, 1788.

cussion of solutions of this problem among themselves.[111] The Quakers were praised for the liberation of their slaves, and French newspapers pointed to them as an example worthy of imitation. Raynal's *Histoire des deux Indes* was very critical of the slave system; Condorcet's *Réflexions sur l'esclavage des nègres* revealed his deep sympathy for the slaves. These works indeed, were the most influential in molding public opinion on this issue. A postscript to Condorcet's work had a table of antislavery legislation in the American states.

In a letter to the Abbé Raynal, Benezet called for a united attack on slavery "so contrary to humanity, reason and religion." [112] Jefferson's remarks in favor of freedom for the Negro slaves drew French attention to his *Notes on Virginia.* In 1788 Les Amis des Noirs was organized with Condorcet and Lafayette as members; abolition was supported by Mirabeau and Brissot as well. Brissot de Warville was the soul of the society, wrote a member to Franklin, including at the same time copies of various discourses and letters and a list of members, also adding that a memoir was to be presented to the Estates General to examine the question of abolition.[113] Brissot wrote with enthusiasm to the group in Philadelphia that he was sure of the National Assembly's support in suppressing the slave trade.[114] Jay wrote Sharp that Brissot was in New York to set up a correspondence with the antislavery group "and to collect such information as may promote our common aims." Brissot, Lafayette, and Sharp were elected honorary members of the New York society; Brissot, it is clear, was the main link in the Anglo-American French antislavery movement. Members of Les Amis des Noirs were in correspondence with Dr. W. Thornton in America, who had plans for an independent Negro state in Africa, similar to the English Sierra Leone project.[115] Pitt hoped to get the important commercial powers to join in

[111] E. D. Seeber, *Anti-slavery Opinion in France during the second half of the Eighteenth Century* (Baltimore, 1937), 84, 116, and *passim.*

[112] Vaux, *Memoirs of Benezet,* 42, July 16, 1781.

[113] F. Monaghan, "Anti-slavery Papers of John Jay," *Journal of Negro History,* XVII (1932), 481–496; *Calendar of Franklin Papers,* III, 387, April 17, 1789.

[114] *Penn. Abolition Soc., Comm. of Corr. Letter Book 1789–1794,* Jan. 20, 1790, Hist. Soc. Penn.

[115] Johnston, III, 344, 357, June, 1788, Sept. 1, 1788.

the abandonment of the slave trade; England wanted co-operative action lest other powers inherit the lucrative commerce she contemplated dropping. Clarkson himself went to France to work with the reform group there, but although his efforts were unsuccessful the French Revolution, which came at this time, swept into the discard, along with many other things, the trade and slavery itself.[116]

Friends of the Negro marshaled evidence to controvert the argument that he was an inferior being. Anthony Benezet furnished the English abolitionists with this type of material, and sympathetic magazines printed similar contributions. William Dillwyn, American-born pupil of Benezet, formed a little group in London which was a center for propaganda. His American experience enabled him to refute the objections of slave-trade protagonists, and his knowledge was of use to Clarkson in the latter's own work.[117] American Friends wrote to English coreligionists about the school for Negroes in Philadelphia, where proofs were given by the colored students of their capacity to learn; the same letter brought the proud declaration, "the members of our Society in these parts are now mainly clear of holding any of these people in bondage." A free school for Negroes was opened in Providence, Rhode Island, and those enrolled were reported as proficient as the whites. "[This] may be reckon'd, among the numerous Evidences of their being Men capable of Every Improvement with ourselves where they [are] under the Same Advantages," wrote Moses Brown to James Phillips.[118] Years earlier the *Gentleman's Magazine* had extracted a section from Dr. Beattie's *Essay on Truth* which defended the intelligence of primitive races and pointed out that Negro slaves had become excellent craftsmen and musicians.[119] A volume of *Letters on Slavery,* published in London quoted the testimony of American authorities on the proficiency of the Negro in various capacities.[120]

---

116 Pettigrew, II, 236, 497, 516, 520; F. J. Klingberg, *The Anti-Slavery Movement in England* (New Haven, 1926), 59–99.

117 Clarkson, 131–141.

118 *Letters to and from Philadelphia,* I, Jan. 20 and 21, 1780; Mss. Port. 23 (44), March 5, 1791, Friends House, London.

119 *Gentleman's Magazine,* XLI (1771), 595.

120 William Dickson, *Letters on Slavery* (London, 1789), 40 note, quoting Franklin's *Thoughts on Peopling of Countries.*

The Bee, in Edinburgh, printed a lengthy account of an American Negro, Benjamin Banneker, whose almanac gained wide fame. The writer in the Scotch press thought this "a fresh proof that the powers of the mind are disconnected with the colour of the skin." Jefferson wrote to Banneker that he had sent a copy of the almanac to Condorcet, because he considered it "as a document to which your whole colour had a right, for their justification against the doubts which have been entertained of them." [121]

Ethnological studies, especially by Americans, were levied upon to refute the argument that there were different species of man. Physical differences, it was maintained, were largely explainable by variations in climate. A treatise by Professor Samuel S. Smith of Princeton on the causes of the variety of complexion and figure in the human species said that Negroes (and whites too) had undergone physical changes since their transplantation across the sea. Negro customs of dress, marriage, and religion were compared with those of western European society and found not inferior. "Where is the difference between the Pagan Negro who worships an evil Spirit, and uses a few ceremonies at a Funeral; and the superstitious Christian who worships God from a fear of the Devil, and connects his future Happiness with a Sacrament before, and a Funeral right after, his Death?" [122]

London Quakers were anxious to convince their fellow countrymen that manumission was compatible even with the temporal interest of communities. They felt that American brethren could supply them with the necessary evidence on this point to defeat the opposition even on what seemed its strongest ground. Benezet argued that the abolition of slavery would permit the British to trade freely with Africa, whose raw materials could be exchanged for English manufactures. The English abolitionists thereafter adopted this argument as their own.[123]

Interest in the slavery question was stimulated by special articles

[121] *The Bee,* XIII (1793), 291–293, 331–334; Jefferson, *Writings,* VIII, 242, Aug. 30, 1791.

[122] Dickson, 71–72, 82; *A Vindication of the Address . . . on the Slavery of the Negroes in America.* By a Pennsylvanian (Philadelphia, 1773), 30–31.

[123] *Letters to and from Philadelphia,* I, Dec. 2, 1785, Nov. 3, 1786; Benezet, *Some Historical Account of Guinea . . .* (London, 1788), 63.

and references in periodicals and books which had a general appeal The *Gentleman's Magazine* devoted some of its space sympathet ically to antislavery activities.[124] Cowper's poetry against slavery wa a weapon in this fight, and its influence was greatly widened wher Lindley Murray included it in his very popular texts for schools The *European Magazine* contained prose and poetry in oppositio to slavery.[125] The *Scots Magazine* extracted "Some Account of th State of Negroes in South Carolina" from Crèvecoeur, which gav the editor an opportunity to indicate his sympathy for the slaves whose condition, he declared, called "loudly for redress," not onl in America but also in the British West Indies.

Thus the leading magazines in England and Scotland, by th many items they printed, indicated the progress of the antislaver movement. Once it was the prohibition of slave imports into Vir ginia, then it was a memorial of the Pennsylvania Abolitionist So ciety to Congress, and later it was news of the Edinburgh Society which, influenced by Clarkson's writings, believed in immediat abolition. A reviewer in the *Gentleman's Magazine* of Clarkson' *Essay on the Slavery and Commerce of the Human Species* men tioned the importance of Woolman, Benezet, and the Quakers gen erally in the effort to abolish slavery.[126] Priestley told his Birming ham congregation of American state action on the slavery issue, and recognizing Quaker priority in this campaign, he said it would b an honor "to this country . . . if the example should be followe here."[127] The report of the committee of the Pennsylvania Assem bly was printed as a model for Parliament, lest a loosely worded ac defeat the purpose of benevolence and "encourage evasion, perjur and all kinds of roguery."

The author of *The American Oracle,* published in London, wa very bitter in his judgment of the slave trade. Why did not othe

---

[124] *Gentleman's Magazine,* LIII (1783), 534; LIV (1784), 121; LV (1785), 67 LVIII (1788), 211, 212, 311, 545.

[125] *Eur. Mag. and Lond. Rev.,* V (1784), 455; VI (1784), 325; X (1787), 133 XIII (1789), 98.

[126] *Scots Magazine,* XLIV (1783), 573–575; XLIX (1788), 43, LII (1791 616; *Gentleman's Magazine,* LVI (1786), 590–591.

[127] J. Priestley, *A Sermon on . . . the Slave Trade . . .* (Birmingham, 1788 30–31.

countries, he asked, follow the legislatures in some of the states which had liberated their enslaved Negroes? [128] In the same year the *Baptist Annual Register* reported that Robert Carter of Virginia had emancipated his 442 slaves. "If this be true, vote him a triumph, crown him with laurels," the editor exclaimed. To the first volume of Tilloch's *The Philosophical Magazine,* Dr. Rush contributed an account of the sugar maple in the United States, the product of which, he contended, was superior to cane sugar, and he added that its use would obviate the need for slaves in the West Indies. The editor appended a footnote to the article in which he called attention especially to the information on the slave trade. Franklin's essay *On the Slave Trade* was extracted for the benefit of the readers of the *European Magazine.*[129]

The American Geography of Jedidiah Morse, which was reprinted in London and was consulted by Europeans for many years as the standard authority on America, was opposed to slavery. In the English edition of 1792, the belief was stated that "all slaves in the United States will in time be emancipated." William Guthrie's *Geographical, Historical and Commercial Grammar,* a very popular work, which in later editions owed much to Morse for its material on America, was very critical of Virginia, whose "indolence and luxury" were called the "fruit of African slavery." [130] Josiah Wedgwood, the maker of the famous Wedgwood ware, sent to the Pennsylvania Abolitionist Society a few cameos whose subject was the abolition of slavery.[131]

The younger generation was also inoculated with the antislavery virus. The Friends in London went directly to the schools so that "just notions of Slavery might be instilled into the tender minds of Youth." [132] Lindley Murray, whose books were widely used, indoctrinated students at an early age. In *The Universal Gazeteer,* John Walker, a former Quaker schoolmaster, lashed out at "the Mer-

[128] Stearns, *The American Oracle,* 252.

[129] *Baptist Annual Register,* I (1791), 220; *The Philosophical Magazine,* I (1798), 182–191; *Eur. Mag. and Lond. Rev.,* XXIV (1794), 45–48.

[130] Edinburgh, 1798, 889.

[131] *Calendar of Franklin Papers,* III, 369, Feb. 29, 1788; 372, May 2, 1788.

[132] *Letters to and from Philadelphia,* I, Dec. 2, 1785; Woodson, "Anthony Benezet," *Journal of Negro History,* II (1917), 37.

chants of Liverpool who have disgraced themselves . . . by their iniquitous exertions in the *man trade;* and they seemed to wish the incorrigible butchers, to perpetuate their infamy by giving African names to the new and improved parts of their town." [133] Jefferson had urged Richard Price to address a tract to the students of William and Mary College whose influence, he felt, would be "perhaps decisive" in the future solution of the slave question.[134]

English Friends were writing optimistically to America that people of all classes were now interested in the movement and that petitions against the slave trade were being sent to Parliament from many parts of the country.[135] Ministers of various denominations found slavery a live subject for their sermons, in which they acknowledged indebtedness to the Quakers.[136]

In the last few years of the century reports from London were less enthusiastic, but Quakers did take steps to withdraw political support from any Parliamentary candidate friendly to the slave trade.[137] American Friends continued to write to individual English correspondents of progress in Congress and of attempts to strengthen antislavery sentiment in regions outside Pennsylvania.[138] In a restrained mood Ezra Stiles wrote in his diary that little would be done, yet public discussions of the subject in Congress, in Parliament, in France, and in other European countries might "ripen such a general Conviction as may prepare for future Abolition." [139] In a tone of patient resignation the Pennsylvania Abolition Society wrote to the London group that only gradual progress could be hoped for. "Long habits & Strong Interests are not to be overcome in an Instant, but we nevertheless believe that conviction will spread

---

[133] John Walker, *The Universal Gazeteer* (London, 1795), art., "Liverpool."

[134] Jefferson, *Writings,* V, 57, Aug. 7, 1785.

[135] *Letters to and from Philadelphia,* I, Feb. 29, 1788.

[136] Samuel Bradburn, *An Address to . . . Methodists concerning the Wickedness of Encouraging Slavery* (4th ed., London, 1792); W. Mason, *An Occasional Discourse preached in the Cathedral of St. Peter in York . . . on the . . . Slave-Trade* (1788).

[137] *Letters to and from Philadelphia,* I, July 30, 1790.

[138] Gibson Mss., IV, 73, Jos. Gilpin to James Philips, Nov. 26, 1792; II, 15, Dec. 31, 1799.

[139] Stiles, *Diary,* III, 381, Feb. 17, 1790.

from man to man until a large majority of the People of America will think it safe as well as just to let the oppressed go free." [140]

The exchanges between Americans and Europeans always recognized the advantage of mutual aid. Moses Brown told James Phillips that American abolition societies had prepared addresses to the coming Congress, in 1791, but before then, he added, "We hope to hear the British Parliament has set the Example." [141] That example was not to be set by the British Parliament, despite some show of promise the next year, because of hostility from the West Indies, and because the radical tendencies of the French Revolution frightened conservatives into opposition against all reform movements.

William Dillwyn, a collaborator of Clarkson in this campaign, watched the votes in Parliament closely, and he thought that the bill asking for abolition of the slave trade would have stood a better chance had it provided for gradual rather than immediate elimination. The West Indian merchants, he said, had won against the wishes of the rest of Britain.[142] The British merchants and planters opposed abolition, fearing it would give their rivals in French Santo Domingo a superior competitive position. Not until the early years of the nineteenth century, after the French had lost their colony and when the British planters suffered from the effects of overproduction, could a prohibitory law by Parliament against the slave trade be enacted.[143] A request came from the London reformers to controvert an argument advanced in England that should she abolish the slave trade America would step in and take it over.[144] But this was a dark age for social reform, and the desertion of the slave cause by Parliament "in contradiction to their resolution in 1792" saddened many Friends in Philadelphia.[145] Almost a whole generation of reformers was to be saddened in the following years, for theirs was the way of humiliation with triumph long deferred.

---

[140] *Penn. Abolition Soc., Comm. of Corr. Letter Book 1789–1794,* Feb. 28, 1790.

[141] Mss. Port., 23 (44), March 5, 1791, Friends House, London.

[142] Dillwyn to his daughter, April 30, 1791, April 4, 1792, Ridgway Library.

[143] Williams, 148–149.

[144] *Penn. Abolition Soc., Comm. of Corr. Letter Book 1794–1809,* July 10, 1794.

[145] *Letters to and from Philadelphia,* II, March 17, 1796.

Americans would have termed premature the enthusiastic English judgment that their young government had "settled into a system of mercy" in its penal legislation. In this, as in so many other respects, hopeful Europeans saw what they wished to see in the American states. It is true they did see there some substance whose greatly enlarged shadow blotted out for them the glaring faults that still existed in American society, but such vision has always been vouchsafed the pessimist at home who looks optimistically abroad. The uncertain human spirit seeks support wherever it thinks it may find buoyancy, and Americans and Europeans found it in each other in the generation after the War for Independence.

CHAPTER VII

Scientific Relations between Europe and America

THE American colonies were settled in an age which witnessed a tremendous growth of interest in science. The utilitarian significance of science was immediately appreciated by the many who were animated by practical considerations. Apart from its meaning for the advancement of business enterprise, however, science had numerous supporters who looked to it for guidance in unearthing the secrets of the universe. It has been largely a joint enterprise from the seventeenth century on, and to the layman as much as to the academician in these early years is due the accumulation of masses of scientific and near-scientific data. To mention one instance, plans were made for English and American groups to make a co-operative study of vegetable colors and in general to aid each other in the study of natural history.[1] In a retrospect of the eighteenth century, a writer in a popular magazine of the time observed that an international scientific correspondence prevailed and that in the promotion of utilitarian devices "the world is but as one Family. . . . The scientific theorist and the practical labourer have shaken hands and minted into one common stock the result of their labours." [2]

Scientists began writing in the vernacular, thus reaching a larger audience. Europeans and Americans strongly urged the abandonment of Latin, and the number of books on natural history written in the classic tongue declined rapidly in the eighteenth century. In

[1] Smith, *Corr. of Linnaeus,* I, 385, Dr. A. Garden to Charles Whitworth, April 27, 1757.

[2] *Gentleman's Magazine,* LXX (1800), 1273–1274.

writing for the populace care was taken to avoid technical language and, when necessary, authors took pains to define even simple terms. One of the first great popular successes was Buffon's *Histoire naturelle* which sold over twenty thousand copies and was to be found scattered over Europe and America.[3] Books on natural history sold better than any others in England, so Linnaeus was informed.[4] In America the more popular channels of scientific communications were the newspapers and the almanacs, the latter reaching an annual circulation of many thousands.[5] Magazines extracted articles from the *Philosophical Transactions* of the Royal Society, which thus reached a vastly larger group. The Newbery publishing house, famous for its children's books, saw to it that even very young readers were informed on motion, water, fire, vision, etc. There must have been a good demand for these publications, for some of them ran into several editions.[6] In one work published for the use of school children the latter were advised to "make it a rule to see for [themselves]." [7]

Scientific lectures were widely attended in America and Europe, with women as well as men in the audience. Dr. Henry Moyes was in America in the 1780's, and it was reported from Philadelphia that "people of every description, men and women, flock to the lectures. They are held at the University three evenings a week." [8]

Americans were to be found on the rolls of many European societies that welcomed overseas contributions to the advancement of science. Europeans, on the other hand, considered it an honor to be elected to membership in the American Philosophical Society. Count Rumford, an exile from his native America after the Revolution, established medal awards by the Royal Society and the Amer-

---

[3] D. Mornet, *Les Sciences de la Nature en France au XVIIIe Siècle* (Paris, 1911), 2–4, pt. III, chap. i.

[4] Smith, *Corr. of Linnaeus,* I, 18, April 16, 1747.

[5] See C. E. Jorgenson, *New England Quarterly,* VIII (1935), 555–561; on almanacs in Europe, see P. Smith, II, 391.

[6] Welsh, 302.

[7] *Botanical Dialogues between Hortensia and her Four Children . . . for The Use of Schools.* By a Lady (London, 1797), with a commendatory letter by Erasmus Darwin, 229.

[8] Darlington, 535.

ican Academy of Arts and Sciences for leading contributions in heat and light. He was, incidentally, the first winner of his own award in England.[9]

War was held to be no bar to an exchange of scientific communications between citizens of opposing countries. Joseph Willard, writing from Harvard during the Revolutionary War to the secretary of the Royal Society, maintained that "political disputes should not prevent communications in matters of mere science"; he did not see how any one could "be injured by such an intercourse." [10] The distinguished naturalist, Sir Joseph Banks, told Franklin he was sure that the American was "incapable of being led astray by the influence of political opinions. I respect you as a Philosopher & solicit the continuance of your friendship." [11] During the earlier war between the French and English, naturalists in both countries had agreed to return specimens that had been captured by enemy warships.[12] Near the end of the century the bitter conflict with the government of the French Directory did not prevent an English captain from extending courtesies to a scientist who was returning from America with a vast collection of plants, and who was permitted to run the blockade.[13]

In an earlier day a "virtuoso" had been described as one who "trafficks to all places" with correspondents in every part of the world. "He values a Camelion, or Salamander's Egg, above all the Sugars and Spices of the West and East-Indies," and he seeks fossil shells and teeth in mines and quarries. Interested in these things for their own sake, the virtuoso is a "man for whom learning is the means to dispose of wealth and leisure in the happiest fashion—and with the comforting assurance that he may also be serving the desiderants of philosophy, history, or art." The first museum of natural history in London, the model for all others in England,

[9] Ellis, *Memoir of Sir Benjamin Thompson, Count Rumford,* 241, 246, 250–258.

[10] *Phil. Trans.,* LXXI, Feb. 16, 1781; see also Franklin to Alexander Small, July 22, 1780, in Smyth, *Franklin, Writings,* VIII, 120.

[11] Mss. in Amer. Phil. Soc.

[12] Smith, *Corr. of Linnaeus,* I, 85, Ellis to Linnaeus, May 31, 1757.

[13] *Gentleman's Magazine,* LXVIII (1798), 716.

including the later British Museum, was born out of Buckingham's concern with the accumulation of specimens from America and the East Indies. John Tradescant and his son of like name were largely responsible for the creation and enlargement of this first collection, to which Virginia made many contributions.[14]

Two significant personalities, Charles Morton and Samuel Lee, graduates of Oxford, were important figures in cultivating the scientific spirit in New England at the close of the seventeenth century. Lee's popular treatises, *Joy of Faith* (Boston, 1687) and *Day of Judgement* (Boston, 1692), were more than the devotional manuals they seemed to be. They contained news of the latest scientific discoveries, which were celebrated as proving the greater glory of God. A close, but cautious, student of Lee says he may have had some influence among his contemporaries, but it is probably more accurate to say that "the stage of thought which appears in his books also appears in New England at approximately the time of his arrival." [15] Morton, as the author of a manuscript textbook of science, *Compendium physicae* (also called *Natural Philosophy*), which was superior to manuals then available to English readers, exerted a deep influence on New England students. His book, says the historian of Harvard, "was the first to inculcate among [its] students that observing and curious attitude toward the physical world which, in modern times marks the educated man." Lee and Morton are among the little-known agents through whom America came into contact with the scientific ideas of the seventeenth century.[16]

The limited number of scientists in the seventeenth century were to be multiplied in the next, and systematic, co-ordinated scientific activity in several fields may be noted. For some time, though, most sciences were in the collecting stage of their history, accumulating data for ultimate classification. Naturally it was the novel specimen which was most eagerly sought. The contributions of American members, now a larger group, to the Royal Society's *Transactions* were continued, and among the most active members in the colonies

---

[14] W. E. Houghton, Jr., "The English Virtuoso in the Seventeenth Century," *Journal of the History of Ideas,* III (1942), 69.

[15] T. Hornberger, "Samuel Lee 1625–1691 . . ." *Osiris,* I (1936), 351.

[16] Morison, *The Puritan Pronaos,* 258–259; Morison, *Harvard in the Seventeenth Century,* I, 249.

was Cotton Mather.[17] He was said to have had at one time fifty correspondents overseas. Individuals of equal or lesser fame sent their communications abroad, and the publications of several European societies paid tribute to American activity.

This energy was mainly expended in the field of natural science, with special emphasis on botany. It is no mere coincidence that great progress should have been made in botany when a new floral world was revealed to the European investigator. The thousands of specimens, hitherto unaccounted for, stimulated students to remarkable efforts. One of the earliest books on North American plants appeared in 1635—*A History of Canadian Plants,* by J. P. Cornut, describing those which had been brought back to Europe. Not long after, John Josselyn, the traveler in New England, described its native plants and other "rarities." Josselyn included a list of plants introduced by the English, and like other observers he noted that while some transplanted products fared worse in America, the greater number were "bigger and better" in the colonies.[18] The observations and collections of John Banister of Virginia, engaged there as a missionary in 1680, were catalogued in the *History of Plants* by John Ray, eight years later.

William Vernon of Cambridge University and Dr. David Kreig, contemporaries of Banister, made a trip to Maryland for botanical specimens, which eventually came into the possession of Hans Sloane. Vernon looked forward on his return to a weekly discussion of the new specimens with Sloane and some other cronies.[19] The Sloane Herbarium was also enriched by William Houstoun, who gathered plants in the West Indies and Mexico. Mark Catesby stayed in the colonies for a number of years under the patronage of several noted botanists. He wrote frequently to his patrons, keeping them informed of his travels in "one of the Sweetest Countrys I ever saw"

---

[17] G. L. Kittredge, *Amer. Antiq. Soc., Proc.,* n.s. XXVI (1916), 18–58, 23; Kittredge, *Col. Soc. Mass., Publ.,* XIV (1911–1913), 81–114; Hornberger, *American Literature,* VI (1934–1935), 413–420; R. P. Stearns, "Colonial Fellows of the Royal Society of London, 1661–1788," *William and Mary Quart.,* Ser. 3, III (1946), 208–269.

[18] John Josselyn, *New Englands Rarities Discovered* (London, 1672), 85, 90; F. Mood, *Col. Soc. Mass., Publ.,* XXVIII (1930–1933), 24 ff.

[19] Brit. Mus., Sloane Mss., 4037, July 24, 1698.

(South Carolina), and sending them large quantities of plants an seeds.[20] On his return, in 1726, Catesby began work on his massiv publication, celebrated by an eighteenth-century historian as "th most splendid of its kind that England has ever produced." [21]

In the work of the leading botanists of this period may be trace the New World contributions. To professional botanists the perio from 1694 to 1735 is known as the "Tournefortian Period," after th author of one of the most important books in botany. Tournefort' debt to investigators in North America was large; the obligation o Linnaeus, who gave *his* name to the next period in botanical sci ence, was far greater.[22]

Men on both sides of the ocean were alive to the need for sub sidized expeditions to America. William Byrd II, hinting broadly t Sir Hans Sloane to advance such support, said a man could not "d a greater good to mankind, than to bestow a handsome stipen yearly upon a well qualifyed Naturallist to come and make Dis coverys in these Parts of the World." [23]

At a meeting of the Royal Swedish Academy of Sciences, Lin naeus suggested that someone be sent to North America to collec seeds of plants which would "improve the Swedish husbandry, gar dening, manufactures, arts and sciences." Peter Kalm, who wa chosen for the task, not only published an interesting work on hi travels in the American colonies, but he raised many of the seeds h had collected in his private garden, sending others to be cultivate in the Botanical Garden at Upsala. Linnaeus, in his *Species o Plants,* carefully noted the findings of Kalm. The great naturalis further enriched his knowledge by visiting the collections of Si Hans Sloane and Mark Catesby, gathered for the most part in Nort America.[24] In all, Linnaeus described some two thousand plants an

---

[20] Royal Soc. Library, Sherard letters, II, 163–185, Catesby to Sherard, May 5 1722–January 10, 1724–1725.

[21] Richard Pultney, *Historical and Biographical Sketches of the Progress o Botany in England* (London, 1790), II, chap. xliv, 55–57. Other American con tributions are mentioned in II, 276–278.

[22] P. A. Rydberg, *N.Y. Botanical Garden Contribs.,* IV, no. 100 (1907).

[23] April 10, 1741, *William and Mary Quart.,* ser. 2, I (1921), 186–200.

[24] Catesby correspondence in Sherard letters in Royal Society Library Mss.

ıundreds of animals from North America in his *Species of Plants* .nd *System of Nature*.[25]

After visiting a garden in Amsterdam, Linnaeus wrote to a friend: We are all devoted to the love of exotic plants, especially those rom America." [26] The heavy indebtedness of Linnaeus' *System of Vature* (in its last edition) to Dr. Alexander Garden, of South Caroina, was noted by other scientists. "No name occurs there more requently," said one authority.[27] Professor Joseph C. Mutis of Bogotá familiarized Linnaeus with South American botany; Mutis ınd his pupils produced a volume on Peruvian flora. From every part of the world, wrote Collinson to Linnaeus, new and rare discoveries are brought to "your door, . . . your agents bring you ribute from every quarter." [28]

Expeditions came to America from Vienna and from Italy, but he most important was probably that of André Michaux, sent over by the French government in 1785. Michaux traveled all over the country and sent back to France more than sixty thousand living woody plants and many boxes of seeds. His own discoveries included some three hundred species of flowering plants. Part of his mission n America was to study trees for possible use in French naval construction. His son, François André, then a youngster of fifteen, started a long, fruitful, scientific career with this expedition. His botanical interests centered in America, which he visited on three occasions, and his writings are of major importance in the literature of her natural history. His relations with American scientists were close, and from the fund he gave to the American Philosophical

---

II, May 5, 1722, Dec. 9, 1722; see elaborate publication by Catesby, *The Natural History of Carolina, Florida and the Bahama Islands* (2 vols., London, 1731–1743); Edward Edwards, *Lives of the Founders of the British Museum* (London, 1870), section on Sir Hans Sloane.

[25] Rydberg, *loc. cit.;* J. A. Allen, *Annals of the New York Academy of Sciences* XVIII (1908), 9–19.

[26] Smith, *Corr. of Linnaeus,* II, 242, to Albert Haller, May 1, 1737; see also Rydberg, *Science,* XXVI (1907), 66 ff.

[27] *Transactions of the Linnaean Society,* I (1791), introductory discourse by J. E. Smith; also Smith, *Corr. of Linnaeus,* I, 309, Garden to Linnaeus, June 2, 1763. Garden was elected to the Royal Society at Upsala.

[28] Smith, *Corr. of Linnaeus,* I, 34, April 10, 1755.

Society (of which he was a member) a gracious memorial of oak was established in Philadelphia.[29]

Michaux worked in friendly rivalry with a British naturalist John Fraser, who was in South Carolina seeking plants and grasses useful to his homeland. Fraser returned home with thirty thousand dried specimens of plants, as well as some living plants, and a new grass for meadowland or pasture. He also wrote a book in which he acknowledged the important assistance given him by Thomas Walter, a local resident. Walter was without books or learned collections of natural history, said Fraser, but he "made his descriptions with an accuracy that is allowed to be by no means inferior to the most eminent botanists in Europe." [30] Fraser sent seeds of a plant to Jefferson, hoping America would adopt it; he called it Jefferson's Pine Apple Apricot. Fraser also sent over the best cucumber seed in England.[31] It is worth noting that a study of foreign plants stimulated a closer examination of native products in Europe.[32]

While Linnaeus and other European students benefited directly by investigations of fellow countrymen traveling abroad, they also felt obligated to Americans with whom they corresponded. No American was held in higher esteem than the self-taught Quaker, John Bartram. He was wholly devoted to his researches, writing simply, "I love Natural History dearly." To an English correspondent he wrote, "I am often exposed to solitary and difficult travelling beyond our inhabitants, and often under dangerous circumstances, in passing over rivers climbing over mountains and precipices, amongst the rattlesnakes, and often obliged to follow the track, or path of wild beasts, for my guide through the desolate and gloomy thickets." [33] Collinson, a merchant trading with America, introduced Bartram to John Custis in Virginia with the light-hearted warning that he was "a down right plain country man—he may be

[29] R. H. True, "F. A. Michaux, the Botanist and Explorer," *Amer. Phil. Soc., Proc.*, LXXVIII (1937–1938), 313 ff.

[30] John Fraser, *A Short History of the Agrostis Cornucopiae: or the new American Grass* . . . (London, 1789), 3–5.

[31] April 13, July 21, 1789, Coolidge Coll., Mass. Hist. Soc.

[32] Cf. *Mémoires de l'Académie Royale des Sciences* (Paris, 1701), 209.

[33] Darlington, 176, Bartram to Collinson, April 23, 1746; 324, May 26, 1742; see also letter of Lewis Morris to Collinson, *N.J. Hist. Soc., Colls.*, IV (1852), 146, May 24, 1742.

. Quaker too into the Bargain . . . you'l not look att the man but ıis mind for my sake." Bartram thought that Custis' garden was the ›est he had seen, next to John Clayton's.[34]

All the first-rate botanists in Europe were acquainted directly or ndirectly with Bartram's work. In a letter to Collinson Bartram vrote: "To my friends Doctor Dillenius and M(ark) Catesby, I sent ny observations on such things as will be proper materials to assist hem in composing their fine histories, for which they promised me ›ne of their books." Dr. J. J. Dillenius, professor of botany at Ox- ord, deferred printing his *History of Mosses* until he could see what 3artram, Clayton, and John Mitchell might send from America.[35] ohn Frederick Gronovius of Leyden, then printing a new edition ›f one of his works, wrote to Bartram: "You shall find (therein) the ıames of all the minerals and fossils you ever had sent to me, with ın encomium and thanks of all the benefits You have bestowed ıpon me." [36] Bartram urged Gronovius to write in English—"I can nake but a poor hand of Latin." [37]

Philip Miller, superintendent of the Chelsea Garden, whose *Dic- ionary of Gardening* was the best-known work of its kind and a nodel for the first American book on the subject, was another who :nriched his collections because of Bartram's activity. The Garden ıt Chelsea displayed many of the specimens sent over by Bar- ram, who in turn received numerous contributions from Miller.[38] Through Collinson, Bartram was employed by a number of pa- rons on an annual basis to furnish them with seeds and plants. In ıis earlier years his financial position was so precarious that he once vrote with great relief to Collinson thanking him for the money ent him, "which came in the nick of time, when I wanted to pay he mortgage interest." [39] In the 1750's he was supplying flora to ome fifteen patrons, including the Prince of Wales, at a charge of ive guineas each. Of three hundred new American plants intro-

---

[34] Dec. 29, 1739, Jan. 21, 1739, Curwin papers, II, Amer. Antiq. Soc.

[35] See G. C. Druce, *The Dillenian Herbaria* . . . (Oxford, 1907), and J. J. Dillenius, *Historia Muscorum* (London, 1768), viii.

[36] Darlington, 358, July 2, 1750.

[37] Gibson Mss., IV, 21, Friends House, London.

[38] N. G. Brett-James, *The Life of Peter Collinson* (London, 1926), 108–109.

[39] Darlington, 122–123, 1739.

duced into England from 1734 to 1776 Collinson was responsibl for forty, most of which came from Bartram; of two hundred or sc credited to Philip Miller, many had likewise been sent over b Bartram. The latter, it may be mentioned in passing, was one of th first to produce hybrid plants, then called "mules." [40] Collinson ar ranged with Custis in Williamsburg for a continuous exchange o plants and seeds so that each could enlarge his collections. Collinson thought the climate of Virginia better than that of England fo plant life.[41]

Within less than half a century America, said Catesby, "has fur nished England with a greater variety of trees than has been procured from all the other parts of the world for more than a thou sand years past." [42] A London society that met in the 1720's t discuss new plants published a catalogue of trees imported int England; a majority of those recorded came from the American col onies.[43] A similar society was formed in Edinburgh to import Amer ican seeds (subscribers to pay two guineas each) and to draw up catalogue of American and Canadian plants and trees which coul flourish in Britain; a correspondence was also to be maintained wit Americans interested in botany.[44]

The work of others besides Bartram was gratefully remembere by European contemporaries. Cadwallader Colden's catalogue o plants found on his New York estate was published by Linnaeus in the transactions of the Academy of Sciences at Upsala. The pro ficiency of the New Yorker's daughter, Jane Colden, attracted atten tion abroad. Peter Collinson wrote Linnaeus that she was the onl woman he had heard of who was "scientifically skilful in the Lin naean system," and he recommended her example "to the ladies o every country." [45] Collinson forwarded to Peter Kalm in Sweden

---

[40] *Peter Collinson, Mss. Note Book,* British Museum Natural History; Ernes Earnest, *John and William Bartram* (Philadelphia, 1940), chap. iv and p. 38.

[41] Dec. 5, 1737, Jan. 25, 1738/39, Curwin papers, II, Amer. Antiq. Soc.

[42] M. Catesby, *Hortus Europae Americanus . . .* (London, 1767), preface.

[43] J. R. Butler, "America . . . a hunting ground for Eighteenth Centur Naturalists," *Bibliog. Soc. Amer., Papers,* XXXII (1938), 6–7.

[44] *Scots Magazine,* XXVI (1764), 83; XXVII (1765), 395.

[45] Darlington, 20; "Jane Colden," in *N.Y. Botanical Garden Contribs.,* IV no. 88 (1907); Smith, *Corr. of Linnaeus,* I, 45, April 30, 1758; W. Smallwood an M. Smallwood, *Natural History and the American Mind* (New York, 1941), 92

naterial on natural history that had been sent from America by the lder Colden.[46] The *Virginia Flora* published by Gronovius was based on observations made by Clayton; a later edition included the vork of Colden, Mitchell, and Kalm as well. John Mitchell of Virinia was credited with important discoveries, and his name was specially drawn to the attention of Linnaeus.[47] Mitchell, who was one of the ablest scientists in America, labored for years on a comprehensive natural and medical history of the colonies. It was lonely vork for Americans widely scattered along the seacoast and in the back country, wanting in books and in stimulating companionship. They eagerly sought out one another and craved the stimulation of the European botanical fellowship.[48]

Humphry Marshall, a younger cousin of John Bartram, was also n correspondence with Europeans; his book on American trees and hrubs received the stamp of scientific approval by translations for oreign students. John C. Lettsom was interested in forming a group o subsidize Marshall for a year to gather specimens from American voods and mountains. He told Franklin he was already sponsoring a European naturalist then traveling through America.[49] William Bartram, son of John, was a skilled naturalist who knew how to portray in words and colors the phenomena he met with in his expeditions to the southern colonies. Sponsored by the noted English physician Dr. John Fothergill, Bartram spent five years in these regions and sent collections and drawings to his English Maecenas. Noted botanists sought his correspondence. The Bartrams, father and son, made rich contributions to an American literary tradition of writing about nature with authority and distinction.

Marshall's *Arbustum Americanum* (1785) was the first strictly American botanical work written by a native American and printed n this country. It was republished in Germany, where foresters believed that the more rapidly growing American trees, if transplanted, might augment the dwindling supply of German timber.

---

[46] Colden to Collinson, June 15, 1751, Huntington Library.

[47] Smith, *Corr. of Linnaeus,* I, 9, Collinson to Linnaeus, January 18, 1743–1744; II, 442, Mitchell to Linnaeus, April 16, 1747; Smallwood, 123.

[48] Nichols, *Literary Anecdotes of the Eighteenth Century,* I, 483 note, Dr. A. Garden to Dr. J. Parsons, May 5, 1755.

[49] Sparks, *Franklin, Works,* X, 267, August 14, 1786.

There had been for some time a considerable demand for American plants in Germany. Friedrich A. J. Von Wangenheim published a work on American trees (1781) and their adaptability to Germany; he had served with the Hessian forces in the American Revolution.

Declining timber supplies in several western European countries prompted experimentation with American trees. Englishmen, for example, planted locust trees in large quantities for making ships and rail fences.[50] After returning from America an Italian nobleman, Luigi Castiglioni, published his travels and included observations on overseas plants with advice on their acclimatization. Wangenheim, a critical student of American woods, planted on his estate in Thuringia a section of forest land which he called "America." [51]

Interest in natural history was not restricted to the scientifically elect; it was a fad in which nearly all classes of society satisfied the desire to collect things. Collinson wrote to Bartram: "There is a [great] spirit and love of [gardening and planting] amongst the nobility and gentry, and the pleasure and profit that attends it, will render it a lasting delight." [52] Some of the nobles who could afford it, literally transplanted a bit of America to England. Collinson described the collection of Lord Petre, a patron of Bartram: "The trees and shrubs . . . are grown to great maturity. Last year Lord Petre planted out about ten thousand Americans . . . which make a very beautiful appearance. When I walk among [his nurseries] one cannot help thinking he is in North American thickets, there are such quantities." [53]

Collinson's own garden was internationally famous, and it pleased him to share its rarities with many botanists. His contagious enthusiasm awakened the love of gardening among many young men of means. In retrospect he once remarked, "I often stand with wonder and amazement when I view the inconceivable variety of flowers, shrubs and trees now in our gardens, and what there were forty years ago." [54] Dr. John Fothergill wrote to Linnaeus, "Our Collinson

---

[50] Young, *Annals of Agriculture,* VII (1787), 197; VIII (1787), 158, Pownall, "On the Acacia or Locust-Tree."

[51] *Penn. Germ. Soc., Proc.,* VII (1897), 28–29.

[52] Darlington, 183, April 24, 1751.

[53] Darlington, 144, Sept. 1, 1741.

[54] L. W. Dillwyn, *Hortus Collinsonianus* (Swansea, 1843), vii; N. G. Brett James, 106, 225.

ught me to love flowers, and who that shared his comradeship ould do other than cultivate plants?" Collinson learned much om Americans, but he also taught them, says Fothergill, urging iem to raise flax, hemp, grapes, etc.[55]

Bernard de Jussieu, professor of botany at the garden of the rench king, told Dr. Thomas Bond, an American visitor, that he iould feel at home among so many of his native plants, which had een brought from America by the professor himself.[56] The Sloane Ierbarium and the Herbarium of Joseph Banks (both of which ere incorporated in the British Museum) were enriched by plants ent over by Bartram, Catesby, Mitchell, John Clayton, and lesser otanical explorers.[57]

Books and articles were written to give instructions on the proper iethods for packing and sending plants from America, and in the 780's a magazine was established to display in natural colors the oreign specimens cultivated in England.[58] A French manual said nterest in natural history was so widespread and travelers so often ent specimens home that they needed instructions in gathering and acking them.[59] An English author, J. R. Forster, who felt that the vork of Gronovius made other compilations unnecessary, neverthe-ess wrote his own book, for he thought that English readers should earn about American plants in their native language.[60] B. S. Barton vrote to William Bartram from Edinburgh that American natural iistory was a particular favorite of European readers and that there-

---

[55] J. Fothergill, *Some Anecdotes of the late Peter Collinson* (London, 1785), 5–18.

[56] Darlington, 316, Feb. 20, 1739.

[57] E. Ray Lankester, ed., *The History of the Collections contained in the Vatural History Departments of the British Museum* (London, 1904), I, 81, 83, 40.

[58] J. C. Lettsom, *The Naturalist's and Traveller's Companion* (London, 1772; rd ed., 1799); Wm. Curtis, *The Botanical Magazine . . . in which . . . Foreign Plants . . . will be accurately represented in their natural Col-ours . . .* (London, 1787). I looked through ten volumes of Curtis' work, which ontains pictures of many American plants.

[59] *Mémoire Instructif sur la manière de rassembler . . . curiosités d'histoire iaturelle . . .* (Lyon, 1758).

[60] J. R. Forster, *Flora Americae Septentrionalis, or a Catalogue of the Plants of North America . . . in their Different Uses, and the Authors who have De-scribed and Figured them* (London, 1771).

fore Bartram's works would be assured of a popular reception i
published abroad.[61]

Botanical studies expressed aesthetic as well as utilitarian objec
tives. But husbandry was almost entirely a practical matter. Th
advances made in the seventeenth century, largely under Dutc
leadership, were as halting steps compared with the giant strides c
the next hundred years. The achievements of Bakewell, Towr
shend, and Jethro Tull helped revolutionize agriculture; societie
for the dissemination of their views were familiar institutions i
England and America. Improved breeds of livestock were an impor
tant British contribution to American agriculture. French influenc
on colonial American agriculture was marked, especially in estab
lishing culture of the grape. So successful in fact were immigran
Frenchmen in this enterprise that the homeland feared the rise o
America as a formidable rival.[62] Americans shared with Englishme
in the awards given for improvements in agriculture and the me
chanical arts by the London Society for the Encouragement of Arts
Manufactures and Commerce.[63] Postmasters in New York an
Charleston actively propagandized in behalf of the London so
ciety.[64]

Italian reformers also followed American proposals for promot
ing agriculture.[65] But Americans were as much debtors as they were
creditors to Europe for agricultural knowledge. While minister to
France, in 1787 Jefferson made a tour through southern France and
northern Italy, carefully observing agricultural conditions—the
various crops, prices of food, labor costs, etc. He even smuggled ou

---

[61] Feb. 19, 1788, Bartram Mss., Hist. Soc. Penn.

[62] R. C. Loehr, "The Influence of English Agriculture on American Agricul
ture 1775–1825," *Agricultural History,* XI (1937), 3–16; A. H. Hirsch, "Frencl
Influence on American Agriculture in the Colonial Period . . . ," *Agricultura
History,* IV (1930), 1–10.

[63] Wm. Bailey, *The Advancement of Arts, Manufactures, and Commerce, o
Descriptions of the useful machines and models contained in the repository o
the Society for the Encouragement of Arts, Manufactures and Commerce* . .
(London, 1772), I.

[64] *American Letter Book 1773–1783,* 24, Anthony Todd to Foxcroft and Fin
lay at New York, June 1, 1774; Mss. in G.P.O., London.

[65] *Opuscoli Scelti sulle scienze e sulle arti,* X (Milan, 1787), 321.

Piedmont rice for his friends in South Carolina. From his vast ore of knowledge, patiently acquired, he was constantly enriching ıe practice of agriculture.

Arthur Young, editor of the *Annals of Agriculture* and chief pre-ptor of the new agriculture, had for his schoolroom America as ell as the British Isles.[66] George Washington was an eager disciple; ıe notes he assembled from Young's publication and Tull's *Horse-oeing Husbandry* indicate his indebtedness. Young taught him oil conservation and sent to Washington English plows and various pes of seeds. In his last annual message as President, Washington ecommended the establishment of a board of agriculture to award remiums and assist generally in diffusing information on the latest nprovements. This proposal clearly followed the example of the nglish Board of Agriculture and revealed once more the influence f Young and Sir John Sinclair.[67] Sinclair, president of the English oard of Agriculture and correspondent of Washington and other istinguished Americans, had proposed such a plan to embrace all urope and the United States; his hope was that scientific communi-ations would be exchanged among the agricultural departments f every nation.[68] Rewards made up of a fund subscribed to by every ountry were to be given to those making useful discoveries in rural Economy" as well as in medicine and the "Useful Arts." n addition to the immediate practical advantages for science and ndustry that Sinclair anticipated would result from this interna-ional correspondence, he hoped too that it would promote the cause f peace.[69]

Americans contributed to the debates, which filled the pages of oung's publication, on the merits of various fertilizers. They were ery enthusiastic (at least for a time) over the effect of plaster of Paris n rejuvenating their worn-out fields. It was Young who convinced

---

[66] *Letters from . . . George Washington to Arthur Young* (London, 1801), –6, especially Aug. 6, 1786.

[67] P. L. Haworth, *George Washington, Country Gentleman* (Indianapolis, 915), chap. v; *The Correspondence of Sir John Sinclair,* I, xxiv, 279.

[68] Young, *Annals of Agriculture,* XXVII (1796), 42–48.

[69] Sir John Sinclair, *Plan of an Agreement among the Powers in Europe, and he United States of America, for the Purpose of Rewarding the Discoveries of General Benefit to Society* (London, 1795).

Jefferson of the advantages of increasing the number of sheep c his farm at Monticello.

Americans acknowledged the superiority of English husbandr but they too felt capable of aiding its progress, especially in tl invention of agricultural machinery. News came to Young fro Philadelphia of a machine for threshing and cleaning grain in or operation, delivering six bushels an hour "fit for the miller." Benjamin Gale of Connecticut was awarded a prize by the Londo Society for the Encouragement of Arts for his improvement of tl drill plow.[71] Jared Eliot, the best-informed writer on agriculture i colonial America, wrote his own *Essays,* because American cond tions were so different from those in the mother country that bool for English farmers were of little use overseas. He complained of tl clumsy apparatus devised by Tull for drilling and immediately s to work to make a simpler and more efficient machine.[72] Eliot *Essays* were known abroad, where advanced agriculturists held the in admiration.[73] Americans thought Eliot's work, based on person experience, superior to that of recent English writers who were a leged to plagiarize from one another and thus offer very little th was new.[74]

Jefferson's mechanical ability, applied to agriculture especiall is well known. His most important achievement in this field was h invention of a new plow with a more efficient moldboard. The su periority of this device to existing implements was soon mad known to progressive agriculturists in England. Europeans ev dently kept watch on American technical advances. Years afterwar William Cobbett, the stormy petrel of Anglo-American journalism wrote to a Long Island nurseryman asking for a machine for shel ing corn that he had once seen in New York. "It shelled a bushel o ears in a minute." Cobbett had eleven acres of corn and expecte twelve hundred bushels. "This will now be an *Indian-Corn Coun try,"* he wrote from Kensington. "It is *already* a Locust-Tree Coun try." [75]

---

[70] *Annals of Agriculture,* XVII (1792), 206–207.

[71] *Calendar of Franklin Papers,* I, 114, Dec. 10, 1770.

[72] R. H. True, *Agricultural History,* II (1928), 193–206.

[73] Smyth, *Franklin, Writings,* III, 58, to Eliot, Dec. 10, 1751.

[74] *Ibid.,* III, 52, Sept. 12, 1751.

[75] Cobbett to George Woodward, Sept. 10, 1828, Huntington Library.

Strikingly modern ideas were bandied about. A Parisian correspondent asked Franklin's opinion about a primitive incubator.[76] A Frenchman projected an incubator, and a Scotsman anticipated present-day horticulturists by suggesting the possibility of accelerating vegetation by electricity.[77] But it was an uphill struggle for the reformer. As in England, so in America, wrote one of them to Young, "Prejudices in favor of antient modes are laid aside with difficulty." [78]

None of the phenomena of nature so stirred the European in America as did the sight of new birds and animals. No European commentary was complete without reference to the beauty of the hummingbird or the fascinating horror of the rattlesnake. Poets rhapsodized over the hummingbird and the mockingbird, and apparently veracious witnesses testified to the power of the rattlesnake to charm the unwary. English and Scottish newspapers attested to the general curiosity about rattlesnakes and other American fauna. A Boston correspondent wrote to the Royal Society about a local frog as big as "a *Penny loaf* which cries exactly like a *Bull.*" [79] John Bartram sent over to Fothergill large bullfrogs and playfully suggested they be put in St. James Park pond, where they "woud surprise & divert all the adjacent inhabitants of London," but on sober second thought he believed Kew Gardens would be better as "being more private." [80] John Custis gave Collinson directions on how to raise "Possums."

Several correspondents sent to the Royal Society their descriptions of American moose, pigeons, and whales. The Society wanted from Cotton Mather a study of the relationship of winds to the migration of pigeons. He was asked for additional information (with which he was always ready) about the "Mouse Deer," "what we have hitherto had," said the Society, "being very imperfect & not to be depended on." [81] Paul Dudley wrote with scientific under-

[76] *Calendar of Franklin Papers,* I, 153, Nov. 25, 1773.

[77] *London Magazine,* XVI (Feb., 1747); Fox, 69.

[78] *Annals of Agriculture,* XIX (1793), 245.

[79] Benj. Bullivant, Jan. 15, 1697–1698, Royal Soc. Library, Mss. B 2, 46.

[80] Bartram Mss. letters, November 28, 1769, British Museum of Natural History.

[81] Royal Soc. Library, Mss., W. 3, 77; W. 3, 79, 1713; M. 2, 35, June 21, 1714.

standing about whales but emphasized particularly their economic value. "I am Endeavouring after a short natural history of our whales," he told Dr. Jurin. Within a few months he sent a fascinating description of the spermaceti whale and the nature of ambergris.[82] This was made use of by a German professor of chemistry in a lengthy contribution on ambergris published in the Royal Society's *Transactions.*

George Edwards' attractive British publication, *A Natural History of uncommon Birds and of some other rare and undescribed Animals* (1743–1751) owed considerable to American students of ornithology; the author was aided, too, by observing live specimens in London. In another work Edwards spoke of the importation of large numbers of the painted finch, either for gifts or to be sold.[83]

It was regretted that no satisfactory description or collection of the fish and insects of America had been made, and to answer that need Samuel Stearns in *The American Oracle* included such material.[84] For the more learned there were numerous articles on American phenomena in the *Philosophical Transactions.* Franklin had already asked John Bartram to do what he was best fitted to achieve—the writing of a "natural History of our country." [85] In a catalogue of North American animals brought out by J. R. Forster in 1771, the author remarked that many of the newer specimens he listed had come from a large collection of American animals belonging to a Lancashire lady. Forster realized the inadequacy of his catalogue. The writings on natural history of Benjamin S. Barton of Pennsylvania were known abroad, where special notice was taken of his observations on the connection between the migration of birds and seasonal changes.[86] Jefferson, then minister to France helped educate the Count de Buffon in American natural history and ordered specimens to be sent over from Virginia.[87] Professor

[82] Royal Soc. Library, Mss., D. 1, 80, Oct. 3, 1724; D. 1, 85, April 5, 1725.

[83] George Edwards, *Gleanings of Natural History* . . . (London, 1758), 132-133.

[84] *The American Oracle,* 331–338; see statement on the need for such a work *Eur. Mag. and Lond. Rev.,* XII (1787), 274.

[85] Darlington, 402, Jan. 9, 1769.

[86] *Monthly Review,* enlarged ser., XXXVI (1801), 351.

[87] Jefferson, *Writings,* V, 244, to A. Cary, Jan. 7, 1786, VI, 21, to F. Hopkinson, Dec. 23, 1786.

lumenbach sent his thanks to the American Philosophical Society r the gift of an opossum, the first he had ever seen alive. After its eath he used the cadaver for his lectures in comparative anatomy.[88]

Naturalists in Europe and America were deeply interested in the ssils discovered in the Ohio Valley in the 1760's, although half a ntury earlier Cotton Mather had sent to John Woodward, paleon- logist and secretary of the Royal Society, bones and fossil teeth.[89] 'hese were mastodon remains, and Mather's communication to the *hilosophical Transactions* seems to be the first published notice of ich fossils in the colonies. Catesby also made known information bout similar bones and teeth, which Negro slaves in Carolina iden- fied as elephant grinders. A French party had discovered large ones along the Ohio in 1739 and had shipped them to France, here they were studied by Buffon and others. One supposition as that the huge animals arriving at the salt licks in a wet season sank so deep as not to be able to rise out & the others out of Sym- athy or some other Cause not being willing to leave their Com- anions in distress have shared the same fate." [90]

George Croghan, the Indian trader on the American frontier, ent to Collinson some fossil teeth; and a close examination was nade, by the distinguished anatomists John and William Hunter, f some bones sent to the Royal Society. It was concluded that they ere not the bones of an elephant, as had been imagined, but of a ifferent kind of animal.[91] On comparing the teeth sent over by Croghan with those from Asia and Africa, Collinson concluded they vere "what is called Mammot's Teeth from Siberia." [92] Franklin nade similar observations and then went on to note the fact that 'elephants now inhabit naturally only hot countries, where there is no winter, and yet these remains are found in a winter country; which looks as if the earth had anciently been in another position

[88] Blumenbach to P. Tidyman, April 10, 1803, Amer. Phil. Soc.

[89] F. E. Brasch, *Scientific Monthly,* XXXIII (1931), 348–349.

[90] Thomas Hutchins to Brigadier General Haldimand, Nov. 15, 1768, *Journal rom Fort Pitt to the Mouth of the Ohio in the Year 1768,* Brit. Mus., Add. Mss., 21686 (f. 39–42).

[91] *Phil. Trans.,* LVII (1767), 464; LVIII (1768), 34; *Mémoires de L'Institut National des Sciences et Arts,* II (1796), 1–23; *Stralsundisches Magazin,* I (1768), 179–189. Other German and Italian publications referred to these fossils.

[92] Darlington, 299, Collinson to Bartram, May 17, 1768.

and the climate differently placed from what they are at pre ent."[93]

Jefferson was anxious that "very exact descriptions" be made these finds, but he warned against premature theorizing: "The m ment a person forms a theory, his imagination sees, in every objec only the traits which favor that theory." More facts must be co lected, he insisted, before theories could be advanced as to the fossil finds.[94] In these years the foundations of vertebrate paleonto ogy were being laid, and while the more important studies we made in England and France, Americans, notably Caspar Wista soon made contributions of genuine significance.

Within a short time fossils were added to the geological divisio of the British Museum and, as was the fashion in popularizing sc ence in the eighteenth century, books for the general public r ferred to these finds.[95] Fossils as well as minerals and "curiosities were exchanged between the Royal Museum at Copenhagen an Yale College. From the Prince of Parma came a proposal to swa specimens so that Italian and American museums might thereb be enriched.[96] A French official in Philadelphia who saw Peale mounting of the skeleton of a mammoth was deeply impressed bu at the same time scornful of Americans who neglected their men c genius. Peale's son, it was reported, planned to exhibit anothe mounted skeleton in Europe to raise funds for future research. The discovery of fossils provoked many questions, particularly re lating to their identification and origin. The conflicts between th rationalists and upholders of the old order were accented by thes problems and separated sharply those who defended and those wh attacked the story of Genesis.

---

[93] Smyth, *Franklin, Writings,* V, 39, Franklin to Croghan, Aug. 5, 1767.

[94] H. F. Osborn, *Science,* n.s. LXXXII (1935), 533–538. See the excellen paper by G. G. Simpson, "The Beginnings of Vertebrate Paleontology in Nort America," *Amer. Phil. Soc., Proc.,* LXXXVI, no. I (1942), 130 ff.

[95] Lankester, 200–201; Morse (3rd ed. 1798), 55; Guthrie, *A New Geograph cal Historical and Commercial Grammar* . . . (17th ed., 1798), 899–900.

[96] Stiles, *Diary,* III, 254, Feb. 7, 1787; *Penn. Mag. of Hist. and Biog.,* XXVII (1904), 136, Jefferson to Peale, June 5, 1796.

[97] *The Philosophical Magazine,* XIII (1802), letter from C. Roume, Jan. 4 1802.

A sounder scientific basis for physical anthropology than had previously existed was created in the eighteenth century by Linnaeus and Buffon with a study of the comparative anatomy of the races of man. Toward the end of the century Professor Johann F. Blumenbach at the University of Göttingen, who was especially distinguished in these investigations, found it helpful to read accounts of voyages and travels. His work, fundamental in the development of the classification of man, was well known to Americans.[98] His researches included a study of the bodily conformation and mental capacity of Negroes. One of his specimens was a skull brought to him from New York by a physician (Michaelis) who had served with the Hessian soldiers. Blumenbach concluded that Negroes themselves differed in color and facial structure and were not mentally inferior to the rest of the human race. With respect to the skull from America he said, cautiously, that if all Negroes had its peculiarity of a projecting upper jawbone "one might be tempted to suppose that they had another first parent than Adam." [99] As for American Indians, they were alleged to be the descendants of the lost tribes of Israel, and the Cherokees who visited London in 1762 were solemnly said to belong to the line established by Meshek.[100]

The natives of Central and South America were studied by lay and clerical observers for the light they might shed on comparative cultures. Soon after the conquest, Guatemala in its College of Santo Tomás (afterwards San Carlos) established a department of Indian languages. Various religious orders which provided for studies in native languages compiled manuscript dictionaries and grammars, a few of which were published. Among Protestants, Moravian missionaries were very active in this work.[101] A London reviewer of Jefferson's *Notes on Virginia* agreed with his view that language

[98] D. J. Cunningham, "Anthropology in the Eighteenth Century," *Jour. of Royal Anthropo. Inst. of Gt. Brit. and Ireland,* XXXVIII (1908), 14–23.

[99] *London Med. Rev. and Mag.,* III (1800), 199–203. Michaelis was Blumenbach's source for much material on American natural history.

[100] *An Enquiry into the Origin of the Cherokees in a letter to a Member of Parliament* (Oxford, 1762).

[101] E. G. Squier, *Monograph of Authors who have written on the Languages of Central America, and collected Vocabularies . . .* (London, 1861, printed at Albany, N.Y.), xiii–xiv, appendix.

was the best proof of the relationship of peoples. But he scoldec Americans for having permitted Indian tribes to disappear withou recording at least the rudiments of their languages.[102]

Many lay scientists in Europe and America found a strong stimu lus to philological studies in Indian languages. Sir William Johnson who knew as much about northern Indians as any man in America spoke of the "noble . . . strong images" and attractive allegory ir their speech. Analyzing their language he said that an adjectiv or article could be contained in the noun by varying the ending.[10 Franklin assisted European scholars in their studies of native lan guages, and A. C. de Gébelin, one of the earliest *Américanistes* ir France, consulted him when the volumes of *Le Monde Primiti* were going through the press. The erudite Jesuit, Hervás y Pan duro, in a comprehensive work published at the end of the eight eenth century, *Idea dell' Universo,* included several volumes on the world's languages, and one of them dealt with American Indiar tongues. The whole project has been described as the "first reall modern linguistic work on a large scale." [104]

Jonathan Edwards' observations on the language of the Mohegar Indians were said to have given philologists on both sides of the Atlantic sounder ideas on the structure of Indian tongues and tc have corrected at the same time numerous errors.[105] John Horne Tooke, the English political radical, had other interests as well, and among them was philological reform. He stated that adjectives though convenient as abbreviations, are not necessary and thus are not to be classified as parts of speech. To support his contention Tooke quoted Edwards' study of the Mohegans, who were said tc use no adjectives in their language.[106] A New Jersey clergyman Joseph Morgan, was another who thought the study of philology would be best advanced by a study of Indian languages.[107] The learned he said, had often altered their language and pronunciation

[102] *European Magazine and London Review,* XII (1787), 276.

[103] Johnson in *Phil. Trans.,* LXIII (1773), 142.

[104] C. U. Clark, ed., "Jesuit Letters to Hervás on American Languages and Customs," *Journal de la Société des Américanistes,* n.s. XXIX (1937), 97.

[105] *Mass. Hist. Soc., Colls.,* ser. 2, IX (1832), 230.

[106] M. C. Yarborough, *John Horne Tooke* (New York, 1926), 137.

[107] March, 1732, m. 3.36, p. 77, Royal Soc. Library.

'to make it more *neat;* but the unlearned speak as it comes. And of all, I think our *American Indians* the Suitablest to learn it from, having never had their Language nor Pronunciation altered by conquest nor commerce." He sent to the Royal Society his linguistic observations on the Pequots and other Indians.

One of the best of the American works in this field was by Samuel S. Smith of Princeton. It was quickly and favorably known abroad. His original purpose was to uphold religious orthodoxy as against Lord Kames's skepticism, but apart from that objective his approach to anthropology was generally far more scientific than that of most contemporaries. His emphasis was on physical and cultural environments in effecting societal change, and of the two he thought culture the more important. His *Essay on the Causes of the Variety of Complexion and Figure in the Human Species* was recommended to British readers by the editor as an antidote to the observations of Jesuits and others who were the undependable, principal sources for information about primitive man—information on which faulty hypotheses of European scientists had been founded. During the last sixty years, said the editor (1788), more data concerning the natural history of man have been collected than in all preceding ages; much has come and will continue to come from Africa and America.

Smith showed how descendants of Europeans had changed in complexion and hair texture under the different climate of America. Whites who lived like Indians began to look like them; American Negroes were changing also. Field slaves, as contrasted with domestics, retained their African aspect longer. He concluded that if Negroes were free and participated equally in white society they would change their African physique and culture much faster. There were differences in beauty of face and figure between the wealthy and poorer classes of society, accounted for by different food, leisure, etc. Such distinctions, said Smith, "are, as yet, less obvious in America, because the people enjoy a greater equality; and the frequency of migration has not permitted any soil, or state of local manners, to impress its character deeply on the constitution."

Smith was contemptuous of credulous European philosophers who believed all sorts of fantastic tales. Travelers, he observed, judge of appearances in a new country in keeping with their native prejudices and habits. "Since America is better known," he said "we find no cannibals in Florida; no men in Guiana with heads sunk into their breasts; no martial Amazons [and] the giants of Patagonia have disappeared." Smith said that Indians thus far had been observed by people—traders, soldiers, etc.—who "had object very different from philosophy in their view." He then went on to suggest a program which has been advocated anew in our own time by such anthropologists as Malinowski. He asked that learned societies send investigators to Indian tribes who had had no intercourse with Europeans, to live with them familiarly, dressing as they did, "and to observe them when they should be under no bias or constraint." We should then be able to make a better comparative study of habits, languages and degrees of civilization among the Indians. "But above all," he said, "we should discover . . . their religious ideas, which have been ascertained with less accuracy than others, by travellers who have not known to set a proper value upon them." [108]

Americans and Europeans became more critical in their approach to ethnological studies. John Mitchell, of Virginia, discussing the coloration of races, was Buffon's "only rival in treating man as to some extent an evolutionary product." [109] Mitchell sent to Collinson "An Essay upon the Causes of the Different Colours of People in Different Climates," which was later printed in the *Philosophical Transactions*.[110] Even popular works taught a more scientific view. Europeans and American natives were not of different species, it was pointed out. Differences in environment and culture produce variations, said Guthrie, "but the great outlines of humanity are to be discovered among them all, notwithstanding the various shades which characterize nations and distinguish them from each

---

[108] M. Kraus, "Charles Nisbet and Samuel S. Smith—Two Eighteenth Century Educators," *The Princeton University Library Chronicle,* VI (1944), 22–23.

[109] P. Smith, *A History of Modern Culture,* II, 106; cf. the work of the South American scientist, Francisco José de Caldas (1771–1811), *On the Influence of Climate on Organic Beings.*

[110] Royal Soc. Library, I, 286, April, 1743; *Phil. Trans.,* XLIII, no. 474 (1744), paper iv.

other." [111] According to Morse's widely used American geography it was highly probable that America was originally peopled from northeast Asia.

Dr. Benjamin Waterhouse, in thanking Dr. Lettsom for the gift of Clavigero's *History of the Mexicans,* said the author had shed new light on the aborigines who apparently had progressed from north to south. Waterhouse then went on to tell Lettsom of an incident which strengthened his belief in the derivation of American Indians from Asiatics. An American painter who had gone to study in Florence, Italy, saw what he took to be three portraits of North American Indians. He expressed surprise at seeing such paintings *there,* but his hosts told him that he was mistaken; they were paintings of three Tartars, sent as gifts from Empress Catharine of Russia. This, said Waterhouse, was another bit of evidence "that our Indians and the Tartars were the same people." [112] Yale students debated the questions whether America was peopled from Asia and whether different climates were the principal cause of the "different Geniuses of Mankind." George Edwards, the well-known naturalist, believed that people as well as birds common to the two worlds crossed over from Asia to America.[113] The peopling of America was a question discussed for many years in the scientific circles of practically every European country.

Hannah Adams, a writer on American history, drew attention to the phenomenon of a declining population among the Indians whenever they adopted the religion and manners of Europeans. How do we account for that fact? she asked Ezra Stiles.[114] And long before Miss Adams, Cotton Mather had written an English correspondent that it was easier to talk about "anglicising the Indians" than to do it.[115] The material culture of Indians was being made known to a larger number of people by building up collections in

[111] Guthrie, *A New Geographical, Historical and Commercial Grammar . . .* (4th ed., London, 1774), 616.

[112] Pettigrew, II, 457, Dec. 4, 1791.

[113] Stiles, *Diary,* III, 112, Feb. 23, 1784; 264, May 29, 1787; G. Edwards, *Essays upon Natural History and other Miscellaneous Subjects . . .* (London, 1770), 85.

[114] Adams, Nov. 2, 1794, Gratz Coll., Hist. Soc. Penn.

[115] Mather to Sir Wm. Ashurst, Dec. 10, 1712, Huntington Library.

museums, but this was an activity largely reserved for later generations.[116]

A large part of the history of the scientific interrelations of Europe and America in the latter half of the eighteenth century can be written around the personality of Benjamin Franklin. It is quite impossible to appreciate the amazing diversity of his contacts with science and the confidence its students placed in him unless one reads the thousands of letters written to him and by him. Individuals on both sides of the Atlantic refrained from publishing till he had criticized their work, and a writer was happy indeed could he send forth his book dedicated to Franklin. He was one of the most important channels through which Americans and Europeans kept abreast of each other's achievements. He saw to it that scientific instruments for Americans were made by the best English and Scottish manufacturers. He was better known abroad than at home, said the *Scots Magazine;* look in the foreign publications on electricity, it urged, where will be found on almost every page the terms Franklinism, Franklinist, and the Franklinian system. He was, said one English biographer, the "American Newton." [117]

Americans were little familiar with European electrical experiments when Franklin's interest in them was awakened. His theory, the single-fluid theory, made understandable the phenomena of electricity—attraction and repulsion and the mysteries of the Leyden jar.[118] Collinson first made Franklin's name known to the English when he published in book form some of the letters his American correspondent had written on electricity. Within a few months, Collinson was writing in excited exaggeration: "All Europe is in agitation verifying electrical experiments on rods." [119]

Franklin's experiments early commanded the attention of the curious everywhere, and for the better instruction of a non-English

[116] D. I. Bushnell, "The Sloane Collection in the British Museum," *Amer. Anthropologist,* n.s. VIII (1906), 671–685.

[117] *Scots Magazine,* XLV (1783), 174–176; same article in *Eur. Mag. and Lond. Rev.,* III (1783); *Gentleman's Magazine,* LX (1790), 572.

[118] I. B. Cohen, ed., *Benjamin Franklin's Experiments . . .* (Cambridge, Mass., 1941), 60 and *passim.*

[119] *Calendar of Franklin Papers,* I, 6, Sept. 27, 1752; *Phil. Trans.,* XLVII, 202–211, 289, 565–567.

reading public translations of his writings were rapidly made. Priestley's work was begun and carried on with Franklin's encouragement. The article on electricity in the first edition of the *Encyclopedia Britannica* (1771) was largely dependent on Franklin's writings. Proponents of his lightning rods were more numerous in America than in Europe, but during his stay abroad in the decade of the seventies Franklin encouraged their wider adoption. From London he wrote to Professor Winthrop of Harvard, one of his firmest supporters, that he had answered the questions of Nevil Maskelyne, the Royal Astronomer, relating to lightning rods: "I have likewise given sets of directions for erecting them to several persons who desired it." "I purpose to follow your advice," he told Winthrop, "and draw up a more compleat instruction to workmen than I have yet given, to be inserted in the Magazines. St. Paul's Church is now guarded . . . and many gentlemen's houses round London are now furnished with conductors." Winthrop replied that he had spoken and written in advocacy of lightning rods: "They are now becoming pretty common among us." [120]

A pamphleteer was confident that Englishmen would rapidly take to conductors, but rising political tension helped to divide scientists on this question.[121] A magazine recommended to the inhabitants of St. Bride's, London, Winthrop's letter criticizing the repair of a church steeple without using a conductor: "Philosophy, we fear, in vain lifts up her still and gentle voice, and unavailingly calls out across the Atlantic." [122] Jean Baptiste Le Roy urged the French to use the rods, and Franklin proudly noted that in Tuscany and in Venice they had been erected.[123] The Austrian Emperor put conductors upon gunpowder magazines as well as other structures, and that dramatic figure of the French Revolution, Robespierre, appears more prosaically in correspondence with Franklin asking advice, so that as a lawyer he might argue with intelligence the question of the legality of lightning rods. Voltaire's example in putting

---

[120] *Mass. Hist. Soc., Proc.,* ser. 1, XV (1876–1877), 11–13, Franklin to Winthrop, June 6, 1770, October 26, 1770.

[121] Benjamin Wilson, *Considerations to prevent Lightening from doing Mischief* . . . (June 24, 1764), Brit. Mus., Add. Mss. 30094 (f. 106); (f. 238).

[122] *Monthly Review,* XLII (1770), 199–210.

[123] Smyth, *Franklin, Writings,* VI, 106, Franklin to Winthrop, July 25, 1773.

a rod on his own house reassured many of the timid.[124] An Italian Jesuit sent his publication on lightning rods to Franklin, proudly acknowledging his indebtedness to him.[125]

In later years, during Franklin's stay in France, letters came to him from all over Europe requesting advice on the construction of lightning rods. While Americans may not have known much of European work in electricity, it was the complaint of patriotic Americans that their achievements were inadequately recognized in European treatises on the subject. Americans, said Ezra Stiles, had gone far beyond European scientists in this field: "The Electrical Kite, the pointed Rods, the positive & negative state of Electy &c belong to Philada." [126]

Frederick E. Brasch has recently written on the close relations that existed between the Royal Society and its correspondents in the colonies who supplied some of the data basic to the structure of eighteenth-century science. Another present-day student of colonial intellectual life asserts that "no new scientific idea that won general acceptance with the leaders of European thought failed of quick adoption in New England parsonages." [127] Newton, wrote Cotton Mather to the Society, was "the perpetual Dictator of the learned World." [128] The Newtonian system made its way among a few American savants and into colonial colleges whose students gradually became acquainted with the new science. James Logan, a close student of mathematics, and prominent in Pennsylvania political affairs, seems to have had the first copy of the *Principia* in the colonies. His collection of books on mathematics and the physical sciences was the finest in America. The Americans, it may be said, were not behind Europeans in accepting the work of the great English scientist.[129]

---

124 *Calendar of Franklin Papers,* I, 210, January 29, 1777; Smyth, *Franklin, Writings,* I, 9, 104, 105.

125 Sparks, *Franklin, Works,* VI, 351, J. B. Toderini, Aug. 15, 1772.

126 Stiles, *Diary,* II, 529, April 13, 1781.

127 C. K. Shipton, "The New England Clergy of the 'Glacial Age,'" *Col. Soc. Mass., Trans.,* XXXII (1933–1937), 37.

128 Royal Soc. Library, Mss., to Richard Waller, M. 2.29 (letter 2).

129 F. E. Brasch, "The Newtonian Epoch in the American Colonies (1680–1783)," *Amer. Antiq. Soc., Proc.,* XLVIII–XLIX (1938–1939), 314; Brasch, "James Logan, a colonial mathematical Scholar . . . ," *Amer. Phil. Soc., Proc.,* LXXXVI (1942–1943), 343.

The earth and the seas and the heavens, too, were probed for their ecrets. Massachusetts seemed to the distant Londoners a field for esearch with especial promise, and her fertility in the wonders of ıature seemed to them to surpass other regions of America.[130] Frank-in half seriously urged Sir William Herschel to come to America, vhere skies were brighter and the chances for astronomical discov-ries thus greater. In gratitude for his election to the American Philosophical Society, Herschel sent a catalogue of one thousand ıew nebulae and clusters of stars.[131] Long before Franklin, Amer-cans were adding to the store of astronomical knowledge.

In the seventeenth century the observations of Thomas Brattle of Boston on the comet of 1680 (Halley's comet) were made use of by Newton. Cadwallader Colden and James Alexander sent several observations of the "Eclipse of the first Satellite of Jupiter . . ." as ın aid in determining the longitude of New York. They had already letermined its latitude.[132] Paul Dudley, also of Boston, whose con-ributions to the Royal Society were nearly always written in a truly scientific spirit, sent a history of New England earthquakes.[133] An-drew Oliver, Jr., of Massachusetts received an appreciative and crit-ical response from Joseph Priestley, to whom he had sent his *Essay on Comets.*[134] Franklin's explanation of the aurora borealis was hailed as one of the first to be based upon the "sound principles of reason and philosophy." [135]

Probably the ablest scientist in America, and Newton's most dis-tinguished disciple this side of the Atlantic, was Professor John Winthrop of Harvard. He contributed some eleven papers to the Royal Society and his investigations ranged from studies of seismo-logical disturbances to observations on the transits of Venus in 1761 and 1769. One of his correspondents was James Bradley, astronomer royal, to whom Winthrop wrote modestly but confidently of his researches, leaving to him the decision whether or not to publish

---

[130] Brit. Mus., Add. Mss., 14936 (f. 99b), no date; *General Instructions for collecting Natural Curiosities in your Voyage & the Countries you go to.*

[131] Sparks, *Franklin, Works,* VI, 569, Feb. 18, 1787.

[132] Royal Soc. Library, Mss., Classified papers, VIII, 1, 76, Aug. 9, 1723.

[133] Royal Soc. Library, Mss., D. 1, 94, Nov. 13, 1727.

[134] *Mass. Hist. Soc., Proc.,* ser. 2, III (1886–1887), 13, 14, Feb. 12, 1775.

[135] *London Review of English and Foreign Literature,* XI (1780), 233–236.

his work on comets.[136] His countryman Ezra Stiles thought Europ had not his equal in mathematics and natural philosophy.

David Rittenhouse of Pennsylvania added to the value of th co-operative studies of the transits of Venus, in which English an French astronomers joined.[137] These observations resulted in greatly improved estimate of the astronomical unit of distance—th distance from the earth to the sun. Rittenhouse's observations wer thought to be among the best that were made.[138] The volume pub lished by the American Philosophical Society containing the paper on the transit of Venus was reviewed with enthusiasm in Englanc and the Americans' frankness and openness in giving full details o their research were commended as an example to "those Europea Astronomers, who are so very *shy* of giving particulars." [139] Anothe English reviewer thought the Americans "were no less skilful an diligent in improving and applying this curious phenomenon [th transit of Venus, 1769] to useful purposes than their associates i other quarters of the globe." [140] It led him to expect great thing from America. A French expedition went to California to partici pate in this study of the transit of Venus, and its report was issuec in an English translation. Nothing, it said, "gives a higher notior of the compass of the human mind, than that art, now brought t such perfection, of steering safely over the trackless ocean . . . tc traverse immense spaces. . . ." [141]

The Royal Academy of Sciences in France dispatched several ex peditions overseas at an early period, the first within a few years o its founding. The great value of comparing astronomical observa tions made in widely scattered places the world over was clearly

[136] Bodleian Library, Bradley Mss. 44 (f. 147), Sept. 21, 1761; 46 (f. 4), Apri 18, 1760 (f. 18), May 19, 1760; F. E. Brasch, "Newton's First Critical Disciple ir the American Colonies—John Winthrop," in *Sir Isaac Newton 1727–1927*, His tory of Science Society (Baltimore, 1928), 301–338.

[137] Rittenhouse's death was mourned abroad. He was America's greates astronomer, said C. D. Ebeling, *Amerikanisches Magazin*, I, 165 (pt. III, 1796)

[138] S. A. Mitchell, "Astronomy during the early years of the American Philo sophical Society," *Amer. Phil. Soc., Proc.*, LXXXVI, no. I (1942).

[139] *Gentleman's Magazine*, XLI (1771), 416–417.

[140] *Monthly Review*, XLVII (1772), 333–347.

[141] Jean Chappe d'Auterrche, *Voyage en Californie pour l'observation du passage de Vénus sur le disque du soleil . . . 1769* (Paris, 1772; Eng. ed., Lon don, 1778), 14.

ecognized, and the Academy issued general instructions for geo-raphical and astronomical observations to be made by voyagers.[142] This pioneer research carried Jean Richer to Cayenne, from 1672 to 673, and according to a recent study it truly inaugurated the long ine of modern scientific expeditions. It was, says Dr. John W. Olm-ted, "the prototype of the best modern scientific expeditions, the irst notable example of a new and distinctive kind of expedition argely inspired by and devoted to the investigation of specific sci-ntific problems." A fundamental task of the day was finding longi-ude at sea, and in the search for a process it was held that marine endulum clocks needed more testing. It was recognized that ob-ervers should be placed in different parts of the world and their ecords co-ordinated. Richer's findings revealed to contemporaries he vast dimensions of the solar system with its enormous sun and lanets. The average mind was overpowered by the contemplation of the incredible distances and masses involved. He established too 'the shortening of a seconds pendulum near the equator," and this act was of great service in analyses of the shape of the earth by Huygens and Newton. Richer's work led to later expeditions, one of which brought M. de la Condamine to the west coast of South Amer-ica in 1735; the objective was to determine the configuration of the earth by measuring an arc of the meridian.[143]

A later scientist, Johann David Schoepf, made signal contribu-tions to American geology in the *Beytrage zur mineralogischen Kenntnis des östlichen Theils von Nordamerika und seiner Ge-bürge*. This was only one of Schoepf's many-sided contributions to American science. In the dedication to his old teacher, Hofrath Schoeber at the University of Erlangen, he wrote, "As I left Europe in 1777 [with the German mercenaries] you gave me the commis-sion to investigate the arrangement of soil and rock beds in America and to discover to what extent the sequence established by von Ohain and Ferber held good also for the New World." It is the ver-dict of a modern student that the instructions were conscientiously carried out.[144]

---

[142] *Mémoires de l'Académie Royale des Sciences,* VII (1666–1699), 432 ff., 457.

[143] J. W. Olmsted, "The Scientific Expedition of Jean Richer to Cayenne 1672–1673," reprinted from *Isis,* XXXIV, pt. 2, no. 94 (1942), 117–128.

[144] G. H. Williams, in *Geological Soc. of America, Bull.,* V (1893), 593.

Studies of wind and weather obviously had great usefulness in an age of sailing ships, and Americans joined enthusiastically in compiling the valuable data. Dudley sent to the Royal Society his four year record on winds and weather, the better to make comparative studies.[145] Spurred on by the ailing Cotton Mather, Isaac Greenwood, then Hollis professor at Harvard, offered to send the Royal Society an annual meteorological account of New England. He proposed to send over accounts of eclipses, for he had good instruments he wrote, and his advanced students would also aid him. Greenwood suggested that societies in London and Paris get extracts from the journals of sea voyages and reports from sailors on winds and weather: "it is not impossible that we should be able to make a probable Judgment of the Effect and Influence of the Wind upon the Weather." [146] These joint observations were to lead to the composition of a treatise on the weather, a project which was apparently approved by the Society.

A writer in the *Gentleman's Magazine* asked that Americans keep systematic tables of meteorological observations which might explain manners, customs, diseases, and "the fall of countries." Proper tribute was paid to the work of Dr. John Lining, of Charleston, in this field, but much more was hoped for, especially from college presidents in the colonies.[147] Lining sent to the Royal Society rain records for fifteen years in Charleston, which, if long continued, he believed might aid in revealing the climatic changes caused by clearing the land.[148] Jefferson had once hoped to establish a national weather service in America with the American Philosophical Society as co-ordinator. These studies, he thought, might determine the direction of the winds. The American Revolution, however, intervened and, as he wrote to Volney with understatement, he had been since "far otherwise engaged." [149] An international meteorological society founded at Mannheim in 1780 had members in

---

[145] April 12, 1733, to Dr. Mortimer, Royal Soc. Library.

[146] Royal Soc. Library, Mss., G. 2.6, May 1, 1727; G. 2.7, May 10, 1727; D. 1 8, May 10, 1729.

[147] *Gentleman's Magazine,* XX (1750), 493–495.

[148] April 9, 1753, Royal Soc. Library, II, 374.

[149] Letter Jan. 8, 1797, quoted in Browne, "Thomas Jefferson and the Scientific Trends of his Time," *Chronica Botanica,* VII (Nov., 1943), 17.

nearly every European country, Greenland, and the United States, whose observations were printed in many volumes.[150]

News of Thomas Godfrey's invention of the sea quadrant was sent to Halley from Philadelphia by James Logan; Halley had developed his own independently. Thomas Pownall, once governor of Massachusetts, where he had learned much of value for North Atlantic navigation, contributed an important paper to the Royal Society: "Hydraulic and Nautical Observations on the Currents in the Atlantic Ocean." Some of his information came from Franklin, and other sources were American shipmasters who, thought Pownall, were superior to European mariners and thus made "shorter & better passages." [151] The list of treatises on navigation lengthened rapidly with the extension of geographical discovery and the opening of new channels of overseas trade. Bowditch's *New American Practical Navigator* (1801) superseded European manuals.

Near the end of the eighteenth century a German bibliographer compiled a list of contemporary British and American authors, many of whom had made contributions to scientific knowledge. It is a long list, including the names of some three hundred Americans who were authors of books or articles published in a variety of periodicals. The great and the humble are here, and standing together with their contemporaries across the sea they remind us once more of the international character of scientific fellowship.[152] Dr. Benjamin Rush of Philadelphia understood it so when he wrote to that thoughtful friend of America, Richard Price: "In science of every kind men should consider themselves as citizens of the whole world." [153]

---

[150] F. Cajori, *The Early Mathematical Sciences in North and South America* (Boston, 1928), 133.

[151] Royal Soc. Library, Mss., L. 6.59, May 25, 1732; H. E. Gillingham, *Penn. Mag. of Hist. and Biog.*, LI (1927), 291; Royal Soc. Library, Mss., letters and papers, Decade VIII, 189.

[152] J. D. Reuss, *Alphabetical Register of all the authors actively living in Great Britain, Ireland and . . . North America, with a Catalogue of their publications* (Berlin, 1791–1803). Dates of publications 1770–1803.

[153] *Mass. Hist. Soc., Proc.*, ser. 2, XVII (1903), 342, April 22, 1786.

CHAPTER VIII

American and European Medicine

In few fields of scientific enterprise in the eighteenth century did Americans feel so much the equal of Europeans as they did in medicine. In the early years of the century medical education was of a very uncertain character in America, and even in Europe a large proportion of the physicians had gained their knowledge by a short apprenticeship to a doctor who might serve on occasion as an apothecary. The word "doctor" seems to have secured no general American usage until about 1760. It has been estimated that of 3,500 individuals practicing medicine in the colonies on the eve of the Revolution, only some 200 had medical degrees. It should be noted that the apprenticeship system in America had certain advantages. It gave American students practical instruction in the sickroom at a time when their European contemporaries were heavily emphasizing theoretical medicine. Americans enjoyed an additional advantage because the tendency in their country was to train the student in both medicine and surgery, whereas in Europe a strong antagonism still prevailed between these two fields.[1]

Americans had much to learn, however, and with the return of youths from Edinburgh and other European medical centers, a great improvement in education and practice quickly occurred in the colonies after the middle of the century. It should be noted that a large fraction of the practicing physicians in America, even before this period, had received some European training.

Beginning with John Moultrie in 1749, forty-one colonials regis-

[1] H. E. Sigerist, "Boerhaave's Influence upon American Medicine," *Nederl. Tijdschrift voor geneeskunde,* Jaargang 82, no. 40 (1938); H. B. Shafer, *The American Medical Profession* (New York, 1936), 20.

tered at Edinburgh before 1775, fourteen of whom were Virginians. The Revolution seemed to place no serious obstacle in the way of Americans who wished to study in Scotland, and between 1776 and 1800 seventy-six more young men registered at Edinburgh, of whom thirty said they came from Virginia. All told, in the half century before 1800, one hundred and seventeen Americans satisfied the requirements for the M.D. at Edinburgh. Some fifteen or twenty Americans might be in attendance at any one time in the crowded Edinburgh halls. In pre-Revolutionary days students named the colony whence they had come, although at the time of the Stamp Act, Samuel Bard from New York and two or three others called themselves Americans. As time went on more and more overseas students registered as Americans, but the pride of the Old Dominion continued to express itself to a late day in the registration of prospective doctors who signified they had come from Virginia.[2]

Noted Americans provided students with letters of introduction to sympathetic guardians on the other side of the Atlantic. Dr. Robert Whytt, a specialist in studies of the nervous system, took care of young Samuel Bard, who had come recommended by Dr. Cadwallader Colden of New York. Bard communicated information of his progress to his sponsor and added an acknowledgment of Colden's instruction in botany, which now stood him in good stead. The professor of botany at the University, John Hope, thought Bard's collection of some four hundred Scottish plants would win him distinguished recognition at school. Sir Hans Sloane was on familiar terms with many Americans, and it was to him that Zabdiel Boylston of Boston commended his son, who intended to study medicine in London.[3] A message came to Sloane from Rhode Island (with a gift of maple sugar) asking him to intercede for one Coker, so that he could get a license to practice medicine. Many quacks abounded, and America needed good doctors, Sloane was told.

Everywhere Franklin lent assistance to young students, his "American children," and during one of his sojourns in England he was able to smooth the path for Shippen, Rush, John Morgan, and others. The kindly John Fothergill, Franklin's doctor in London,

[2] *New Eng. Hist. and Genealog. Reg.*, XLII (1888), 159 ff.

[3] Sloane Mss., Dec. 19, 1737, 4055 (f. 248); Will Walker, R.I., March 5, 1740, 4056 (f. 211).

was the particular guardian for these Americans. Morgan and Rush came under his watchful eye, and Benjamin Waterhouse, later the distinguished if somewhat eccentric Harvard professor, began his studies in England under the same supervision.[4] Waterhouse wrote Franklin that he intended to practice in Boston and added his belief (after a visit to the medical center at Leyden) that it was not necessary for young men to go to Europe in order to cure the diseases of their next-door neighbor. Characteristically he wrote at the same time that he had learned much during his stay with his relative, Dr. Fothergill. The latter expressed the hope to Franklin that Waterhouse might some day teach in the projected Massachusetts College of Medicine, although Fothergill thought him still too young and inexperienced.[5]

Dr. John Pringle, a pupil of Boerhaave, was another who was held in high regard by American doctors, and his advice in various matters was eagerly sought, Franklin usually acting as an intermediary. When the prominent Philadelphian, Dr. Thomas Bond, was contemplating sending his son Richard abroad to complete his medical studies, he desired Pringle's advice on the comparative merits of the schools in Edinburgh, Paris, London, Leyden, and Vienna.[6] In later years Dr. John Coakley Lettsom was the guide for many Americans and when they in turn achieved professional distinction they did not fail to remember his kindly aid.[7]

From their work in private offices of distinguished surgeons and from experience gained in English hospitals young Americans, such as P. S. Physick, fitted themselves for careers of eminence.[8] John

[4] *Colden Papers, N.Y. Hist. Soc.*, VI (1918–1937), 219; *Thomson Papers, N.Y. Hist. Soc., Colls.* (1878), 17; W. Pepper, *The Medical Side of Benjamin Franklin* (Philadelphia, 1911), 41–44; R. H. Fox, *Dr. John Fothergill and his Friends* (London, 1919), 371–375.

[5] *Calendar of Franklin Papers*, II, 324, 326, Dec. 16, 1780, Dec. 25, 1780.

[6] *Ibid.*, I, 122, July 6, 1771.

[7] Pettigrew, I, 100–101; see B. S. Barton, *Collections for an Essay toward a Materia Medica of the United States* (Part second, Philadelphia, 1804), dedicated to Lettsom.

[8] Sir D'Arcy Power, "How the tradition of American surgery came to America," *Trans. Amer. Surgical Assn.*, XLII (1924), 23–24; Sir William Osler, *The Evolution of Modern Medicine* (New Haven, 1921), 196–197.

Hunter, who was credited with making surgery a real science, and who in Osler's judgment combined the qualities of Vesalius, Harvey, and Morgagni, had a great influence on American surgeons, devoted exponents of his methods. James Lloyd, who had studied with Hunter and William Smellie, carried back to Boston the results of his London training. Lloyd is said to have been the first physician in America to practice obstetrics scientifically. Thomas Chalkley James, reputed to be the foremost obstetrician of his time, was one of Hunter's many students.[9] Physick, a noted disciple of Hunter, thought the master was "the greatest man that ever adorned the medical profession."

Even before students began to return from European medical schools, colonial Americans had made some efforts to create societies to publish communications or to establish systematic courses of lectures. In his early days in Philadelphia Colden had suggested a course of medical lectures, but the learning dispensed by Dr. John Kearsley, Sr., in his local office was the nearest approximation to a systematic education available in the colonies. The elder Kearsley seems to have been a successful mentor, for his students included the most famous colonial physicians—William Shippen, Sr., Cadwallader Evans, John Bard, John Kearsley, Jr., and John Redman. A number of medical societies were established in America about the middle of the century as a result of the initiative of men like Colden, Dr. William Douglass, and others scattered through the colonies.[10]

These haphazard means of gaining a medical education were incapable of satisfying the demands of a growing professional class that was already conscious of its importance in the community. It was at Edinburgh that the American medical schools were born in the minds of Shippen, Morgan, and Samuel Bard, three fellow students. Bard wrote to his father of the proposals of his companions to

---

[9] J. M. T. Finney, "The Influence of John Hunter upon early American surgery" (address to Hunterian Society, London, 1927), Ms. copy in possession of Mr. M. Woolf of the Society; F. R. Packard, *The History of Medicine in the United States* (New York, 1931), II, 992–993.

[10] M. Kraus, *Intercolonial Aspects of American Culture on the Eve of the Revolution* (New York, 1928), chap. vii.

start a school in Philadelphia. He was sorry that they were not to live in New York, but he saw no reason why a similar institution should not be established in his own city.

Both plans waited on the passage of time, but individuals were already holding classes in various colonial towns. Before his return to Philadelphia, Dr. William Shippen II, who had studied with John Hunter, had been urged by Fothergill to give a course of anatomical lectures; these he delivered with the aid of drawings supplied by his English guide.[11] Dr. William Hunter, related to the more famous London brothers of that name, gave some lectures in Rhode Island. In Boston and New York dissections by experienced physicians were made for the instruction of a few students, but for some time to come prejudice on both sides of the Atlantic opposed such realistic medical teaching. Plans for a Harvard medical school that had been proposed before the Revolution, inspired in large part by Morgan's work in Philadelphia, matured in 1783 under the prodding of John Warren.

The establishment of schools in America did not have the effect of lessening the desire for additional medical training abroad. Before professional schools existed in the colonies it was customary to get medical training by association with some distinguished physician, who himself had probably been abroad. The young doctor, if he wished for distinction in his profession, then made every effort to attend courses of lectures in Europe, or visit the hospitals in the capitals on the Continent and in England to observe at first hand the finest techniques of the day. It was exceedingly fortunate that so many students went to Edinburgh, probably the best school of its time, founded as it was by the pupils of Boerhaave. There they were instructed in the principles prescribed by the great Dutch master. They carried home to America his books, applied his teachings in their practice, and passed them on to their apprentices. Boerhaave's ideas in medicine were dominant in America till near the close of the century.[12]

The number of Americans who attended medical lectures in Paris, Leyden, and other Continental centers, while not large, was not negligible. Some twenty-three Americans studied at Leyden be-

[11] Packard, I, 306–319.

[12] Sigerist, 4.

ore 1800, fifteen of them taking their degrees there. John Redman and Benjamin Morris had received degrees from Leyden; Thomas Bond had studied at Paris. These were the mentors of the group in Philadelphia who journeyed abroad later in considerable numbers. It is worth noting that before their departure from America they underwent some apprentice training. After the Revolution France attracted many of the prospective doctors from the United States.

Some Americans went overseas to complete their medical training without taking degrees in any of the universities, but these too contributed an important share to the improvement of American medicine. Although the records are incomplete, it is fairly certain that few doctors after 1760 achieved distinction without some instruction in Europe—or guidance from someone himself trained in a European school. From the most important center of medicine in America, Philadelphia, students carried the ideas of Benjamin Rush through the length and breadth of the United States.[13] In a period of about forty years after 1770, some three thousand students (counting apprentices and college pupils) learned their medicine from him. Dr. Lettsom compared Rush very favorably with the illustrious Sydenham. Americans who were familiar with medical training at home and in Britain soon began to write from England that medicine was "taught more scientifically in Philadelphia than in London." It was alleged, too, that teachers in England were not as attentive to the needs of their pupils.[14]

Nevertheless, American resources were as yet inadequate for advanced training. There was a lack of variety of operations and not enough dissection. Dr. Thomas Bond once wrote complainingly that he could scarcely find material for his clinical lectures in Philadelphia; either the people were too healthy, or else they shunned hospitals.[15] Americans at Edinburgh benefited greatly from discussions in their medical societies, which were cosmopolitan groups of Europeans, and some believed they gained more from these associations than from classroom lectures. William Cullen's influence at Edinburgh was profound, and Americans generally idolized him. On his

[13] Goodman, *Benjamin Rush,* 128.

[14] W. S. Ruschenberger, *An Account of the College of Physicians of Philadelphia* (Philadelphia, 1887), 17.

[15] Bond to Franklin, Sept. 24, 1779, *Calendar of Franklin Papers,* II, 145.

retirement, the American Physical Society of Edinburgh joined with others in expressing its warm regard for him.[16] The two years that Rush spent at Edinburgh he considered the most important in his life for their effect on his character and conduct.[17]

It was not American attendance at European medical centers alone that enhanced the prestige of American medicine; it was also the result of migration of European doctors to the colonies. Drs. Alexander Garden, Lionel Chalmers, William Douglass, and Cadwallader Colden were a few of those who brought medical knowledge and often a general intellectual distinction to colonial groups with whom they made their homes.

While America was largely a debtor to Europe for education in medicine the balance was partly redressed by the free exchange between them of proposals for the advance of medical science. In the initial issue of a London medical journal it was pointed out that valuable information could be secured from the colonies, "where there are physicians of great experience and abilities." [18] Years before this publication was urging transatlantic medical correspondence, Dr. John Lining, of Charleston, had forwarded the results of observations and experiments he had been making to find the causes of epidemic diseases which returned regularly with the seasons.[19] English and American doctors wrote pamphlets advising the prospective emigrants to the southern colonies and West Indies how to make their adjustments to the warmer climate to avoid illness.

John Mitchell, a versatile scientist, exchanged ideas with Cadwallader Colden on the origin of yellow fever in the colonies, indicating a desire (which he lived to realize) to write on the medical

---

[16] W. J. Bell, Jr., "Philadelphia Medical Students in Europe, 1750–1800," *Penn. Mag. of Hist. and Biog.*, LXVII (1943), 1–30.

[17] L. A. Biddle, *A Memorial . . . of Dr. Benjamin Rush . . . written by himself* (publ. privately, Lanoraie, 1905), 24.

[18] *Medical Observations and Inquiries,* By a Society of Physicians in London (1757), I, preface v–vi. Dr. Fothergill was very active in behalf of this publication (Packard, II, 1121 note 1).

[19] Royal Soc. Library, Mss., letters and papers, Decade I, 188, April 11, 1741, Jan. 22, 1740/41; I, 374, Jan. 29, 1743; see *Phil. Trans.* XLII (1742–1743), 491–510.

phenomena as well as natural history of North America.[20] John Fothergill's "classic" description distinguishing scarlet fever from other fevers was anticipated by ten years in William Douglass' work, *The Practical History of a New Epidemical . . . Fever . . . 1735 and 1746.* This work was summarized in the journal published by the doctors of Edinburgh.[21] Colden sent to Dr. Fothergill studies on throat distemper which had originally been supplied by Douglass.[22]

Many of the individuals who were physicians by profession were very much interested in natural science, which accounts for their appreciation of the contributions which allied scientists could make to the art of healing. Fothergill questioned John Bartram about the medicinal plants "in use among [American] practitioners; or even celebrated among the vulgar." Bartram replied that there were very many roots, herbs, and barks used in America which had been discovered by the Indians, but remarked that inexpert use made people discard them when they were seemingly ineffective. A half-century earlier Dr. Nehemiah Grew, a pioneer in the study of sex in plants, conducted a correspondence with Americans in Rhode Island and Virginia which indicated an active interest in medical practice among the Indians.[23]

One of the better-known American contributions was the snake root, which was regularly exported from Virginia. Bernard de Jussieu, Royal Professor of Botany at Paris, told Dr. Bond that the root had been "sent him with a recommendation and method of use in pleurisies and repeatedly tried with surprising success [so that it] was in the highest esteem with him and many other physicians." William Byrd likewise spoke highly of the rattlesnake root, a considerable quantity of which his friend, Dr. John Tennent was taking over to Europe for experimental purposes. The Edinburgh medical fraternity were soon to become familiar with Tennent's

---

[20] Mitchell to Colden, London, March 25, 1749, Huntington Library.

[21] *Medical Essays and Observations* by a Society in Edinburgh, IV (1737), 490.

[22] *Medical Observations and Inquiries,* I (1757), 211.

[23] Darlington, March 22, 1743–1744, July 24, 1744; *Col. Soc. Mass., Trans.,* XIV (1911–1913), 145. James Logan of Pennsylvania did work of sufficient distinction on the sexuality of plants to win European commendation (F. B. Tolles, *Meeting House and Counting House* [Chapel Hill, 1948], 216–217).

work on the snake root.[24] His pioneer studies familiarized British and French physicians with the plant, which was later cultivated in Europe.[25]

John Bartram wrote a preface to an American edition of Dr Thomas Short's *Medicina Britannica,* a popular plant materia medica. Bartram's notes, scattered through the work, told where many of the specimens described could be found in America, and he indicated, too, the virtues of a number of plants indigenous to the New World. Governor William Gooch of Virginia sent to London a specific which was supposed to cure venereal diseases. Next to the service humanity might expect from it, wrote the Governor, "I wish it may be an encouragement to one of the traveling Phisitians to take a Tour into America, where he'll profit much more than by a jaunt to France and Italy." [26] William Byrd urged Dr. Hans Sloane to endow traveling fellowships for English doctors to familiarize themselves with valuable plants. It was the noted traveler-scientist Peter Kalm who brought to the attention of his master Linnaeus a reputed Indian cure for venereal disease.[27] It may have been the sarsaparilla root that Governor Gooch had sent over. At any rate some years later a military surgeon, William Fordyce, was experimenting with this root, and he confirmed the optimistic claims that had been made for it.[28]

Europeans were constantly searching for medicinal plants. Fothergill wrote to Humphry Marshall in Pennsylvania praising sassafras bark but regretting the lack in medical practice of a dependable

[24] Sloane Mss., May 31, 1737, Add. Mss. 4055, f. 112; *Medical Essays and Observations* V (1744), pt. II, 906, 1006; Tennent, *An Epistle to Dr. Richard Mead concerning the epidemical Diseases of Virginia* . . . [and] *the Seneca Rattle-Snake Root* (Edinburgh, 1738), particularly 97–98 giving cases.

[25] W. Woodville, *Medical Botany* . . . (London, 1790–1793), II, 253–255; *Mémoires de l'Académie Royale des Sciences* (Paris, 1739), 135, 139; *ibid* (1744), 37 *et seq.;* see also W. B. Blanton, *Medicine in Virginia in the Eighteenth Century* (Richmond, 1931), 135–151.

[26] *Virginia Mag. of Hist. and Biog.,* XXXII (1924), 229, June 29, 1729. There are a number of references in eighteenth-century correspondence of Indian remedies for venereal diseases, e.g., *Gentleman's Magazine,* XXVII (1757), 405–406.

[27] Sloane Mss., 4055 (f. 112), May 31, 1737; Smith, *Corr. of Linnaeus,* II, 225, Jussieu to Linnaeus, Feb. 19, 1751.

[28] *Medical Observations and Inquiries,* I (1757), art. xvii, 149.

diuretic. Marshall was asked to be on the watch for a plant that would answer the purpose.[29] Quinine, as well as most of the other drugs known in the Anglo-American world, were also familiar to the Spanish-speaking colonies. Spain's scientists organized expeditions for researches in botanical medicine in the New World; quinine had for them a special attraction.[30] Sloane asked William Byrd to look around for "ipecocanua": "I dare say you will find plenty of it and you will save so much money as goes from hence to Portugal and Spain on this Occasion." An English play dealing with the Indians said they were the "first botanists in the world," and they were reported to have remedies (including antidotes to all venomous bites) for almost every one of their native diseases.[31] A very large work on medical botany by William Woodville (1790) included many exotic plants and paid tribute to American initiative in introducing them to Europe. J. D. Schoepf, the German scientist who had studied in America, brought out a *Materia Medica Americana* in 1787, with an acknowledgment of the work of American writers who had long preceded him.

The publications of the period and the correspondence of physicians often refer to medicinal plants introduced into Europe from America. With some literary license, Addison wrote in *The Spectator* (1711), "We repair our bodies by the drugs from America"; and a contemporary with equal enthusiasm said that "every new discovery, every new plantation, every new branch of trade furnisheth some new thing, some rarity in nature, some specific in physic for the relief of a distempered world, which long hid till navigation carried us to America." [32]

On the other hand it must not be forgotten that most of the drugs used by American doctors in their practice generally came from London. Such doctors as Sylvester Gardiner in Boston and Simeon Smith of Connecticut kept large stocks of drugs imported from England and the Continent, which they then distributed to other

[29] Darlington, 503, Fothergill to Marshall, Feb. 11, 1771.

[30] Garcia del Real, "The Discovery of America: its influence on medicine," *Revista de las Españas,* nos. 89–91 (1935), 16–27.

[31] Sloane Mss., 4068 (f. 54), Dec. 7, 1709; James Bacon, *The American Indian; or Virtues of Nature* (London, 1795), 42.

[32] Gillespie, *Influence of oversea expansion on England to 1700,* 222.

American communities.[33] Lord Sheffield said that quack nostrum
were consumed in large enough quantities in the southern colonie
to form no inconsiderable article of commerce.

Publications on both sides of the Atlantic frequently include
correspondence exchanged between practitioners. A Scottish pe
riodical drew the attention of its readers to the "famous America
Receipt for the Rheumatism." *An Essay on Fevers,* by Dr. Lione
Chalmers, of South Carolina, was drawn upon shortly by an Englis
doctor who strongly endorsed Chalmers' proposals for purging an
sweating "as the most effectual means of stopping the progress o
fevers." [34] When a new periodical, the *Medical Observations and In
quiries,* was started in London, it expressly indicated that it counte
on important contributions from America "where there are physi
cians of great experience and abilities."

An American doctor observed that his countrymen had long bee
borrowers from Europe. "As the terms granted us have been libera
and advantageous, it is time for us," he said, "to think of reimburs
ing the loan." And with a certain pride he stated that American
were prepared to cancel, in part, their "weighty obligations." It wa
claimed, for example, that febrile diseases were better understoo
in America than elsewhere.[35] Certainly no one aided more than di
Benjamin Rush in canceling those obligations. "His opinions ma
not always be the most maturely weighed," said a London writer
but it was recognized that he had often added new facts to the gen
eral stock of knowledge, and his ingenuity in particular was highl
praised.[36] It was Rush who urged British doctors to send their tuber
cular patients to America, whose climate, he said, was more likely t
effect a cure.[37] He was one of the first to speak authoritatively of th
natural basis of insanity. After many years of treating the insane, i
his office and in the Pennsylvania Hospital, Rush wrote his pionee

---

[33] J. Thacher, *American Medical Biography* (Boston, 1828); H. E. Smith
Colonial Days and Ways (New York, 1900), 333.

[34] *The Weekly Magazine, or Edinburgh Amusement,* V (1769), 210; *Reflec
tions on the General Treatment and Cure of Fevers* (London, 1772), 49.

[35] C. Caldwell, ed., *Medical theses, selected from among the Inaugural Dis
sertations of the Univ. of Penn.* (Philadelphia, 1805), lx.

[36] *Monthly Review,* enlarged ser., XIX (1796), 413.

[37] Pettigrew, III, 191, June 15, 1790.

work, *Medical Inquiries and Observations upon the Diseases of the Mind* (1812), which remained a classic for long years thereafter.

When Rush was a younger man his friend Samuel Bard commiserated with him after learning of the former's dispute with other Philadelphia doctors because of his "chemical Pathology"; Rush was attempting to substitute the principles of Cullen for those of Boerhaave. Bard, however, thought controversy quite all right; it spurred the discussion of new ideas. "I very well remember," he added, "we always fared the better at Edinburgh when our masters quarrelled." [38]

The publication of medical literature increased with great rapidity in America. Just over fifty items have been catalogued down to 1750 in the colonies; in the next half-century more than five hundred items are listed, a good many dealing with the terrible yellow-fever epidemics of the 1790's. Rush was an important contributor to this fast-growing volume of medical writings, and it is worth noting that European medical journals paid especially close attention to American publications on epidemics.[39]

The sentiment of nationalism which animated so many aspects of American life in these years affected medical education too. With the opening of the Harvard Medical School in 1782, Waterhouse, himself educated abroad, acknowledged the value of scientific contacts with foreign countries, but he said an independent United States "should blush to be indebted to foreign seminaries for *first principles of professional instruction.*" [40]

The thought of utilizing electricity in healing human ills occurred to a considerable number of doctors. A magazine item of 1749 told of a German professor's experiments in applying electricity in his medical practice. Franklin and Dr. Cadwallader Evans used electric shocks in an attempted cure, and they communicated the details of their experiment to the physicians of London.[41] Dr. Robert Whytt and Dr. John Pringle, both of whom kept in close touch

[38] Bard to Rush, June 24, 1770, Ridgway Library.

[39] Charles Evans, *American Bibliography* (Chicago, 1903–1934), I–XII.

[40] Quoted in Curti, *The Growth of American Thought,* 144.

[41] *Gentleman's Magazine,* XIX (1749), 452–453; *Medical Observations and Inquiries,* I (1757), 83.

with American medical progress, discussed the use of electricity i
the cure of a palsy. Franklin had sent some observations on the e
fects of electricity in paralytic cases to Pringle, noting, however, th
the improvement appeared temporary. He suggested that mo
permanent benefits might be achieved if the electric shocks we
accompanied by proper medicine and regimen. Pringle on one occ
sion asked Franklin to assist him in treating a patient with electri
ity.[42]

The medical faculty in Paris watched closely the effect of ele
trical treatment on paralytics, and Franklin was kept informed.
dissertation at the medical school in Lyons, referring to electr
therapy, frequently mentioned Franklin and Ebenezer Kinnersle
(of Philadelphia). Ingenhousz, the noted Viennese doctor and frien
of Franklin, suggested that the insane might have their mental fa
ulties restored by electrical shock.[43] John Wesley was an enthusiast
believer in the use of electricity in curing ailments, claiming t
have treated hundreds of patients. Wesley's electrotherapeut
measures found a strong supporter in the distinguished scientis
Joseph Priestley.[44]

Within a period of twenty years a number of doctors had becom
accustomed to using electric machines in their practice.[45] Specialis
had arisen claiming particular skill in the construction and use c
these machines.[46] One of the advantages claimed for the applicatio
of electricity was that it would be useful in resuscitating person
rescued from drowning. Dr. Perkins, inventor of metallic tractor
gave his name to a cult, Perkinism, which created a furore in Europ
and America at the turn of the century. Doctors and laymen exper

---

[42] *The Works of Robert Whytt* (Edinburgh, 1768), 483–487; Smyth, *Fran lin, Writings,* III, 425, Dec. 21, 1757; *Calendar of Franklin Papers,* I, 19, 1758.

[43] J. B. Bonnefoy, *De l'Application de l'Eléctricité a l'Art de Guérir* (Lyor 1782); Ingenhousz to Franklin, Aug. 15, 1783, *Calendar of Franklin Papers,* II 96.

[44] North, *Early Methodist Philanthropy,* 44–45; H. A. Colwell, *An Essay o the History of Electrotherapy and Diagnosis* (London, 1922), 24.

[45] *Medical Observations and Inquiries,* V (1776), art. 1.

[46] See advertisement of G. Adams in W. Cadogan, *An Essay upon Nursin* (1772); John Birch, *Considerations on the Efficacy of Electricity in removin Female Obstructions. To which is now added a Description of the Manner c Applying it* (2nd ed., London, 1780), iv note.

mented and discussed the theories of Perkins, and the conclusion was that, although medicine had little to gain from Perkinism, the study of physiology might be aided.[47] Certainly many quacks were now claiming to cure ailments by electricity.

Political differences between England and the colonies had no important effect on the friendly relations that existed between doctors on both sides of the Atlantic. Younger men like Dr. Samuel L. Mitchill of New York were in frequent correspondence with European practitioners. Collaboration between them was, if anything, closer after the Revolution than before. In the pages of *The London Medical Journal,* beginning with the first volume in 1781, are to be found many signs of this interactivity. Studies of hydrophobia, for example, were underscored by inclusion of American knowledge sent from New York and Philadelphia.[48] There were a great many cases of this dread disease in the United States in the 1780's. James Mease's *Dissertation on the Disease produced by the Bite of a Mad Dog* (Philadelphia, 1792) was considered of sufficient importance to be republished in London the next year, sponsored by Dr. Lettsom. This London reprint partook of the character of a symposium on hydrophobia and tetanus, containing as it did opinions of English and American doctors which each had communicated to the other. The contribution of Dr. Lionel Chalmers, of Charleston, on tetanus was adjudged superior to that of any contemporary.[49] Daniel Coxe, a loyalist still critical of America but unable to restrain a sentimental attachment to her, wrote to an old-time friend suggesting that Philadelphia pipe her water supply to every house, as in London, to avoid epidemics.[50]

The observations of American army doctors were communicated to English colleagues, and articles appearing in American scientific publications were reprinted in England.[51] Barnabas Binney's noted

---

[47] Rev. Samuel Glasse, *A Sermon in Favour of the Humane Society* (London, 1793), 45; *The Philosophical Magazine,* II (1798), 188; Colwell, 47.

[48] *London Med. Journal,* V (1785), 286–289; also X (1789), letter of Thomas Percival to Dr. Haygarth.

[49] *Encyclopedia Britannica* (1797), art. "Medicine," 253.

[50] Dec. 9, 1798, Rush Mss., Ridgway Library.

[51] *London Med. Journal,* VII (1786), 291–305, 424–434.

case of a gunshot wound led the reviewer in the *Scots Magazine* to say that surgeons who were not certain of the utility of their operations had better follow Binney and "leave a desperate disorder in the hands of nature, than through too great an officiousness proceed on doubtful and precarious grounds." [52] A London journal in a review of *The Medical Repository of New York,* which had been sent over by Dr. Mitchill, lamented the limited intercourse with the Western World but hoped now that this publication would keep England in touch with American medicine. Very proudly Ezra Stiles sent to Edinburgh copies of the earliest published memoirs of the New Haven Medical Society.[53] The medical school in Philadelphia, following the trend of scientists toward writing in the vernacular, apparently inaugurated the practice of permitting theses to be written in English, a fact that caught the attention of a London journal.[54] By the end of the century all American medical schools were permitting their graduates to write their dissertations in English.

From England, France, and Germany Franklin received requests for the details of a cure for dropsy mistakenly attributed to him. His aid was valuable to Dr. Thomas Percival of Manchester in studying the correlation between smoke and the increase in pulmonary complaints. Franklin, who participated in a fresh-air campaign for the sick and for the healthy, wrote to a French doctor that physicians "have begun to discover that fresh air is good for People in the Smallpox, and other fevers." He hoped they would in time find out "that it does no harm to People in Health." [55]

American doctors were rather favorably known in France, partly as a result of Franklin's good offices. The Royal Society of Medicine in recognition of the especial achievements of some American doctors conferred upon them the title of correspondent, and its pub-

---

[52] *Scots Magazine,* L (1788), 602, reviewing *Memoirs of the Academy of Arts and Sciences,* Boston.

[53] *The London Med. Rev. and Mag.,* VI (1801), 133–134; Stiles, *Diary,* III, 328, Aug. 30, 1788.

[54] *Medical Facts and Observations,* I (1791), 204 note.

[55] *Calendar of Franklin Papers,* I, 211, 311, 427, Feb. 1, 1777, Nov. 21, 1777, May 20, 1778; Smyth, *Franklin, Writings,* I, 118–119, 61–62, June 22, 1773, to J. B. LeRoy.

ications included papers written by American physicians.[56] In the ·arly years of the nineteenth century Paris was beginning to sup- ›lant Edinburgh in the esteem of American doctors.

In the establishment of hospitals Americans naturally followed amous European models which were newly founded or had re- ently been reorganized. Franklin sent news of the founding of the ›ennsylvania Hospital to Sir Alexander Dick (president of the Col- ege of Physicians at Edinburgh), believing the Scotsman would be lelighted to know that Americans had "imitated the Edinburgh In- titution of an Infirmary." For the benefit of the hospital Franklin 'isited several British institutions and sent back to Philadelphia heir rules of procedure. David Barclay and John Fothergill gen- ·rously assisted in financing the Pennsylvania hospital and sent over ›ooks for its medical library.[57] In equipping the hospital Fothergill uggested the use of iron bedsteads. When the Society of the Hos- ›ital in the City of New York was established in 1771, Dr. Fothergill vas one of the incorporators. Through his effort and that of Sir Villiam Duncan money was raised in London for the American nstitution. The founding of the Philadelphia Dispensary to ad- ninister to the poor followed directly upon the suggestion of Dr. Ienry Moyes, the energetic organizer of humane societies in vari- ›us parts of the world.[58]

A very profitable result of the scientific relations between the olonies and England was the mutual encouragement offered in he adoption of inoculation against smallpox. Although Cotton Aather, who was responsible for its adoption in America, is sup- ›osed to have learned about it from an article in the Royal Society's *Transactions,* it is clear that he knew about the value of this prac- ice from a slave who testified that it had long been in use in Africa. Vith that crusading spirit so typically his, Mather wrote to Dr. John Voodward of the Royal Society: "How does it come to pass, that no nore is done to bring this operation, into experiment and into ashion in England? . . . I beseech you, Syr to move and save more

[56] *Calendar of Franklin Papers,* II, 287, Sept. 7, 1780.

[57] Smyth, *Franklin, Writings,* IV, 2, 95, Jan. 3, 1760, Feb. 26, 1761; A. M. Gummere, *Friends Hist. Soc., Bull.,* I (1906), no. 1, 20–21; Packard, 220–221.

[58] Ruschenberger, 124–125.

Lives than Dr. Sydenham. For my own part, if I should live to se
the Small-Pox again enter into our city, I would immediately pr
cure a consult of o^{r} Physicians, to Introduce a Practice, which ma
be of so very happy a Tendency. But could we hear, that you hav
done it before us, how much would that embolden us!" [59] Five yea
after this letter was written Mather, spurred to action by an ep
demic, carried out his part by urging the physicians of Boston t
adopt inoculation, but all were opposed, with the exception o
Zabdiel Boylston. Mather was able to report soon after that th
success of inoculation in Boston despite the opposition was suc
that "we need nothing from the other side of the Atlantic to em
bolden our proceeding." [60]

Boylston went to London and lectured to the Royal College o
Physicians and to the Royal Society on his experiences. His pub
lished report of *An Historical Account of the Small Pox . . . i
New England . . .*, a very careful record, is spoken of as a "ma
terly clinical presentation," "the first of its kind from an America
Physician." [61]

To his diary Mather confided the hope that his writings on th
subject, addressed to an audience in England, where they were pub
lished, would make her adopt the practice. Mather's hope was t
some extent realized. Sir Hans Sloane, to whom one of these wri
ings was dedicated, was much interested in inoculation. Englis
writers quoted Mather, among them Dr. James Jurin, Secretary o
the Royal Society, who kept in close touch with developments i
New England. Charles Maitland, who inoculated Lady Montagu
children, was urging Englishmen to adopt the practice, "new in
deed, and utterly unknown here till of late" though long known i
Turkey.[62] At the same time London papers were presenting to
larger public news of the Boston epidemic and the experiments i
inoculation.

---

[59] G. L. Kittredge, "Lost Works of Cotton Mather," *Mass. Hist. Soc., Proc*
XLV (1911–1912), 422, letter of July 12, 1716.

[60] Royal Soc. Library, *Inoculation letters and papers,* Mather to Dr. Jurin
May 21, 1723, 48.

[61] H. R. Viets, "Some Features of the History of Medicine in Massachuset
during the colonial period," *Isis,* XXIII (1935), 389–405.

[62] *Mr. Charles Maitland's Account of Inoculating the Small Pox* (London
1722), 2.

The use of this medical practice was far more quickly adopted in ıe colonies, however, than in Europe. After a few years of consid-rable progress the practice seemed to have fallen into disuse in ngland. Twenty years after Mather's correspondence with London hysicians, Peter Collinson wrote John Bartram: "I hear [that small-pox inoculation] is very successfully operated with you—but ob-ains little with us." [63] However at just about the time Collinson was riting in so discouraged a tone to Bartram, the favorable accounts ıat kept coming from America inspired a revival of interest in reat Britain. The establishment of an Inoculation Hospital in ondon helped gradually to break down resistance to the novel ıedical practice.[64] A charitable institution for inoculating the oor recorded that in four years only one of almost six hundred ıoculated died, whereas among those getting smallpox naturally ıe mortality rate was one in seven. Londoners were told that in one utbreak of smallpox in South Carolina in 1738 more than eight undred people were inoculated, of whom only eight died.[65] Not ntil the second half of the century, when prominent doctors like ohn Fothergill became its protagonists, was this practice generally dopted in Britain. The London Medical Society was strongly in ıvor of inoculation; the objections to it were thought so trivial as) be unworthy of notice.[66]

The whole conflict over the adoption of inoculation against mallpox was fought along parallel lines in Europe and America. 'he same opposition on religious grounds had to be overcome on oth sides of the Atlantic, and the Reverend Cotton Mather punc-ıred the arguments of those who enlisted God in their behalf. "It ; *cavilled* . . . that this *New Way* comes to us from the *Heathen,* nd we *Christians* must not *Learn* the *Way* of the *Heathen.*" Mather ıen asks if Hippocrates were not a heathen? "And whether we ave not learnt some of our very Good Medicines from our In-

---

[63] Darlington, 147, Feb. 3, 1741/42.

[64] W. Woodville, *The History of the Inoculation of the Small-Pox in Great 'ritain* . . . (London, 1796), *passim.*

[65] *A Representation from the Governors of the Hospital for the Small Pox nd for Inoculation,* Jan. 28, 1756; J. Kilpatrick, *An Essay on Inoculation* . . . ondon, 1743), first printed in South Carolina.

[66] *Medical Observations and Inquiries,* III (1767), preface vi–vii.

dians? . . . And, Gentleman Smoakers, I pray, whom did you lear to Smoke of?" [67] Increase Mather said that many of the clergy, no tably among the younger group, were in favor of inoculation. Bu Dr. William Douglass, who opposed inoculation, said it was Mathe who had stirred up the clergy to preach in favor of it.[68]

In England one champion derided the injunction to trust i Providence alone. Providence, he replied, "has given Heads an Hands to contrive and execute what is most for our advantage. . . To trust in Providence is to do all we can for ourselves, and then t believe we shall be taken care of." The *Gentleman's Magazine,* ob serving the obstacles to the adoption of inoculation, suggested tha Englishmen turn their eyes to New England "and see what success i has there found and whether the mother may not be instructed b the daughter." [69]

There was a constant interchange on the subject of inoculatio and improved methods in its practice. One of those credited wit reviving its use in England was Dr. James Kilpatrick, who had prac ticed in America and had returned to London, where he publishe a pamphlet on the success of inoculation in South Carolina. Dr Kilpatrick had apparently won a distinguished reputation, for h was asked by the leading French nobility to inoculate them agains smallpox.[70]

The use of mercury as a preparative for inoculation was know to Americans in the 1740's (it was employed by Dr. Thomas of Vir ginia and Dr. George Muirson of Long Island) and was communi cated to England's doctors by Dr. Benjamin Gale of Connecticut.[71]

---

[67] *Some Account of what is said of Inoculating or Transplanting the Sma Pox by the learned Dr. Emanuel Timonius and Jacobus Pylarinus* . . . (pub by Z. Boylston, Boston, 1721, but Mather's work). See also Royal Soc. Librar *Inoculation letters and papers,* Mather to Dr. Jurin, May 21, 1723, 38–40.

[68] I. Mather, *Several Reasons proving that Inoculation . . . is a Lawfu Practice* (Boston, 1721); Douglass to A. Stuart, Royal Soc. Library, D. 2.2., Sep 25, 1721.

[69] David Hartley, *Reasons why the Practice of Inoculation ought to be intro duced into . . . Bury . . .* (1733), 18; *Gentleman's Magazine,* XXIII (1753 414.

[70] Kilpatrick, *The Analysis of Inoculation* . . . (London, 1754), 110–11 Woodville, 306.

[71] Muirson told Ezra Stiles he had gotten the hint from Boerhaave, Stile *Diary,* III, 127, June 17, 1784; Packard, I, 501.

)r. Gale had sent his pamphlet on inoculation to a Dr. Andrew of :xeter, pointing out that before the general use of mercury and ntimony in preparing people for inoculation, one out of a hundred f the inoculated died, whereas with their use the mortality rate vas only one in eight hundred.[72] To advance the cause Benjamin 'ranklin wrote a propaganda pamphlet, in 1759, for the use of Dr. Villiam Heberden of London, which drew upon American experince. Swedish doctors were soon familiar with the practice of Philalelphia physicians who used mercury in conjunction with antinony.[73] Daniel Bernoulli calculated that the general adoption of noculation had added three years to the average longevity of Euopeans.[74]

The victory of the proponents of inoculation elsewhere in Euope was made easier by the example set by Americans. It is supposed that Dutch physicians gained in confidence after the publicaion of Dr. J. V. B. Tennent's thesis, presented to the faculty at the Jniversity of Leyden. In his *Dissertatio . . . de Insitione Varioarum* (1764), Dr. Tennent, who had come from New Jersey, spoke f the new methods used in inoculation, and he included a table of noculations performed in several of the colonies. He observed that ut of over eight thousand inoculated, only nineteen died.

Wherever the fight went on Americans participated or their exerience was drawn upon, and, while sometimes the verdict was ostile, in the main the reactions were favorable. One of the first otices in France of inoculation quoted its good effects in Boston.[75] I. de La Condamine, in a memoir read to the Royal Academy of

[72] Woodville, 339–343; see Benj. Gale, *Historical Memoirs relating to the 'ractice of Inoculation in New England* (1765), in Royal Soc. Library, letters nd papers, IV, 261, sent to Dr. Huxham.

[73] J. A. Murray, *Historia Insitiones Variolarum in Suecia* . . . (Gottingae, 767), 156–157, referring to a Stockholm publication by Nils von Rosenstein 1764).

[74] P. Smith, *A History of Modern Culture*, II, 118; but R. H. Shryock, *The 'evelopment of Modern Medicine* (New York, 1947), 103–104, noted that while ıfant mortality showed a sharp drop, adults did not show any increase in life xpectancy in England. Tuberculosis and other diseases kept up a high adult eath rate.

[75] M. De La Coste, *Lettre sur L'Inoculation* . . . (Paris, 1723), 36, 37. An arlier one, J. B. Boyer, 1717, to the medical faculty at Montpelier went unoticed.

Science in France, urged the adoption of inoculation. Anoth
French writer drew attention to Dr. Adam Thompson's publicatio
on inoculation, pointing to its success in Boston in 1752. Thom
son's method of preparing the patient prior to inoculation—a ligh
nonstimulating diet, administering of mercury and antimony, mo
erate bleeding and purging—became known in Europe and in th
colonies as the American method. Dr. Thompson preferred to i
oculate on the leg so that the reaction should take place at th
greatest distance from the brain and other vital organs.[76]

Voltaire spread the gospel after seeing the results of inoculatio
in England. (When inoculation became the rage Parisian wome
always in search of novel fashions, began wearing *bonnets à l'inoc*
lation, decorated with ribbons having dots in imitation of poc
marks.) Dr. M. Gatti in a tract published in Brussels also gave
strong endorsement to inoculation.[77] By the middle of the centu
or shortly thereafter, inoculation had been introduced to the Net
erlands, the German states, Austria, Scandinavia, and Russia. D
Jan Ingenhousz, a close friend of Americans, inoculated the roy
family in Austria, and in Russia Catherine the Great set the e
ample for her subjects.

Dr. Thomas Bond, in a pamphlet published in Strasbourg, r
vealed a detailed knowledge of the progress of this medical practi
in England, France, and America, noting especially the similariti
of English and American methods.[78] A Society for General Inocul
tion was established in London, which was hailed by Dr. Lettsom
contributing greatly to popularizing this medical practice. Faci
ities for inoculation of the poor were established in a number of th
provincial towns of England after London had given the lead.[79]

---

[76] M. De La Condamine, *Mémoire sur L'Inoculation de la petite véro*
(Paris, 1754); M. Tissot, *L'Inoculation Justifiée . . .* (Paris, 1773, writte
1754), 24, 25; M. C. Leikind, "Variolation in Europe and America," *Ciba Sy*
posia, III, no. 10 (Jan., 1942), 1101.

[77] M. Gatti, *Nouvelles Réflexions sur la pratique de L'Inoculation* (Brusse
1767).

[78] T. Bond, *Défense de L'Inoculation et Relation des Progrès qu'elle a fa*
à Philadelphie en 1758 (Strasbourg, 1784); *Recueil de Pièces concernant L'I*
oculation de la petite Vérole, & propres d'en prouver la sécurité & l'utili
(Paris, 1756), 43 *et seq.*

[79] J. C. Lettsom, *A Letter to Sir Robert Barker and George Stacpoole, upo*

Dr. Benjamin Waterhouse engaged in a correspondence with Dr. ohn Haygarth, of England, on the subject of smallpox, in which he ave a number of details of treatment used in preventing its spread. Vaterhouse, who felt that Americans knew more about the disease han Europeans, said that the practice in his country, particularly n New England, was to have nearly everyone inoculated. Haygarth, who was engaged in the movement for the adoption of inoculation and had been writing to Franklin on the subject), informed others n Europe of the contents of his correspondence with Waterhouse. For example, in writing to the Council of Health in Geneva, Haygarth said, "The letters of Professor Waterhouse exhibit an excellent picture of a country, where the casual small-pox is justly dreaded and inoculation eagerly sought by soldiers, sailors, and every other class of people." [80] During the Revolution, hospitals for noculating the American troops were set up, and this large-scale noculation was undoubtedly the greatest mass experiment of the kind up to that time.

Waterhouse is, of course, better remembered for his work in behalf of vaccination as a more efficient preventive against smallpox. t was that good angel of Americans, Dr. Lettsom, who sent Waterhouse Edward Jenner's *Inquiry into the causes and effects of the . . Cow Pox.* On reading this work, said Waterhouse, he "was truck with the unspeakable advantages that might accrue to this country, and indeed to the human race at large, from the discovery of a mild distemper that would ever after secure the constitution rom that terrible scourge, the small-pox." He then drew up an account of cowpox, which was printed in an American newspaper.[81] Waterhouse, strongly supported by Jefferson, embarked on a campaign of public education in which he used information collected rom various English physicians. He requested some of the vaccine

General Inoculation (London, 1778); *An address to the Inhabitants of Liverpool on the subject of a General Inoculation for Small Pox* (Liverpool, Sept. ., 1781), 3–4.

[80] J. Haygarth, *A Sketch of a Plan to exterminate the casual Small-Pox from Great Britain . . . to which is added a correspondence . . .* (London, 1793), 359–364, 516, 562.

[81] *The Columbian Centinel,* March 12, 1799. Waterhouse had known Jenner n England ("Extracts from the Journal of Benjamin Waterhouse," in *Cambridge Hist. Soc., Publ.,* IV [1909], 24).

(which Dr. Haygarth sent him) and inoculated his own children with it. The people of New England, he said, had "set a noble example to their older brethren of Old-England, in adopting . . . inoculation for small pox, in 1721. Now, the English, in their turn lead the way in a practice still more salutiferous"; and he urged Americans to adopt it.[82]

Waterhouse, called "The American Jenner," was largely responsible for spreading a knowledge of vaccination through the states sending vaccine to doctors in Philadelphia, New York, New Hampshire, Charleston, and Virginia. A fellow Bostonian, Dr. James Jackson (who had studied vaccination with William Woodville in London) was also active in familiarizing Americans with the new medical treatment. In Baltimore, Dr. John Crawford, a founder of the local dispensary, was another of the pioneers in the practice of vaccination.[83] Doctors in New York formed a Vaccine Institution patterned after the one in London. By his English contemporaries Waterhouse was classed with Jenner, John Ring, and others in effecting the adoption of vaccination, and Jenner himself valued highly the judgment of the American doctor.[84]

The king of Spain sent vaccine to his colonies in this period, and the report of the famous vaccine expedition was sent to Jenner. Within a few years the practice of vaccination on a large scale had spread to rather remote Spanish areas in the American Southwest.[85] A New York doctor told Dr. Lettsom that the practice of vaccination had gained headway with great rapidity, even in regions far

[82] B. Waterhouse, *A Prospect of Exterminating the Small-Pox; being the History of the Variolae Vaccinae or Kine-pox* . . . (Boston, 1800); John Ring, *A Treatise on the Cow-Pox; containing the History of Vaccine Inoculation* . . . (London, 1801), 458.

[83] Packard, I, 437, II, 978; M. C. Leikind, "An Episode in the History of Small Pox Vaccination in New Hampshire," *Bulletin of the History of Medicine,* VII (1939), 671–687.

[84] B. Waterhouse, *A Prospect of exterminating the Small Pox* (Cambridge, Mass., 1802), part II; this was inscribed to Lettsom and Jenner; Lettsom, *Hints designed to promote Beneficence, Temperance and Medical Science* (London, 1801), III, 25, 66.

[85] P. K. Brown, "A Review of the Early Vaccination Controversy . . . and the spread of vaccination to the Spanish possessions of America," *California State Journal of Medicine* XIII (May, 1914); Josef Larrañaja (1815–1819) New Mexico, Mss. *Record of Vaccinations,* Huntington Library.

removed from the large cities. From a small Ohio community, a correspondent told Lettsom that he was taking some vaccine to near-by Indians.[86]

The problem of eradicating smallpox, first by inoculation and then by vaccination, was the central one in transatlantic medical communications. The success that attended this American-European co-operative attack on one of humanity's worst scourges was a promise of greater victories to come in the war against disease.

---

[86] Pettigrew, II, 174, 327.

CHAPTER IX

America and the Utopian Ideal

UTOPIA has nearly always been in the past or the future. Rarely has it coincided with the present. Europeans with Utopian dreams had the striking good fortune to find them apparently materialized in the lands beyond the western horizon. Thomas More in his *Utopia* and Montaigne in his *Essays* were but two of many writers who revealed the stimulating effects of the New World discovery on the Old World's imaginative life. Onto America was projected the blueprint of a society far removed from the European reality.[1]

It was not, however, until the later period of colonization that America and the Utopian ideal existed actively in the consciousness of the mass of people whose yearning was more real than that of the litterateur. Letters from pioneer settlers, as well as books, pamphlets, and articles with biased or accurate information, all told Europeans of advantages overseas. Those who had found Utopia were more vocal than those who had sought it in vain. With the ingratiating language of a real-estate promoter, South Carolina was spoken of as a country which might not attract the gay, amusement-loving rich, but for those who like solitude, gardening, "and the like innocent Delights of plain simple Nature . . . there can scarce any Place in the British Dominions be found, that will better answer their Expectation." [2] American settlers belonged to the class of

---

[1] Sidney Lee, "The Call of the West," *Scribner's*, XLII (1907), 316; G. Atkinson, *Les Relations Voyages du xvii*e *Siècle et l'Evolution des Idées* (Paris, 1925), 9 ff.

[2] *A Letter from South Carolina* . . . (dated June 1, 1710) written by a Swiss Gentleman to his Friend at Bern (2nd ed., London, 1732), 56.

simple folk, men of nature, whom it pleased eighteenth-century philosophers to idealize.

In recalling a sophisticated society to simplicity the Indians played an important part. These "noble savages" were a guide to a new moral order, and curiosity about them was enormous. To a century steeped in classical traditions, these modern pagans suggested comparisons with the Greeks of old. The Indians were portrayed as possessed of classical beauty, and a common impulse attributed to them the moral qualities of their ancient prototypes. Lafitau, in his widely known *Les Moeurs des Sauvages,* emphasized the similarity between Indians and the inhabitants of ancient Greece by placing statues, bas-reliefs, medals, and scenes of American life alongside those of Greek life. This confusion in thought was worse confounded when the American settlers were alleged on occasion to have become "Indianized" and at the same time possessed of the virtues which drew attention to them as creatures in a Grecian idyl. Cotton Mather, when sending some squash seed, etc., by his son to Sir William Ashurst, said, "It comes by a *Tame Indian* for so the Europeans are pleased sometimes to denominate the children that are born in these Regions." [3]

Americans were, to the ordinary European understanding, Indians. Writers found it necessary to emphasize the point that, when referring to Americans, they did not mean Indians, but rather descendants of European parents. By an easy transference in thought, phrases descriptive of aboriginal characteristics were also used to describe traits of white neighbors. In a large number of books, some issued for popular consumption, it was written, "Liberty . . . is the prevailing passion of the Americans" (i.e., Indians); the *Encyclopedia Britannica* characterized the New Englanders in similar language.[4] In the fateful year 1776, in a small, inexpensive *History of North and South America,* appeared like thoughts: "The darling passion of the Americans is liberty, and that in its fullest extent; nor is it the original natives only to whom this passion is confined; our colonies sent thither seem to have imbibed the same principles." Hessian officers in the midst of the Revolution spoke of the "in-

[3] Mather to Ashurst, Dec. 10, 1712, Huntington Library; see also Mather to Royal Society, M. 2.46, Royal Soc. Library.

[4] *Encyclopedia Britannica* (1797), 544, 548, 664.

domitable ideas of liberty" possessed by Americans, who were "bold unyielding and fearless." [5]

British publications said American whites had copied various customs from the Indians which gave them a physical distinction matching the Greek ideal of beauty. Children born in America of European parents were said to have escaped the ailments afflicting youngsters in the Old World.

The *Scots Magazine* one year printed extracts from an American work, and, although much of it was misinformation, it revealed what people willed to believe. In New England, it said, "The greatest care is taken of the limbs and bodies of infants, which are kept strait by means of a board; a practice learnt of the Indian women who abhor all crooked people; so that deformity is here a rarity . . . The women are fair, handsome, genteel. They have, indeed adopted various customs of the Indian women." [6] In a very elaborate London publication that had almost a thousand subscribers, and whose words were often repeated in works of lesser note, the Greek ideal of physical beauty was said to have been realized by the Indians and American settlers: "The Indians of America are tall and straight beyond the proportion of most other nations." Indian women were said to bear children more easily than English mothers. "The descendants of the Europeans in Carolina," the writer continued, "are a straight, tall well-limbed and active people, whose children are seldom troubled with rickets, or with the many other distempers with which the Europeans are afflicted." The women, who were as well proportioned as any in the world, were very fruitful. "They seldom miscarry, and have very easy labours." [7] A letter to the widely circulated *Gentleman's Magazine* (1752) said that American-born women of British parents "in point of beauty and merit . . . seemed rather . . . to have improv'd, than degenerated by being transplanted into another climate."

More than one hundred years before, in the early days of the

[5] Anon., printed for J. Whitaker (London, 1776), I, 58; *Letters from Major Baurmeister to Colonel von Jungkenn . . . 1777–1778* (B. A. Uhlendorf and E. Vosper, eds., Philadelphia, 1937), 41.

[6] *Scots Magazine,* XLIV (1782), 337–340.

[7] Fenning and Collyer, II, 643, 666–673. There was much talk in Europe (and even in America) about people and animals degenerating in the colonies.

Massachusetts Bay settlement, William Wood had written, in his *New England's Prospect,* that Indian women had enjoyed easy childbirth, and that white women had recovered more speedily after childbirth in America than they had when living in England.

In other respects, too, this development in European minds of a multiple Indian-Graeco-Roman-American personality may be noted. A writer was thus stirred to eulogistic comment on the capture of Louisburg by the colonials: "When I consider the coolness and bravery with which they marched to action, and their return from victory to their several occupations, I take into my mind the great image of the ancient Romans leaving the plow for the field of battle, and retiring after their conquests to the plow again." [8] Thomas B. Hollis of the family that lavished gifts on Harvard wrote its president, Joseph Willard, in 1788: "Our papers mention that there is an intention of having the Olympic Games revived in America. All her friends wish it and say they are capable of it, and having acted on Greek principles, should have Greek exercises." [9]

It was among the Cherokee Indians with whom he had lived for seven years that a German, one Christian G. Priber, brought to fruition communistic ideas that had been budding for a long time during his stay in Saxony and England. His "Kingdom of Paradise," which he hoped would later be imitated by France, provided that women as well as men be sharers in the liberty accorded by this commonwealth of Indians. Priber was only one of many who were dreaming of a society to be organized on an equalitarian and communistic basis.[10]

Travel reports of the seventeenth and eighteenth centuries, particularly those of the Jesuits from South America told eager Europeans of ready-made Utopias. The communal settlements of the natives of Paraguay, under Jesuit supervision, had a remarkable appeal for Europeans. But these distant Utopias were rather vague, and it needed the shock of personal contact with people more like themselves, engaged in the renovation of society, to awaken Euro-

[8] *Gentleman's Magazine,* XV (1745), 422.

[9] *Mass. Hist. Soc., Proc.,* XLIII (1909–1910), 629.

[10] V. W. Crane, "A Lost Utopia of the First American Frontier," *Sewanee Review,* XXVII (1919), 50–58; André Lichtenberger, *Le Socialisme Utopique: Etudes sur quelques précurseurs inconnus du socialisme* (Paris, 1898), 217–218.

peans from dreaming to doing. In their own world of the eighteent century eyes turned first to England; then after the middle of th century they turned to Corsica; America next thrilled the Europea imagination; and finally Utopian hopes were centered on France.

Voltaire and Montesquieu made it fashionable to locate the lan of liberty in England, although some of her own residents wer more skeptical. In the literature of social criticism England was use as a weapon of assault against the existing social order on the Conti nent. But the struggle of Corsica and its leader Pascal Paoli wa more than a mere footnote to a literary device that ridiculed con temporary society. The conflict helped crystallize liberal sentimen and sharpened the line of division from conservative thought.[11] Englishmen wrote poems in praise of Corsicans, Goethe was deepl impressed by their leader, and Americans, already political dis senters themselves, delighted to honor the name of Paoli. He was a inspiration to the colonial Sons of Liberty, some of whom gave hi name to their children. The fire whose fuel was gathered in Eng land and kindled by Corsica was further fed from America.

America already held within itself the seeds of destruction for th Old World's social structure, although a changing industrial mech anism and altered intellectual outlook in Europe were, in them selves, sufficiently powerful to disrupt a world. But the vague aspi rations of Europeans toward a new society were given solidity by th concrete appearance of the world of tomorrow in the thirteen col onies. The fortunes of the many thousands who had sailed from Europe to seek a new homeland, with all their fears and hopes, ha become part of the stream of consciousness of those who were left be hind. For those who had missed the "Mayflower," there was at leas the hope that on her return trip she would bring back some mani festation of that new spirit rising overseas—new wine to be poure into old bottles. It was the American Revolution, says the well known British historian, Professor Reginald Coupland, which wa the "chief factor in the collapse of the Georgian reaction."

[11] C. B. Tinker, *Nature's Simple Plan* (Princeton, 1922), chap. ii; G. P. Ander son, "Pascal Paoli," *Col. Soc. Mass., Trans.*, XXVI (1924–1926), 180–210; F. H Reinsch, *Goethe's Political Interests prior to 1787* ("Univ. of Calif., Publ. i Mod. Philology," X, 1920), 199.

England was not alone in feeling the impact of distant events. Scotland, Ireland, France, Belgium, the German states, the Dutch Netherlands, the Scandinavian countries, and others to the east and south, and Latin America too—all these were stirred. John Adams was right when he said that a complete history of the American Revolution would be a "history of mankind during that epoch." Near the end of his life he told a correspondent that the Revolution was no common event: "Its effects and consequences have already been awful over a great part of the Globe; And when and where are they to cease?" The American Revolution and its effects so faded into the more momentous French Revolution that the particular influence of America has often been overlooked. But the contemporary European did not miss its significance.[12]

News from America after 1760 received much more space than formerly in European periodicals. Political news, especially, attracted readers. Papers sometimes doubled their sales in times of acute political controversy, but the journals which failed to keep up to the minute with news reports on American developments found their readers drifting away. The letters of "Anti-Sejanus" against Lord Bute in *The Public Advertiser* of London, increased daily sales from 1,500 to 3,000 copies. Average daily sales of papers had grown from 23,600 in 1753 to 41,600 in 1775, and, despite the extra tax of a half-penny in 1776, sales rose to over 45,000 in the next few years. Papers which did not present up-to-date news were severely handicapped. A Scottish periodical suspended publication for a time, with the explanation that its inadequate materials on the American Revolution were "ill calculated to satisfy a curiosity so ardent or an anxiety so natural at the present momentous crisis." [13]

Resistance to the Stamp Act won for America an important position in the English press, and special sections were set up in newspapers to deal with news from the colonies. A new department

---

[12] This, and the preceding paragraph, come from M. Kraus, in *The Era of the American Revolution: Studies inscribed to Evarts B. Greene,* 332–333. Adams' correspondent was H. Niles, Feb. 13, 1818.

[13] Stephens, IV (1761–1770), 370; W. J. Couper, *The Edinburgh Periodical Press* (1908), II, 120–121; A. S. Collins, "The Growth of the Reading Public during the 18th Century," *The Review of English Studies,* II (1926), 433.

called the "American Budget," which promised to make a special effort to collect and impartially present colonial news, appeared in the *London Packet* in 1774, and other newspapers adopted similar plans.[14] A large part of the first three volumes of *The London Review of English and Foreign Literature,* which began publication in 1775, was devoted to reviews of books relating to the struggle with America.

After the conclusion of the War for American Independence the London press showed a continued interest in the former colonies, which were a subject of everyday talk. Many hundreds of publications connected with the American Revolution were issued in the years 1760 to 1790. The Revolution was a powerful stimulus to historical writing in Europe and, of course, in America. In general it strengthened the concept of the idea of progress in historiography, already enunciated by earlier eighteenth-century historians.

Europe's children had grown to manhood overseas in a new world of their own making, and to liberals in the Old World it was intolerable that this structure should be destroyed. Uncertain lines in Europe rallied on receipt of the news of revolt in America, and the revolutionaries were heartened by the response that came from well-wishers in nearly every country. English and American Whigs joined hands in opposition to the administration. The Boston Sons of Liberty were cheered by the support of John Wilkes. One of these radicals wrote to him, "If anything short of a miracle can save Great Britain and the colonies (for it seems to me they must stand or fall together) my hopes are placed on you, & a few more brave, Just & Tenacious Men." American sympathizers visited Wilkes in prison, where they talked of common action against military authority. Some of them named their sons for him. French women, in 1770, wore handkerchiefs à la Wilkes.[15]

Revolutionary ideas in America were stimulated by native pe-

---

[14] J. F. Hinkhouse, *The Preliminaries of the American Revolution as seen in the English Press 1763–1775* (New York, 1926); see also C. L. Carlson, *The First Magazine, A History of the Gentleman's Magazine* (Providence, 1938), chap. vii.

[15] Wilkes Mss., Brit. Mus. Add. Mss., 30870 (f. 77); 30871 (f. 34); Wilkes to Wm. Palfrey, *Col. Soc. Mass., Trans.,* XXXIV (1937–1942), 411–428; C. H. Lockitt, *The Relations of French and English Society, 1763–1793* (London, 1920), 76.

riodicals, and many readers were told about such distinguished liberal friends in England as Wilkes, Chatham, and Mrs. Catharine Macaulay. Ezra Stiles assured Mrs. Macaulay that Americans all believed that "providence intends a glorious English Empire" in their land. "We suck it in with our Mothers milk," he said, "it grows up with us, it propagates with increased vigor." And when American population shall have doubled and redoubled, her enemies will be unable to chastise her. Hoping Mrs. Macaulay would come to America, he prepared an itinerary enabling her to meet all the colonial liberal and radical leaders, starting with Christopher Gadsden in South Carolina. The gallant Charles Lee urged Mrs. Macaulay to have as many daughters as possible, made in her image, "and some descendants of Catharine Macaulay may attribute the salvation of the state to your progeny." [16]

Horne Tooke defended the American colonists in a political speech to fellow Englishmen: "The Security of their Freedom and their Rights is essential to the enjoyment of our own. We should never for a moment forget this important truth, that when the people of America are enslaved, we cannot be free; and they can never be enslaved whilst we continue free. We are stones of one arch, and must stand or fall together." [17] Granville Sharp feared that Parliamentary ignorance of the British Constitution might lead to imperial disaster. He warned America against letting the British troops become a standing army, "the Bane of all Societies . . . as dangerous to the *Liberties of America itself* as to the Peace and Commerce of Great Britain." In a friendly caution to Benjamin Rush, Sharp said, "Beware of an American Cromwell." [18]

The Scottish minister, John Erskine, in a pamphlet entitled *Shall I go to War with American Brethren,* said that victory for the British was not at all a foregone conclusion. The colonials would use unorthodox tactics—guerrilla warfare and the like, similar to Indian practices—which might wear down a standardized army. American military practice did, in fact, suggest a new mobility and

---

[16] C. A. Greenough, "New England Almanacs 1766–1775 and the American Revolution," *Amer. Antiq. Soc., Proc.,* n.s. XLV (1935), 316; Stiles Mss., Nov. 13, 1772; *Memoirs of the Late Charles Lee* (New York, 1793), 199, May 2, 1767.

[17] Yarborough, *John Horne Tooke,* 78; see Hinkhouse, 87, 193–201.

[18] Sharp to Rush, Jan. 31, July 18, 1775, Ridgway Library.

aggressiveness to older European armies. The New England vic
tory at Louisburg in 1745, said Erskine, furnished Britain "with a
price to purchase peace, after a most disastrous and unsuccessfu
war." Erskine was especially fearful of the establishment of a mili
tary government in America; the precedent would be alarming, fo
it might extend ultimately to Britain herself. "Nothing," he said
"can so much tend to prevent the establishment of despotism in th
British empire, as every part of that empire considering it as at onc
their interest and duty, to guard against encroachments on th
right of every other part." [19]

The assembly of South Carolina sent £1,500 to the Supporter
of the Bill of Rights, a radical English society, to be used in defens
of subjects of the British Empire, particularly those "who by as
serting the just rights of the people have or shall become obnoxiou
to Administration & suffer from the hand of power." The Englis
Whigs, sometimes against their more sober judgment, were pushe
farther along a more radical path because of their support of th
American cause.[20] John Almon, close friend of Wilkes, was con
stantly reprinting papers and pamphlets sent him from America
His *Remembrancer* was designed to keep all relevant document
and writings bearing on the Revolution in one publication. His own
belief was that the governmental measures against the colonies orig
inated, not in the ministry, but in a junto of American and English
traitors.[21]

An Irish song and poem said the hope of relief from Brit
ish tyranny lay in victory for Americans. A partisan of Ireland's
cause was certain that America's independence was assured by 1778

---

[19] John Erskine, *Shall I go to War with my American Brethren* (London,
1769); Gershoy, *From Despotism to Revolution,* 163; H. Kohn, *The Idea o
Nationalism* (New York, 1944), 379.

[20] Wilkes Mss., 30871 (f. 7); see also papers by G. H. Guttridge, "The Whig
Opposition in England during the American Revolution," *Journal of Modern
History,* VI (1934), 1–14; "English Liberty and the American Revolution,"
Pacific Coast Branch, *Amer. Hist. Assn., Proc.,* V (1930), 151–159; *English Whig
gism and the American Revolution* ("Univ. of Calif., Publ. in Hist.," XXVIII,
1928), 142–144.

[21] J. Almon, *Memoirs of a late Eminent Bookseller* (London, 1790), chap. iv,
32–35, 121.

out, he asked Franklin, "When will Ireland's turn come?" [22] Rich-
rd Price's *Observations on Civil Liberty,* strongly supporting the
olonies, sold sixty thousand copies within a year, was translated for
Dutch and German readers, and brought the author an invitation
o settle in America. In it, he asserted, "we are not maintaining but
iolating our own constitution in America." [23]

It was in the years of the Wilkes crisis that it became popular to
hold open meetings, where public opinion could express itself on
great political questions. There was a sharpening of the political
consciousness of Englishmen, who began to watch their representa-
ives in Parliament more closely. It was becoming more and more
difficult to ignore the weight of public opinion.[24]

American progressives and their English counterparts were in
ntimate contact during these years and continually reinvigorated
each other. Their exchange of correspondence, their common understanding and warm sympathy account for the similarity in the
organization and sentiments of the radical associations on both
sides of the Atlantic. The debt that each owed to the other is im-
measurable. American propagandists, notably Franklin, kept the
political pot a-boiling. Cartwright, Jebb, and many others wrote in
behalf of the colonies; Cartwright displayed the Declaration of Independence in a conspicuous position in his own home. Opposing
the claim of Parliament to tax the colonies, Cartwright said that
America and Ireland should be considered as sister kingdoms: "I
would cement a lasting union with them as between the separate
branches of one great family." He defended the Boston Tea Party
and spoke of its "glorious *illegality,*" terming it an act of "absolute
moral and political *necessity.*" Half a century after these events,
Cartwright still maintained his ties with America in correspondence
with Jefferson and others.[25]

---

[22] *Col. Soc. Mass., Trans.,* XVIII (1915–1916), 205–206; XIII (1910–1911), 254–257; *Calendar of Franklin Papers,* I, 379, MacMahon, March 22, 1778.

[23] Roland Thomas, *Richard Price* (London, 1924), 73–87; Price, *Observations on Civil Liberty* . . . (London, 1776), 49.

[24] W. E. H. Lecky, *England in the Eighteenth Century* (London, 1878–1890), III, 189, 247–248.

[25] D. M. Clark, *British Opinion and the American Revolution* (New Haven, 1930), 158, 175–178; V. W. Crane, "Certain Writings of Benjamin Franklin on

John Jebb who urged the Americans to be firm at once to avoi
bloodshed later, nevertheless pinned his hopes on legal solutions
Among the group of reformers led by Jebb and Cartwright wa
Thomas Day, author of the popular *Sandford and Merton*. He ha
studied law at the Middle Temple in the company of American
who kept him posted on the colonial side of the controversy. H
was particularly friendly with John, son of Henry Laurens, whos
influence was important in strengthening Day's political liberalism
and humanitarianism. The latter's *Ode for the New Year, 1776* wa
a strong defense of the colonies, whose cause he again espoused, dur
ing a particularly gloomy period, in *The Desolation of America.*[2]
In the list of those in England who threw their weight on the sid
of the colonials special mention should be made of the Dissenters
for they were very close to the American revolutionaries, and thei
own agitation for political and social change was given greater so
lidity by American success.

In the general struggle to broaden the area of freedom in the
eighteenth century, the movement for a freer press is of first impor
tance. A powerful impetus to free expression of opinion came from
the Zenger case in New York. Many years after the event, court-
rooms and legislative halls in England and America echoed the arguments of Andrew Hamilton in defense of Zenger, charged with
publishing a criminal libel against the colonial governor. Hamilton
claimed that the right to criticize and complain of acts of governors
was a natural right, a right claimed by all free men. In opposition
to the prosecution, which quoted English precedent that publication of itself was libelous (its truth or untruth being irrelevant),
Hamilton retorted that truth ought to govern the whole matter of
libels and that the jury should judge the facts in the case. Further-
more, he went on to say that it was "strange doctrine to press every-

---

the British Empire and the American Colonies," *Papers of Bibliog. Soc. of America*, XXVIII (1934), 1–27; John Cartwright, *American Independence, the interest and glory of Great Britain . . .* (London, 1774), 13, 61; F. D. Cartwright, *Life and Correspondence of Major Cartwright* (London, 1826), II, 265–276.

[26] G. W. Gignilliat, *The Author of Sandford and Merton—A Life of Thomas Day, Esq.* (New York, 1932), 50, 121, 132, 139.

hing for law here [in America] which is so in England," for what was often good law in the mother country was not necessarily of equal value in the colonies. Hamilton's address to the jury, which acquitted Zenger, became a classic on both sides of the Atlantic. The proceedings of the trial were reprinted a number of times in America and England during the rest of the century. It need hardly be added that conservative opinion was startled by the novelty of Hamilton's plea, which it found subversive of authority.

Legal authorities recognize that the trial was of the greatest significance in the development of the law of criminal libel and in establishing the freedom of the press. An important principle was laid down, contrary to prevailing legal practice, that newspapers must be free to make comments, even severely critical, upon the acts of government officials. News came from London of the considerable interest shown there in the trial, and the speech of Zenger's advocate was hailed as a splendid assertion of public liberty, for his words defended as well the rights and privileges of Britons.[27]

The English followed the case closely after Zenger's arrest had been chronicled in the London papers. Pamphlets and newspaper extracts emphasized the meaning of the trial and its outcome as a check against despotic power. It was no mere coincidence that a new edition of Milton's *Areopagitica* appeared in 1738 while the Zenger case was on the front pages of the press.[28]

The Zenger precedent was seized upon by British and American writers to protect defendants in similar cases. A British bookseller, William Owen, was prosecuted in 1752 for publishing an item charged as libelous. The jury, in opposition to the judge, determined the matter of law as well as the matter of fact and voted not guilty. A dissertation on libels, upholding Hamilton's principles, was published at this time and in it the Zenger and Owen cases were quoted as precedents. In reviewing the history of the Owen case,

[27] S. Kobre, *The Development of the Colonial Newspaper* (Pittsburgh, 1944), 67–68; for the whole case see L. Rutherford, *John Peter Zenger* (New York, 1904). R. B. Morris, "Massachusetts and the Common Law," *Amer. Hist. Rev.*, XXXI (1926), 451, points out that a Massachusetts law of 1645 was an overlooked precedent which might have been invoked by Hamilton.

[28] *The Daily Journal,* Jan. 23, 1735; *The Country Journal: or The Craftsman* (London), Jan. 21, 1738; *Gentleman's Magazine,* VIII (1738), 35; XV (1745), 373–374.

the *Monthly Review* spoke of the frequent republication of the Zenger trial, which, it said, was too well known to require any extended comment. The magazine praised the jury in the Owen case for judging "(which it was their GREAT DUTY to do) as to *fact, law* and *justice* of the whole &c." In presenting to the public a narrative of both Zenger's and Owen's trials, a foreword said, "In an age of persecution, when few people dare to write and fewer still to print, these Trials ought to be universally read by every True Friend to English Liberty, who will here see two of the most noble stands which have been made since the Revolution 1689, in Defense of Constitutional Freedom." [29]

The Irish press, too, following closely the events in America in the Revolutionary era, scrutinized all threats to liberty. The *Freeman's Journal* printed a "Letter . . . to be read by all Jurymen" on the subject of libel, and the action of the American jury in declaring Zenger not guilty was held up as a noble example. A vigorous campaign in favor of freedom of the press was carried on in succeeding issues of the paper, which published a long story of the Zenger case, including the celebrated speech of Hamilton. British writers, looking back over the sequence of events which culminated in the Revolution, pointed to the Zenger case to show that long before 1775 Americans were bent on opposing the will of the British government and had been striving continuously to be ruled by their own laws. Early in 1770 in New York, in the midst of political turmoil in which Captain Alexander MacDougall, the "Wilkes of America," was charged with authorship of libelous material, the booksellers reprinted the proceedings of Zenger's trial.[30]

Many years passed before the principles for which Hamilton argued were incorporated into English law. It was not until 1792 that a bill, introduced by Charles James Fox and passed by both

---

[29] *Gentleman's Magazine,* XXIII (1753), 203; Joseph Towers, *An Enquiry . . . whether Juries are . . . Judges of Law, as well as of Fact . . .* (London, 1785); *Monthly Review,* XXXII (1765); *The Trial of John Peter Zenger . . . to which is now added . . . the trial of Mr. Owen, Bookseller . . .* (London, 1765).

[30] *Freeman's Journal,* Feb. 21, 1764; David Loch, *Essays on the Trade, Commerce, Manufactures and Fisheries of Scotland . . .* (Edinburgh, 1778–1779), III, 134–197; A. Mackraby to Sir Philip Francis, March 10, 1770, *Penn. Mag. of Hist. and Biog.,* XI (1887), 493.

Houses, provided that the jury might give a verdict of guilty or not guilty upon the whole matter at issue and should not be required or directed by the judge to find a defendant guilty merely on the proof of publication of a paper held to be criminally libelous. A German very familiar with England wrote at this time that England's press was much freer than it had been twenty years earlier. In England and elsewhere the American Revolutionary era had loosened the official ties that had long restricted freedom of expression.[31]

The close association between American and English radicals was only one of the threads that linked Europe's destiny with America. France too found support for a liberal position in American developments. French literature on America was more voluminous after 1770, although much of it had appeared before this date, inspired by Huguenot visions of a Utopian settlement. No one did more to stimulate an interest in foreign lands than the Abbé Prévost, whose *Manon Lescaut* had for its background the far-off colony in Louisiana. Works relating to America were very well known in France, which regarded them less as gems of literature than as propaganda. French officers, returned from the Revolutionary War in America, published accounts of the new country; translations of travel books and histories of the states further served to spread a knowledge of America.[32] Lafayette in particular, was a most important channel through which the American Revolutionary spirit was communicated to France.

Into a restless French society Benjamin Franklin threw some elements that combined to make a turbulent mixture. His remarks and his writings, keen and most often good-humored, were making accepted traditions ridiculous. It was one of Franklin's great honors, said Richard Price, that he had contributed much to bring on the

---

[31] R. L. Crosman, "The Legal and Journalistic Significance of the Trial of John Peter Zenger," *Rocky Mountain Law Review*, X (1938), 258–267; F. A. Wendeborn, *A View of England towards the close of the Eighteenth Century* (London, 1791), II, 25.

[32] G. Chinard, *Les Réfugies Huguenots en Amérique avec une Introduction sur le Mirage Américain* (Paris, 1925); Pierre Heinrich, *L'Abbé Prévost et la Louisiane—Etude sur la Valeur Documentaire de Manon Lescaut* (Paris, 1907); B. Faÿ, *Ouvrages Français Relatifs aux Etats-Unis, 1770–1800* (Paris, 1925).

Revolution in France.[33] Jefferson too had a great deal to teach th
French, who considered him "the apostle of the religion of liberty.'
French literature on America, often colored by Franklin's influence
was full of enthusiasm and moral precepts.

The Abbé Raynal's liberal study of European colonies has bee
thought by some to have had as much influence on the French Revo
lution as Rousseau's *Social Contract*. Condorcet, who was intensel
aware of the implications for Europe of the American Revolution
celebrated it with lyrical enthusiasm.[34] In the opinion of Joh
Adams, the American Revolution was possibly as influential i
bringing on the Revolution in France as were the writings of Dide
rot, D'Alembert, Voltaire, and Rousseau. His view was sustaine
by a contemporary German writer's admonition to those who wer
tracing the origins of the French Revolution to the writings o
Rousseau *et. al.* to remember the *acts* of the American Revolutio
and their stimulating suggestiveness.[35]

The new American state constitutions, especially Virginia's, wit
its declaration of rights and its notable passages on tolerance an
liberty, were brought to the notice of Frenchmen, who were one da
to write their own declaration of the rights of man. La Rochefou
cald d'Enville, a liberal duke very friendly to America, was amon
the first to publish translations of the American constitutions whic
had been given him by Franklin. The state constitutions wer
thought infinitely superior to those of the famous republican gov
ernments of Greece and Rome, which were said to be in many re
spects "unjust and immoral." The latter promoted "a ferocious and
contracted patriotism," which was little better than the spirit of
union that held together a band of robbers, who talked of fidelity
and honor among themselves but were "the plunderers and mur
derers of all beyond the pale of their community"—this was the

[33] Price to Rush, June 19, 1790, Ridgway Library.

[34] Chinard, *Thomas Jefferson*, 216; Faÿ, *The Revolutionary Spirit in France and America*, 158–159, 194, 264–267; Anatole Feugère, *L'Abbé Raynal, un précurseur de la Révolution* (Angoulême, 1922); J. Salwyn Schapiro, *Condorcet* (New York, 1934), chap. xii; L. M. Gidney, *L'Influence des Etats-Unis D'Amérique sur Brissot, Condorcet et Mme. Roland* (Paris, 1930).

[35] Adams to F. A. Van der Kemp, April 19, 1790, Hist. Soc. Penn., Mss.; H. S. King, *Echoes of the American Revolution in German Literature* ("Univ. of Calif., Publ. in Mod. Philology," XIV, no. II, 1929), 89.

udgment of the translator of the Abbé de Mably's work on America. The Abbé examined the laws of the several states, and, though a ittle fearful of too much democracy himself, found mainly words of praise for the new governments.[36] It is important to remember hat America was debtor as well as creditor to France, whose leading iberals and radicals were widely known overseas in American pe-iodicals, colleges, and legislative halls.[37]

The German states too were brought within the orbit of Amer-can revolutionary influence. Though the bartered blood of Hes-ian mercenaries that flowed from east to west sought to quench he fires of revolution, ideas that moved from west to east proved tronger. In fact many of the Hessians sent to fight Americans de-erted or were given permission to remain at the war's end, pre-erring life in America to existence under petty German princes. One must not expect German princes outside Prussia, in league with a Hanoverian descendant on the English throne, to favor ex-pressions of sympathy with America. But America did not lack sup-porters. German interest in America was of long standing, and, hrough articles and books in the hundreds, Germany was in-formed of developments overseas. During the Revolution, Germany kept in close touch with America; in her periodicals could be found a continuous record of the war.[38]

Young Germany saw in America a political Utopia, and some of her youthful writers thought to emigrate thither. In the works of Goethe, Lessing, Klopstock, Wieland, Herder, Schiller, and Kant may be found enthusiastic expressions of interest in America. The German magazines printed many contributions that spoke of Amer-

[36] Chinard, in *The Amer. Philosophical Soc., Library Bulletin,* 1943, 90–91; Abbé de Mably, *Observations on the Government and Laws of the United States of America . . .* (London, 1784), translator's preface, *passim.*

[37] See M. M. Harrison-Barr, *Voltaire in America 1744–1800;* P. M. Spurlin, *Montesquieu in America, 1760–1801* (Baton Rouge, 1940); R. F. Harvey, *Jean Jacques Burlamaqui; a Liberal Tradition in American Constitutionalism* (Chapel Hill, 1937).

[38] P. B. Baginsky, *German Works Relating to America 1493–1800* (New York, 1942); also E. E. Doll, *American History as Interpreted by German Historians from 1770 to 1815* ("Trans. Amer. Philos. Soc.," n.s. XXXVIII, pt. 5, 421–534; Philadelphia, 1949).

ica as an escape for the disheartened and disinherited. In printing the constitution of Pennsylvania in 1777, a Leipzig publication wrote hopefully: "Perhaps we shall attempt in the future to test this thing thoroughly, according to the fundamentals of political science and the general law of the land." Berlin had two newspapers which appeared every other day, and both had strong sympathy for Americans. The American Revolution prompted the German press to speak with greater boldness, and, among other matters, the traffic in soldiers came under severe criticism. A sharp political alertness is apparent in Germany in this period; while monarchy still had its majority of supporters, there were many who believed with Kant that to develop the entire mass of the body politic democracy was the highest form of government that had yet been devised.[39]

A fiery spirit in German poetry burned bright at this time. In *Sturm und Drang,* whose scene is laid in America at the beginning of the Revolution, Klinger's hero cries, "Ah, let me but stand securely on American soil, where all is new." In *Die Freiheit Amerikas* (1783) European peoples are adjured to look to the model of American liberty, now made secure. Schubart in his semiweekly, the *Deutsche Chronik,* during the years 1774 to 1777, wavered between love for England and love for America. Some ten years later in the *Vaterlandische Chronik* he definitely favored America as the only country where the oppressed might find asylum, since England, Holland, and Switzerland had become inhospitable. In America, said Schubart, thirteen "golden gates are open to the victims of intolerance and despotism."

Friedrich L. Stolberg, in *Die Zukunft* (1782) said that not only North America but also South America would be free. Would the Old World, he asked, then be content to remain in darkness? *Ueber Nordamerka und Demokratie* (1782) by J. C. Schmohl was a very influential book. The author, having penetrated to the core of American ideas, had gone to America to fight for them. Though not hostile to England, Schmohl believed that America was destined to guide Europe out of political and social disintegration and bring it freedom. Despite the apparent imminence of fundamental social

[39] T. S. Baker, in *Amer. Germanica,* I (1897); *Ephemeriden der Menschheit . . .* (Leipzig, 1777), I, 40; King, *Echoes of the American Revolution in German Literature,* 36–37, 82, 174, 181–184.

change in Germany as expressed in her literature, no such change occurred. It was, in these years, mainly an intellectual movement (and German intellectuals are not distinguished for starting revolutions); those who might have given it something of a mass basis had abstracted themselves from the German population and gone to America.[40]

While Swiss sentiments generally favored England, the thought was often expressed that Europe was about played out, that in America would be found the future home of liberty. Johannes von Müller, close friend of Francis Kinloch, an American in Europe, who lectured him on America's destiny, was writing his history of Switzerland and studying the British colonies at the same time. He became convinced that his generation was standing on the divide between two ages; it was his duty, he felt, to write history in the service of the coming age. But he abhorred violence, believing rather in the peaceful evolution of political institutions. In fact Müller looked forward to the evolution of Great Britain and her colonies into a British Commonwealth.[41] Ischiffeley, a Swiss liberal dedicating the remainder of his days to the political welfare of society, thought nothing could contribute better to this end than the diffusion of the new American state constitutions among all peoples. He planned to translate them for the people of his own land and for those of Germany and Italy.[42]

Italian patriots, too, found fuel for their fervor in the American struggle, particularly in the writings of Franklin, which were collected in numerous editions before and after 1800. At Venice, 1797, appeared *Il buon uomo Riccardo e la costituzione di Pensilvania, Italianizzati per uso della Democratica Veneta Restaurazione.* A student of Franklin's influence on Italy writes: "[His] works and

---

[40] *Penn. Germ. Soc., Proc.,* XIII (1904), pt. XIII, 56–57; J. A. Walz, "The American Revolution and German Literature," *Mod. Lang. Notes,* XVI (1901), 458–462; J. T. Hatfield and E. Hochbaum, "The Influence of the American Revolution upon German Literature," *Amer.-Germanica,* III, nos. III, IV (1899–1900), 338–385; J. A. Walz, "Three Swabian Journalists in the American Revolution," *Germ. Amer. Annals,* n.s. I (1903), 211–212; King, 33, 34, 95–96. Schmohl was drowned on his way to America.

[41] King, 163–167, 186.

[42] *Calendar of Franklin Papers,* I, 469, Ischiffely, Aug. 1, 1778.

name passed from the library to the political assembly at the end of the eighteenth century." A large number of editions of Poor Richard's Almanac appeared within a few years in Italian cities. The Virginia agent, Philip Mazzei, who wrote propaganda material for the American cause in Paris and Florence, was certain that the vast mass of Italians were strong for America; they "feel greatly for our cause," he said, "and dare call it aloud the *cause of mankind,* although they live under despotick governments." [43]

Joel Barlow, who played a role in Europe similar to that of Tom Paine, exhorted Italy to adopt French and American revolutionary principles. "Italy is destined to form one great republic," he wrote. "The boundaries which nature has given it are peculiarly suited to this purpose and as long as we follow nature, in politics as well as morals, we are sure to be in the right." In free governments boundary questions can be settled without great difficulty, as the United States has shown; this would prove, said Barlow, "that the doctrine I here advance, as one of the effects of liberty, is not chimerical." Reports of the American Revolution were printed in Italian newspapers, and, as in Germany, George Washington stirred the imagination. Alfieri composed odes on *L'America Libera* and sent one to Washington, to whom he dedicated his tragedy *Brutus I.*[44]

In Holland, John Adams was in close touch with the Dutch patriots and was deeply concerned over their welfare. The great leader of the Dutch patriots was J. D. Van der Capellen, whose support of America took unusual courage at a time when the success of the Revolution was problematical. So grateful were Americans for his stand that members of Congress, as well as others, wrote him their appreciation. Adams discreetly made use of the Dutch press to advance the American cause. *The Gazette de Leyde,* one of the most influential papers in Europe, threw its weight on the side of Amer-

[43] L. Rava, "La Fortuna di Beniamino Franklin in Italia," *Nouva Antologia,* CCXXI (1922), 16–34; R. C. Garlick, *Philip Mazzei, Friend of Jefferson* (Baltimore, 1933), 42; H. R. Marraro, "Unpublished Mazzei Correspondence, 1780–1783," *William and Mary Quart.,* ser. 2, XXIII (July, 1943), 315–316.

[44] Barlow, *A Letter . . . to . . . Piedmont, on the Advantages of the French Revolution . . .* (London, 1795); E. Goggio, "Italy and the American War of Independence," *Romanic Review,* XX (1929), 25–34; Goggio, "Benjamin Franklin and Italy," *ibid.,* XIX (1928), 307.

:a. The historian and publicist A. M. Cerisier also added to the ery welcome support tendered the Americans. One of the Dutch atriots, Francis A. Van der Kemp, was introduced to Franklin by afayette, who spoke of his efforts and suffering in the abortive Dutch Revolution and urged Americans to aid him. Van der Kamp, ho eventually reached America, thought Adams too conservative, nd we have the interesting spectacle of a European *philosophe* at-empting to "radicalize" a leading American.[45] The Dutch refugee, vatching the American scene closely, called Daniel Shays "the Wat Tyler of the Massachusetts."

Conservative Belgium, too, felt the impact of new thought and ction overseas. She developed the American fever largely through ontact with Holland and France, although a small American col-nly lived in Brussels. Belgium's neutral press received its news ltered through England, with whom her rulers were officially riendly; nevertheless the items that were printed in the papers kept heir readers informed about the progress of the political contro-ersy between the American colonies and the mother country. The vents of the war itself were followed closely, but the more impor-ant significance of America for Belgium came during the latter's wn revolutionary period from 1787 to 1790. The American fight or freedom was pictured as one in which Europe's liberty was also t stake. Coupled with the impetus supplied by France, the events of these years were decisive in creating a revolutionary psychology n the Austrian Netherlands. Here, as elsewhere, American heroes aptured the imagination. To Belgians an especially impressive eature of Washington's career was his consistent refusal to use his position for personal aggrandizement. Local heroes were given added stature by being fixed in an American image—General Van der Mersch was called the "Washington Belgique," and Henri Van der Noot, the "Franklin des Belges." At least one participant in the Belgian Revolution, Colonel Jean-Pierre Ransonnet, had been in America long enough to be indoctrinated with liberal ideas.

The constitutions of the several American states were made

[45] F. Edler, *The Dutch Republic and the American Revolution* ("Johns Hop-kins Studies in Hist. and Pol. Sci.," XXIX), 31–33, 169 notes 4 and 5, 229; letters of Adams to Van der Kemp, especially Feb. 7, 1790, letter of Lafayette, March 6, 1788, Hist. Soc. of Penn.

known to the Belgians and urged as a precedent in modifying pro
vincial governments. Provinces announced their severance from th
Habsburg Empire by a Declaration of Independence à l'Amér
icaine, with a similar long list of unredressed grievances. The mani
festo of Flanders even repeated the very text of the American Decla
ration, and the Articles of Confederation were levied upon by th
Belgians in drawing up their own Treaty of Union. But like sc
many other budding plans all over Europe, the frosts of reactior
delayed the ripening till well into the nineteenth century.[46]

No people were more deeply stirred by developments in Americ
than the Irish, whose political difficulties with Parliament strikingl
paralleled those of the colonies. All Ireland, said Horace Walpole
was "America mad." Irish resentment against England had an an
cient history, but it was the events of the American Revolutionar
era that crystallized amorphous plans into definite programs pro
posing a change in imperial relationships. The new British imperia
policy after 1763 evoked the same responses in Ireland as in Amer
ica, for it was believed that coercion in America was part of a more
comprehensive, ominous plan which included Ireland as well. Fear
of an augmented British military establishment haunted both
peoples. Like English Whigs, American and Irish leaders were say
ing that the King was being betrayed by his advisers.

Emigration to America emphasized the disabilities under which
Irishmen suffered in land tenancy. So many were leaving that it was
prophesied manufactures would be hurt and landlords ruined. Lists
of vessels with their thousands of passengers leaving from Irish ports
for America were published with a warning to the government—an
admonition emphasizing joint English, Irish, and American discontent. "Read this, Ye! Men in Power, and relieve this oppressed, sinking and Betrayed nation. Repeal the Boston Port Bill. . . . Restore to the Middlesex Freeholders [Wilkes' constituents] their
Birth-rights. Restore the Charter of Boston." In Ireland and in
America there were Hearts of Oak Boys and Hearts of Steel Boys
who were very effective in expressing hostility to the *status quo*.
Irish readers kept track of the Sons of Liberty in America and

[46] T. K. Gorman, *America and Belgium* (London, 1925), 20–35, 41–42, 53–54, 58, 62–63, 107–109, 155–156, 176, 237–240.

ounted the number of men in the colonies who were able to bear rms. It was hinted that a civil war in America and in Ireland would e too much for the administration to bear.

When political debate in the colonies was succeeded by armed truggle excitement in Ireland ran high. Irish seaports gave shelter nd supplies to American privateers; the American flag, writes the istorian James A. Froude, "was seen daily fluttering in insolence rom the Irish coast anywhere between Londonderry and Cork." resbyterians in northern Ireland were said to be Americans in heir hearts, while Catholics in southern Ireland were thought to be waiting aid from France or Spain. Irishmen boasted that their insmen in the American army were largely responsible for the de-eat of the English at Saratoga. In Ireland itself, Irish Volunteers ractically took over the military authority of the country after most f the regular troops had been sent overseas.

To wrest concessions from England, Irishmen adopted American echniques. They resolved to wear their own manufactures, and, when shopkeepers were suspected of failing to abide by the non-importation agreements, they were, "after the American fashion," tarred and feathered. The British administration was warned that if it continued to follow a restrictive policy many individuals would transfer to America the woolen and linen manufactures "to the great prejudice of those trades in England, Scotland and Ireland." Propaganda, much of it prepared by Franklin, told the Irish that Americans grieved with them over the heavy load of pensions they had to shoulder, the many well-paid sinecures, and the privileged position of the military.

Henry Grattan, a very distinguished figure in the Irish Parliament, challenged the right of the British Parliament to make laws for Ireland. He summoned his fellow countrymen to rise to the dignity of statehood: "Before you decide on the practicability of being slaves forever look to America. . . ." And then in a warning to England he said, "What you trample on in Europe will sting you in America. When America sends forth her ambassadors . . . to Europe and manifests to the world her independency and power do you imagine you will persuade Ireland to be satisfied with an English Parliament making laws for her?" John Jebb, agitating for parliamentary reform, favored the same for Ireland; "If the liberties

of Ireland be extinguished," he said, "the boasted liberties of En
land may not long survive." He looked upon reform of the Iris
Parliament as facilitating a similar reform in England.[47]

Richard Price said all Ireland should continue to exert pressu
on England, and he believed that Catholics should be given equ
voting rights with Protestants as a way of breaking the hold of th
aristocracy. To prevent any such collaboration between the tw
religious groups, the laws against Catholics were considerably r
laxed. Along with modifications in the laws against Catholics, th
Irish did win great economic and political concessions, with auto
omy for their own parliament. Well might Grattan say that "th
American war was the Irish harvest." But the harvest was followe
by many lean years, and it was mainly the sustenance from Americ
that kept alive a frustrated spirit in a body whose native diet wa
little more than hope and cold fury.

It seemed providential that a new land existed overseas to receiv
those who could act on their dreams. And of dreams there wer
many in these years. There was a dream of equality. In a perio
when traditions counted for a great deal, it was daring to think on
could achieve greatness even though the family name were of n
significance. Franklin's career made it less daring. He was the mos
important forerunner of that long list of self-made Americans. It i
striking that articles and biographies should have made a specia
point of his rise from an humble origin. An English magazine sai
in a leading article, "Doctor Franklin, now one of the first character
in the philosophical and political world, owes his present elevate
rank in life entirely to himself." A German series of biographies o
great men started off with *Dr. B. Franklin's Leben,* emphasizing hi
self-dependence, implying he was without any family inheritance t
smooth his path.[48]

[47] *The Works of John Jebb . . .* (London, 1787), I, 207, II, 530–531. Thi
material on America and the Irish revolutionary movement comes mainly fro
the paper of the same name by M. Kraus in *The Era of the American Revolu
tion: Studies inscribed to Evarts Boutell Greene.* See also L. F. Stock, "The Iris
Parliament and the American Revolution," a reprint, from *U.S. Catholic His
torical Records and Studies,* XXX (1939), which he kindly sent to me.

[48] *Eur. Mag. and Lond. Rev.,* III (1783), 163; *Dr. B. Franklin's Leben* (Tübin
gen, 1795); also *Benjamin Franklin's Kleine Schriften* (Weimar, 1794).

Americans generally made a fetish of equality. As the *Encyclo-
edia Britannica* put it, "Every man thinks himself at least as good
; his neighbor, and believes that all mankind are or ought to be
qual." [49] Travelers took note of this prevailing sentiment and re-
orted on it, caustically or favorably, depending on their own polit-
:al alignment.

Joel Barlow wrote in one of his studies addressed to a revolution-
ry Europe: "The word *people* in America has a different meaning
om what it has in Europe. It there means the whole community,
nd comprehends every human creature; here [in Europe] it means
omething else, more difficult to define." [50] That staunch friend of
merica, Thomas Pownall, thus differentiated between European
nd American liberty:

he liberty of the People of America is not merely that share of Power,
hich an Aristocracy permits the People to amuse themselves with and
hich they are taught to call Liberty. It is not Domination with which
ie People govern in a Democracy, and therefore call Liberty. It is not
iat share of Domination which a political Monarch throws into the
ands of the People, in order to ally their power to his Force, by which
) govern the Aristocracy. The genuine Liberty on which America is
ounded is totally and intirely a New System of Things and men. . . .
Every Inhabitant of America is, de facto as well as de jure, equal in his
ssential inseparable rights of the individual to any other individual; is,
i these rights, independent of any power that any other can assume over
im; over his labour or his property; this is a Principle in act and deed,
nd not a mere speculative Theorem.[51]

There were some in Britain who caustically remarked that the
merican war was undertaken to provide subjects in America as
vell as in Ireland and India. But these intentions were defeated, the
ritish were told, "and a hundred millions of your money spent."
nglishmen were advised to look to America, where such characters
s now dishonored the British name "would soon be taught the

[49] *Encyclopedia Britannica* (1797), art. "New England," 665.

[50] Barlow, *Advice to the Privileged Orders* (London, 1792), pt. I, 33. Had
arlow known the phrase, he might, like Arnold Toynbee, have spoken of the
internal proletariat."

[51] T. Pownall, *A Memorial Addressed to the Sovereigns of America* (London,
783), 54–55.

meaning of the word *People*." The Irish too had lessons to teach th
English, who were consigned to a gloomy future did they refuse t
learn from their neighbors.[52]

Crèvecoeur's *Letters from an American Farmer,* widely reprinte
in its entirety or in extracts, strengthened the revolt against fate—
man could will his own world. With all the hardships labor, bot
free and bound, had to face in the colonies, the area of freedo
available to it there was greater than in Europe. In America, Crève
coeur wrote in a noble phrase, the poor "are become men," and thi
metamorphosis was performed by their laws and their own industry
"Every farmer has the air of a gentleman," wrote a German ob
server. The dignity of man depended not on artificial classificatio
but on his inherent worth. Letters from Germans who had fough
in America emphasized this characteristic. Steuben was pleased wit
American equality, which permitted careers to talented individual
regardless of class. "Unser General der Artillerie," he said, "wa
Buchbinder in Boston," and, what was more to the point, under
stood his duties. The fact that in America a mere bookbinder coul
gain recognition as a military leader delighted him.[53] The *Bosto
Magazine* mentioned with a somewhat mistaken pride that the for
bidding division between rich and poor in older countries had no
yet occurred in America, a factor of real significance in her govern
ment: "The middle class of people," it said, "hold the reins unde
the direction of the multitude, and the poorest member of the com
munity feels and exercises the pride of prerogative." [54]

Love of equality was said to be a trait characteristic of all Amer
icans—Indians as well as whites. J. Long, an Indian trader, said
"The Iroquois laugh when you talk to them of obedience to kings
for they cannot reconcile the idea of submission with the dignity o
man. Each individual is a sovereign in his own mind; and as he con-

[52] *Letters on Political Liberty, and the Principles of the English and Irish Projects of Reform, addressed to a member of the House of Commons* (3rd ed., London, 1789; written 1782–1783), 82, 89.

[53] Crèvecoeur, *Letters from an American Farmer,* 52; J. T. Kohler, *Sammlung Neuer Reisebeschreibungen aus Fremden Sprachen Besonders der Englischen* (Göttingen, 1767), I, 372; King, 49.

[54] *Boston Magazine,* Nov., 1785, 403–405. Although not accurate, it must be remembered this statement was made against the oligarchical background of Europe.

ceives he derives his freedom from the Great spirit above, he cannot be induced to acknowledge any other power." Oglethorpe wrote that Indian Kings could "do no more than perswade"; while Daniel Falckner pointed out that Indian kingship was not inheritable—the king was merely the wisest, as well as the finest hunter among equals. Speaking of the American whites, Dr. Samuel Smith of Princeton said:

> You seldom see a superior treat an inferior with haughtiness, but you see all, even to the lowest of the landholders, act with a certain air, that indicated they are sensible that they are not in any degree dependent on you. . . . The truth is, every man seems to carry about with him a consciousness that he is an independent citizen of an independent state.[55]

German immigrants, who were more acutely conscious of the existence of old-world kings than were their English neighbors, delighted in their own little personal "kingdoms" established on American soil. From New Jersey in 1789 came the cheerful message that it was a land "where every one is a king in his own domain, and only his own faults can bring misfortune; where an adequate livelihood is not rare on such fruitful soil, and commerce can be freely pursued with the whole world, unrestrained by monopoly. In this respect America will always be especially valuable to all men." [56]

European governments feared the influence of those who had returned from America, for they frequently caused dissatisfaction at home and spurred emigration. A German province, Nassau-Dillenburg, decreed in 1773 that those returning from America must have permission to enter and were given only a limited time to transact whatever business they had there. Some of these travelers were emigration agents, and it quickly became clear that they, with their rosy accounts, were more successful in convincing people to undertake the fearsome journey to America than were agents who had never been overseas. These agents, who worked on a commission basis, and who handled mainly indentured servants, were the most potent force in promoting European emigration. Several German states issued decrees against their activities, but in one way or

---

[55] J. Long, *Voyages and Travels of an Indian . . . Trader* (London, 1791), 30; *Gentleman's Magazine*, III (1733), 413–414; *The Bee*, XII (1792), 225.

[56] *Amerikanisches Magazin*, I (1796), 143.

another they got the emigrants out. The Swiss in the canton of Berne, when emigration was especially great (1754–1770), feared an almost complete depopulation. Though many restrictions were placed on emigration few proposals were made to eradicate its causes. The use of undivided lands and of forests for the very poor was suggested in Switzerland. Some talked of starting industries to employ prospective emigrants, but little materialized. Though nothing much of importance was achieved in ameliorating conditions for the lowly, the effect of emigration was to create a deeper concern with social problems.[57]

The discontented Belgians, who knew about cheap American lands, circulated a pamphlet attacking Joseph II's policy hindering emigration. The Emperor was reminded that a happy, contented people needed no compulsion to stay at home, but they would gravitate to wherever favorable conditions beckoned them. It was so with Germans, Scotch, English, French, and Irish, and so eager were they to go that many were even willing to sell themselves into indentured servitude for some years to reach the promised land. That people gladly assumed these heavy burdens should be a lesson to monarchs, Joseph was told: "Princes who wish to keep their subjects, should seek to govern them well." [58] Like the medieval peasant who "bought his blood," the eighteenth-century emigrant bought his future, and at heavy cost also, but his descendants remember with gratitude his sacrifice.

In order to quiet prospective emigrants from Scotland, a few clan leaders relieved impoverished tenants at the expense of mortgagers and other creditors. This apparently had some influence among the tenants headed by General MacLeod, but even so, large numbers continued to leave. It was reported in the 1770's that landlords were forced to behave more circumspectly toward tenants. Twenty years later further migrations prompted a Scottish journal to urge the government and landed proprietors to do something about alleviating conditions, and it offered a plan already put in operation by one landowner.

---

[57] J. D. Brite, *The Attitude of European States toward Emigration to the American Colonies and the United States 1607–1820* (Univ. of Chicago, Ms. dissert., 1939), 131–222.

[58] Gorman, 143.

In the Hebrides in 1773 James Boswell had been asked to join in a dance called "America," whose motif was the infectious nature of emigration. One resident told him that, in the previous year, when a vessel left for America, relatives on shore waving good-by were "almost distracted." "This year," he wrote, "there was not a tear shed. The people on the shore seemed to think that they would soon follow. This indifference," concluded Boswell, "is a mortal sign for the country." [59]

In Utopia life must be more secure, happier, and longer. English interest in these aspects of Utopia was quickened by fears of a steady depopulation at home. The fruitfulness of American marriages was recorded by travelers, and statistics of population growth were well known to Europe. The *London Medical Journal,* commenting on a paper dealing with this question (which appeared originally in the *Memoirs* of the American Academy of Arts and Sciences), said that either the climate or the manner of living on the seacoast of New England was very favorable to life. A paper by William Barton in the *Transactions* of the American Philosophical Society noted the rapid population growth in the United States. His country, he said, possessed "in a superior degree, an inherent radical and lasting source of national vigor and greatness." At every age, he maintained, the probabilities of life in the United States were higher than in Europe.[60] Malthus' epoch-making work (in its second edition) paid tribute to Franklin's American population studies.

A German author, whose work was translated for French readers, used Barton's essay to prove his point: the American environment was most favorable to humankind, "because after the most careful observations, we are convinced that the mortality among the inhabitants of the American states is much less than in our hemisphere." Against one hundred births were set eighty deaths in England, over seventy in Sweden, and in Paris, over ninety-seven. In the small villages of Salem and Hingham, Massachusetts, deaths did "not exceed

[59] *The Bee,* IV (Aug. 24, 1791); E. C. Guillet, *The Great Migration: The Atlantic Crossing by sailing ship since 1770* (New York, 1937), 1–2, 43.

[60] *London Med. Journal,* VII (1786), 316–321, E. Wigglesworth, "Observations on the Longevity of the Inhabitants of Ipswich and Hingham," *Amer. Phil. Soc., Trans.,* III (1793), 25–50.

48 or 49, and 50 at Philadelphia, that is to say, just about less than half the mortality of Paris." With rare judgment, he estimated in 1797 that the population of the United States within 120 years would be 126,000,000. A publicist estimated that the best lands in America cost a third of what the poorest sold at in Germany. Because labor was relatively well paid, marriage was easier and therefore more common, and it occurred at an earlier age, than in Europe.[61]

The pursuit of happiness had ended in its capture. At least so wrote the *Encyclopedia Britannica:* "It may in truth be said, that in no part of the world are the people happier . . . or more independent than the farmers in New England." The New Jersey German quoted previously added, "The thought that the ground on which we and our children stand belongs to us, that our bodies are not the possession of a single individual and his whims, will always refreshen with an inner satisfaction the European who comes here."

The quest for economic security seemed ended for those willing to work. From a Pennsylvania farmer came the comment, "For the lazy good-for-nothing, dissolute and scandalous, this land is of as little value as their Fatherland." America was no East Indies or Peru where wealth might easily be gathered, "but . . . a very beautiful country" which guaranteed "to the industrious and ambitious worker a peaceful existence, a comfortable income and an independent prosperity." In Arthur Young's influential *Annals of Agriculture* were reports of American conditions. One traveler from New Jersey commented, "You see no marks of poverty in lower orders of society, and they are therefore exempt from that abject cringing so common in the poor of England"; nor did the government burden the farmer with taxes.[62]

British workmen heard of the high labor rates paid in Boston, New York, and Philadelphia, but they were assured that labor outside the main colonial centers received no more than English workers. Skilled craftsmen were being restrained from migrating overseas, but higher wages, opportunities to open independent

[61] E. A. W. Zimmerman, *Essai de Comparaison entre la France et les Etats Unis* (Leipzig, 1797), 269–272; Doll, *loc. cit.*, 438.

[62] *Amerikanisches Magazin*, I (1796), 26; Young, *Annals of Agriculture*, XIX (1793), 230–231, 254–257.

businesses, or easy acquisition of a homestead continued to be inducements to emigration. It is estimated that the real wages of a workman in the colonies were from 30 to 100 per cent more than the wages of his contemporary in England. The American advantage continued after the Revolution.[63] In a long letter from New York an Irish immigrant rhapsodized over the New World with its high wages for all kinds of work: "Ah Dear Sir, theer is braw living in this same Toon. The young Folk in Ereland are aw but a Pack of Cowards for I will tell you in short this is a bonny Kintry & aw things grows here that ere I did see grow in Ereland. . . ." [64]

Ministers in Scotland complained of the loss of many parishioners who had gone to America and were able to send money home to aid further emigration. Letters arrived comparing the superior American conditions with Scottish demoralization and thus excited other Scots to leave home. Emigrants, many of whom were departing from the economic waste of Paisley, when questioned why they were leaving, generally answered, "for Poverty and to get Bread." Some left because of an increase in rents, dearness of provisions, or unemployment. Occasionally a lighter note is struck in the answers of prospective emigrants. Agnes Adair was leaving Scotland because she could not get a husband; another went to keep his friends company; some went for curiosity, others to make their fortunes or to be with relatives; Andrew Brown, "gentleman," left for his health. The great majority said they would not have left could they have supplied their families with food. Scottish feudalism appeared starkly anachronistic when measured by American opportunities. A British minister traveling through the States in the 1790's said that in Richmond, Virginia, no family was so poor but had beef, pork, bacon, Indian corn, potatoes, and wheat flour.[65]

Franklin, in his correspondence with the noted Spanish reform

[63] Mitchell, *The Present State of Great Britain and North America . . .*, 298–299 note; Morris, 26–28, 45, 46.

[64] James Murray to Rev. Baptiste Boyd, New York, March 18, 1767, Port., 4 (22), Friends House, London; an amusing letter, possibly parodying American enthusiasts.

[65] V. R. Cameron, *Emigrants from Scotland to America 1774–1775* (typescript, N.Y. Hist. Soc.). No one gave "religion" as a reason for leaving Scotland for America, but this is not surprising in a population largely Presbyterian; *Toulmin's Journal*, 73.

minister, the Count of Campomanes, said that two opinions prevailed in Europe which were harmful to national happiness—that useful labor was dishonorable, and that families may be perpetuated with estates. "In America," he wrote, "we have neither of these Prejudices, which is a great advantage to us." Washington struck a balance in favor of America in comparing her agriculture with England's. "Commons, Tithes, Tenantry (of which we feel nothing in this country)," he wrote to Sir John Sinclair, "are in the list of impediments . . . to perfection in English farming . . . and taxes are heavy deductions from the profit thereof." English agriculture, he granted, was superior technically but more expensive, so that "when the balance at the end of the year is struck in the two countries, no doubt can remain in which scale it is to be found." [66]

Time after time America is referred to as the "asylum" for the oppressed, an escape from a cruel, unreasonable world. Emigration, that had been hindered by war, was resumed in the 1780's, wrote William Bingham to Richard Price; people were coming from all of Europe, but the largest number were arriving from Germany.

> From being in a state of vassalage in their own country, mere hewers of wood and drawers of water, they find themselves entitled to all the rights of citizenship in a free country, and with a small pittance enabled to purchase a freehold estate for themselves and family. It is really fortunate for human nature, that there is a country where the oppressed of all nations may find a secure asylum.[67]

It was a familiar fact that workmen in America, after accumulating some money, often abandoned their jobs to become independent landowners. Indeed the advantages of getting land in freehold tenure often outweighed the drawing power of higher wages for many Europeans.

The later years of the eighteenth century produced more careful analyses of the place of America in the world. The disadvantages as well as the advantages of emigration were more frequently noted,

---

[66] Smyth, *Franklin, Writings,* IX, 221, 240, June 5, 1784, July 26, 1784; *Letters from . . . George Washington to Sir John Sinclair . . .* (London, 1800), 21–28, July 20, 1794. Washington wrote in similar vein to Arthur Young.

[67] *Mass. Hist. Soc., Proc.,* ser. 2, XVII (1903), 361; Morris, 48, 49.

the former often prompted by political hostility. But even when the highly colored emigrant propaganda literature was being challenged by more realistic treatments, redemptioners could not be dissuaded from leaving for America. Conflicting reports reached Europe of conditions in the States which were straining to adjust themselves to new constitutions and create a new nation.

Warm-hearted Richard Price was among those who rejoiced when peace came and America's independence was secured, for her institutions, he told Franklin, were humanity's brightest star. He had often spoken to Lord Shelburne in this vein, and he hoped the latter would be able "to produce such a reformation in our Parliament as shall make it a *real* representation instead of such a mockery and nuisance as it is [at] present. . . ." Pownall too was pleased with the war's end, and sending to Franklin his *Memorial . . . to the Sovereigns of America* he spoke of "the two Branches of the English Nation now two separate Dominions and governments." Thomas Day said the future association between Great Britain and the United States must be based on ties of friendship and mutual interest. The success of America, he believed, was a great warning to the wielders of arbitrary power.[68]

Price said European interest in the American struggle had stirred so general a fermentation of political ideas that the "silly despots of the world are likely to be forced to respect *human* rights and to take care not to govern too much lest they should not govern at all." Henry Flood, the noted Irish spokesman, calling for Parliamentary reform, said that both Americans and Irishmen had been told they were "virtually represented" in Parliament. Virtual parliaments and an inadequate representation have cost enough abroad already, he said, referring to America. "Take care," he warned the Commons, "they do not cost you more at home, by costing you your Constitution." [69]

Price said that the technique of arousing mass support for reform

---

[68] Price to Franklin, Jan. 7, 1782; Pownall to Franklin, Oct. 6, 1783, Amer. Phil. Soc., Mss.; Thomas Day, *Reflexions upon the present state of England, and the Independence of America* (London, 1782), 90, 98; Morris, 320 note 15.

[69] Price to Franklin, Sept. 26, 1787, Sparks, *Franklin, Works,* X, 320; *The Speech and Proposition of the Rt. Hon. Henry Flood . . . on a Reform of . . . Parliament* (London, 1790), 11–13.

by committees of correspondence, etc., borrowed from America, was frequently resorted to at this time. Jebb urged this procedure and, in writing at the war's end, which he called a victory for liberty, he expressed the hope that "the acts of freemen on the other side of the Atlantic will inspire our countrymen on this with a similar spirit. . . ." American independence, he felt, was an essential condition of freedom in England.[70]

Price was grateful to Franklin for reassurance on conditions in the States; "for the sake of the world I wish them [the American states] all possible prosperity." He told a New York correspondent that Europe believed the States were falling apart and were likely to regret their independence. "But the hope of the friends of Virtue and Liberty," he added, using the language of Benjamin Rush, "is that, whereas the kingdoms of Europe have travelled to tranquility through seas of blood, the United States are travelling to a degree of tranquility and liberty that will make them an example to the world, only through seas of blunders. God grant this may prove the truth."[71]

Utopians in Europe looked with an anxious eye to Americans and exhorted them to hold fast to their ideals. Let the United States, wrote Pownall,

> respect the rights and liberties of Mankind; that by a free commerce they diffuse to the World at large the surplus portion of these good things which they must be continuously creating in their own World; that they consider themselves as the means in the hands of Providence, of extending the Civilization of human Society . . . If they take up this Character within themselves, and hold out its operations and effect to the Old World, they will become a Nation *to whom all Nations will come.*

Price was fearful that the United States was imitating European desires for luxury; and he strongly criticized some of the state constitutions for including religious tests. For his own people he said the Revolution began a new era, "a revolution by which Britons themselves will be the greatest gainers if wise enough to improve properly the check that has been given to the despotism of their

---

[70] *The Works of John Jebb,* I, 171–172, 188; III, 314–317, 361.

[71] Price to Franklin, Bache Coll., Amer. Phil. Soc., March 21, 1785; *Gentleman's Magazine,* LVII (1787), 631; Price borrowed this phraseology from Rush; see Price's letter, Jan. 26, 1787, Ridgway Library.

ministers, and to catch the flame of virtuous liberty which has saved their American brethren." [72]

Price urged with vigor the creation of a federal government to decide disputes, regulate commerce, "to institute an union that shall have weight and credit." The present power of Congress in Europe, he said, was an "object of derision, rather than of respect." A plan must be worked out, he asserted, which would give real power to a central agency "without encroaching too much on the liberty and independence of the confederate states." [73]

Men like-minded with Price sought to warm hopes chilled by contempt and indifference at the "flame of virtuous liberty." The Reverend Christopher Wyvill, a liberal pamphleteer, in *A Defence of Dr. Price and the Reformers of England* (1792), agreed that American citizens were better off than those of Great Britain. They possessed the benefits though not the corruptions of civilized society, and their state would soon "rank on a footing of equality with the first Empires in the World." Opposed as he was to revolution, Wyvill argued that America must be used as a model for gradual change in England.

On the three hundredth anniversary of the discovery of America, an American, Elhanan Winchester, delivered an oration in London wherein he proudly listed the lessons his country had taught the world:

1. A large country could be ruled by a republican form of government without monarchy or an aristocracy.
2. Religious worship needed no legal establishment; "to allow all to think freely for themselves in matters of religion, and worship God according to the dictates of their own Consciences is the best policy."
3. Church and state could subsist without alliance.
4. Milder punishment for crimes tends to prevent them.
5. People are happier and more contented under a "mild and equi-

---

[72] Pownall, 137–138; Price, *Observations on the Importance of the American Revolution and the Means of Making it a Benefit to the World* (London, 1784), 2, 47–48.

[73] Price to Rush, Jan. 1, 1783, Sept. 2, 1787, Ridgway Library; see also C. B. Cone, "Richard Price and the Constitution of the United States," *Amer. Hist. Rev.*, LIII (1948), 726–748.

table government," which is far stronger than arbitrary governments and in less danger of being overturned.

6. America had also shown the world "that to admit the Jews to all the privileges of natural born subjects, is far from being a dangerous experiment, as has been generally supposed."

The orator hoped that the time was not far distant "when all the world shall learn and practice these lessons in a still more perfect manner than they are yet practised in America itself." [74]

That the world at least took notice of these lessons, even if it did not learn and practice them, is proved by the extended review of them in the *Gentleman's Magazine,* which said it was surely a glorious boast of Winchester that his country was "the very birthplace of civil and religious liberty." To one conservative British observer Washington's second election seemed to add significance to lesson number one—a republic could exist even in a large country. From Philadelphia, after attending the administration of the oath of office to the President, the secretary to the English minister wrote: "Our innovating demagogues in England will, I suppose, draw strong inferences in favour of the electing of the first executive magistrate from this instance, which is certainly an uncommon one, of an unanimous choice of a whole people repeated in his favour." Jefferson's election and inaugural address heartened the European liberal and gave opportunity to repeat the moral of the lesson which taught that people were happier under mild and just governments. An Englishman prefaced his publication of Jefferson's message with the remark that the constitution of America was obviously "the most free one we know of; the Government of the New World is stronger, because juster, than any we witness in the Old." With this example Englishmen were urged to reform peacefully their own abuses.[75]

In the decades immediately following the Revolution, and for long years thereafter, America was a factor of varying weight in the

---

[74] Elhanan Winchester, *An Oration on the Discovery of America* (London, 1792), 27–28.

[75] *Gentleman's Magazine,* LXIII (1793), 433–434; "Letters of Edward Thornton," *Penn. Mag. of Hist. and Biog.,* IX (1885), 219; *The Speech of Thomas Jefferson . . . with a few Remarks on its Probable Effects* (London, 1801), by an Englishman.

minds of Englishmen. Radicals and antiadministration men down to 1800 were pro-American, while conservatives belittled the success of the new institutions arising overseas. The very promise of success for these institutions, as time went on, made conservatives even more acidulous in their comments. They watched closely for signs of impending disaster in the States, believing that the former colonies would then come back to the Empire. But European radicals were as optimistic as the most sanguine of Americans. Scottish delegates, in convention to urge parliamentary reform, toasted the American Congress and said that the American people had taught them to assert their rights. Following a time-honored practice of disavowing alien influence, one expositor of the principles of English radicals said the latter acted not on French precedents but on old English political ideas. Washington and his fellow American patriots had behaved in accord with the same principles.[76]

The American constitution was received with respect by the English press, which saw in it a strong likeness to Britain's unwritten constitution. A defender of the *status quo* compared England with less favored regions and said that even in America whatever was desirable in that vast continent was to be found only in the United States, "which have derived from us both their character and constitution." [77]

On several leading occasions the United States was a point of constant reference in the verbal warfare of this period. Burke begot one controversy with his questions about the right of revolution and of people to govern themselves. "Burke leads you wrong, the world is not his own," warned Joel Barlow in *The Conspiracy of Kings.* Paine was quickly involved in this debate, and his *Rights of Man* initiated many separate discussions about the nature of government. His insistence on the need for a written constitution was strongly supported by other radical publicists. Barlow's *Advice to the Privileged Orders* and Paine's *Rights of Man* were prized texts for British radicals. Barlow and Paine were advisers also, to the French revolutionaries.

---

[76] L. Fraser, *English Opinion of the American Constitution and Government (1783–1798)*, (New York, 1915), 34; R. Dinmore, Jr., *An Exposition of the Principles of the English Jacobins . . .* (Norwich, 1796), 13–14.

[77] John Smith, D.D., *An Affectionate Address to the Middling and Lower Classes of British Subjects on the Present Alarming Crisis* (Edinburgh, 1798), 7.

Thomas Spence, the British radical, quoted frequently from Bar low, reminding his readers that the belief that people needed ruler was merely a superstition. The ignorance of the masses, said Spenc (with Barlow's support), was the foundation of privileged group and fostered by them designedly. The American government, h maintained, was inexpensive and was founded on a system of rep resentation. "No man in his sober senses," said Spence, "will com pare the character of any of the kings of Europe with that of Genera Washington." Barlow was again called upon to substantiate th thesis that people in general get nothing from military conquests The latter enriched only a few at home and strengthened them ove the mass of the people.[78]

Burke was set upon by critics who compared his views at thi time with his once friendly attitude toward the American Revolu tion. "You felt none of those alarms then," he was reminded, "tha now disturb your repose." And that former period, said one writer was more dangerous than the present (1790). With a final whiplash Burke was told that there was no opinion he had held, no doctrin he had supported through a long political life which his pamphle did not contradict. Another writer remembered predictions that ha been made about America's falling into disorder when England' protecting hand was withdrawn. France, too, he said, will develop a stable structure and contribute to the world another exampl showing "at how small a charge every object of good governmen may be obtained." The Americans were "Republicans *on prin ciple*"; they had their emissaries everywhere; and they were openl supported by leading men in Britain.[79]

In several important particulars American political wisdom wa defended against the attacks of her detractors. Among the principa objects of reform in Britain were listed the expenditure of the pub lic money, the representation of the people, and the national estab lished church. In these respects, it was asserted, America had show

---

[78] Thomas Spence, *Pigs' Meat; or Lessons for the Swinish Multitude* (3rd ed. London, 1793–1795), I, 13, 68; II, 219; II, 219. The Huntington Library cop has Francis Place's bookplate.

[79] [Sir Brooke Boothby], *A Letter to the Right Hon. Edmund Burke* . . (London, 1790), 38–39; *Thoughts on Government; Occasioned by Mr. Burke' Reflections &c. in a Letter to a Friend* (London, 1790).

a praiseworthy superiority. A pamphlet urging emigration estimated that, on the average, a family of six in a European state paid in taxes about £17 annually; a family of the same size in America, the writer said, paid only thirty shillings. Yet in America, life, liberty, and property were just as secure. European inhabitants were generally *subjects,* not *citizens,* a situation that did not exist in America. Emigration, it was argued, would serve to awaken European countries to a realization of the need for reforms.[80]

Britain's involvement in war with Revolutionary France brought to the fore a comparison of European and American political institutions. The fact that the United States had achieved greater political democracy and had largely succeeded in divorcing civil from religious authority, all without a collapse of society, strengthened the convictions of radicals whose joint Anglo-American struggle had started with John Wilkes. This was a thirty-year war which came to an abrupt end with the trials for treason instituted after 1794 by a nervous, ghost-seeing government.

America as a great experiment in dynamic social organization was a continual source of energy to the radical. Americans, said Priestley, went far beyond the Glorious Revolution of 1689; "they formed a *completely New Government* on the principles of equal liberty and the rights of man—without Nobles, without Bishops and without a King." Conservatives on the other hand, were forced to a re-examination of their position and new rationalizations of their privileges. Conservatives were taunted for their inconsistency in concluding from French experience, after only a brief time had elapsed, that republicanism was akin to anarchy, while at the same time they were denying that the experiment in America was old enough to offer reliable deductions.

The movement for Parliamentary reform which had antedated the American Revolution was tremendously stimulated by it, but this proposal became part of a much broader program involving religious toleration, a free press, freedom of assembly, and free right of petition. Advocating an appeal to reason as against precedent, one writer said it was "not impossible that the nations of the earth

[80] *The Political Crisis; or a Dissertation on the Rights of Man* (London, 1791), 23, 73, 124; *Thoughts on Emigration. To which are added Miscellaneous Observations relating to the U.S.A.* (London, 1792), 7, 11–14, 17.

would have been . . . sunk in apathy and ignorance" had not the American Revolution promoted a spirit of inquiry and discussion that made men long for freedom.[81] The more radical reformers wanted universal suffrage and abolition of primogeniture, while individuals like Thomas Spence went even further to speak of the uselessness of an aristocracy to society.

The audiences for such men as Spence and Paine were larger than is usually imagined. By this time workingmen were gathered in adult education groups—book clubs, reading societies, and discussion circles. Paine indicted the civilization of his day as productive of great affluence combined with great misery, and, following the lead of earlier celebrants of the "noble savage," he urged a study of the American Indian to see how these twin evils could be avoided. While Paine acknowledged that the natural state of man was without the advantages that flow from agriculture, arts, science, and manufactures, he did go on to say that poverty had become hereditary and that it was next to impossible for the poor to get out of this condition by themselves. Anticipating Karl Marx he said that this mass of poor was continually increasing in so-called civilized countries: "More persons fall annually into it, than get out of it." To find a way out of this blind alley Paine urged a national fund to get young people started in life at twenty-one and also old-age pensions to begin at fifty years. Like so many of his contemporaries Paine was desperately anxious to realize in the relations among men and nations the law and order of Newton's universe.[82]

It was when such agitation spread to the lower classes in English society, and at a time when discontent had reached the combustion point, that the government throttled discussion and banished bitter critics. Price, Wyvill, Priestley, and the like were middle-class liberals, whose audiences were not potentially as dangerous as the groups reached by Paine, Thomas Hardy, and Joseph Gerrald. The least-educated ear could tingle to the inflammatory phrases of Tom Paine. Wyvill, comparatively moderate now, criticized Paine's counsel to rebuild a new political structure on the model of America, as

---

[81] Henry Yorke, *Reason urged against Precedent* . . . (Derby, 1793?), 39.

[82] Paine, *Agrarian Justice, opposed to Agrarian Law, and to Agrarian Monopoly* . . . (London, 1797), 10, 27; H. H. Clark, "The Influence of Science on American Ideas, 1775 to 1809," reprinted from *Wisconsin Acad. Sci., Arts and Letters, Trans.*, XXXV (1944), 314.

being "conveyed in the most dangerous shape, and far more likely to make an impression on those to whom it is chiefly addressed, than if it had been delivered in a more classical composition." Paine would then have avoided "the grossness of indecent language" and would not have excited "the lowest class of People to acts of violence and injustice." [83] Arthur Young, probably exaggerating, numbered the membership of the radical Corresponding Societies at 100,000, and he pointed to their militant distribution of the writings of Paine and others "into the kitchens of so many ale and pot-houses." "Blasphemy, sedition, treason, distributed for a penny," complained Young, "their antidotes for a shilling, or half a crown." [84]

The Corresponding Societies, inspired by American and French precedents, were so deep a threat that their meeting in Edinburgh in 1793 was dissolved by the government and the leaders were charged with sedition. One of them, Joseph Gerrald, who was sentenced to fourteen years' exile, had in earlier life lived in America. In the courtroom, under charge of sedition, he defended his espousal of universal suffrage and similar measures by a reference to his experience in Pennsylvania, where he had resided for four years. Contradicting those who said a wider suffrage would lead to social disorders, he said he had seen many elections held in America without riots.

> For in truth, gentlemen [he told the court], the representative had no interest distinct from his constituents; the office which he undertook was rather a burden than a benefit, and as the government was too poor to purchase, and the people too virtuous to barter away their liberties—so the deputy had no temptation to sell his constituents. What then has been found by experience to be wholesome food for Americans, can never prove hurtful or poisonous to Britons.

On another occasion Gerrald had written that Americans were not weighted down with taxes to support royalty or an insolent nobility. No lordly peer trampled down the corn of the farmer in America;

---

[83] Rev. Christopher Wyvill, *A Defense of Dr. Price and the Reformers of England* (London, 1792), 55–56.

[84] Arthur Young, *An Enquiry into the State of the Public Mind amongst the Lower Classes . . .* (London, 1798), 8 and note on p. 10. But Hannah More had been writing conservative propaganda to reach poorer people to counteract revolutionary ideas. Many tracts were sold at a low price, 1792–1795; see A. S. Collins, *The Profession of Letters . . .* (New York, 1929), 78.

"no proud prelate wrings from him the tythes of his industry. They have no chicanery in ermine." [85]

The interrelationship of American, British, and French radicalism was the constant preoccupation of the spokesmen of the day. American and French revolutionary symbols were embroidered onto the older British fabric. Citizen Lee, at the British Tree of Liberty, Haymarket, sold a pamphlet complaining of high prices and asking for a more representative Parliament. "This balance of power between the Rich and the Poor," it said, "would be productive of a thousand times more consolation to this Nation than the chimerical nonsense of court-jugglers, 'the balance of power in Europe.' " Kings can do no good, Barlow told the Convention in France; monarchy and hierarchy, he prophesied in September, 1792, would be "buried in the same grave" within a few months. British publishers even reprinted old publications on the American Revolution, adding new material on the French Revolution. Pamphlets in behalf of the Catholics in Ireland were likewise republished, stressing the revolutionary examples of America, Poland, and France as worthy of emulation. "In America," said Wolfe Tone, "the Catholic and Protestant sit equally in Congress, without any contention arising, other than who shall serve his country best; so may it be in Ireland." [86]

The correspondence of the British societies with French clubs reveals the frequent recurrence of the theme that America, Great Britain, and France must be in alliance for the freedom of humanity. A celebration of the French Revolution at Belfast, 1792, omitted England's banner in the parade and made the triumvirate America, France, and Ireland. Everywhere in the British Isles it was Amer-

[85] Joseph Gerrald, *The Defence of Joseph Gerrald on a charge of Sedition at . . . Edinburgh* (London, 1794), 12; *Authentic Biographical Anecdotes of Joseph Gerrald . . . written by a Friend* (London, 1795), 14. It is an interesting fact that American sympathizers helped Scottish political exiles in Australia to escape, 1796 (G. S. Veitch, *The Genesis of Parliamentary Reform* [London, 1913], 295).

[86] *The Rights of Swine—An Address to the Poor* (London, 1795?); Barlow, *A Letter to the National Convention of France . . .* (London, 1792), 15, 25; T. Wolfe Tone, *An Argument in Behalf of the Catholics of Ireland; Reprinted by the Society of United Irishmen . . .* (Belfast, 1791), 29–30.

can and French inspiration that fired radical sentiment. "We ar-
lently wish," said one, "the triple alliance (not of crowns but) of the
eople of America, France and Great Britain to give freedom to
urope and peace to the whole world." [87]

Robert Hall, who had drunk deeply at the American fount of
iberty, wrote in behalf of freedom of the press and against the sup-
ression of Paine's writing. Upholding the latter's sentiments,
Iall, writing in 1793, said that the French Revolution had always
ppeared to him "the most splendid event recorded in the annals
f History." Thomas Spence estimated the probable influence of
his event on the liberties of Europe; if successful, he thought "the
pirit of extreme Democracy" was likely to spread over all Europe,
wallowing up "in a volcanic eruption, every remnant of monarchy
nd of nobility in the civilized world." If it were unsuccessful it
vould mean for a long time to come the survival of reaction and
nonarchy. A new song, quoted by Spence, reveals the intermingling
n radical minds of French, English, and American developments.
The song by W. D. Grant, "The Americans happy without the As-
istance of *Royal Proclamations*" says:

> There liberty is law
> And joy o'erspreads each cheek,
> No more 'tis "vive le roi!"
> But "vive la République!" [88]

In America support for the French Revolution during its first years was very vigorous. It is "but the first chapter of the history of European liberty," said Jefferson, who foresaw its wide effects. The Revolution revitalized radical activity among dormant English and American groups and stimulated the establishment of new democratic societies. As Hugh H. Brackenridge expressed it, "If kings combine to support kings, why not republics to support republics?" Many Americans feared that a conquest of France would be followed by the launching of an attack by the victorious monarchies upon the United States. The attitude of the Washington adminis-

---

[87] Fraser, *English Opinion of the American Constitution and Government*, 72.

[88] R. Hall, *An Apology for the Freedom of the Press, and for General Liberty* (London, 1793), 107; Spence, *Pigs' Meat* . . . , II, 184–185, 283.

tration toward France, cautious and reserved as it was, stung ardent Francophiles to the quick. To the Irish, interested in any revolution that weakened Britain, American reluctance to go to the aid of France seemed gross ingratitude and an example of shortsighted national policy. "As long as the great nations of the world profess their present habits," wrote a correspondent to Mathew Carey, "the pacific Quakerly system of America is Utopian if she intends to command respect proportionate to her natural consequence." [89]

The theater in France during the Revolution dramatized the earlier struggle in America as a spur to the French in their own battle with reaction. A tableau introduced an American Quaker who told the French workers and peasants the affecting story of his own group's fight for liberty. Americans, on the other hand, were reminded that they had obligations to aid a Revolutionary France in exchange for the services of Lafayette and Rochambeau. Englishmen realized the need for creating national solidarity in these perilous days, and some writers, believing that Parliamentary reform was essential to secure it, tried to scare Pitt into action by raising the specter of a Franco-American alliance.[90]

Conservatives everywhere, of course, hated the French Revolution, especially after the first flush of general enthusiasm had passed. Its violence was horrifying, but, more specifically, its attacks on property rights and its equalitarianism frightened and angered them. They disliked intensely celebrations favoring French Revolutionaries, a custom joyfully followed in America. "The great pox [syphilis] is supposed to have been imported from America into Europe," wrote Charles Nisbet, conservative president of Dickinson College. America, he said, received the smallpox in exchange. Something of the same kind was going on at present, he wrote in 1793. "The Great Pox of liberty has been sent from America to France, and the Small Pox of equality is likely to be sent over to us

[89] E. P. Link, *Democratic Republican Societies 1790–1800* (New York, 1942), 55; John Chambers to Carey, Mar. 26, 1794, Aug. 2, 1794, Lea and Febiger Coll., Hist. Soc. Penn. Jefferson's remark is in Dumbauld, *Thomas Jefferson, American Tourist,* 213.

[90] G. M. Fess, *The American Revolution in Creative French Literature, 1775–1937* ("Univ. of Missouri Studies," XVI, no. II), 88, 98–99; *A Letter to the Right Hon. William Pitt,* by the Rev. Christopher Wyvill (2nd ed., York, 1793), 37–38.

in exchange." [91] Nisbet and a host of others were glad when the counterrevolution came, for so they interpreted the establishment of the French Directory.

Radical Dissenters, the spearhead of advanced thought in England at this time, who had been agitating for years for specific sectarian objectives, now envisaged a broad plan for a great organization of the unprivileged—Jews, Protestant Dissenters, and Catholics—to be united on the fundamental basis of the rights of man and citizen. A wave of progressive thought in behalf of religious, economic, and humanitarian reforms reached a climax in the early 1790's. But the defeat of the bill to repeal the Test and Corporation Acts and the failure of slave trade abolition marked the recession of the progressive wave. It broke against the barrier of an English conservatism made hysterical by the ogre of a Revolutionary France. A distrust of France in revolution, shared by conservatives in England and in America, made for a tenuous bridge of understanding. The British Minister to the United States, George Hammond, was instructed to aid the anti-Jacobin forces in America. With a note of derision for his Federalist opponents, Jefferson asked if the English government got the idea of suppressing the democratic societies in Britain from America? [92]

When John Adams succeeded Washington in an orderly election, the doubters and evil-wishers in England seemed finally convinced that the merits in the American government were sufficient to promise it an enduring life. American hostility to France (later developments of the French Revolution altered earlier American friendship) warmed conservative British hearts and made them see virtues where only shortly before they had seen defects. Arthur Young, who in former days had sometimes been moderately critical of America, now reminded gentlemen farmers that "as the danger of commotions increases in Europe, the eyes of mankind will necessarily be turned to the region [United States] where *Property* remains re-

---

[91] Nisbet to Wm. Young, Mar. 16, 1793, Misc. papers, N.Y. Public Library.

[92] A. Lincoln, *Some Political & Social Ideas of English Dissent 1763–1800* (Cambridge, Eng., 1938), 183, 236; Jefferson to W. B. Giles, Mar. 19, 1796, Jefferson, *Writings,* IX, 326; B. Mayo, ed., *Instructions to the British Ministers to the United States, 1791–1812* ("Ann. Rep. Amer. Hist. Assn. for 1936") III, 66, Aug. 8, 1794.

spected." Jefferson's inaugural was, of course, saluted as a tocsin to liberals everywhere: "The language of the new Trans-Atlantic President may confirm the wavering patriot on this side the ocean. . . . The now confirmed government of America will be, perhaps, to the framers of constitutions, henceforward, a normal school, a model for statesmen to work by." [93] But at best it was a grudging acceptance by the ruling classes, for not very deep under the surface was the gnawing fear of America as a perpetual ideological threat and a potential economic rival to Europe.

Upholders of conservative British traditions always remembered the disintegrating force of American Revolutionary ideology. Long after the Revolutionary era a correspondent, in a warning to W. C. Plunkett, a supporter of the Catholic emancipation fight in Parliament, gave him a history of the attacks on the British constitutional position. They came originally from America, he said, and the effect of the Revolution was to establish overseas a democratic government in direct contrast and opposition to the constitution of Great Britain; for it had no king, no aristocracy, no national religion, no established church. Every office in the state was open to every citizen, suffrage was widespread, and all power was considered as flowing from the people. The American political system, this close observer went on to say, "did not fail to produce consequences momentous and calamitous to this country."

Democratic principles, simple and intelligible even to the least educated, soon found their way to Ireland, spreading there with incredible rapidity, especially among the Dissenters in the North; "their greater intercourse with America, prejudice against episcopacy and their strong leaning . . . to republicanism" made them peculiarly accessible to American principles and theory. American success validated these principles in Irish eyes, which looked with a sense of immediacy to impending changes. Plunkett was asked to recall the many meetings, newspaper essays, speeches, etc., which spread the principles of democracy among large masses of people, from which contagion had risen the Society of United Irishmen. Paine's *Rights of Man* also aided in the work of subverting the

[93] Young, *Annals of Agriculture,* XIX (1793), 247; *The Speech of Thomas Jefferson . . . with a few remarks on its probable effects* (London, 1801), by an Englishman, prefatory remarks.

British constitution. The adoption of these principles by the National Assembly in France, and the Revolution there, further aided in perplexing and unsettling the political opinion of the country and giving currency to democratic ideals.

Despite all this infection, however, the body politic of Britain remained fundamentally healthy, it was asserted; most people remained attached to the British constitution. "You mistake, and you confound the disorder and the distemper of the age for illumination and Liberality," Plunkett was told. "It is America, it is Paine, it is democracy, it is Jacobinism from which this illumination has sprung." The correspondent concluded with a presentation of alternatives, offered by conservatives down to the twentieth century; the question under debate, ostensibly toleration for Catholics, was really that same question and no other which had been at issue since the American War: "whether we shall adhere to British laws, British principles, British system, and the British Constitution; or whether we shall exchange these for the principles, the system and the constitution of the United States of America." Thus was stated, baldly and no doubt too extremely, a fundamental factor in the evolution of the nineteenth century.[94]

In the years when imperfect man dared believe in his perfectibility, America made it seem less visionary. Into the texture of his dream was woven a thread that bound all mankind into a community of understanding fellowship. Of Pennsylvania it was written that it afforded "a beautiful prospect to see men take and give an equal liberty: to see them live, if not as belonging to the same church, yet to the same Christian religion; and if not to the same religion, yet to the same fraternity of mankind." [95] A liberal in Belgium looking across the Atlantic urged the adoption of the new political ideas in his homeland in a work called *Représentants légitimes du Peuple*. After remarking that this publication portrayed the Americans as the "wisest and most virtuous people of the world,"

[94] *A Review of a Celebrated Speech on the Catholic Claims . . . in a letter addressed to the Rt. Hon. W. C. Plunkett* (London, 1820), 10–13, 25–26, 30.

[95] Fenning and Collyer, *A New System of Geography*, II, 657; see also Edith Phillips, *The Good Quaker in French Legend* (Philadelphia, 1932), especially, chap. iv.

one reader said that he seemed to see in it a modern version of Plato's *Republic* or More's *Utopia.*[96] In the later eighteenth century and down through the nineteenth, Utopias under different names continued to be cherished. The Pantisocracy of Coleridge and Southey, Brook Farm of the New Englanders, and the many Utopian communities scattered over America poignantly revealed the craving of humanity to make its dreams come true.

---

[96] Gorman, 249.

Some of the material in this chapter has already appeared in "America and the Utopian Ideal in the Eighteenth Century," *Miss. Valley Hist. Rev.,* XXII (1936), 487–504. Gilbert Chinard has valuable material in his paper "Eighteenth Century Theories on America as a Human Habitat," *Amer. Phil. Soc., Proc.,* XCI, no. 1 (Feb., 1947).

CHAPTER X

Nationalism and Cosmopolitanism

IN THE middle and later years of the eighteenth century, Americans became more and more conscious of how different they were from Europeans. They stressed what they believed to be the uniqueness of their civilization—a new experiment in human relations. Their rate of growth, outstripping European countries, and their security, protected by the Atlantic, gave them an almost overweening confidence in their future. Their boastfulness naturally grated on European ears, particularly ears of the traditional English ruling groups. The latter were willing to grant to Americans, though reluctantly, a special mechanical aptitude. In the early years of the century, Cotton Mather sent a plan of a "land ship" (wagons with sails, originated by the Reverend Joseph Morgan) to the Secretary of the Royal Society. At that time Mather made a strong plea for the practical application of science; if obscurantists, he wrote, "had not Inspired people with a Disposition rather to Ridicule, than to *Cultivate*, well projected Inventions for the good of the World, we should before now have seen the World in much better circumstances than it is. We try for *Machines* to render the *Wind* as well as the *Water Serviceable* to us; and extend our Empire into all the Elements." [1] The secretary of the British Minister to the newly constituted federal government criticized American vanity, which pretended to primacy in the arts, etc., but he added, "if they have any genious or original invention . . . it is in the mechanic arts." He insisted,

[1] Royal Soc. Library, M 2 (41), June 7, 1723. Morgan invented an ice boat; see letter to Royal Society, Dec. 22, 1732, M. 3.39; for nationalism, see Merle Curti, *The Roots of American Loyalty* (New York, 1946), 22.

however, that for the most part they copied English models.[2]

British periodicals told their readers of the many machines being produced and perfected in America which revealed a mechanical proficiency that "far surpasses Europe." Ingenious mechanics were said to have enriched the American states with an incredible variety of useful machines of which "Europe has not the smallest idea." [3] Lord Sheffield said that American axes were thought so superior that British manufacturers sold their own product as of New England make.[4] Jefferson returned the compliment when he spoke of the mechanical arts in London being "carried to a wonderful perfection." [5] But he was jealous of America's reputation in invention. New Jersey farmers, he said, had followed the practice of making the circumference of a wheel of one single piece. Franklin had suggested this procedure to a London workman, and now, wrote Jefferson, it is claimed as an English invention.

American hustle and bustle, even if aimless, were already fixed in the national grain. From Charleston, Dr. Alexander Garden wrote:

We are a set of the busiest, most bustling, hurrying animals imaginable, and yet we really do not do much, but we must appear to be doing. And this kind of important hurry appears among all ranks, unless among the gentleman planters, who are absolutely above every occupation but eating, drinking, lolling, smoking and sleeping, which five modes of action constitute the essence of their life and existence.[6]

Some Englishmen, however, thought that Americans, in their forums, were direct and purposeful. The *Gentleman's Magazine* assumed that the English were superior orators, but the debates in the Constitutional Convention, it said, showed that Americans "as men of business [and] speaking on a subject they thoroughly understand . . . are really more worthy of attention than the flowery speechifiers on this side of the water." [7]

[2] "Letters of Edward Thornton to Sir J. B. Burges," June 11, 1792, *Penn. Mag. Hist. and Biog.*, IX (1885), 215–216.

[3] *Scots Magazine,* LX (1798), 236–239, reprinted from the *Monthly Magazine.*

[4] Greene, *The Revolutionary Generation,* 61.

[5] Jefferson, *Writings,* V, 305, to John Page, May 4, 1786; VI, 54, to Crèvecoeur, Jan. 15, 1787.

[6] Smith, *Corr. of Linnaeus,* I, 519–520, Nov. 19, 1764.

[7] *Gentleman's Magazine,* LVIII (1788), 1096–1097.

The observant German scientist Johann D. Schoepf, traveling in the United States in the 1780's, thought that the large majority of Americans, while rather indifferent to formal learning, had a good natural intelligence and revealed "a better expression of their understanding than people of the same rank in Europe." Americans comparing themselves with Europeans felt they had a keener grasp of the essentials of political life. Soliloquizing in a Paris simmering with subversive talk, Barlow thought there were not five men in all Europe "who understand the nature of liberty and theory of government as well as they are understood by five hundred men in America." [8]

Awareness of one's own characteristics is always sharpened by acquaintance with the habits of other peoples. Most Europeans who traveled in America were almost painfully aware of an insistent social equality. John Adams, a staunch republican, in friendly correspondence with the noted Scotsman, Sir John Sinclair, urged him to come to America, promising cordial treatment "notwithstanding your title." [9] Americans did not like the use of the word "servant," and it was noted that native men would not act as domestics. If a servant were asked if his master were home, he might reply: "Master! I have no master; do you want Mr. Such-a-one?" It startled the upper-class traveler from Europe to see the coachman eat at the same table with the passengers. The effect on English servants created a "problem" for the English aristocracy.[10]

At the end of the seventeenth century the Reverend Hugh Jones, talking about Maryland, observed with some astonishment that it had been chiefly settled by poor people "whose Industry hath raised them to great Estates." [11] It need hardly be added that he was speaking only of the most fortunate. Almost a hundred years later, another English clergyman, the Reverend Henry Toulmin, commenting on the beneficent laws in America, spoke of the practice of parents buying land for their children so that all might share equally, for a

[8] Curti, *The Growth of American Thought,* 141; P. H. Boynton, "Joel Barlow advises the Privileged Orders," *New England Quarterly,* XII (1939), 477–499.

[9] *The Correspondence of Sir John Sinclair,* II, 36, March 2, 1793.

[10] R. Parkinson, *The Experienced Farmer's Tour in America . . .* (London, 1805), I, 19.

[11] *Phil. Trans.,* XXI (1699), 436.

parent would "shudder at the thought of making 5 children slaves or beggars for the sake of making the sixth a gentleman." At a time when English writers were saying that a fundamental condition for a prosperous state was "a large and solid basis of the lower classes of mankind" at the bottom of the social pyramid, a Yankee editor urged his readers "to prevent the execution of that detestable maxim of *European* policy amongst us, *viz.:* That the common people, who are three quarters of the world, must be kept in ignorance, that they may be slaves to the other quarter who live in magnificence." [12]

Franklin, John Jay, Jefferson, and others were very conscious of the differences between America and Europe, and they frequently told their countrymen of the superior civilization enjoyed by them. From Madrid, John Jay wrote to a friend, "I never loved or admired America so much as since I left it." He was glad to learn that the anniversary of American independence had been celebrated in Amsterdam: "If I am not much mistaken the time will come when that day will be considered as one of the most important in modern history." Franklin and other Americans so influenced Dr. Jan Ingenhousz, physician to the Habsburg ruler, that he became a partisan of the Revolutionary Americans and transmitted a highly favorable report about them to his royal patron. Comparing Europeans with Americans he said that the former were generally illiterate, ignorant about affairs of government, worn and tired from their daily tasks. Such people could easily be led by the nose to follow a few designing leaders on a path prejudicial to their own interest. The North Americans, on the other hand, because of superior economic conditions, have leisure enough to acquire culture and learn about their relations to government. They are therefore less easily led by a "few evilly intentioned individuals." Their laws and regulations were usually far wiser than those of other peoples.[13]

The American loyalists, refugees in England, themselves gave proofs of the swift-rising tide of nationalism. Their disappointment

---

[12] *Toulmin's Journal,* 18; Morris, 52–53.

[13] Jay to Benson, March, 1781, to R. Morris, April 25, 1782, to De Neufville and Son, July 16, 1781, Johnston, *John Jay, Correspondence and Public Papers,* II, 6, 55, 195; "New Franklin Letters add to History," *N.Y. Times Magazine,* April 29, 1928.

n the Old World, their pride in their colonial homes are vivid reve-
ations of how different Americans had become from Englishmen.
Samuel Curwen, formerly of Salem, Massachusetts, resented English
aspersions on America and was angered by a British officer's state-
nent that Yankees in battle were cowards.[14] Americans, even those
who had lived in England for a long time—artists and others—
ound it difficult indeed to take root. They had become aliens in a
amiliar world.

American youngsters compared themselves with boys recently arrived from Europe and thought themselves to be superior in every
type of competition, "corporeal and mental." Male American descendants of English forbears generally surpassed their fathers in
tature, wrote a careful doctor. Another physician, Dr. Lionel
Chalmers, whose work was widely and favorably known in European scientific circles, writing on the natives of South Carolina, said
they were "forward in genius, and thought capable of receiving instruction earlier than children in Britain commonly are." [15] Half a
century later Alexis de Tocqueville said Americans spoke almost
as if they belonged to a distinct race of mankind. Nevertheless Joel
Barlow, so vigorous a spokesman for nationalism, doubted that
Americans had as yet formed a "national character." [16]

Americans and many Europeans believed that America was to be
the seat of empire vacated by England. One light-hearted author
even visualized the dispatch overseas of all imperial records from a
London fallen into decay.[17] Another prophet of decadence and cele-
brant of America's rise, spoke in words similar to those Tennyson
used a century later:

> Puissant America! whose gen'rous sons
> From British fathers sprung, have rais'd thy name
> Beyond the Greek and Roman fame, and shall

---

[14] Lewis Einstein, *Divided Loyalties* (Boston and New York, 1933), 216.

[15] *Autobiography of Charles Caldwell* . . . (Philadelphia, 1855), 43, 44; L. Chalmers, *An Account of the Weather and Diseases of South Carolina* (London, 1776), I, 37–38.

[16] Barlow, *Advice to the Privileged Orders* . . . pt. II, 46.

[17] *Anticipation, or the Voyage of an American to England in the year 1899* . . . (London, printed for W. Lane, 1781), 78.

> Extend they empire to the utmost bounds
> of this Globose.[18]

There were many who apparently agreed with Bishop Berkeley on the westward movement of empire. As skeptical Andrew Burnaby, who had traveled in America, expressed it, "every one is looking forward with eager and impatient expectation to that destined moment when America is to give the law to the rest of the world." A recent arrival in New York, the Reverend Archibald Laidlie, wrote to his brother in Scotland that North America "bids fair for being one day the greatest Empire in the world"; his only regret was that he would not live to see it. Turgot and others prophesied that separation of the colonies from England would be followed by separation of all America from Europe. He also thought that ease of escape for Europeans from bad governments would force their rulers to adopt more enlightened policies. The Abbé Galiani of Naples, long a partisan of the Americans, said that the Revolution would decide whether America was to rule over Europe or the latter was to continue ruling over America. He was wagering in favor of America, and he lightly warned a friend not to buy a house in Paris but rather in Philadelphia. "My trouble," he said, "is that there are no abbeys in America." Another clergyman, the Abbé Gregoire, who foresaw the building of an isthmian canal, said that the United States would "change the face of the commercial world and the face of empires." "Who knows," he asked, "if America will but then avenge the outrages she has received and if our old Europe, placed in the rank of a subaltern power, will not become a colony of the New World." [19] Horace Walpole, in hyperbolic style, wrote, in the month of America's Declaration of Independence, that the little island of England would some day look back proudly to "its former brave days, and swear its capital was once as big as Paris, or—what is to be the name of the city that will then give laws to Europe—New York or Philadelphia?" [20]

---

[18] Thomas Lyttelton, *Poems* (London, 1780), "The State of England, in the year 2199" (written 1771).

[19] Charles Sumner, *Prophetic Voices concerning America* (Boston, 1874), *passim;* Laidlie, Nov. 5, 1773, Laidlie papers, New York Hist. Soc.

[20] "Walpole on America," *Mass. Hist. Soc., Proc.,* ser. 2, VII (1891–1892), 7–10.

Jefferson wanted Americans to visit Europe if only to see by contrast how superior America was; it would make them adore their own country, he said, "its soil, its climate, its equality, liberty, laws, people & manners." Americans, he felt, did not sufficiently appreciate their blessings, which no other peoples enjoyed. Europeans came to live in America, but he was positive that no American would remove to Europe for permanent residence. Abigail Amelia Adams thought Americans and Englishmen very much alike, but she believed that a greater degree of politeness and civility existed in her own country. As for the "lower class of people in America [they] are infinitely superior to the lower class of people here" in England. Jefferson was willing to admit that Frenchmen were more temperate than Americans, better mannered, and shone with especial distinction in the fine arts. Americans, he insisted, were much happier than Europeans, whose fate he considered most deplorable: "In science, the mass of the people are two centuries behind ours; their literati, half a dozen years before us. Books, really good, acquire just reputation in that time, and so become known to us, and communicate to us all their advances in knowledge." [21]

Many Americans were critical of parents who sent their children abroad to study and insisted that if they must study in Europe it should at least be in a Protestant country. Noah Webster wanted Americans to travel in their own land, but if they had to go abroad he preferred their journeys to be preceded by an education at home. Jay wrote in similar fashion to Robert Morris who had sent two sons overseas.[22] Education in Europe might alienate them from their native home, Jay thought, and thus make for a difficult adjustment in mature life.

The accent on Americanism led to newspaper ridicule of the returned traveler from England who brought with him modes of speech and behavior too loose and wanton for some natives. Among the accomplished beaux the colonial "has learned these elegant expressions, Split me, Madam; By Gad; Dam me," and he uses them on all occasions. "So entirely is he taken up with England, that he

[21] Chinard, *Thomas Jefferson,* 217; Roof, 108; Jefferson, *Writings,* V, 153, Sept. 30, 1785.

[22] Hansen, 249–251; Johnston, II, 351, Oct. 13, 1782.

always mentions guineas when he speaks of money." [23] Like an English fop, he boasts of his vices and sneers at virtue. South Carolina's young men, returned from English schools, were said to be "little more improved & much more dissipated than they went." [24] Jefferson did acknowledge that his daughter could get a good education in Paris, where she went to a school attended by Protestants and Catholics together. Doubtless the school, which he thought the best of its kind in France, appealed to him because nothing on religion was spoken of in classes.[25] A number of well-to-do Catholic families sent their children abroad for education.

So strong was the American nationalistic temper in the Revolutionary era that foreign education even for advanced students was frowned upon. This was a subject on which Noah Webster had vigorous opinions. Other observers also made interesting comments on this theme. Just prior to the Revolutionary War, William Eddis, not long arrived from England, said that as the growth of higher education in America lessened the need for study abroad, the attachment of the colonies to Great Britain would gradually weaken, "and a less frequent intercourse will tend to encourage those sentiments of self-importance which have already taken too deep root," and which he feared could never be wholly eradicated.[26] A few years later, Baron von Steuben told Franklin that the scientific work at the university in Leipzig, from which he was writing, was not superior to that in the college at Philadelphia.[27] Silliman of Yale thought it fairer to compare one of the American colleges with an individual college in the English universities. While he believed that English schools were superior in classical learning and philology, some American colleges were their peers in mathematics, ethics, and the physical sciences. It has been estimated that at the outbreak of the Revolution, one out of every thousand colonists had had some college edu-

---

[23] E. Singleton, *Social New York under the Georges* (New York, 1902), 373–374.

[24] Quoted in Greene, *The Revolutionary Generation,* 378.

[25] Jefferson papers, Mass. Hist. Soc., July 23, 1787.

[26] Eddis, 146–149, Oct. 4, 1773.

[27] B. M. Victory, *Benjamin Franklin and Germany* ("Amer. Germanica," no. 21, 1915), 143, Oct. 12, 1781; see also J. Foulke to Franklin, Leipsic, Oct. 12, 1781, *Calendar of Franklin Papers,* II, 400. Foulke had taken his M.D. at Philadelphia.

ation. But the proportion was much higher among the *leaders* of American life, many of whom had studied in Europe. Almost without exception, every noted political leader in Charleston, South Carolina, had been educated at the Inns of Court.[28]

Although Jefferson usually discouraged people from studying abroad (except for medicine), to those who pressed him for his views his judgment was that Geneva and Rome were the best European educational centers. He was unfriendly to Geneva in 1785 because of the reactionary revolution there, but a few years later he told a correspondent that the Swiss city was far beyond all others on the Continent. In the British Isles, Edinburgh was his enthusiastic choice; he thought it the finest school in the world, especially for Americans because of its spirit of republicanism. It was, he said, the best place for the "acquisitions of real science." To his kinsman Peter Carr, he wrote a note urging the study of Spanish: "Our future connections with Spain and Spanish-America will render that language a valuable acquisition." [29] John Adams felt much the same as did Jefferson about the virtues of education at home. He wanted his son, John Quincy, who had started at Leyden, to be educated at Harvard, for he believed that "no American can be any where so well educated as in his own Country." Even though Adams encouraged Joseph Willard, president of Harvard, to study European universities, believing some good would come from such an educational trip, he hoped Harvard would remain essentially unchanged.[30]

Though Adams wished Harvard to remain unchanged, Dr. Benjamin Waterhouse of that college wanted to borrow some of the academic customs of Cambridge, England, and wrote to Dr. John Haygarth for details. Waterhouse wanted to know the form of a diploma for a bachelor in medicine, for Harvard expected to create several, he said, "and as *our* university was formed on the model of *your* University of Cambridge, we should prefer their form of Diploma to any other." [31]

[28] Greene, 123–124; Bowes, 52.

[29] Jefferson, *Writings*, V, 185, to J. Bannister, Jr., Oct. 15, 1785, VI, 257, to Carr, Aug. 10, 1787; VIII, 274, to Mr. M'Alister, Dec. 22, 1791; to Mr. Elder, Paris, Nov. 25, 1785, Jefferson papers, Mass. Hist. Soc.

[30] Adams to Willard, Sept. 8, 1784, *Col. Soc. Mass., Trans.*, XIII (1910–1911) 14.

[31] Haygarth, 336–364, letters, 1789.

Despite the disapproval of the elders, young men still went abroad to study, especially if they were interested in law and medicine, as they had all through the eighteenth century. Edinburgh continued to draw the larger share of medical students. The study of law at the Inns of Court drew many from the States, particularly from South Carolina. Much smaller in number were those who went to Continental schools, but here and there among American medical men could be found evidences of Viennese, Genevan, Dutch, and Parisian training. A few American names appeared on the rolls of the University of Göttingen, but it was in the nineteenth century that this German school was to do much to stimulate young minds from the United States.[32]

Like nearly every other institution, education came under close scrutiny in the Revolutionary era. A French correspondent wrote Franklin of a proposed national academy of education, a journal of education, and the creation of a hall of fame.[33] The plans for national education in America, drawn up by Benjamin Rush, Nathaniel Chipman, and others, are fairly familiar. Rush told Richard Price of his ideas and asked the Englishman to further these plans by writing to Congress.[34] To be long-lived, republics must invest in popular education, Rush told Price. Republics, he said, "are slow in discovering their interest, but when once they find it out they pursue it with vigor and perseverance." Little could be done by American public bodies, said Rush, until they carried the people along with them. And because the means at hand for spreading knowledge were still scanty, the movements of these representative bodies were marked "with appearances of delay and procrastination. To remedy these inconveniences, colleges, newspapers, and posts are establishing in all our States." [35]

Related questions were discussed by college faculties and students. President Stiles's students at Yale debated such questions as whether a public education was preferable to private schooling;

---

[32] D. B. Shumway, "The American Students of . . . Göttingen," *Germ. Amer. Annals*, n.s. VIII (1910–1911), 172 ff.

[33] Le Roux to Franklin, Feb., 1779, *Calendar of Franklin Papers*, II, 23.

[34] "Price Letters," May 25, 1786, *Mass. Hist. Soc., Proc.*, ser. 2, XVII (1903), 343.

[35] Goodman, *Benjamin Rush*, 310–311.

"whether female academies would be beneficial"; whether Latin and Greek were studied too much in America, and whether agriculture should be introduced into colleges as a "classical study." [36]

American civilization was held up as a possible stimulus to a new kind of schooling. But the record of that civilization must be carefully kept, said Dr. Fothergill, and revised every twenty years. "If the history of the actions of men in civil life are of any use to posterity, what advantages might not be gained by thus taking time by the forelock?" Unfortunately, said the Quaker doctor, our whole education is suffused with the history of warfare, "and no character is thought equal to that of a hero, a Licenced Wholesale murderer; we are taught to be in love with [classical military leaders] and in solemn prose with the lives of Men who made themselves illustrious by slaughter." Most students never free themselves from the influence of this teaching: "How much happier is it for those who have none of these Learned prejudices to eradicate, but like a Tabula rasa, are open to the impression of every useful bias that humanity and philanthropy exult in." [37] Nathaniel Chipman, advocating a new system of education for his American countrymen, wrote in the same vein as Fothergill. History-writing in the future he asserted, should not be so exclusively concerned with wars and the intrigues of statesmen. It should deal rather with man in society and the development of the human mind.

A Scottish periodical in a discussion of American affairs urged that small academies instead of colleges be founded in the new states. Sunday Schools, it believed, should be everywhere established for the instruction of servants and the working class. The education of women, it said, should be "particularly attended to, and the fatal error avoided, that a woman's chief excellence consists in being able to make a pudding." [38] American writers were also placing considerable emphasis on education for women.

The Lancastrian system of schooling (older boys acting as guides

---

[36] Stiles, *Diary*, II, 545, July 3, 1781; III, 10, March 5, 1782; III, 152, March 14, 1785; III, 355, June 2, 1789.

[37] Fothergill to W. Bartram, copy, Sept. 10, 1766, Port. 38 (86), Friends House, London.

[38] *The Bee*, III (May 25, 1791), 96–101.

and teachers to younger ones) quickly made its way to America soon after its founding by Joseph Lancaster. He began it in 1798 writing and speaking in behalf of a national system of education to be based on a nonsectarian principle. He invoked the magic name of Franklin to show how older youths might influence younger schoolmates. Thomas Eddy, the American reformer, who received from London Lancaster's pamphlet advocating his educational system, immediately had one thousand copies printed in New York and Philadelphia.[39] He was certain it would be adopted in American schools; it had the definite advantage of providing education for the masses at low cost. Philadelphia and New York soon had these schools, and others were established in Washington, Alexandria, and Nashville, and in Vermont.

It was natural that the nationalistic temper in the United States should have expressed itself in a desire for textbooks written by Americans. Jedidiah Morse capitalized on it, but the best-known figure in the field was Noah Webster. His *Grammatical Institute of the English Language* challenged the continued use of Dilworth "or any other Spelling Book" by Englishmen. Webster's objective was to emancipate America from what he believed to be the constraining cultural traditions of Europe. Only then, he thought, could a truly national American character be created.

The great model for scientific societies was, of course, the Royal Society. American scientific societies go back to the close of the seventeenth century, with the organization formed by Increase Mather and his friends. Shortly before the creation of the American Philosophical Society in its final form, Ezra Stiles projected an American Academy of Sciences (1765) which was to maintain a world-wide correspondence. It was to have memoirs patterned after those of the Royal Society, and its first president was to be Harvard's noted professor, John Winthrop. Reflecting the rising self-consciousness in the colonies, it provided, among other objectives, for the collection of materials on American history, but Stiles's plan waited for fulfillment till after the Revolution.[40]

---

[39] Joseph Lancaster, *Improvements in Education, as it respects the industrious classes of the Community* (London, 1803), introduction and 51–52; Knapp, 206–207, June 20, 1804.

[40] R. S. Bates, "The Rise of Scientific Societies in the U.S.," *Harvard Univ*

A few years before Stiles was drawing up his plans, Hollis had written to Mayhew urging the establishment of scientific societies in the colonies. Mayhew's conversations with fellow Bostonians indicated that in their opinion America was not yet ripe for such societies, whereupon Hollis replied that neither did England think herself ripe for the Royal Society in 1660. "A museum at least," he urged, "with a public library, and a botanical garden annexed to it . . . might certainly be instituted, which may assume the name of The British Museum, or if a more extensive title should be liked, the New England Museum and will serve as an example from you to the mother colony, and a noble one to every other colony." Hollis wrote in after years of his pleasure that a society for promoting arts and commerce had been finally established in Boston. To a similar society in Charleston, Hollis sent a set of publications issued by a like organization in Berne, Switzerland.[41]

With the establishment of the American Philosophical Society the colonies had for the first time an important organization of their own to stimulate and co-ordinate scientific activity. But in addition to this body there were medical and agricultural societies which did their share to raise standards and initiate new achievements. Williamsburg in 1773 boasted a Society for the Advancement of Useful Knowledge which had some able members in it, including John Clayton, the naturalist. The Charleston Museum dates from the same year; it was founded by a few South Carolinians educated in England and familiar with the collections in the British Museum. Du Simitière, a man of diverse interests, who had come to the colonies via the West Indies, settled in Philadelphia shortly before the Revolution. There he began a museum containing books, antiquities, fossils, paintings, etc., which was open to the public on three days during the week.[42] It was a forerunner of Peale's Museum, and it played its small part in shaping the public taste for the formal historical societies and learned academies that later were established.

Summaries of Theses 1938 (Cambridge, 1940), 127; Stiles Mss., *Plan of an American Academy of Sciences,* Aug. 15, 1765.

[41] *Memoirs of Thomas Hollis,* Mayhew to Hollis, May 21, 1760, 90, 294, 319.

[42] W. J. Potts, "Du Simitière, Artist, Antiquary," *Penn. Mag. of Hist. and Biog.,* XIII (1889), 343 ff.; also on Du Simitière, see *ibid.,* LXIX (1945), 315–325, art. by Hans Huth.

The American Academy of Arts and Sciences was a product of the Revolutionary generation; so too was the Massachusetts Historical Society. When John Erskine of Scotland was elected to the latter group he suggested an annual publication to print the results of its members' inquiries. The work, he said, should be divided into two branches: natural history, medicine, etc., and civil and literary history. In passing, he said that although Cotton Mather's *Magnalia* had mistakes, it made him feel regretful that Scotland had no similar compilation to celebrate the deeds of her own clergy and statesmen.[43] When Thomas Brand Hollis was elected to the American Academy he sent to it the *Memoirs of Thomas Hollis,* recalling that the elder Hollis had always desired such an institution to be established in America, "for he held it as a maxim that societies and nations flourish more by the wisdom and magnanimity of individuals, the leaders of them, than by their numbers." Richard Price was also elected to the Academy, and in acknowledgment forwarded information about Herschel's discovery of a new planet.[44] On receipt of the Academy's *Memoirs,* Price wrote to Willard that "the new world opened a new field for enquiry" and he hoped that as a result of these efforts and the absence of all restraints on free discussion "the American Revolution will in the end prove the means of extending much farther than ever human investigation and improvement."

In Europe and America the large number of learned societies already established increased rapidly in the second half of the eighteenth century.[45] Proposals were made and even carried out (at least in short-lived publications) to print an account of all that was going on in learned societies throughout the world. The problem of co-ordinating the mass of materials in widely scattered publications was even then a serious one, and Americans and Europeans strove unsatisfactorily (as we do today) to solve it.

---

[43] Feb. 27, 1793, Corresponding Secretary 1791–1798, Mass. Hist. Soc., archives.

[44] "Willard Letters," *Mass. Hist. Soc., Proc.,* XLIII (1909–1910) 612, T. B. Hollis, Aug. 15, 1783, Sept. 3, 1783; *ibid.,* 614, Price to Willard, Oct. 6, 1783; *ibid.,* 624, July 24, 1786.

[45] B. Faÿ, "Learned Societies in Europe and America in the 18th Century," *Amer. Hist. Rev.,* XXXVII (1932), 265.

If John Adams' recollections in old age are to be trusted, it was he who pushed forward the project of the American Academy, and it came about, he said, as the result of international crosscurrents. He had been awakened to an interest in natural history by the collections of a fellow American, one Arnold, in Norwalk. When Adams was in Europe in 1778 and 1779, he saw other collections which suggested to him the need for American studies in this field. French Academicians queried him about the American Philosophical Society, praising its work. He concluded, with a dash of local pride, what could be done in Philadelphia could also be done in Boston. He then set Dr. Samuel Cooper, a distinguished intellectual, to stirring up sentiment for the proposed Academy, and shortly thereafter the Massachusetts state legislature voted it into existence.[46] The pro-Gallic bias of these years, it may be noted, gave tremendous prestige to French mathematicians in America for half a century or more thereafter.[47]

There were other societies projected in these fruitful years, but many of them were abortive. One of the most interesting of them was an academy planned by the Chevalier Quesnay de Beaurepaire in 1786, for Richmond, Virginia. The Chevalier had served in the American Revolutionary army in Virginia. He stayed for a while, traveled through the country, and dreamed of bringing over French culture and the fine arts. The idea of founding an academy in America had been suggested to him in 1778 by John Page, later governor of Virginia. Quesnay, who was to head the Academy, was to bring over European professors, and he perceived that this was a good opportunity to draw closer France and America. The elaborate plan was in the nature of an American edition of the French Academy of Arts and Sciences with branches to be located in Baltimore, Philadelphia, and New York. It was to have international affiliations as well. In its various ramifications the Richmond Academy was to be the nerve center of an Atlantic world of scientists and, as Sara Bache expressed it to her father, Benjamin Franklin, it was to be a school

[46] G. B. Goode, "The Origin of the National Scientific and Educational Institutions of the U.S.," *Amer. Hist. Assn., Papers,* IV, pt. II (1890), 9–11. Stiles's project of 1765 should be recalled.

[47] L. G. Simons, "The Influence of French mathematicians . . . in American Colleges," *Isis,* XV (1931), 104–123.

of postgraduate studies. But the structure never rose higher than the foundation (it was actually laid), for with the outbreak of the French Revolution the support for it, which had been generously promised, quickly vanished.[48]

The rising sentiment of nationalism prompted the suggestion that the American Philosophical Society be organized on a federal plan with committees of learned men in the separate states and the parent body in Philadelphia acting as a clearing house. There had long been an understanding that several American libraries should be the depositaries for the transactions of every learned society in Europe.[49]

Before leaving Paris for home in 1789, Jefferson wrote to President Willard of Harvard, "What a field have we at our doors to signalize ourselves in!" American botany was incompletely known, its mineralogy untouched, and its natural history distorted, he said. It was the task of her own colleges and other learned institutions to

> do justice to our country, its productions and its genius. It is the work to which the young men, whom you are forming, should lay their hands. We have spent the prime of our lives in procuring them the precious blessing of liberty. Let them spend theirs in showing that it is the great parent of science and of virtue; and that a nation will be great in both, always in proportion as it is free.[50]

An unfulfilled plan for a federal university supported by the nation had some elements similar to that of the proposed Richmond Academy. Several young men were to be sent abroad to study the latest developments in the mechanical arts and to report back to their native country. Exploratory studies of natural resources at home were also to be made by students of the national university.[51]

At the end of the century the American Philosophical Society pleaded for state aid for the advancement of science and asked espe-

---

[48] R. H. Gaines, "Richmond's First Academy projected by M. Quesnay de Beaurepaire, 1786," *Va. Hist. Soc., Colls.*, n.s. XI (1892), 168–173.

[49] Lewis Nicola, 1780, Amer. Phil. Soc., archives; see Library Co. of Phila. to Franklin, Jan. 25, 1771, *Calendar of Franklin Papers,* I, 117.

[50] C. A. Browne, "Thomas Jefferson and the Scientific Trends of his time," reprint, *Chronica Botanica,* VIII (Nov., 1943), 23.

[51] Appendix to Goode, *loc. cit.*

cially for expenditures on modern books and instruments. Americans needed to keep in touch with European discoveries, men of talents must be furnished with "materials from the other side of the Atlantick." And then to reassure the Pennsylvania State Assembly, the secretary of the Society added, "We are *Modern Philosophers of the New School.* . . . Since 1785 I have neither heard nor seen Politicks introduced." Priestley wrote from Pennsylvania to an English friend that America had many advantages, "the press is perfectly free," and no country in the world was making such rapid progress, but nevertheless "we have not the same advantages for literary and philosophical pursuits that you have in Europe." It was hoped that European troubles would cause the migration of libraries to America.[52]

Americans were honored with degrees from noted schools and by election to distinguished European societies. A number of Americans received honorary degrees from abroad, most of them from Scottish universities. But such was the reputation of American organizations that membership and correspondence with them was, in return, eagerly sought by European savants. The list of foreign members of the American Philosophical Society grew from 24 in 1771 to 70 by 1793, at which time Erasmus Darwin's name was on the roll. Darwin had long been an enthusiastic admirer of Franklin.[53] John Hunter, in acknowledging election to the American Philosophical Society, stated his desire to send scientific contributions, but the pursuits in which he was then engaged, he said, "rather require assistance from America which contains an almost inexhaustible treasure hardly begun upon, consequently much is to be expected from the labours of the society." John Hyacinth de Magellan, F.R.S., well-known instrument maker, scientist, and descendant of the great navigator, nervously awaited election to America's leading learned society. He sent his writings to it and left a fund for the award of a medal, preferably for notable achievements in navigation. The Royal Society of Valencia, with famed Spanish lavishness, added the whole roster of the American group (which it

---

[52] John Vaughan to George Fox, Jan. 20, 1800, Mss., Univ. of Penn.; *Gentleman's Magazine,* LXVII (1797), 23.

[53] L. Hussakof, "Franklin and Erasmus Darwin," *Science,* n.s. XLIII (1916), 773–775.

called the "Anglo-American society") to its roll of honorary members.[54]

The ties between American and European education became much closer in the nineteenth and twentieth centuries. American financial aid to European institutions in these later years repaid something of the debt contracted in the colonial period. American students in large numbers went abroad, and Europeans began to enter American schools. It has been a story of mutual aid from the beginning and is one of the brightest chapters in the history of Western civilization.

English booksellers were delighted at the prospect of an increased demand for their products from a growing population in America, but purists in speech were prophesying the day when the two countries would no longer have a common tongue. If the present tendency continued, wrote one English traveler early in the nineteenth century, in another hundred years the dialect of Americans would become unintelligible to Englishmen. It was reported that Americans during the Revolution referred to their tongue as the "American Language." John Witherspoon (who was hostile to deviations from the mother tongue) claimed to have coined the word "Americanism." Witherspoon and his fellow purists were helpless, for the generation after the Revolution was a period of great invention in the language spoken by Americans.[55]

An English review of William Bradford's book on crime and punishment in America praised its purity of language, so different from many contemporary American productions, whose "licentious innovations, and unidiomatical combinations of words . . . threaten . . . to convert the English which is written and spoken on the different sides of the Atlantic into two different languages." [56] The critical secretary to the British Minister wrote from Philadelphia that Americans in the eastern states had retained the "local idioms

[54] Hunter, Dec. 2, 1787; Magellan, June 17, 1783, Valencia, Nov. 22, 1796, Amer. Phil. Soc., archives (also published *Amer. Phil. Soc., Trans.,* II [1786], xix; III [1793], 366).

[55] Mesick, 244–245; H. L. Mencken, *The American Language* (4th ed., New York, 1937), 6, 12.

[56] Quoted in Rich, *Bibliotheca Americana Nova,* 394.

and barbarisms" of their English ancestors, and "thus a barbarous dialect becomes a national language, and its corruption is perpetuated." [57] His staunch conservatism waxed indignant at the new words adopted by Americans and their continued use of old ones: "They plead, I presume, revolution and the rights of man for these innovations in language, and the liberty of talking in bad English, I suppose considered as indefeasible as that of doing wrong, when the people unite in such a resolution." He was very uncertain as to the eventual language of this people gathered from the ends of the earth.

Some writers, including William Eddis, a recent arrival in Maryland from England, were more friendly to American speech. Eddis observed that whereas England had wide variations in dialects, in Maryland and near-by provinces a striking similarity of speech universally prevailed, and the pronunciation of all classes of people "has an accuracy and elegance that cannot fail of gratifying the most judicious ear." Contrary to the expectations of those who believed that the diverse origins of Americans would beget a polyglot tongue, the language of the immediate descendants of so promiscuous an ancestry, said Eddis, was "perfectly uniform." He confessed himself at a loss to account for "the apparent difference between the colonists and persons under equal circumstances of education and fortune resident in the mother country." Witherspoon thought the common people in America spoke better than the comparable class in England, because their migratory habits prevented them from becoming too much addicted to local peculiarities. Benjamin Silliman, after traveling through much of England was likewise convinced that the Americans as a people talked better English than did the masses in Great Britain.[58]

Philologists in England and America discussed the advisability of establishing academies to maintain the purity of the language; and at least one Englishman, discouraged by apathy at home, thought

---

[57] James Hutton, ed., *Letters and Correspondence of Sir Bland Burges* (London, 1885), 222; also M. M. Mathews, "Notes and Comments made by British Travelers and Observers upon American English 1770–1850," *Harvard Univ., Grad. School of Arts and Sciences, Summaries of Theses, 1936*, 341–344.

[58] Eddis, 57–62, June 8, 1770; Greene, 183; Silliman, *Journal of Travels*, II, 237, 239.

of first fixing the standard of the language in America. Once set there, he hoped American example would communicate its good effects to England. John Adams also thought that establishment of an academy for speech in America might prompt the British to do likewise.[59]

The English language in America, enriched by additions from Indian, French, and Dutch sources, brought words and expressions into the language often frowned upon by the pundits. But the *Gentleman's Magazine* approved of a London reprint of Noah Webster's essays, with their Americanisms, and a new Oxford dictionary of the English language which proposed to devote some space to American English was immediately asked to find explanations for "caucus" and "Yankee." One English scientist thought Americans had improved the language by introducing "some words and phrases very energetic and concise, instead of diffuse circumlocution." Americans sometimes turned the tables on the critics of their language. When he described his agricultural activities to Dr. Lettsom, Dr. Waterhouse of Massachusetts wrote, "I *grew* (to use an *Anglicism* which we *Yankees* smile at) about 160 bushels of [Indian corn]." Long before 1800 travelers noted the many new terms and novel uses of old words by American farmers.[60] Americans and Englishmen have continued to smile at each other, and eighteenth-century prophecies have been partly fulfilled, for today individuals of both nations sometimes stand bewildered by sheer inability to comprehend each other's language.

Although the language was changing from its parental stem, the literature fashioned from it remained largely unchanged from its English models. Perhaps the criticism against literary dependence upon Europe went too far; declarations of literary independence

[59] A. W. Read, "Suggestions for an Academy in England in the Latter Half of the 18th Century," *Mod. Philology,* XXXVI (1936–1937), 145–156; Read, "American Projects for an Academy to Regulate Speech," *PMLA,* LI (1936), 1141–1179.

[60] *Gentleman's Magazine,* LXVIII (1798), 415; LVII (1788), 92; *Eur. Mag. and Lon. Rev.,* XII (1787), 114 note; Pettigrew, II, 497, March 9, 1801; A. W. Read, *Dialect Notes,* VI, pt. VI (1928–1939), 313–335; Read, "The Comment of British Travellers on early American terms relating to Agriculture," *Agricultural History,* VII (1933), 99–110; Mencken, 104–113; Silliman, I, 234.

then and later seem somewhat ridiculous. After all, Americans were a part of European civilization, and it was a sign of good taste to choose the best literature available on which to model their own. If you want to read poetry, James Otis said to a kinsman, read only good poetry—Shakespeare, Milton, Dryden, and Pope.[61] German literature as well, in the eighteenth century, was indebted to Englishmen—Sterne and Richardson—and English literary superiority was openly acknowledged by Herder, who wondered why Germany had no Shakespeare, Swift, Addison, Fielding, or Sterne. What was deplorable was the slavish adherence of American writers even in the matter of materials, for they seemed utterly oblivious to their native wealth. European critics scored Americans for their failure to root themselves at home. "From a country like America, where nature sets before the eyes of the poet the most luxuriant and the most terrific scenes," wrote a reviewer, "we might expect wild effusions of fancy, and those nervous glowing thoughts and expressions, whose irregular beauty and sublimity set criticism at defiance." But instead of emulating nature, they have slavishly borrowed "from her copyists, and those Europeans"; in the words of many American contemporaries, the writer concluded, "Till they shake off the trammels of Europe in poetry as well as European government, they will not rise above mediocrity." [62]

There were Americans who, though unable to do much about it, were aware of the problem. In the rising temper of national feeling a young Yale commencement orator had spoken of the decline of belles-lettres in England because of pedantry and "luxurious effeminacy." Her writers "are great admirers of antiquity and followers in the path of servile imitation. They sacrifice ease and elegance to the affectation of classic correctness, fetter the fancy with the rules of method and damp all the ardour of aspiring invention." [63] A lively young lady, Juliana Smith, editor of a literary journal in Connecticut, begged for prose contributions with "new thoughts." "Of course odes and Sonnets would be very fine if they were *poetical,* but, oh, my dear Jack," she wrote to her brother at Yale, "I fear me

[61] Tyler, *Literary History of the American Revolution,* I, 37.

[62] *Eur. Mag. and Lond. Rev.,* X (1786), 256.

[63] *An Essay on the Use and Advantages of the Fine Arts delivered at the Public Commencement in New Haven* (1770), 11.

there is very little promise that any of your Friends will prove to be Shakespeares or Miltons." [64] Some Americans agreed with European critics and were delighted that instead of babbling about "dells and dingles, the Alps and Apennines and the River Po," local writers were finding their images in their own national scene.[65]

Charles Brockden Brown gave several reasons for the "extremely superficial" nature of American literature. He listed them as occupation with business, a defective system of college education, lack of competition in scholarship, little reward for authors, scarcity of books and difficulty in getting them. To which other critics added another—politics.[66] The very criticism of a traditionalist like Joseph Dennie may have implied progress. Conservative in outlook, regretting the separation of America from England, and intensely desirous of European recognition, he bemoaned the quality of American writing: "To imagine that a refined and classical style of writing will be encouraged here," he said, "is as absurd as for a Thief to break into a Log House in the expectation of stealing Silver Tankards." [67]

Dramatists more quickly than others rooted themselves in the American scene. In the Revolutionary era practically every native play had realistic characters in plots based on current issues. Actors in certain roles were already endowed with the essential characteristics of the American—independence, directness of action, blunt speech, quick decision, a constant activity directed to practical ends, and a cheerful, rather obvious sense of humor. The accent on nationalism in the theater was not quite so strong in the years immediately following the end of the war, for the number of plays that contained characters taken from American life was less than in the preceding period.[68]

---

[64] H. E. Smith, 282.

[65] Krout and Fox, *The Completion of Independence 1790–1830,* 349.

[66] Mott, *A History of American Magazines, 1741–1850,* 187.

[67] L. G. Pedder, *The Letters of Joseph Dennie 1768–1812* ("University of Maine, Studies," ser. 2, XXXVI), 157–159, April 26, 1797.

[68] P. I. Reed, *The Realistic Presentation of American Characters in Native American Plays prior to Eighteen Seventy* ("Ohio State University, Contribs. in Lang. and Lit.," Bull. XXII no. I).

The escape from provincialism so much sought after in letters was more speedily achieved in the realm of religion. Here as in political philosophy the spirit of America entered more fully into the currents of world affairs. But as always it was the effect of a two-way European-American relationship, with America in this instance giving probably more than she received.

The struggle for religious toleration, and then for complete separation of church and state, took on added strength when it was tied in with the revolutionary thought of the latter half of the century. Acknowledging the gift of a new edition of Toland's life of Milton, sent over from England by the generous Thomas Hollis, Jonathan Mayhew wrote that the principles the great poet advocated in politics generally prevailed in New England, "though bigotry in religious matters has far too much place among us; so much as almost makes me ashamed of my country." But to British readers New England was held up as superior to old England in matters that affected church and state. In answer to the charge made in Parliament that the Anglicans were being persecuted in New England, Benjamin Franklin (signing himself "A New England Man") challenged, "Let us see how this *persecution account* stands between the parties." [69] In New England, where the legislative bodies were made up almost entirely of Dissenters, he found: (1) there was no test to prevent Anglican churchmen holding offices; (2) the sons of churchmen had the full benefit of the colleges; (3) the taxes for support of public worship, when paid by churchmen, were given to the Episcopal minister. In old England he reminded his readers: (1) Dissenters were excluded from all offices of profit and honor; (2) the benefits of education in the universities were appropriated to the sons of Churchmen; and (3) the dissenting clergy received none of the tithes paid by their people, who were at the additional expense of maintaining their own separate worship.

The open sympathy of English Dissenters for Americans during the Revolution was cause for bitter recrimination. New England, it was said, was "more the country of their hearts than the England wherein they were born and bred." Priestley observed that artic-

[69] *Memoirs of Thomas Hollis*, 1762, 108; *Scots Magazine*, XXXV (1773), 9–10.

ulate disaffection coincided with the Wilkes agitation, so much so that the words "dissenter" and "Wilkite" were used synonymously. The Dissenters were the spearhead of aggressive journalism and political clubs; the sermons of their ministers, in England and America, had more to do with the kingdom of earth than with the kingdom of heaven.[70]

Mayhew's liberalism made him very sensitive to the shortcomings of New England, but Pennsylvania afforded to the world such an example of amicable living amid religious diversity that countless Europeans felt impelled to speak of it. In prescribing behavior for Nova Scotia, the *London Magazine* pointed to the amity existing among Pennsylvanians who professed all the religions in Europe: [71]

> These people entertain a laudable and religious charity towards one another, and consider that tho' they differ in form they are all in motion towards the same point; and who worship in sincerity in any way what soever, is esteemed a good man and honest neighbour. If it were practicable to bring over the Gallo-Scotians into a sensibility of universal charity in religion, like these wise people of Pennsylvania and to entertain a good opinion of British government Nova Scotia would became altogether as happy.

Many British publications, popular as well as select, pointed out to their readers interesting information about religious conditions in the colonies. One of them which catered to the luxury trade praised Rhode Island, where liberty of conscience was "granted in the fullest extent. . . . Here is little bigotry, that every man is left to think and act for himself; and while he observes a good moral conduct, no body give themselves any trouble about his religious principles for which he is only accountable to God." [72] Writers of all stripes found much to praise in Rhode Island and Pennsylvania, but quite naturally it was the Dissenters who took fullest advantage of the opportunity. The good Quaker was possibly the finest symbol

---

[70] Lincoln, 24–42.

[71] *London Magazine,* XVIII (April, 1749), 184. One Friend, compiling a history of Quakers, was skeptical toward unrelieved adulation: "Voltaire's Quaker, I imagine, must be generally looked upon as the creature of his fancy, rather than a real being" (John Gough to J. Phillips, Jan. 22, 1783, Gibson Mss., I, 131, Friends House, London).

[72] Fenning and Collyer, II, 652.

America had to offer to anxious European eyes. Part of the English regard for Pennsylvania's religious liberalism, it should be mentioned, came from mercantilist appreciation of the value of toleration in promoting economic growth.[73]

During the Revolutionary era the popular churches, the Baptist and the Methodist, progressed rapidly, making inroads among the Presbyterians and Episcopalians. A few of the Anglican clergy themselves aided in the spread of Methodism, notably the Reverend Devereux Jarratt in Virginia, so that the way was prepared for the popular preachers who soon came along. "Blessed be God for Field-preaching!" J. Pilmoor wrote from America to Wesley. In New York he reported large congregations, "and we have the pious of most congregations to hear us, which makes the Presbyterian bigots mad!" [74] But more preachers were asked for, especially for service in frontier districts, and aid was sought in England for their support.[75]

Transatlantic thought dealing with the relations between church and state had often expressed itself even before the events of the Revolutionary era focused more intense interest upon it. In the previous century Roger Williams, on a trip to England during the Puritan Revolution, injected the New England controversy into the debates on toleration then being pressed by Presbyterians and Independents. Isaac Watts and Benjamin Colman engaged in a discussion arising from reading a work on the subject of toleration, and Watts (though preferring Christian towns and governments) asked, "But if a few heathens or Mahometans are found amongst them, must they be banished and excluded from the publick protection?" [76] The union of church and state made him uneasy—"knowing what eternal mischiefs it has wrought thro all Europe in all ages, and is every day working throughout the world."

Isaac Norris, visiting in England, informed a fellow Quaker

---

[73] [F. Hall], *The Importance of the British Plantations in America to this Kingdom* (London, 1731), 89.

[74] *The Arminian Magazine,* VI (Oct. 31, 1769), 276; VII (May 5, 1770), 223. Coke remarked on the great number of children given the name of Wesley.

[75] Tyerman, *Wesley,* III, 116–117.

[76] "Letters of Dr. Isaac Watts," *Mass. Hist. Soc., Proc.,* ser. 2, IX (1894–1895), 368–369, Nov. 13, 1739.

about the recent publication, *The Rights of the Christian Church Asserted,* by Mathew Tindal, which gave the Established Church a body blow. It showed, said Norris, that the Church of England, established by law, was "a mere creature of the people and civil power." The book rested upon principles expounded by Locke and Sidney, continued Norris, maintaining that it was "absurd and inconsistent with the very being of a government to have two independent powers in the same society; that the clergy's endeavouring at it, is upon Papal principles and inconsistent with the Christian religion . . ." Norris was quite carried away with its logic, erudition and boldness.[77]

The attack on religious establishments took a more sinister turn with the growth of deism and free thinking, which frightened the orthodox. " 'Tis a melancholy truth," reported Governor William Gooch from Virginia to the Bishop of London, that "the Church & Clergy have many Enemies in this Country, free thinkers multiply very fast having an eminent Layman for their Leader, and the Current runs in some places almost without opposition." [78] Deists made use of the familiar device of the Indian spokesman answering a missionary's sermon. One such essay which was widely known raised the question of the relative viciousness of Indians and Christians and concluded that the Christians were more depraved, which explained why they needed God's beneficence more than did the Indians. Certainly one objective of missionary activity as reported by a contemporary periodical could hardly have contributed to piety. It was suggested that the Indians, once Christianized, would advance to a civilized state and thus be in a position to require many manufactured articles from England.[79] Franklin's parable on persecution was given wide reprinting in Europe, especially after it had been strongly endorsed in Lord Kames's *Sketches of the History of Man.*

It was, of course, the events of the Revolutionary era which crys-

---

[77] *Correspondence between William Penn and James Logan,* II, 210–211, Norris to Joseph Pike, Bristol 24, 2d mo., 1707. A number of Quakers were interested in deistic literature (Tolles, 171–174).

[78] *Virginia Mag. of Hist. and Biog.,* XXXII (1924), 332–333, July 8, 1735.

[79] *Scots Magazine,* XXIII (1771), reprinted from *London Magazine; Scots Magazine,* XXXIV (1772), 460.

talized thought about church and state, religious liberty, and the role of religion in modern society. European reformers in religion, as in other phases of contemporary thought, were immensely stimulated by the changes in American state constitutions, which severely limited established churches, and which provided for a greater degree of religious freedom than was generally the rule in their own lands. Publications of all types familiarized their readers with the latest developments in religion in the new American states. At the same time the loosening of rigid orthodoxy in European religious circles communicated its effects to Americans. Liberals believed in the value of hands across the sea and were quick to recognize and appreciate support wherever it appeared even during the Revolutionary War. The *Gentleman's Magazine,* the best-known periodical in England, paid tribute in verse to Hollis' print of Dr. Mayhew of Boston. The rhyme observed that Mayhew could not be bought by England:

> Religious liberty with honest pride
> Living he cherish'd, and triumphant died.[80]

The same magazine spoke of the spirit of toleration which prevailed in America to so great an extent that it "has caused a vast diversity of sects to be settled on this continent," resulting in its being called "the land of sectaries." [81] Even conservative readers would find in their favored authors such sentences as this on Pennsylvania: "There is no Ecclesiastical Establishment: every mode of worship is allowed and no man acknowledging the being of a God, is deprived or abridged of any civil right as a citizen." [82] A reviewer of Jefferson's *Notes on Virginia,* referring to the appendix which included the famous act for establishing religious freedom, said it was "framed on very liberal principles indeed." Along with praise went admonition. Price was pleased with the Massachusetts constitution, which stipulated that "every denomination of Christians . . . shall be Equally under the protection of the law," but he

---

[80] *Gentleman's Magazine,* LII (1782), 133.

[81] *Ibid.,* LXVI, 770.

[82] Anthony Stokes, *A View of the Constitution of the British Colonies . . . down to the present Period* (London, 1783), 83.

would have admired it more if it had been extended to include men of all religions.[83]

Correspondents exchanged information about many details in the rapidly changing society of the closing eighteenth century. From Scotland came the query, "Are all sects equally regarded by your government, and equally eligible to civil offices? or is there any exception made with regard to Roman Catholics?" And from Princeton went the reply: "There is no exception, and we find the Roman Catholics make zealous and attached citizens to the new states. Their religious principles we do not fear. The American sense of liberty is so high, that we are sure they would not wish to give themselves a master even in the Pope." [84] The Continental Congress, though exploiting anti-Catholicism on the one hand, assumed a different tone when wooing the French Canadians, in its *Letter to the Inhabitants of Quebec.* There it naturally preferred to speak of the successful association of Protestant and Catholic cantons in the Swiss Confederation. In general, it may be said that the Revolutionary era brought with it a lessening of animosities against Catholics.[85] The *Scots Magazine* praised the liberalism of legislation in America, but it charged that genuine piety was almost completely absent. Young people, it alleged, went to church purely for the economic and social advantages to be derived from attendance.[86]

Ezra Stiles of Yale and Joseph Willard of Harvard were in close touch with English Dissenters, exchanging notes of encouragement in the fight for greater religious freedom. Under Stiles's auspices seniors debated the problem of state support for religion and the more extreme question, "Whether Liberty for all Religions, Pagan & Mahometan as well as Xtian ought to be allowed in the United States?" Willard congratulated Price on the wide tolerance displayed at his school in Hackney (England) and emphasized the especial importance of educating Dissenters. They in particular, said Willard, were the ardent promoters of religious as well as civil

---

[83] *Eur. Mag. and Lond. Rev.,* XII (1787), 382; Price, *Observations on the Importance of the American Revolution,* 47–48.

[84] *The Bee,* XII (Dec. 19, 1792), 283–284, S. Smith to C. Nisbet, Feb. 4, 1785.

[85] Greene, *Religion and the State,* 77.

[86] *Scots Magazine,* LX (1798), 236–239.

liberty, and could be counted on to be in the vanguard of the struggle in England.[87]

Outside of the colleges and universities of Scotland, the academies run by Dissenters gave the best instruction obtainable for youth in Britain. The Dissenters were more than teachers; they were the ablest theorists in education of their time, a contribution which has been inadequately recognized. The English dissenting academies in earlier years had close ties with Holland, but, toward the middle of the eighteenth century and after, their associations veered strongly toward Scotland and America. Priestley described these schools as places "where youth are taught the most liberal principles both in religion and politics." Robert Hall, a leading radical of these years, it was said, owed "his undying passion for liberty" to his schoolmaster at Northampton, the Reverend John Rylands, who ardently supported the American cause in the Revolution.[88]

English radicals, critical of the whole social structure, found ammunition in America for their attacks on the Establishment. America, said one, "affords an example that government can do better without an established church, than with it." The London Quakers continued to report to Philadelphia of their unsuccessful attempts to get relief from the tithe laws. Henry Wormall, in prison for not paying tithes, testified in moving words to the aid sent him by his Quaker coreligionists in America.[89]

A pamphleteer in behalf of English Dissenters spoke glowingly of the Virginia act respecting religious liberty and of the sixth article of the federal Constitution stating that no religious tests were to be imposed for officeholders. The writer believed that no country was more indulgent to religious diversity than the United States, the majority of whose people were Dissenters, and he argued therefore that this showed the modern temper of Dissenters was not intolerant. The warning was held up that just as in Ireland, so too in

---

[87] Stiles, *Diary,* III, 124, June 7, 1784; III, 147, Jan. 10, 1785; III, 250, Dec. 11, 1786; "Price Letters," *Mass. Hist. Soc., Proc.,* ser. 2, XVII (1903), 371, Nov. 19, 1788.

[88] Lincoln, 66, 86, 88 note 2.

[89] G. Dyer, *The Complaints of the Poor People of England* (London, 1793), 37.

England, large depopulation would ensue unless the Test Act were repealed.[90] Charles James Fox, speaking in Parliament for the repeal of the Corporation and Test Acts, called attention to the American example, "the imitation of which," he said, "would reflect the highest credit upon ourselves." [91]

The Dissenters in England and America were a powerful force in effecting the gradual secularization of politics. Broadening the base of their appeal so that on it could stand all the massed array of the unprivileged Jews and Catholics as well, the Dissenters now opposed toleration as too narrow a concept, urging, rather, complete liberty as a right to be demanded, not as a privilege granted by the state.[92] In this they had been anticipated by American nonconformists, who opposed any kind of religious establishment. The latter, it was said, implied a claim to infallibility, such as that upheld by the Roman Catholic Church.

It was Richard Price, that devoted friend of America, who did most to spread the news of religious developments in the States. Americans and Englishmen sought his aid in advancing religious freedom, believing he had more influence with American legislators than had any other person in Great Britain. On one occasion a Philadelphia correspondent urged him to write a pamphlet addressed to Congress and the state legislatures, which he felt would "have more weight . . . than a hundred publications thrown out by the Citizens of this country." In communicating the famed Virginia act to the *Gentleman's Magazine,* Price wrote that it afforded "an example of legislative wisdom and liberality never before known, and must please all the friends of intellectual and religious liberty . . . Had the principles which have dictated it been always acted upon by civil governments . . . most of the evils which have disturbed the peace of the world . . . would have been prevented." His enthusiasm for Virginia's measure was unbounded: "It is the first of the kind that was ever pass'd," he told Rush, and it was a

---

[90] Samuel Heywood, *The Right of Protestant Dissenters to a Compleat Toleration assisted* . . . (2nd ed., London, 1789), 60–63, 79–80.

[91] *Two Speeches delivered in the House of Commons* . . . *in support of his motion for a Repeal of the Corporation and Test Acts* (London, 1790), 40–41.

[92] Lincoln, 254–255.

'happy omen of the benefit to mankind that may arise from the American Revolution." [93]

Rush wrote to Price that Pennsylvania had repealed its test law, thus putting all citizens on a basis of equality. "The success of the friends of humanity in this business should encourage them to persevere in their attempts to enlighten and reform the world. Your letter to me," he said to Price, "upon the subject of that unjust law was the instrument that cut the last sinew." William Hazlitt, father of the essayist, wrote from Boston that he expected in that community, within a generation, as much freedom of thought on religious subjects "as there is at present amongst the Dissenters in England. Dr. Mayhew . . . led the way to this." [94] Price, in his noted pamphlet, *Observations on the Importance of the American Revolution, and the means of making it a Benefit to the World,* discoursed on the evils of religious establishments, including the English, and then gave thanks that they were absent in the new American states. He was, however, critical of the religious tests still to be found in some of the state constitutions. Colonel William Smith, son-in-law of John Adams, concluded after hearing Dr. Price preach that he was "the most liberal Christian [he] ever met with. I have taken him as my Father Confessor." [95]

Americans directly aimed a propaganda barrage at Europe, and no propagandist was more vigorous than Joel Barlow. Liberty (i.e., equal rights) was incompatible with the existence of a national or preferred church, he argued. Then he went on to state proudly that because the United States had no national church, her government was thus distinguished from all others "that ever existed; it ensures that unembarrassed exercise of religion, the continuation of public instruction in the science of liberty and happiness, and promises a long duration to a representative government." Ezra Stiles in conversation with a prominent Frenchman pointedly expressed the hope that the example of American religious as well as civil liberty

---

[93] Lincoln, 133 note 1; *Gentleman's Magazine,* LVII (1787), 74–75; Price to Rush, July 30, 1781, Ridgway Library.

[94] "Price Letters," *Mass. Hist. Soc., Proc.,* ser. 2, XVII (1903), 341, April 22, 1786; *ibid.,* 322, Hazlitt to Price, Oct. 19, 1784.

[95] Roof, 95.

might lead France to relax restrictions on the Huguenots.[96] There seems little doubt that American example did help. Those who aided in the adoption of the edict of 1787 granting civil rights to French Protestants were strong Americanophiles. It was with great joy that Lafayette wrote to Washington about the achievement.[97]

Jefferson proudly wrote to his colleague Madison that Virginia's act for religious freedom had been enthusiastically received in Europe, not by the governments, he said, "but by the individuals who compose them." It had been widely reprinted in translation in many publications. "It is honorable for us," he added, "to have produced the first legislature who had the courage to declare that the reason of man may be trusted with the formation of his own opinions." Hollis told the president of Harvard that the Virginia act, which he called a declaration against intolerance, went far beyond anything of its kind in Europe, "and gives us an example of what we may expect from men emancipated from subjection, perfectly free with the powers of the human mind at full liberty to range through the civil and intellectual world, and pursue truth and knowledge and follow their dictates." Europe expected much from Americans who had advantages the old world never had. America had Europe's experiences to build on and, it was hoped, the wisdom to avoid her follies.[98]

Communications from Kentucky Baptists to England underscored the joyful news: *"Liberty of conscience is unlimited among us";* "The Lord deliver you from the civil state of dissenters in England." A South Carolina correspondent observed, gratefully, that churchgoing was made easier because "our poorest people have a horse to ride." [99]

While believers on both sides of the Atlantic strengthened each other's hands, it should be mentioned that doubters too sought com-

[96] Barlow, *Advice to the Privileged Orders,* pt. I, 69; Stiles, *Diary,* II, 372, Sept. 11, 1779.

[97] H. C. Rice, "Cotton Mather speaks to France," *New England Quarterly,* XVI (1943), 232.

[98] Jefferson, *Writings,* VI, 10, Dec. 16, 1786; Hollis to Willard, "Willard Letters," *Mass. Hist. Soc., Proc.,* XLIII (1909–1910), 622.

[99] Rippon, *Baptist Annual Register* (London, 1790–1793), 106, 117; *ibid.* (1794), 201.

fort in each other's unbelief. Deism and rationalism flourished on both sides of the ocean, and though they rose and fell in appeal they left a permanent mark on the civilization of the Atlantic peoples. In the early years of the century the young graduates of Yale were cautioned against the new philosophy (associated with the names of Boyle, Locke, and Newton), "that of late was all in vogue," because it threatened to bring in "a new Divinity and Corrupt the pure Religion of the Country." [100]

In later years, in devious ways as, for example, through *An Essay on Punctuation,* students were exposed to the new thought. Among samples of short sentences needing no comma were the following: "The earth is a mere atom in the universe. Innumerable worlds lie beyond this visible scene." Commas were required in "Comets, it is certain, do not presage any calamity." [101] Linnaeus wrote to a correspondent that in the future only valuable materials would be admitted to the transactions of the learned society at Upsala—on medicine, natural philosophy, mathematics, etc.—but "no theological nonsense" (meaning doctrinal controversies). The secretary of the Royal Society in England wrote to Professor Greenwood at Harvard that the "part of Philosophy the least known & where there is a great deal worth knowing is Rational Chymistry, divested of its Rosicrucian Jargon. . . ." [102]

The liberal clergyman, John Clarke of Boston, agreed with Price that the Mosaic history of the creation and fall of man "was not to be understood according to the literal sense of the words." But Americans, especially in smaller communities, were careful lest their neighbors pry into their reading. Pack the books, wrote a correspondent from Northampton to Henry Knox in Boston, so "they may be intirely concealed when they arrive here." [103]

Contact with new people, such as the American Indian, provoked

---

[100] E. C. Smyth, "The 'new philosophy' . . . Yale College . . . in 1714," *Amer. Antiq. Soc., Proc.,* n.s. XI (1896–1897), 252; see also H. M. Morais, *Deism in Eighteenth Century America* (New York, 1934), chaps. ii–iv.

[101] *An Essay on Punctuation* (printed by Jos. James, Philadelphia, n.d.).

[102] Smith, *Corr. of Linnaeus,* II, 371, May 29, 1744; Feb. 18, 1729/30, R. 2.36, Royal Soc. Library.

[103] "Price Letters," *loc. cit.,* 345, July 18, 1786; Jos. Clarke to Knox, April 8, 1773 in "Henry Knox and the London Book-store in Boston 1771–1774," *Mass. Hist. Soc., Proc.,* LXI (1927–1928), 250.

comparisons between unlike societies. It mattered little that as scientific ethnologists European observers were often sadly deficient, for they saw what they wanted to see and they wrote what they believed their audiences at home wanted to read. Clever journalists spoke through the mouths of real or fictitious Incas or Cherokees to cast doubt on revelation, for had they not, too, their own traditions of earth's origin? The question was raised whether Indians who had never heard of revelation should be damned. To say that all innocent men had to be punished because of one ancestor's sin, it was maintained, must make the Almighty an ill-natured Being. Indian women were apparently unaware of the curse on Eve, for it was said they bore their children without pain. It was observed with satisfaction that Indians had no ties between church and state.

A London skeptic asked, if the whole globe had been deluged, "how came it then that none of Noah's family were sent to America, to re-people that, if America then existed, or had suffered in the general confusion?" Yale seniors debated the question "Whether Mountains & Vallies, with marine fossils in the Apalachian Hills, & Trees dug up 100 feet deep . . . &c. prove the Deluge?" Other questions for debate were "whether the historical parts of the Bible are of divine inspiration?" and "whether all mankind derived from One Man?" [104] A Maryland correspondent of the Royal Society spoke of the wearing away of Niagara Falls and remarked that if it could be determined at what rate the cataract was eating away the rock, "the Age of the World of the Deluge will be known; it's said . . . to be half a rod a year." [105] In a French dialogue one speaker asserted that the oldest inhabitants and the greater part of the animals found in America were antediluvian. "What!" his companion asks in mock horror, "do you suppose then that the deluge was not universal?" The author of the dialogue believed that "our globe and the universe in general, is of an antiquity more distant than is commonly believed." [106]

---

[104] *Gentleman's Magazine,* LIII (1783), 498; Stiles, *Diary,* II, 569, 571, Dec. 4, Dec. 11, 1781; III, 123, 306, 311, 332, June 1, 1784, Feb. 18, March 18, Nov. 11, 1788.

[105] J. Calder, Jan. 10, 1794, Royal Soc. letters, 1787–1799, Royal Soc. Library.

[106] *Essai sur cette question: Quand et comment L'Amérique a-t-elle été peuplée d'hommes et d'animaux?* par E. B. d'E. (Amsterdam, 1767), preface and 235.

Benjamin Rush fluttered an English reviewer of his *Three Lectures upon Animal Life* because the work appeared to teach that rational beings function merely in response to certain stimuli. This theory, it was charged, thus reduces man to the level of brute creation and, concluded the reviewer, is therefore "subversive of moral and religious principles." [107] More frequently it was European rationalism that stirred the tempest. Joseph Priestley, harried out of England, republished in Philadelphia his *Appeal to the serious and candid Professors of Christianity* (1794), claiming that fifty thousand copies of it had been sold in its original edition.

As is the way in controversy, and particularly in religious controversy, fantastic exaggeration was the order of the day. This was especially true in the continuing crisis of the last quarter of the eighteenth century. Americans thought Frenchmen, as well as other Europeans, murderers of the faith, while Germans with equal inexactness assumed that all New Englanders were atheists, who, for outward conformity, carried the Bible in their pockets six days a week and prayed on the seventh.[108] Over all the clouds of controversy, in the fearful imaginings of conservatives, moved the satanic figure of Tom Paine. John Adams thought that no man in the world had equaled him in influence over a period of thirty years. "Call it," he said disparagingly, "the Age of Paine." [109]

The sharpening of sectarian conflicts was only slightly mitigated by appeals to reason. But with painful slowness, through legislation, through the co-operative enterprise of those able to see above the battle, and from the compulsions of new interests, older religious habits began to give way. While the New World was a vast field in which the various sects competed with one another (sometimes bitterly) for unattached souls, it should be recorded that religious lines were sometimes erased in the fraternity of Christian fellowship. The New World contributed, however slightly, to the modification of denominational differences. A plan for religious and secular education among the German Protestants in Pennsylvania drew large support from Holland, Scotland, and England. Youngsters of all denominations were to be accepted in the schools, which

---

[107] *The London Med. Rev. and Mag.,* III (June, 1800), 352–353.

[108] Ebeling, *Amerikanisches Magazin,* I (1796), pt. 4, 172.

[109] J. Adams to Benj. Waterhouse, Oct. 29, 1805, *Atlantic Monthly,* CXXXIX (May, 1927), 615.

were to teach English and German. In their religious instruction they were to be taught "by such catechisms as their own parents approve, avoiding all compulsion and partiality with respect to particular notions, not essential to true piety and virtue." [110] A "Plan for Social Prayer" in New York which called for co-operation among several of the churches was proposed on the basis of earlier action taken in Great Britain. "Our brethren in Britain of different denominations," it said, "have unified in prayers, on a more catholic plan than what is proposed here, notwithstanding their many obstacles; ought not we to imbibe their spirit, and imitate their example?" [111]

After the Revolution American formal religious ties with Europe became weaker, with the creation of autonomous national organizations freed from European jurisdiction. In the process a reaction developed against the rationalism of European and American clergy, and a Protestant counterreformation once again found sustenance in the springs of evangelicalism. But side by side with this development the steady growth of secularism proceeded.

This gradual secularization of European-American thought moderated the fierceness of sectarian controversy. John Adams urged an investigation of the history of the colonies and their treatment of Quakers and Baptists.[112] In the shaky handwriting of old age he asked, "Why should we not honestly and candidly investigate the errors and crimes of our Ancestors, that we may correct, reform and avoid them?" The growth of secularism in these years may also be measured by the declining enrollment of divinity students in proportion to the total student body. At Edinburgh, medicine seemed to be a stronger attraction; in America it was law as well as medicine.[113] The changing content of college curricula, the wider range of subjects discussed by students, science in particular, and new developments in the arts too, all suggest the mutations occurring in the human spirit in this period.

The changes in Puritan thought and feeling about death and the future life, writes Odell Shepard, are clearly revealed in the head-

---

[110] *Scots Magazine,* XVII (1755), 192–193, taken from *Gentleman's Magazine.*

[111] *The Missionary Magazine* (Edinburgh), III (1798), 490–494.

[112] Adams to Van der Kemp, undated, Hist. Soc. Penn.

[113] Andrew Duncan, *Annals of Medicine* (Edinburgh, 1799), 537, table of Edinburgh students, 1790–1800.

stones of New England. Gravestones of an earlier day insisted upon man's decadence, "the symbolic carvings suggesting little hope of a glorious resurrection"; but, as the years pass,

> the death's head acquires more and more the look of a cherub and the cross-bones give place to wings. By the middle of the eighteenth century the horror of death is so far subordinated that portraits of the deceased not unlike those to be seen on the tombstones of the ancient world occur frequently. Later still, perhaps under French influence, the cinerary urn and cypress which were never used by early Puritans because of their pagan origin, swept aside for a time most of the Christian symbols.[114]

It has been a long, never-ending process, this mutual civilizing of Americans and Europeans. They have aided each other in living up to their common ideals, and when the religious life of one ran sluggish it was often inspirited by the energy that flowed from the other side of the ocean. Americans were proud of their example of peace amid religious diversity, and while they did have much to teach the world, they were not averse to sitting at Europe's feet. The enlightenment originating in Europe severed some from a religious life, but for many it gave a broader basis to religious thought and observance. The limits of the City of God were measurably widened by the builders of the Atlantic civilization.

The heritage of the Revolutionary years left bitter memories in England and America, although manifestations of friendliness persisted which were a countertheme to the dominant note of hostility. Even during the years of hostilities Americans and Englishmen managed on occasion to preserve their social relationships. When Franklin invited Alexander Small to dine with him in his home in Passy, he acknowledged that Small was in the enemy's service but believed that their respective masters were "reasonable enough to allow that differing politics should not prevent the intercommunication of *philosophes,* who study and converse for the benefit of mankind." [115] David Hartley, whose Parliamentary career was given over to the cause of a just understanding with America, continued his friendship with Franklin to the end. Hartley throughout his life

---

[114] O. Shepard, *New England Quarterly,* III (Jan., 1930), 166–167, reviewing H. M. Forbes, *Gravestones of Early New England. . . .*

[115] Smyth, *Franklin, Writings,* VIII, 120, July 22, 1780.

maintained his interest in America, for which he forecast a brilliant future.

Thomas Pownall wrote from London, in 1778, to the Reverend Samuel Cooper and to James Bowdoin, that he hoped the time would soon be at hand when it would "no longer be a crime for the different parts of the English Nation living in G. Britain & America" to correspond with each other. Pownall wanted to know how he would be received if he were to make his home in America; many, he believed would seek new homes there.[116] Quakers in Philadelphia suffering from the British occupation during the war were given assistance by co-religionists in England and Ireland.

There are many evidences that the threads of prewar business and social relations were gradually picked up with the ending of hostilities. Despite the failure to solve disputed questions a slow easing of tension is observable. An amusing example of this relaxation occurred in a British playhouse where an interlude ridiculing America was performed. The scene presented some American officers, without shoes and in tattered uniforms, and each was asked what his trade had been before he entered the army. One replied, "a tailor," another, "a cobbler," etc. The wit of the playlet was to poke fun at them for not keeping themselves better clothed and shod. Before the lines could be spoken, however, an American in the gallery shouted "Great Britain beaten by taylors and cobblers? Huzza!" Even the Prime Minister, who was present, could not help smiling amid a general peal of laughter.[117]

Americans and Europeans have looked at each other with mingled hope and fear since the eighteenth century. After the grant of American independence George Chalmers said Britain should show the United States that she did not require the latter's aid in supplying the needs of the West Indies. But he did add that the British should learn from the New Englanders and the French how to arrange "those miscellaneous cargoes, which are so commodious to the West Indian buyer as well as to the British seller." Future American competition in East Indian waters was to be anticipated.

---

[116] Pownall to Cooper, April 19, 1778, Huntington Library.

[117] *The Bee,* XIII (Jan. 23, 1793), 120.

The profits of freights, said Chalmers, were more valuable to Britain than the mines of Potosí were to Spain.[118]

The author of a popular work on the United States said that the latter would be a formidable economic rival to England, many of whose most valuable mechanics would emigrate to America. "All Europe will feel the shock," he prophesied, "and her power and consequence must naturally dwindle as those of America shall rise." [119] A German publication expressed similar thoughts founded on orthodox mercantilism. America's self-sufficiency would cause a cessation of trade with Europe, which would then experience a profound crisis and eventual decline. To prevent this, it was suggested that America be partitioned and controlled by European powers. A different point of view was expressed by a scholar friendly to the United States. With remarkable prescience Professor Zimmerman said that America would be a vast storehouse always ready to spread its largess over Europe's penury.[120]

The Revolution was looked upon by many in England and America as a civil war, and it was believed that a reconciliation might be effected even though each branch of the empire was now an independent unit. David Hartley devoted years in and out of Parliament to the furtherance of Anglo-American friendship; included in the broad imperial outline he favored was the grant of virtual dominion status to Ireland. He had suggested the same for the colonies during the American Revolution, and even after 1783 he continued to think in terms of an Anglo-American alliance based on commercial reciprocity and strengthened by common culture and traditions. Canada, he believed, was a common factor of interest, and so it has proved to be in the creation of the North Atlantic triangle.[121]

---

[118] G. Chalmers, *Opinions on Interesting Subjects of Public Law and Commercial Policy, arising from American Independence* (London, 1784), 116, 127, 140.

[119] James Franklin, *The Philosophical & Political History of the Thirteen United States of America* (London, 1784).

[120] King, 138; Zimmerman, *Essai de Comparaison entre la France et les Etats-Unis*, 98.

[121] G. H. Guttridge, *David Hartley, M.P., an advocate of conciliation, 1774–1783* ("Univ. of Calif., Publ. in Hist.," XIV, no. III, 1926); J. B. Brebner, *North Atlantic Triangle* (New Haven, 1945).

The associations of American liberals and intellectuals with their English counterparts were scarcely interrupted by the war. In extracting some consolation from the wreckage of the empire one writer saw economic and ideological gains. He believed that Anglo-American trade would thereafter be maintained on "a more rational, permanent and equitable foundation." For a long time to come he expected American agricultural products would be exchanged for European manufactures. "Perhaps this strange and unaccountable American war," he wrote prophetically, "has been appointed as the means of great and glorious revolutions through the world." [122] More than a few Englishmen were impressed by the tremendous resources of the United States for whom an imperial role was forecast in the Caribbean and in South America.

Thomas Pownall, in his perceptive *Memorial addressed to the Sovereigns of Europe and the Atlantic,* told his readers that "the peculiar orbit of every planet of the European system is disturbed, and the center of the general system of Europe is shifted." He called for a "real family compact" between the two Atlantic powers, Great Britain and the United States, urging the creation of a "great marine Atlantic Alliance." George Canning's action leading to the issuance of the Monroe Doctrine was foreshadowed in Pownall's plea that England and the United States join in opening up South America to commerce for all the world.[123] The imperial mind of William Byrd II, long before, had argued against England and the colonies getting mixed up in European wars; with complete faith in the Royal Navy he said, "We should therefore trust to our Wooden Walls altogether & let the Good People in the continent Fight their own Battles." [124]

But Franklin and his circle hoped that no peoples would engage

---

[122] [Thomas Tod], *Consolatory Thoughts on American Independence, shewing the great Advantages that will arise from it to the Manufactures, the Agriculture, and commercial Interest of Britain and Ireland.* By a Merchant. (Edinburgh, 1782), 17–18, 66.

[123] Pownall, *Memorial,* 9, 67–68, 73–74. In calling for joint English and American action in South America, Pownall was anticipated by Tod (see Tod, 55).

[124] W. Byrd II, Mss., Sept. 5, 1740, also Aug. 20, 1739, Huntington Library. This may indicate a lengthier tradition of American isolation than we imagine. See also M. Savelle, *Seeds of Liberty* (New York, 1948), 344–345.

n war. Benezet sent his *Thoughts on the Nature of War* to many ndividuals in America and Europe, including Frederick the Sec- nd. Franklin confided to his friend Richard Price, in the midst of he Revolution, the hope for a plan "that would induce & oblige Nations to settle their Disputes without first Cutting one another's Throats." Somewhat despairingly he wondered if men would ever e convinced that "even successful Wars at length become Misfor- unes" to those who begin them. Another friend, Dr. John Fother- ill, writing to Franklin a few months later, looked for the establish- nent of a college of justice where the claims of sovereigns could e weighed and war would then be levied only on those who refused ubmission to its decrees.[125] While still at Passy, Franklin was aston- shed to receive from Toulon "A Project of universal and perpetual eace written by Pierre-André Gargaz, a former galley slave," which e then printed at his private press. When Jefferson succeeded ranklin, Gargaz corresponded with him also.[126]

Franklin was quick to suggest the example of the federated states f 1787 to Europe's notice. He sent the federal Constitution to one orrespondent and added that if it succeeded he saw no reason why urope could not carry out the project of Henry IV by forming a ederal union of its different states and kingdoms. Robert R. Liv- ngston, inspired by the peaceful settlement of the bitter boundary ispute between Pennsylvania and Connecticut, even went so far s to prophesy European imitation of this American precedent: 'The great cause between Connecticut and Pennsylvania has been ecided in favor of the latter," he wrote Lafayette. "It is a singular vent. There are few instances of independent states submitting heir cause to a court of justice. The day will come when all disputes n the great republic of Europe will be tried in the same way, and America be quoted to exemplify the wisdom of the measure." [127]

[125] Vaux, 62, 71; Smyth, *Franklin, Writings,* VIII, 9, Feb. 6, 1780; *Calendar f Franklin Papers,* II, 326, Dec. 25, 1780. A number of plans for peace were ut forward in the seventeenth and eighteenth centuries; see E. V. Souleyman, *The Vision of World Peace in Seventeenth and Eighteenth Century France* New York, 1941).

[126] Eddy edited this in a New York ed., 1922; *Calendar of Franklin Papers,* I, 25, Feb. 14, 1779.

[127] Francis Wharton, *Revolutionary Diplomatic Correspondence of the United States* (Washington, 1889), VI, 202, Jan. 10, 1783.

James Wilson of Pennsylvania, the Scottish lawyer whose learnin
so impressed such travelers as Chastellux, likewise saw in the federa
Constitution and in the Supreme Court an example to the nation
of the world for the peaceful adjudication of war-provoking dis
putes and set forth his views to his students at the University o
Pennsylvania.[128]

Franklin sought to forestall criticism, and a plea of insuperabl
obstacles to be overcome, by pointing out that the Americans als
had many interests to be reconciled. Washington wrote to Lafayett
that America had sowed "seeds of Liberty and Union that will sprin
up everywhere upon earth. Some day, taking its pattern from th
United States, there will be founded the United States of Eu
rope." [129] Holding up the American states as an example the Frenc
Revolutionary orator, Rabaut Saint-Etienne, in an *Adresse au
Anglais,* asked for a constitution of the United States of Europe, a
objective advocated also by Richard Price.[130] Turgot and Condorce
often talked of a government for a United Europe.

The *European Magazine* drew the attention of its readers to som
interesting provisions in the treaty concluded between the Unite
States and Prussia in 1785; the contracting parties agreed that, i
case any power were to go to war with either of them, "the free intercourse and commerce of the subjects or citizens of the party remain-
ing neuter with the belligerent Powers shall not be interrupted."
"There is another clause in this new compact which does honou
to humanity," the magazine went on to say. "In case of war, no
women, children, men of letters, farmers, artisans and fishermen,
who are not found in arms and who live in unfortified cities, towns
and villages, i.e., all whose vocation tends to the subsistence and
general good of the human race shall have liberty to continue their
respective profession unmolested." Were any of these to suffer loss
they were to be reimbursed by the offending state. Vessels not carrying ammunition were to be protected; nothing was to be done

[128] R. G. Adams, ed., *Selected Political Essays of James Wilson* (New York, 1930), 340.

[129] Smyth, *Franklin, Writings,* IX, 69, letter to F. Grand, Oct. 22, 1787; Souleyman, 207.

[130] Faÿ, 319.

n either side to destroy or even interrupt the freedom of com-
nerce.[131]

There were a number of questions of a humanitarian character, uggested in part by the liberalizing influence of the New World; ne such brought this answer on the usefulness of America to man- ind; "The discovery of America in substituting the spirit of com- nerce for the spirit of conquest and invasion has undoubtedly endered peace infinitely precious to all the governments, but na- ional egoism has not as yet permitted the delicious fruits of this pirit of peace to be reaped." [132]

The historian C. D. Ebeling wrote to Jedidiah Morse, that war nust at long last be held in universal detestation, unless "when a ation is attacked in her own lands." "America," he said, "must give the example to the World." [133] Granville Sharp, who always eared the warlike potentialities of standing armies, as well as their langers to democracies, urged that America adopt rather a kind of national guard, rotating with short periods of service.[134] Condorcet hought that the system of militia in America was proof that wars of onquest were foreign to her ideals. He wanted France to follow the same principle, and he drafted the statement adopted by the Legis- lative Assembly expressing French intentions to take up arms only in self-defense. Condorcet believed that the American Revolution would more than justify itself if it led Europeans to cherish peace. The exchange of communications on the methods of attaining peace led in the nineteenth century to an organized pacifist movement supported on both sides of the Atlantic.[135]

In the many decades since independence, Americans and Euro- peans have been struggling to understand each other. Anti- Americanism has been matched by anti-Europeanism; the latter in

[131] X, 133.

[132] *Le Triomphe du Nouveau Monde Réponses Académiques formant un Nouveau système de Confédération, fondé sur les besoins actuels des Nations Chrétiennes,* I, 26.

[133] Oct. 4, 1796, Morse Mss., Yale Library.

[134] Sharp to Rush, Sept. 11, 1798, Ridgway Library.

[135] C. Phelps, *The Anglo-American Peace Movement in the Mid-Nineteenth Century* (New York, 1930).

its more virulent form has been largely Anglophobia. Contributing to the misunderstanding has been the general practice, until fairly recently, of Englishmen to emphasize the similarities between themselves and Americans and ignore the differences, while the American habit too often has been to stress the differences and ignore the similarities. It hardly helped matters when friendly Englishmen could not avoid distinguishing between Americans of German, Irish, Scottish, and English descent and spoke of the latter as "Anglo-Americans." [136] Fundamental economic and political conflicts created deep fissures in the Atlantic world, and only in our own day after infinite suffering has a partial unity been achieved. The "cosmopolites" of the eighteenth century who transcended national boundaries waited a long time for their spiritual children to be born.

America inspired the growth of nationalism all over the world, but she also contributed greatly to the concept of a common humanity which disregarded national boundaries. The creation of a federal government apparently accommodating differences between antagonistic states gave a more solid foundation for the dreams of European federalists. America's mixed population of diverse origins gradually merging into a homogeneous unity was an example with constant appeal to philosophers and the unlettered alike. Americans, North and South, were producing a new type of man. Crèvecoeur observed it in North America; Bolívar noted it in Latin America. "We differ," he said, "from all the other varieties of the human species."

Men with a world view and a general interest in science—Franklin, Price, Paine, Rush, Turgot, Condorcet—favored some sort of association of nations, whose task would be to build the international community. Their argument, buttressed as it often was by a reference to the world fellowship of scientists, led to a cosmopolitanism which banished boundaries. As Thomas Paine put it:

Men who study any universal science, the principles of which are universally known, or admitted, and applied . . . [for] the common bene-

[136] *Toulmin's Journal,* 94.

> fits of all countries, obtain thereby a larger share of philanthropy than those who only study national arts and improvements. Natural philosophy, mathematics and astronomy, carry the mind from the country to the creation, and give it a fitness suited to the extent. It was not Newton's honor, neither could it be his pride, that he was an Englishman, but that he was a philosopher; the heavens had liberated him from the prejudices of an island, and science had expanded his soul as boundless as his studies.[137]

It is quite fitting that in our own time the foremost heirs to this eighteenth-century tradition should be the scientists who worked on the atomic bomb.

It is a striking challenge that these visionaries in the American Revolutionary era flung at the world. Our world is now planning to give substance to those visions. Franklin and his contemporaries probably would have considered America the logical setting for a United Nations home in which to conjure reality out of their dreams.

---

[137] Quoted in Clark, "The Influence of Science on American Ideas, from 1775 to 1809," *loc. cit.*, 347.

CHAPTER XI

Summary

THE peoples who engaged in the process we call Europeanizing the world were not themselves homogeneous. They took with them differences in religion and in class relationships. In England the middle class had gained a status in conducting the affairs of their homeland superior to that enjoyed by their compeers in Spain or France. Britain had already enlarged the fields of economic and political activity for its bourgeoisie even before they embarked on overseas enterprise at the end of the sixteenth century.

The religious differences among the expansionist powers were more marked than economic differences. In Protestant countries, the authority of ecclesiastical establishments was more limited than in the lands still faithful to Roman Catholicism. Although Protestant countries (as well as those still professing Catholicism) transplanted to new settlements their established churches, Protestants were less successful in exacting conformity. Everywhere among the colonies the social patterns of the respective homelands were reflected.

The expansion of Europe has been a many-faceted experience to the generations affected by it since the fifteenth century. Europeans carried with them to new lands overseas institutions and beliefs of ancient lineage. Those who pulled up stakes to pitch a new encampment on a foreign shore clung with strong attachment to old habits. In a hostile environment, far from familiar scenes, this was the shield that offered comfort. In many of the colonies, however, institutional patterns began to diverge from the homeland models, and it seems that in the British settlements on the North American mainland in particular, the divergences assumed larger proportions than those in other contemporary empires.

Europeans looked to overseas regions as areas for quick economic exploitation, missionary enterprise, and (notably in the case of the British and Spaniards) homes for permanent habitation. While most left Europe willingly, a large number left only under duress; some 30,000 convicted felons were transported in the eighteenth century from Great Britain to the American colonies, where need for laborers seemed insatiable. The demand for workers in the Anglo-American colonies increased rapidly toward the end of the seventeenth century, and it appears that a tacit conspiracy existed between interested individuals in England and America to evade the laws to recruit the necessary labor supply. But even this augmented labor force proved inadequate to the needs of the colonists, especially in the South. The gap was filled with vast numbers of Negro slaves who thus brought their distinctive contributions to that complex called the Atlantic Civilization.

The discoveries had profound effects on the life of Europe. They accelerated economic changes already under way, speeding up the transition to a money economy. Their impact helped make more fluid the relations between social classes. They also stimulated enormously the imagination of poets, philosophers, artists of every kind. The exotic coloring and fantastic imagery which gave especial brilliance to the work of dramatists and poets came from a world strange to European experience. The historian's canvas was broadened, and his speculations were deepened. Political scientists were led to think more critically of the nature of government by comparing their own institutions with those newly found in America and elsewhere. Such subjects as anthropology and ethnology could hardly be said to have existed prior to contact with peoples different from Europeans. The content of the social sciences was greatly enlarged by study of American Indians, who on occasion impishly prodded whites to a re-examination of their own civilization. The scientific spirit found a rich field for investigation in the new treasures found in the waters and earth of remote regions.

To leave domestic hearths for permanent settlement in North America required desperation—and courage: desperation to escape from a life without a future, courage to dare a terrifying ocean voyage to a land without a past. Hardships on the voyage and danger of shipwreck were real enough, but the historian has frequently overemphasized their importance. Anxiety over adjustment to a new environment and sheer boredom with endless days at sea were possibly more disquieting than the imminence of real danger.

Communications were more frequent than is generally imagined. Social exchanges with relatives and friends left in the old country were maintained by correspondence or a rare visit. In addition to these social exchanges were also the ties of business, religious, and common intellectual interests by which inhabitants of the Atlantic community kept in relatively close contact. By the middle of the eighteenth century sophisticated European travelers moving in such urban centers as Charleston, Philadelphia, New York, or Boston found enough congenial company of requisite taste to make their stay pleasurable. The colonial traveling abroad rarely had the same degree of self-confidence in a metropolis such as London but did feel at ease in the smaller cities of Europe.

An important connecting link in the Anglo-American world was the bond between religious groups on both sides of the ocean professing the same beliefs. Anglicans were joined together in a common determination to strengthen the Establishment, and, where they were a minority (it so happened in New England), support from the mother country helped ease their unfavorable position. Dissenters wherever found had at least a common interest in opposing Anglicanism. A consciousness of kind existed to a striking degree among Quakers, whose itinerant preachers brought the glowing word to lacklustre lives. Evangelists among Methodists, Presbyterians, and Baptists tied together their respective sects in the transatlantic community in religious revivals and in joint struggles for religious liberty. Germany was a partner with Britain and America in these enterprises, for from the deep spiritual well of Halle was drawn the refreshing draught that invigorated the life of Protestantism everywhere.

Projects for improving education were discussed in transatlantic communications initiated by Anthony Benezet, one of the most progressive teachers of the eighteenth century. Higher education in colonial America was greatly indebted to Britain for leadership and financial support, which was given in generous measure. European philanthropists enriched American college libraries as well as the collections of books sponsored by religious organizations and other community groups. Americans often regretted the inadequate educational opportunities available to them at home, although these were definitely improving on the eve of the Revolution.

Whatever inadequacy Americans may have felt in education was less painful than the sense of inferiority they suffered when contemplating the superior achievements in art of contemporary Europeans. Americans (in their relationship to art more than in any other activity) even after graduating from their actual colonial status have either been spiritual colonials or chauvinists—they have found it difficult to be natural or at ease about their own art creations. Too often they have been diffident or domineering, as though reflecting an inner uncertainty. Surely this was true of some colonial artists, yet the accomplishments of the best of them were sufficiently meritorious to rank them with the leading European painters of their day. The Americans, notably Copley and West, were acclaimed the finest painters of historical themes, and they, probably more than any other artists, fashioned the public taste for such pictures.

Although Americans apologized to excess for their limitations in the creative arts they exhibited greater confidence in dealing with problems of human relationships. Just as on religious questions they felt they had much to teach Europe, so too, in proposing further tempering of man's inhumanity to man, colonials expressed themselves with assurance. Humanitarian reform, notably penology and the antislavery movement, had as vigorous exponents in America as were to be found in Europe. But there was no especial claim by individuals on either side of the Atlantic to a starring role. Where leadership was clearly displayed, as it was by John Howard in prison reform, there discipleship was freely accepted. Americans, however, were sufficiently independent to advance beyond the master, and the fertility of social invention displayed by them deeply impressed observant Europeans. Americans and Europeans worked jointly to moderate the severity of penal codes; together they inaugurated a plan of campaign which, despite its setbacks, ultimately aided in bringing to successful completion a ban on the slave trade.

The gains recorded by social reformers on both sides of the Atlantic may appear slight in retrospect because of progress made since, but to the people of the eighteenth century the advances in humanitarian endeavor were important. The mutual aid that reformers on both sides of the ocean accorded one another was a heartening demonstration of trans-Atlantic co-operation.

Scientists more easily than others were able to transcend national boundaries and think of themselves as members of a fellowship bound together in common search. The Royal Society in England was the dynamo that generated much of this activity, and it was a signal honor to be granted membership in it. A small number of colonials won the coveted position, and they made significant contributions to the sum of knowledge accumulated by the Society. Careful observations on the habits of animals unfamiliar to Europeans, discovery of many new plants, closer study of the relationship between climate and disease—these were among the communications transmitted from America to England. The circulation of the Society's *Philosophical Transactions* throughout European scientific circles and the publication of extracts of articles in periodicals of general circulation meant that its contents reached a much larger audience than merely the membership of the Royal Society. The only one of the Americans whose reputation ranked him with the eminent scientific figures of the day was Franklin. His place was won by his experiments in electricity but was maintained and strengthened by the general support he offered to the whole scientific community in establishing a rational basis for human existence.

In a period when specialization was not as customary as it is today many physicians engaged in scientific researches, some not directly related to medicine. They were of course alert to the advantages of utilizing the latest finds by botanists and of using electricity in medical treatment. European example set precepts for the training of doctors in America. American contributions to medical literature were of a high order, notably in the discussion of epidemic disease. Americans showed that inoculation could drastically reduce the rate of mortality in smallpox epidemics, and it was their initiative which strengthened the determination of European physicians to adopt this procedure. When at the end of the eighteenth century Jenner proposed vaccination as a more effective preventive of smallpox he had no stronger supporters than doctors in America. The recognition accorded the work of American physicians in Europe seems convincing proof of the quality of their accomplishments.

If any diffidence was evident in the attitude of Americans when they discussed medical problems with Europeans, it completely vanished when the talk veered on politics. Americans who gladly sat at the feet of European masters in art or in science felt that they themselves were masters who could teach Europeans the facts of political life. In this phase of human activity Americans were assertive (perhaps even abusive) in pointing to the deficiencies of European political organization. This was especially true in the Revolutionary era when the success of the War for Independence won an accolade from European liberals who were critical of their own antiquated political structures. The fraternity of believers in human progress lent encouragement to each other in the Atlantic world, and none were more ardent in their beliefs than Americans. American fulfillment of many of their common aspirations spurred Europeans from hoping to daring and then to achievement. The community of interest that was created in the last third of the eighteenth century among liberals everywhere in the Atlantic civilization has been an enduring factor in the life of western society to our own time.

It is a tribute to the persistent vitality of America that even though she often strayed from her own ideals, she continued to fertilize the imaginative life of mankind in the decades that followed the American Revolution. For those who could not enter the land of Canaan the vision itself was stimulus to the frustrated heart. America brought sustenance to the body and to the spirit of millions and gave modern man a real foundation for his Utopian fantasy.

The American Revolution (and of course, the French Revolution) ultimately had a powerful effect on national movements throughout the world. The inspiration afforded by American example in setting up an independent nation reached across to Ireland, Belgium, Italy, and, in our own hemisphere, South America. To our own day the blow that American Independence gave to colonialism has reverberated. But the growth of nationalism was partly offset by the impetus American federalism gave to plans for regional and world organization. Europeans had cherished such hopes for centuries. What was a chimera in Europe, however, seemed a reality in America. George Washington was only voicing the expectations of many humbler Americans in hoping the time would come when Europeans would create a Continental federation. Two centuries ago prophets foretold that the center of gravity in the Atlantic community would shift to the New World. We, in this generation, have the troublesome honor of fulfilling that prediction.

It has been observed by an American poet that Europe is still the biggest fact in North America. It might be just as valid to say that North America has long been the biggest fact in Europe. This is the true meaning of the Atlantic civilization, whose origins go back to the eighteenth century.

Bibliography

SELECTED references are included; others are in the footnotes to the text. To list everything read for this volume would make its bibliography overlong.

The materials were gathered in Europe and America over a period of many years. Manuscripts and primary printed materials are the chief sources, along with authoritative secondary works. For several chapters, manuscripts in the British Museum (especially the Wilkes and Sloane Mss.) were helpful. Probably the richest store of relevant materials came from Friends House, London (particularly for the chapters on religion, education, and humanitarianism), and from the Royal Society library for science and medicine. In our own country Franklin Mss. and others in the American Philosophical Society, Rush letters in the Ridgway Library, the collections of the Pennsylvania Historical Society, the Stiles and Morse Mss. in the Yale library, the Curwin papers and others in the American Antiquarian Society, the Jefferson, Mather Brown, and Winthrop Mss. in the Massachusetts Historical Society—all these were very useful. Other libraries kindly permitted examination and use of their treasures, among them the New York Public Library, the New York Historical Society, the Huntington Library. The Newberry Library, Chicago, with its Ayer collection of Indian materials, was very helpful.

Certain printed materials were of use throughout the volume. *Benjamin Franklin, Writings* (A. H. Smyth, ed.; New York, 1905), I. M. Hays, ed., *Calendar of Franklin Papers* (Philadelphia: American Philosophical Society, 1908) , and A. A. Lipscomb, ed., *The Writings of Thomas Jefferson* (Monticello ed.; Washington, D.C., 1904), were obviously of prime importance; so too, were the Willard letters and Price letters in the *Massachusetts Historical Society Proceedings.* Newspapers on both sides of the Atlantic and magazines (especially the *Gentleman's Magazine,* the *European Magazine and London Review,* and the *Scots Magazine*) were frequently consulted. The collection of English pamphlets in the library of the University of California at Los Angeles was of considerable assistance, notably in the chapter, "America and the Utopian Ideal." For several sections of this book the *Encyclopedia Britannica* (first and third editions) was useful.

CHAPTER I

THE BEGINNINGS OF AN ATLANTIC CIVILIZATION

For economic and social impact on Europe: H. M. Robertson, *Aspects of the Rise of Economic Individualism* (Cambridge, Eng., 1935); E. J. Hamilton, *American Treasure and the Price Revolution in Spain 1501–1650* (Cambridge, Mass., 1934); several articles by Hamilton mentioned in footnotes; J. E. Gillespie, *The Influence of Oversea Expansion on England to 1700* (New York, 1920), J. B. Botsford, *English Society in the Eighteenth Century as influenced from Oversea* (New York, 1924); Eric Williams, *Capitalism and Slavery* (Chapel Hill, 1944); C. M. MacInness, *England and Slavery* (Bristol, 1934); Malachy Postlethwayt, *The African Trade, the great Pillar and Support of the British Plantation Trade in America . . .* (London, 1745); Leo Gershoy, *From Despotism to Revolution* (New York, 1944); *The Present State of the British and French Trade to Africa and America consider'd and compar'd . . .* (London, 1745); D. D. Brand, "The Origin and early distribution of New World cultivated Plants," *Agri. Hist.*, April, 1939.

For impact on European thought, art, etc.: D. Fenning and J. Collyer, *A New System of Geography . . .* (London, 1766); *Le Triomphe du Nouveau Monde: Réponses Académiques formant un nouveau système de Confédération fondé sur les besoins actuels des Nations Chrétiennes . . .* (Paris, 1785); E. A. Baker, *The History of the English Novel* (London, *1924–39*); Pedro Henriquez-Ureña, *Literary Currents in Hispanic America* (Cambridge, Mass., 1945); *Works of Francis Bacon* (Spedding ed., Boston, 1860–1864); Walter Raleigh, *The English Voyages of the Sixteenth Century* (Glasgow, 1910); R. R. Cawley, *Unpathed Waters: Studies in the Influence of the Voyagers on Elizabethan Literature* (Princeton, 1940); J. L. Lowes, *The Road to Xanadu* (Boston, 1927); R. W. Frantz, *The English Traveler and the Movement of Ideas 1660–1732* ("University of Nebraska, Univ. Studies," XXXII–XXXIII); G. Atkinson, *The Extraordinary Voyage in French Literature before 1700* (New York, 1920); P. B. Gove, *The Imaginary Voyage in Prose Fiction* (New York, 1941); G. Chinard, *L'Amérique et le Rève Exotique dans la Littérature Française au xviie et au xviiie Siècle* (Paris, 1934); Mary Serjeantson, *A History of Foreign Words in English* (London, 1935);

H. N. Fairchild, *The Noble Savage* (New York, 1928); B. Bissell, *The American Indian in English Literature of the Eighteenth Century* (New Haven, 1925); P. A. Barba, *The American Indian in German Fiction,* "German-American Annals," n.s., XI; J. F. Hunnewell, "Illustrated Americana," *Amer. Antiq. Soc., Proc.,* VI; Thomas Thomsen, *Albert Eckhout . . .* (Copenhagen, 1938); R. C. Smith, "Frans Post," *The Art Quarterly,* I (1938); C. B. Tinker, *Painter and Poet: Studies in the Literary Relations of English Painting* (Cambridge, Mass., 1938); E. W. Gudger, "George Marcgrave," *Popular Science Monthly,* LXXXI (1912); M. Ornstein, *Scientific Societies in the Seventeenth Century* (New York, 1913); E. Brerewood, *Enquiries touching the diversity of Languages and Religions throughout the chief parts of the World* (London, 1614); H. Grotius, *De Origine Gentium Americanorum,* 1642 (Eng. ed., Edinburgh, 1884); T. Bendyshe, "The History of Anthropology," *Memoirs of the Anthropological Society of London,* I (1863–1864); José de Acosta, *The Natural & Moral History of the Indies* (C. R. Markham, ed., London, 1880); J. L. Myres, *The Influence of Anthropology on the Course of Political Science* ("University of California, Publ. in Hist.," IV).

CHAPTER II

COMMUNICATIONS AND SOCIAL RELATIONS

For this chapter much valuable information came from the *Mss. Treasury Letter Books,* and the *Mss. American Letter Book 1773–1783* in the General Post Office, London. The best secondary source is W. E. Rich, *The History of the United States Post Office to the Year 1829* ("Harvard Econ. Stud.," XXVII); see also William Smith, *History of the Post Office in British North America* (Cambridge, Eng., 1920); J. F. Sachse on Daniel Falckner, *Penn. Germ. Soc., Proc.,* XIV; "An Essay on Emigration," *Edinburgh Magazine and Review,* II (1774); R. B. Morris, *Government and Labor in Early America* (New York, 1946); A. E. Smith, *Colonists in Bondage* (Chapel Hill, N.C., 1947); Carl Wittke, *We Who built America* (New York, 1939); C. K. Shipton, "Immigration to New England 1680–1740," *Jour. Pol. Economy,* XLIV; J. L. Mesick, *The English Traveler in America 1785–1835* (New York, 1921); F. B. Dexter, ed., *The Literary Diary of Ezra Stiles* (New York, 1901); H. Tilghman, ed., "Letters between the English and American Branches of the Tilghman Family 1697–1764," *Maryland Hist. Mag.,* XXIII; K. B. Murdock, *Increase Mather* (Cambridge, Mass., 1925); K. M. Roof, *Col. Wm. Smith and Lady* (New York, 1929); H. R. Marraro (trans.), *Memoirs of the Life and Peregrinations of the Florentine Philip Mazzei 1730–1816* (New

York, 1942); J. H. St. John Crèvecoeur, *Letters from an American Farmer* (New York, 1925); J. R. Masterson, "Records of Travel in North America 1700–1776," *Harvard Univ. Summaries of Theses,* 1936 (Cambridge, 1938); Frank Monaghan, *French Travellers in the United States 1765–1932* (New York, 1933); Wm. Eddis, *Letters from America . . . 1769 to 1777 . . .* (London, 1792); A. B. Shepperson, *John Paradise and Lucy Ludwell of London and Williamsburg* (Richmond, 1942); Charles Whitworth, *State of the Trade of Great Britain . . . from the Year 1697* (London, 1776); Thomas Whately, *Considerations on the Trade and Finances of this Kingdom . . .* (3rd ed., London, 1769); *Political Speculations, or an Attempt to discover the Causes of the Dearness of Provisions, and High Labour in England . . .* (Part the Second, London, 1767) in the Huntington Library; John Mitchell, *The Present State of Great Britain and North America . . .* (London, 1767); Caleb Evans, *A Letter to the Rev. Mr. John Wesley . . .* (London, 1775).

CHAPTER III

RELIGIOUS RELATIONS

The most important materials for this section came from manuscript collections in the London library of the Society for the Propagation of the Gospel; Friends House, London, where were located *Mss. Letters to and from Philadelphia;* the Princeton University Library, which has Samuel Davies' *Diary;* and the Huntington Library. An indispensable source is N. Curnock, ed., *The Journal of John Wesley* (London, 1909–1916). See also G. Fothergill, *A List of Emigrant Ministers to America 1690–1811* (London, 1904); T. G. Wright, *Literary Culture in Early New England 1620–1730* (New Haven, 1920); *A Journal of the Life of Thomas Story . . .* (New Castle upon Tyne, 1747); Samuel Mather, *An Apology for the Liberties of the Churches in New England* (Boston, 1738); E. B. Greene, *Religion and the State* (New York, 1941); C. F. Pascoe, *Two Hundred Years of the Society for the Propagation of the Gospel in Foreign Parts . . .* (London, 1901); John Nichols, *Literary Anecdotes of the Eighteenth Century* (London, 1812); John S. Simon, *The Revival of Religion in England in the Eighteenth Century* (London, 1911); S. G. Dimond, *The Psychology of the Methodist Revival* (London, 1926); Cotton Mather, *Nuncia Bona E Terra Longinqua* (Boston, 1715); William Seward, *Journal of a Voyage from Savannah to Philadelphia and from Philadelphia to England* (London, 1740); L. Tyerman, *The Life and Times of the Rev. John Wesley* (2nd ed., London, 1871): Luke Tyerman, *The Life of the Rev. George Whitefield*

(London, 1876); "The Glasgow Weekly History, 1743," *Mass. Hist. Soc., Proc.*, LIII; John Gillies, *Historical Collections relating to Remarkable Periods of the Success of the Gospel* (Glasgow, 1754); Thomas Milner, *The Life . . . of the Rev. Dr. Isaac Watts* (London, 1834); W. Armistead, *Memoirs of James Logan* (London, 1851); R. M. Jones, *The Later Periods of Quakerism* (London, 1921); Jos. Ivimey, *A History of the English Baptists* (London, 1823): Isaac Backus, *A History of New England . . . Baptists* (Newton, Mass., 1871); *The Life and Character of . . . Jonathan Edwards . . .* (London, 1785); John Rippon, *The Baptist Annual Register, 1790–1793*, London; *Extracts of the Journals of the Rev. Dr. Coke's Five Visits to America* (London, 1793).

CHAPTER IV

ON BOOKS AND LEARNING

This chapter drew on manuscripts in Friends House, London; the Morse and Stiles Mss. in the Yale Library; the Sprague Mss. in the Congregational Library, London; the Colman Mss. and Jefferson papers in the Massachusetts Historical Society; the Ebeling letters in the American Philosophical Society; the Isaiah Thomas papers in the American Antiquarian Society, and the Mss. reports on collections in Britain for New York and Philadelphia colleges, 1763, in the Historical Society of Pennsylvania. See also R. Vaux, *Memoirs of Anthony Benezet* (Phila., 1817); Merle Curti, *The Growth of American Thought* (New York, 1943); E. B. Greene, *The Revolutionary Generation* (New York, 1943); C. Welsh, *A Bookseller of the last century, John Newbery* (London, 1885); Wm. Guthrie, *Geographical, Historical and Commercial Grammar* (17th ed., London, 1798); Jedidiah Morse, *American Geography* (London, 1792): *Memoirs of James Lackington* (London, 1794): S. E. Morison, *Puritan Pronaos* (New York, 1936): Morison, *Harvard in the Seventeenth Century* (Cambridge, Mass., 1936); F. J. Powicke, *The Cambridge Platonists* (London, 1926): *Papers in Honor of Andrew Keogh . . .* (New Haven, 1938): Samuel Miller, *Memoir of the Rev. Charles Nisbet* (New York, 1840); *Memoirs of Thomas Hollis, Esq.* (London, 1780); E. L. Bradsher, *Mathew Carey* (New York, 1912); T. J. Pettigrew, *Memoirs of J. C. Lettsom . . .* (London, 1817); G. Chinard, *Thomas Jefferson* (Boston, 1929); B. C. Steiner, "Rev. Thomas Bray and his American Libraries," *Amer. Hist. Rev.*, II; A. S. Pratt, *Isaac Watts and his Gift of Books to Yale College* (New Haven, 1938); J. T. Adams, *Provincial Society* (New York, 1928); T. J. Wertenbaker, *The Old South . . .* (New York, 1942). Excellent material is to be found in "Henry

Knox and the London Book-Store in Boston 1771–1774," *Mass. Hist. Soc., Proc.,* LXI; White Kennett, *Bibliothecae Americanae Primordia* (London, 1713); G. S. Gordon, *Anglo-American Literary Relations* (London, 1942); H. S. Jantz, "German Thought and Literature in New England, 1620–1820," *Jour. Eng. and Germ. Philology,* XLI. Some of this chapter has appeared in an article, "Literary Relations between Europe and America in the Eighteenth Century," contributed to the *William and Mary Quarterly,* July, 1944, where fuller documentation will be found.

CHAPTER V

GRAPHIC ARTS, MUSIC, AND ARCHITECTURE

Some of the best materials for this section came from the "Smibert-Moffatt Letters, 1735–1752," printed in *Mass. Hist. Soc., Proc.,* XLIX, and from *Letters and Papers of John Singleton Copley and Henry Pelham 1739–1776* (*Mass. Hist. Soc., Colls.,* LXXI); Mather Brown Mss. in Massachusetts Historical Society are very interesting; also useful are William Dunlap, *A History of the Rise and Progress of the Arts of Design in the United States* (F. W. Bayley and C. E. Goodspeed, eds., Boston, 1918); W. T. Whitley, *Artists and their Friends in England 1700–1799* (London and Boston, 1928); T. Bolton and H. L. Binsse, "Robert Feke, First Painter to Colonial Aristocracy," *The Antiquarian,* Oct., 1930. O. Hagen, *The Birth of the American Tradition* (New York, 1940), is provocative. See also E. P. Richardson, *The Way of Western Art 1776–1924* (Cambridge, Mass., 1939) and J. T. Flexner, *America's Old Masters . . .* (New York, 1939). Very helpful is Gordon Washburn in *The Catalogue of Old and New England . . . An Exhibition of American Painting of Colonial and early Republican Days together with English Paintings of the same time . . . in the Museum of Art of the Rhode Island School of Design* (Providence, 1945).

Other references to Anglo-American art relations are found in Hugh Owen, *Two Centuries of Ceramic Art in Bristol . . .* (London, 1873); E. Meteyard, *The Life of Josiah Wedgwood* (London, 1865); R. T. H. Halsey, "Ceramic Americana of the Eighteenth Century," *Art in America,* IV. Of considerable importance are the several volumes of *Catalogue of Prints & Drawings in the British Museum; Political and Personal Satires,* edited first by F. G. Stephens and now carried on by M. D. George (London, 1870–   ).

For music: P. A. Scholes, *The Puritans and Music in England and New England* (London, 1934); J. F. Sachse, "The Music of the Ephrata

Cloister," *Penn. Germ. Soc., Proc.,* XII; R. R. Drummond, *Early German Music in Philadelphia* ("Amer. Germanica," n.s., IX, 1910); L. Keefer, "Hopkinson and the First American Art-Song," *Musical America,* Nov. 25, 1942; C. H. Firth, *An American Garland: being a collection of Ballads relating to America 1563–1759* (Oxford, 1915).

On architecture and sculpture: H. R. Shurtleff, *The Log Cabin Myth* (S. E. Morison, ed., Cambridge, Mass., 1939); Fiske Kimball, *Domestic Architecture of the American Colonies and of the Early Republic* (New York, 1933); H. M. Forbes, *Gravestones of early New England and the men who made them 1653–1800* (Boston, 1927); F. Kimball, "The Beginnings of Sculpture in Colonial America," *Art and Archaeology,* VIII.

CHAPTER VI

THE HUMANITARIAN SPIRIT

Much of the material came from manuscript collections in London and Philadelphia; in the former largely from Friends House, in the latter from the Pennsylvania Historical Society. Important matter was found in such articles as C. A. Moore, "Shaftesbury and the Ethical Poets in England 1700–1760," *Publ. Mod. Lang. Assn.,* XXXI, and in V. W. Crane, "The Promotion Literature of Georgia," in *Bibliographical Essays: A Tribute to Wilberforce Eames* (Cambridge, Mass., 1924). See also B. K. Gray, *A History of English Philanthropy* (London, 1905); P. C. Weber, *America in Imaginative German Literature in the First half of the 19th Century* (New York, 1926); M. D. Learned, *Herder and America* ("Germ. Amer. Annals," n.s. II, no. 9); A. Jorns, *The Quakers as Pioneers in Social Work* (New York, 1931); G. Chinard, ed., *The Common Place Book of Thomas Jefferson* (Baltimore, 1926). *Memoirs of the Life of Sir Samuel Romilly* (London, 1840); S. L. Knapp, *The Life of Thomas Eddy* (New York, 1834); J. A. Krout and D. R. Fox, *The Completion of Independence 1790–1830* (New York, 1944); H. E. Barnes, "The Historical Origin of the Prison System in America," *Jour. Amer. Institute of Criminal Law and Criminology,* XII; O. F. Lewis, *The Development of American Prisons and Prison Customs 1776–1845* (Albany, 1922); R. J. Turnbull, *A Visit to the Philadelphia Prison, 1796;* F. A. La Rochefoucauld-Liancourt, *On the Prisons of Philadelphia* (Philadelphia, 1796); G. Dyer, *The Complaints of the Poor People of England* (2nd ed., London, 1793); E. F. Klein and G. A. Kleinschrod, *Archiv des Criminalrechts* (Halle, 1799); Prince Hoare, *Memoirs of Granville Sharp* (London, 1820); G. E. Ellis, *A Memoir of Sir Benjamin Thompson, Count Rumford* (Boston, 1871); Henry Wansey, *Thoughts on Poor*

Houses . . . (London, 1801); J. A. Krout, *The Origins of Prohibition* (New York, 1925); N. G. Goodman, *Benjamin Rush* (Philadelphia, 1934).

On slavery and abolition: M. S. Locke, *Anti-slavery in America 1619–1808* (Radcliffe College Monographs, no. 11, 1901); Thomas Clarkson, *History of the Rise, Progress and . . . Abolition of the African Slave Trade* . . . (London, 1839); James Ramsay, *Objections to the Abolition of the Slave Trade with Answers* (2nd ed., London, 1788); E. D. Seeber, *Anti-slavery opinion in France during the second half of the Eighteenth Century* (Baltimore, 1937); F. J. Klingberg, *The Antislavery Movement in England* (New Haven, 1926); Wm. Dickson, *Letters on Slavery* (London, 1789); A. Benezet, *Some Historical Account of Guinea* . . . (London, 1788). This chapter is an enlargement of two articles that appeared in the *Pennsylvania Magazine of History and Biography*, January, July, 1936.

CHAPTER VII

SCIENTIFIC RELATIONS BETWEEN EUROPE AND AMERICA

Valuable manuscripts were in the Royal Society Library (not always printed in the *Philosophical Transactions* of the Society); Sloane Mss. in the British Museum were also important. Significant printed sources include J. E. Smith, *A Selection of the Correspondence of Linnaeus and other Naturalists* (London, 1821); Wm. Darlington, *Memorials of John Bartram and Humphry Marshall* (Philadelphia, 1849); *Mémoires de l'Académie Royale des Sciences;* Arthur Young's *Annals of Agriculture*. See also D. Mornet, *Les Sciences de la Nature en France au xviiie siècle* (Paris, 1911); Theodore Hornberger's several excellent articles and a small volume on science in colonial colleges; *Transactions of the Linnaean Society* (1791); N. G. Brett-James, *The Life of Peter Collinson* (London, 1926); *Letters from George Washington to Arthur Young* (London, 1801); P. L. Haworth, *George Washington, Country Gentleman* (Indianapolis, 1915); *The Correspondence of Sir John Sinclair* (London, 1831); F. E. Brasch, in *Scientific Monthly*, XXIII (1931), and in *Amer. Antiq. Soc., Proc.*, Oct., 1939. The bicentennial issue of the *American Philosophical Society, Proc.*, LXXXVI, has several useful articles. See also S. S. Smith, *An Essay on the Causes of the Variety of Complexion and Figure in the Human Species* (Edinburgh, 1788), and M. Kraus, on Smith in *The Princeton University Library Chronicle*, Nov., 1944. On electricity, in addition to Franklin's own writings and the *Philosophical Transactions,* see I. B. Cohen, ed., *Benjamin Franklin's Experiments . . .* (Cambridge, Mass., 1941). F. E. Brasch has an excellent paper on John Winthrop in *Sir Isaac Newton 1727–1927* (Baltimore: History of Science Society, 1928). Some of this chapter appeared in an article in the *Scientific Monthly,* Sept., 1942.

CHAPTER VIII

AMERICAN AND EUROPEAN MEDICINE

Much of the material for this chapter came from manuscripts in the Royal Society, from publications of medical societies, and from pamphlets dealing with the controversy over smallpox. The *Colden Papers,* in the volumes of the New York Historical Society Collections, and the letters of Franklin are important.

See also H. E. Sigerist, "Boerhaave's Influence upon American Medicine," *Nederl. Tijdschrift vor geneeskunde,* Jaargang 82, no. 40 (Oct., 1938); W. Pepper, *The Medical Side of Benjamin Franklin* (Philadelphia, 1911); R. H. Fox, *Dr. John Fothergill and his Friends* (London, 1919); M. Kraus, *Intercolonial Aspects of American Culture on the eve of the Revolution* (New York, 1928); W. J. Bell, Jr., "Philadelphia Medical Students in Europe, 1750–1800," *Penn. Mag. of Hist. and Biog.,* LXVII; L. A. Biddle, *A Memorial of Dr. Benjamin Rush . . . written by himself* (Lanoraie, 1905); F. R. Packard, *The History of Medicine in the United States* (New York, 1931); G. L. Kittredge, "Lost Works of Cotton Mather," *Mass. Hist. Soc., Proc.,* LIV; W. Woodville, *The History of the Inoculation of the Small-Pox in Great Britain* (London, 1796); M. C. Leikind, "Variolation in Europe and America," *Ciba Symposia,* III, no. 10, Jan., 1942; J. Haygarth, *A Sketch of a plan to exterminate the casual Small-Pox from Great Britain . . . to which is added a correspondence* (London, 1793). T. J. Pettigrew, *Memoirs of J. C. Lettsom* (London, 1817) is very important for this section. This chapter has been considerably enlarged and revised since it appeared as "America and European Medicine in the Eighteenth Century" in the *Bulletin of the History of Medicine,* VIII, May, 1940.

CHAPTER IX

AMERICA AND THE UTOPIAN IDEAL

Many eighteenth-century pamphlets, magazines, and manuscripts were used for this chapter; the footnotes in the text refer to them.

See also: G. Atkinson, *Les Relations Voyages du xviie Siècle et l'Evolu-*

tion des Idées (Paris, 1925); F. J. Hinkhouse, *The Preliminaries of the American Revolution as seen in the English Press 1763–1775* (New York, 1926); on America and the Irish Revolutionary movement, see the chapter by M. Kraus in *The Era of the American Revolution: Studies inscribed to Evarts B. Greene* (R. B. Morris, ed., New York, 1939); several papers by G. H. Guttridge mentioned in the notes to the text; Richard Price, *Observations on Civil Liberty . . .* (London, 1776); D. M. Clark, *British Opinion and the American Revolution* (New Haven, 1930); R. L. Crosman, "The Legal and Journalistic Significance of the Trial of John Peter Zenger," *Rocky Mountain Law Review,* X; B. Faÿ, *The Revolutionary Spirit in France and America at the end of the eighteenth century* (New York, 1927); Faÿ, *Ouvrages Français Relatifs aux Etats-Unis 1770–1800* (Paris, 1925); J. S. Schapiro, *Condorcet* (New York, 1934); H. S. King, *Echoes of the American Revolution in German Literature* ("University of California, Publ. in Modern Philology," XIV, no. 2, 1929); Joel Barlow, *A Letter . . . to . . . Piedmont, on the Advantages of the French Revolution . . .* (London, 1795); Joel Barlow, *Advice to the Privileged Orders* (London, 1792); F. Edler, *The Dutch Republic and the American Revolution* ("Johns Hopkins Studies in History and Political Science," XXIX); T. K. Gorman, *America and Belgium* (London, 1925); T. Pownall, *A Memorial addressed to the Sovereigns of America* (London, 1783); J. D. Brite, *The Attitude of European States toward Emigration to the American Colonies and the United States 1607–1820* (University of Chicago, Ms. dissertation, 1939); E. A. W. Zimmerman, *Essai de Comparaison entre la France et les Etats-Unis* (Leipzig, 1797); V. R. Cameron, *Emigrants from Scotland to America 1774–1775* (typescript, New York Hist. Soc.); R. Price, *Observations on the Importance of the American Revolution and the means of making it a Benefit to the World* (London, 1784); Leon Fraser, *English Opinion of the American Constitution and Government 1783–1798* (New York, 1915); E. P. Link, *Democratic Republican Societies 1790–1800* (New York, 1942); Anthony Lincoln, *Some Political & Social Ideas of English Dissent 1763–1800* (Cambridge, Eng., 1938); Edith Phillips, *The Good Quaker in French Legend* (Philadelphia, 1932). Some of the material in this chapter appeared in the *Mississippi Vall. Hist. Rev.,* March, 1936.

CHAPTER X

NATIONALISM AND COSMOPOLITANISM

Much of this section is based on eighteenth-century periodicals and on the writings, mostly published, of leading Americans of that era. See also M. Curti, *The Roots of American Loyalty* (New York, 1946); L. Einstein, *Divided Loyalties* (Boston and New York, 1933); Charles Sumner, *Prophetic Voices concerning America* (Boston, 1874); A. O. Hansen, *Liberalism and American Education in the eighteenth Century* (New York, 1926); B. M. Victory, *Benjamin Franklin and Germany* ("Amer. Germanica," no. 21); several articles by A. W. Read on American English; George Chalmers, *Opinions on Interesting Subjects of Public Law and Commercial Policy, arising from American Independence* (London, 1784); G. H. Guttridge, *David Hartley, M.P., an advocate of conciliation 1774–1783* ("University of California, Publ. in Hist.," XIV); Samuel Miller, *A Brief Retrospect of the Eighteenth Century* (New York, 1803).

Index

INDEX

INDEX

INDEX